30 DAY
MEAL PLAN
RECIPES

MW00946689

GASTRIC
SLEEVE
BARIATRIC
COOKBOOK

The information in this book is not intended as medical advice or to replace a one-on-one relationship with a qualified health care professional. It is intended as a sharing of knowledge and information from the research and experience of Sandra Grant. We encourage you to make your own health care decisions based on your research and in partnership with a qualified health care professional. You may not be familiar with many of the ingredients listed herein. To help, we've included some basic information for many of the more unusual items. However, please note that some of the ingredients are considered medicinal in nature. So, before consuming large quantities of anything you're not familiar with (or, if you have any special medical condition or are taking any prescription medication), please do a bit of research and/or talk to a medical professional when in doubt.

© Copyright 2024

– Sandra Grant -

All rights reserved.

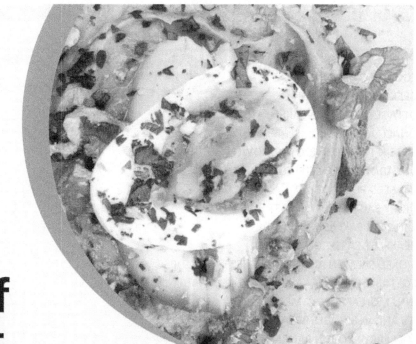

Table Of Content

DINNER 123

CHAPTER 1

THE NEED FOR HEALTHY EATING: A JOURNEY TO A HEALTHIER YOU

Have you heard that more than forty percent of adults around the world battle with being overweight? That is a mind-bogglingly large number, is it not? This problem is caused by a number of circumstances, some of which include bad eating habits, inactive lifestyles, and busy schedules that make it difficult to put our health first in our priorities. The good news, though, is that you have the ability to change that and start on the path toward a healthier version of yourself.

We would like to take this opportunity to welcome you to the bariatric cookbook, which serves as a reference to scrumptious and wholesome meals that have been developed exclusively for people who have had bariatric surgery or who are on a quest to lose weight. In this chapter, we will discuss the significance of eating healthily and how doing so can have a significant impact on your life.

Obesity is a worldwide epidemic that has a negative impact on the lives of millions of individuals all over the world. It has repercussions not only for our physical health but also for our mental and emotional well-being as a whole. But there is still a chance. You may take charge of your health and make progress toward a more healthy weight if you learn to adopt good eating habits.

This cookbook was created specifically to assist you in your quest toward a healthier lifestyle. It is tailored to meet the needs of those who have had bariatric surgery or are currently engaged in a program of weight reduction. The term "bariatric surgery" refers to an operation that modifies one's stomach or digestive system in order to facilitate weight loss in patients. It is a device that can facilitate a new beginning and throw open the doors to a better way of life.

However, there is one important point to keep in mind: bariatric surgery is only the first step. It is crucial to make changes in your eating habits that are lasting if you want to have success in the long run. This is where the bariatric cookbook can be of assistance to you. This is not your typical cookbook by any means. It is a useful resource that provides you with a wide variety of recipes that are both delicious and nutritious and are adapted to your specific requirements.

The major objective of this cookbook is to demystify and simplify the process of preparing nutritious meals. It acknowledges that eating healthily does not require one to forego pleasure or flavor in their food. Instead, it intends to demonstrate to you that healthy meals can be tasty, filling, and even enjoyable to put together in the kitchen.

In the next chapters, we will delve more into the particulars of a bariatric diet, give you a collection of recipes that are sure to whet your appetite, and provide some helpful hints regarding the planning and preparation of meals. You will learn how to make educated decisions about the foods you eat, how to provide your body with the appropriate nutrients, and how to design a lifestyle that is both sustainable and conducive to achieving your weight loss objectives.

Get ready, for we are about to start on an incredible journey together. Put an end to monotonous eating and diets that are too restrictive. You'll discover a whole new world of flavors, textures, and culinary delights thanks to the bariatric cookbook, all while you work towards being a happier and healthier version of yourself. Are you prepared to make changes to your eating routine and open yourself up to the pleasure of consuming meals that are both healthy and delicious? Let's plunge in!

CHAPTER 2

UNDERSTANDING BARIATRIC SURGERY AND THE IMPORTANCE OF A HEALTHY DIET

A. A description of the bariatric surgery procedure:

First things first, let's have a solid grasp on exactly what bariatric surgery entails. Those who struggle with obesity and want to improve their health through weight loss can benefit from bariatric surgery, which is a medical operation. There are several variations of bariatric surgery, but the overarching goal of each procedure is to make adjustments to your stomach or digestive system in order to facilitate eating less food and experiencing satiety more quickly.

The term "gastric bypass" refers to one kind of bariatric surgery that is quite common. During this operation, the surgeon will create a small pouch at the top of your stomach. This pouch will be attached directly to your small intestine after it has been created. This causes a reduction in the amount of food that can be consumed as well as a reduction in the amount of calories and nutrients that can be absorbed because a portion of your stomach and small intestine are bypassed.

The sleeve gastrectomy, often known as the gastric sleeve operation, is yet another kind of weight loss surgery. During this procedure, a significant piece of your stomach will be removed, and in its place, a smaller, sleeve-shaped stomach will be created. The smaller size of the stomach makes you feel full after eating fewer calories, which makes it easier to maintain a healthy weight.

In addition to adjustable gastric banding and biliopancreatic diversion with duodenal switch, there are additional procedures that fall under the category of bariatric surgery. Each surgical procedure comes with its own set of advantages and potential drawbacks; nevertheless, the members of your healthcare team will assist you in making the decision that is most suited to your needs.

B. The significance of nutrition after bariatric surgery

Bariatric surgery is a potent instrument that can assist you in kick-starting your road toward losing weight. However, it is essential to keep in mind that surgery on its own is not a silver bullet for the problem. After having bariatric surgery, it is absolutely necessary to make dietary changes that are both healthy and well-rounded in order to successfully manage one's weight and maintain general health.

Why is eating after surgery so critically important? So, how about we take a more in-depth look? The operation known as bariatric surgery alters the function of both the stomach and the digestive tract. It limits the amount of food that you may consume, and it also interferes with the body's ability to absorb nutrients. If you do not adhere to a healthy diet, it is possible that your body will not be able to obtain all of the vitamins, minerals, and other important nutrients that it requires.

After having bariatric surgery, the focus of a healthy diet should be on supplying the body with the appropriate proportions of nutrients while also watching portion sizes. Your healthcare team will provide you with particular dietary guidelines that you should adhere to, but in the meantime, here are some general principles that you should keep in mind:

Protein: Consuming adequate amounts of protein is of the utmost importance for your health, especially after having bariatric surgery. It promotes healing, protects muscle mass, and helps you feel full while doing all of those things. Make sure that the majority of the protein that you consume comes from healthy and low-fat sources, such as chicken, fish, turkey, eggs, tofu, and legumes like beans and lentils.

Fruits and vegetables are colorful foods that are high in a variety of nutrients, including fiber, vitamins, and minerals. Not only do they supply you with the nutrition your body needs, but they also help you feel full. Your diet should consist of a wide variety of fruits and vegetables because each type of food has a unique set of beneficial effects on your body.

Grains complete: loaves of bread made with whole wheat, brown rice, quinoa, and oats are some examples of grains complete that are good sources of complex carbohydrates. They give you a feeling of fullness in addition to providing prolonged energy and fiber. Stay away from refined grains and choose alternatives made with whole grains instead.

Fats that are good for you: Yes, fats can also be beneficial! Avocados, almonds, seeds, and olive oil all contain beneficial fats that are excellent for your heart and can make you feel more satiated after a meal. These fats can also be found in olive oil. Because fats are so high in calories, it's important to watch how much you consume of them.

Hydration: Water is necessary for the body to operate properly and is vital for hydration. To ensure that your body is properly hydrated throughout the day, be sure to drink enough water. Reduce your intake of sugary beverages and make clean, refreshing water your primary beverage choice.

If you follow these dietary suggestions, you can ensure that your body receives the essential nutrients it needs while also maintaining a healthy weight. Keep in mind that bariatric surgery is an effective method, but it is ultimately up to you to maximize its benefits by embracing a healthy diet and lifestyle after the procedure.

In the following chapter, we will go deeper into the particulars of a diet that is conducive to bariatric surgery, including meal planning, controlling portion sizes, and eating foods that are nutrient-dense. We are going to embark on a journey together to discover a world of delectable and nutritious dishes that will assist you on your path to losing weight and help you maintain a healthy lifestyle. Prepare yourself for a revolution in both your meals and your life!

Chapter 3

NOURISHING YOUR BODY: PRACTICAL NUTRITIONAL GUIDELINES FOR BARIATRIC PATIENTS

An Exposition of the Macronutrients

Now that you understand the significance of macronutrients in a bariatric diet, let's investigate each category in further depth and discover how to combine them in an efficient manner.

In a bariatric diet, proteins are an extremely important component. They are the fundamental components of our bodies and are necessary for maintaining muscle mass, promoting wound healing, and enhancing general recovery following surgical procedures. Consuming an adequate amount of protein helps prevent the breakdown of muscle tissue and promotes a feeling of fullness, both of which are very important following bariatric surgery.

It is essential to incorporate lean sources of protein into each of your meals. Eggs, tofu, Greek yogurt, cottage cheese, lean cuts of beef or pork, chicken, turkey, fish, lean cuts of beef or pork, lean cuts of pork, eggs, and legumes like beans and lentils are all examples of these. Aim to consume a quantity of protein equal to the size of your palm with each meal. If you have trouble getting the amount of protein you need from meals alone, the protein supplements or shakes that have been recommended to you by your healthcare team can be a beneficial addition.

Your body and brain rely heavily on carbohydrates as a significant source of the energy they require. Nevertheless, it is absolutely necessary to direct one's attention toward complex carbohydrates rather than simple carbohydrates. Complex carbs provide prolonged energy and are rich in fiber, which both improves digestion and increases satiety. Complex carbohydrates also contain fewer calories than simple carbohydrates.

Choose foods made with whole grains, such as bread made with whole wheat, brown rice, quinoa, and oats. In comparison to their refined cousins, these grains have undergone a lower level of processing and so retain a greater proportion of their original fiber and nutrients. Include a serving or two of complex carbs in each of your meals so that you can maintain a healthy level of energy without subjecting your body to an excessive amount of calories.

A healthy diet should also include fats; however, it is critical to include the appropriate kinds of fats in the diet. Avocados, almonds, seeds, olive oil, and fatty fish like salmon are all excellent sources of healthy fats, which are great for the health of the heart as well as overall well-being. However, keep in mind that fats are high in calories, so maintaining proper portion management is essential.

Be conscious of the quantity of fat you consume and make it a priority to include meals that include only trace amounts of nutritious fats. This can be accomplished by cooking with olive oil, adding a sprinkling of nuts or seeds to your salads or yogurt, and treating yourself to an avocado slice once in a while. A healthy diet is one in which the consumption of fat, proteins, and carbs is all kept in appropriate proportions.

B. Managing Your Portions and Eating More Often

After having bariatric surgery, maintaining proper portion control and eating regularly become two of the most important components of your new eating routine. Because the size of your stomach has been reduced, you will need to reduce the amount of food you consume in order to alleviate any discomfort and jumpstart your weight reduction.

Consider eating a series of smaller meals more often throughout the day as opposed to the traditional pattern of three large meals each day. This strategy helps to adapt to your decreased stomach capacity and generates a feeling of fullness in your body. Aim for five to six meals and snacks that are both healthy and well-balanced, and spread them out equally throughout the day.

Eating more frequently and in smaller portions will help you keep your metabolism stable and prevent you from overeating. Keep in mind that you should eat slowly and properly chew your meal. This will not only improve digestion, but it will also make it easier for your brain to recognize when your stomach is full, thereby lowering the likelihood that you will consume an excessive amount of food.

When hunger hits, it can be helpful to have some healthy options readily available and to have planned out your meals in advance. This can help you make better food choices and prevent you from making hasty decisions that are less nutritious. You can ensure that your body receives a wide range of nutrients as well as a variety of flavors by eating meals that come from a wide range of food groups.

C. Micronutrient Considerations

In addition to macronutrients, micronutrients like vitamins and minerals are critical to your body's ability to function properly and keep you in good health. It is possible that bariatric surgery will impair your body's ability to absorb certain nutrients, in which case you will need to take dietary supplements.

After bariatric surgery, vitamin B12, vitamin D, and iron deficiency are among the most common micronutrient deficits. To ensure that you meet the necessary intake levels, the healthcare team that you see will tailor a supplement regimen to your unique requirements and write a prescription for it.

It is essential to take your supplements in accordance with the instructions provided in order to maintain a healthy diet and avoid issues. Your nutrient levels will be monitored through the use of routine blood tests, and any necessary adjustments to your supplementation will be made accordingly.

Even though supplements play an important role, it is also crucial to get the nutrients you need from whole foods whenever they are available. A wide variety of necessary vitamins and minerals can be obtained by consuming a diet that is abundant in fruits, vegetables, lean meats, and whole grains.

Always make sure you are drinking enough water to keep yourself hydrated throughout the day. Maintaining a healthy level of hydration is critical to the efficient functioning of your body because it facilitates digestion and the absorption of nutrients.

By adhering to these doable nutritional rules, you will be well on your way to fueling your body and accomplishing your objectives regarding weight loss. In the following chapter, we will discuss meal planning, give you some useful advice for grocery shopping, and showcase a selection of delectable recipes that have been developed specifically for bariatric patients. Get ready to embark on a gastronomic adventure that will not only satisfy your taste buds but also benefit your overall health!

CHAPTER 4

EMBRACING A HEALTHY LIFESTYLE FOR LONG-TERM SUCCESS

A. Promoting Healthy Lifestyles Through Exercise

If you want to keep the weight off, improve your overall health, and feel better overall, physical activity is one of the most important factors to consider. Not only can maintaining a regular exercise routine help you burn calories, but it will also help you build strength, enhance your stamina, and foster a sense of well-being in yourself. Here are some suggestions for suitable activities post-surgery:

Walking: Walking is a low-impact kind of exercise that may be readily included in your everyday routine. Walking is an excellent form of exercise despite its low-impact nature. Walk for shorter distances at first, and work your way up to longer and more intense walks over time. Strive to get at least half an hour of vigorous walking in on most days of the week.

Exercises with low impact: Exercises with low impact are easier on your joints while still offering benefits to your cardiovascular system. Activities such as swimming, cycling, elliptical machine use, and water aerobics are all possibilities. These exercises are gentle on your body while simultaneously helping you burn calories and increase your level of endurance.

Strength Training: Including resistance training activities as part of your regular routine can assist in the development of muscle mass, which can then lead to an increase in your metabolism. Squats, lunges, and push-ups are examples of exercises that can be performed with either resistance bands, modest weights, or even just your own body weight. You should begin with lighter weights and progressively work up to heavier ones as your strength improves.

Before beginning any new workout routine, you should be sure to discuss it with your healthcare provider first. They are able to make individualized recommendations that are based on your particular requirements and constraints.

B. Practices of Mindful Consumption

Your connection with food can be profoundly altered for the better through the practice of mindful eating, which also enables you to select foods that are better for you and helps you keep your diet well-balanced. Incorporating the following practices into your lifestyle can help you become more conscious of what you eat:

Consume your food at a leisurely pace, savoring each bite and completely masticating it while you do so. When you eat slowly, your brain has more time to notice when it's full, which helps prevent you from eating too much. Put down your fork in between mouthfuls so you may engage in conversation or focus on appreciating the meal's many flavors and textures.

Learn to recognize the signs of hunger and fullness. Pay attention to the cues that your body sends you when it is hungry or full. Eat only when your stomach is signaling that it needs food, and stop when you've reached a point where you're no longer hungry. Avoid using food as a way to deal with your feelings or pass the time when you're bored.

Concentrate on foods high in nutrients. You should pick foods that are high in nutrients and provide energy that lasts a long time. Your meals should contain a wide variety of foods, including fruits, vegetables, lean meats, whole grains, and healthy fats. These foods not only provide your body with the nutrients it needs, but they also help you feel more content and give you more energy.

Observe portion control. Be aware of the size of your portions and use smaller plates and bowls to give the illusion that you are more full than you actually are. If you want to correctly measure out your meals, you should use measuring cups or a food scale. When you cook your own meals at home, you can more easily monitor the quality of the components and the quantity of each serving.

C. Assistance Programs and Available Resources
Creating a network of people who will encourage and support you along your journey to a healthier weight is critical to your long-term success. Having a group of people in your network who are able to empathize with your struggles and celebrate your successes with you may be an incredible source of support and inspiration. The following are some resources that may be of assistance to you:

Support Groups: Becoming a member of a nearby support group or going to bariatric-specific support groups gives you the opportunity to connect with individuals who have been through experiences that are similar to yours. You are able to offer and receive emotional support, as well as exchange and trade recipes. These clubs frequently hold regular meetings or maintain online forums where individuals can find direction and inspiration to help them through difficult times.

Communities Online: The internet offers a plethora of online communities and forums where you can engage in conversation with others who are on a path that is analogous to your own. You are able to find support online and communicate with other users by asking questions, sharing success stories, and getting advice. Even if you are in the convenience of your own home, participation in these communities can provide a feeling of belonging as well as support.

Additional Resources: Books, blogs, podcasts, and mobile apps that are focused on bariatric surgery and weight loss can offer helpful knowledge, inspiration, and advice that can be applied in real-life situations. Do some research and look into other sites to find ones that speak to you and can offer you advice on how to improve your nutrition, activity, thinking, and overall well-being.

Keep in mind that you are not traveling this path by yourself. Reach out, look for people who can help you, and make connections with people who understand and share your objectives. You will be able to overcome obstacles, celebrate victories, and maintain your success over the long run if you work together.

In the following and final chapter, we will put everything together by giving you an extensive collection of dishes that are friendly to people who have undergone bariatric surgery and that are both tasty and nutritious. Get ready to go on a gastronomic journey that will not only please your taste buds but also nourish your body and support your commitment to health and well-being for the rest of your life.

MEAL PLAN

Meal Plan: A bariatric diet plan typically consists of an approximate list of dishes that can be consumed throughout the day.

Remember, the bariatric diet plan is tailored to meet individual needs, and it is crucial to consult with your healthcare team to develop a plan that works best for you. Following the plan, making healthy choices, and incorporating regular physical activity can contribute to a successful and sustainable weight management journey after bariatric surgery.

30 DAY Meal Plan 1

MONDAY

Breakfast	Lunch	Dinner	Snacks
VEGGIE EGG MUFFINS	CAULIFLOWER FRIED RICE WITH SHRIMP	GRILLED LEMON HERB CHICKEN BREAST	GREEK YOGURT POPSICLES WITH MIXED BERRIES

TUESDAY

Breakfast	Lunch	Dinner	Snacks
GREEK YOGURT PARFAIT	TURKEY LETTUCE WRAPS WITH AVOCADO	BAKED COD WITH LEMON AND DILL	SUGAR-FREE JELLO WITH A DOLLOP OF WHIPPED CREAM

WEDNESDAY

Breakfast	Lunch	Dinner	Snacks
COTTAGE CHEESE PANCAKES	GREEK SALAD WITH GRILLED SALMON	TURKEY MEATLOAF MUFFINS WITH CAULIFLOWER MASH	CHIA SEED PUDDING WITH COCONUT MILK AND BERRIES

THURSAY

Breakfast	Lunch	Dinner	Snacks
AVOCADO TOAST WITH POACHED EGG	QUINOA SALAD WITH ROASTED VEGETABLES	BEEF AND VEGETABLE STIR-FRY WITH BROWN RICE	FROZEN GRAPES FOR A REFRESHING AND SWEET TREAT

FRIDAY

Breakfast	Lunch	Dinner	Snacks
TURKEY SAUSAGE BREAKFAST BURRITO	TUNA SALAD LETTUCE WRAPS	SPINACH AND FETA STUFFED PORK TENDERLOIN	BAKED PEACHES WITH CINNAMON AND GREEK YOGUR

SATURDAY

Breakfast	Lunch	Dinner	Snacks
QUINOA BREAKFAST BOWL	GREEK YOGURT CHICKEN SALAD LETTUCE WRAPS	EGGPLANT PARMESAN WITH SIDE SALAD	ALMOND BUTTER ENERGY BALLS

SUNDAY

Breakfast	Lunch	Dinner	Snacks
VEGETABLE FRITTATA	QUINOA-STUFFED BELL PEPPERS	GARLIC AND HERB ROASTED PORK TENDERLOIN	CHOCOLATE AVOCADO MOUSSE

30 DAY Meal Plan 2

MONDAY

Breakfast	Lunch	Dinner	Snacks
CINNAMON APPLE OATMEAL	TURKEY AND AVOCADO LETTUCE WRAPS	TURKEY AND VEGETABLE CHILI	PUMPKIN SPICE PROTEIN SHAKE

TUESDAY

Breakfast	Lunch	Dinner	Snacks
BLUEBERRY PROTEIN PANCAKES	GRILLED SHRIMP AND VEGETABLE KEBABS	GRILLED SHRIMP SKEWERS WITH QUINOA	PROTEIN-PACKED CHOCOLATE CHIP COOKIES

WEDNESDAY

Breakfast	Lunch	Dinner	Snacks
TACOS WITH LETTUCE WRAPS	SPINACH AND FETA STUFFED CHICKEN BREAST	ASIAN-STYLE BEEF LETTUCE WRAPS WITH MUSHROOMS	RASPBERRY ALMOND CHIA PUDDING

THURSAY

Breakfast	Lunch	Dinner	Snacks
RICOTTA AND BERRY STUFFED FRENCH	TUNA AND WHITE BEAN SALAD	BAKED CHICKEN WITH ROASTED ROOT VEGETABLES	PEANUT BUTTER PROTEIN BALLS

FRIDAY

Breakfast	Lunch	Dinner	Snacks
BREAKFAST SALAD WITH POACHED EGG	LENTIL AND VEGETABLE SOUP	SPAGHETTI SQUASH WITH TURKEY BOLOGNESE SAUCE	LEMON POPPY SEED MUFFINS

SATURDAY

Breakfast	Lunch	Dinner	Snacks
SMOKED SALMON AND AVOCADO TOAST	GRILLED FLANK STEAK SALAD	MEXICAN CHICKEN AND BLACK BEAN SKILLET	CHOCOLATE PROTEIN ICE CREAM

SUNDAY

Breakfast	Lunch	Dinner	Snacks
EGG WHITE SCRAMBLE WITH VEGETABLES	BAKED CHICKEN TENDERS WITH ALMOND CRUST	STUFFED ZUCCHINI WITH LEAN GROUND BEEF	MINI BLUEBERRY MUFFINS

30 DAY Meal Plan 3

MONDAY

Breakfast	Lunch	Dinner	Snacks
TURKEY BACON AND EGG BREAKFAST BURRITO	BAKED CHICKEN TENDERS WITH ALMOND CRUST	CAULIFLOWER FRIED RICE WITH SHRIMP AND VEGETABLES	CHOCOLATE ALMOND PROTEIN BARS

TUESDAY

Breakfast	Lunch	Dinner	Snacks
QUINOA PORRIDGE WITH BERRIES	TOFU AND VEGETABLE STIR-FRY	GREEK-STYLE STUFFED EGGPLANT WITH GROUND TURKEY	CHOCOLATE COVERED STRAWBERRIES

WEDNESDAY

Breakfast	Lunch	Dinner	Snacks
MINI EGG AND VEGETABLE QUICHES	GREEK SALAD WITH GRILLED SHRIMP	BAKED TILAPIA WITH QUINOA AND ROASTED VEGETABLES	ALMOND FLOUR CHOCOLATE CHIP COOKIES

THURSAY

Breakfast	Lunch	Dinner	Snacks
BARIATRIC-FRIENDLY BREAKFAST SKILLET	CHICKEN AND VEGETABLE KABOBS	TURKEY AND VEGETABLE CURRY WITH CAULIFLOWER RICE	VANILLA PROTEIN SHAKE

FRIDAY

Breakfast	Lunch	Dinner	Snacks
ALMOND FLOUR BANANA MUFFINS	QUINOA AND BLACK BEAN STUFFED TOMATOES	GRILLED SHRIMP AND VEGETABLE KABOBS WITH QUINOA SALAD	PUMPKIN PROTEIN BARS

SATURDAY

Breakfast	Lunch	Dinner	Snacks
BROCCOLI AND CHEESE OMELET	ROASTED VEGETABLE AND HUMMUS WRAP	ITALIAN-STYLE BAKED CHICKEN WITH ZUCCHINI NOODLES	BLUEBERRY ALMOND FLOUR CRUMBLE

SUNDAY

Breakfast	Lunch	Dinner	Snacks
PUMPKIN SPICE CHIA PUDDING	SPICY THAI CHICKEN LETTUCE WRAPS	MEXICAN-STYLE STUFFED BELL	CHOCOLATE AVOCADO PROTEIN PUDDING

30 DAY Meal Plan 4

MONDAY

Breakfast	Lunch	Dinner	Snacks
CHICKEN SAUSAGE BREAKFAST BURRITO	GREEK TURKEY BURGER	GRILLED SALMON WITH LEMON DILL SAUCE	LEMON RASPBERRY PROTEIN MUFFINS

TUESDAY

Breakfast	Lunch	Dinner	Snacks
RICOTTA PANCAKES WITH BERRIES	ROASTED VEGETABLE AND QUINOA SALAD	ZUCCHINI NOODLES WITH TURKEY BOLOGNESE SAUCE	VANILLA COCONUT CHIA PUDDING

WEDNESDAY

Breakfast	Lunch	Dinner	Snacks
MINI VEGETABLE FRITTATAS	BAKED COD WITH ROASTED ASPARAGUS	GARLIC HERB ROASTED PORK TENDERLOIN	ALMOND FLOUR BLUEBERRY MUFFINS

THURSAY

Breakfast	Lunch	Dinner	Snacks
SMOKED SALMON AND SPINACH OMELET	CHICKEN AND VEGETABLE STIR-FRY	BAKED COD WITH ROASTED VEGETABLES AND QUINOA PILAF	CHOCOLATE COCONUT CHIA SEED PUDDING

FRIDAY

Breakfast	Lunch	Dinner	Snacks
CHOCOLATE PROTEIN PANCAKES	GRILLED SHRIMP AND AVOCADO SALAD	SPINACH AND FETA STUFFED CHICKEN THIGHS	RASPBERRY ALMOND FLOUR MUFFINS

SATURDAY

Breakfast	Lunch	Dinner	Snacks
VEGGIE OMELET ROLL-UPS	ROASTED BUTTERNUT SQUASH AND QUINOA SALAD	TURKEY AND VEGETABLE STIR-FRY WITH SESAME	VANILLA COCONUT PROTEIN BALLS

SUNDAY

Breakfast	Lunch	Dinner	Snacks
ALMOND FLOUR WAFFLES WITH BERRIES	SHRIMP AND VEGETABLE SPRING ROLLS	SHRIMP AND BROCCOLI CAULIFLOWER FRIED RICE	BERRY PROTEIN SMOOTHIE BOWL

30 DAY Meal Plan 5

MONDAY

Breakfast	Lunch	Dinner	Snacks
ZUCCHINI AND FETA EGG BAKE	CHICKEN AND BLACK BEAN CHILI	MEXICAN-STYLE STUFFED PORTOBELLO MUSHROOMS	CHOCOLATE PROTEIN MUG CAKE

TUESDAY

Breakfast	Lunch	Dinner	Snacks
HAM AND CHEESE EGG CUPS	QUINOA AND BLACK BEAN SALAD	TERIYAKI TOFU AND VEGETABLE STIR-FRY WITH BROWN RICE	VANILLA COCONUT FLOUR WAFFLES

WEDNESDAY

Breakfast	Lunch	Dinner	Snacks
BREAKFAST STIR-FRY	TURKEY AND VEGETABLE LETTUCE CUPS	TURKEY AND VEGETABLE STIR-FRY WITH GINGER	CHOCOLATE MINT PROTEIN POPSICLES

RECIPES

BREAKFAST

VEGGIE EGG MUFFINS

Nutrition: Cal 150;Fat 8 g;Carb 6 g;Protein 12 g
Serving 2; Cook time 40 min

Ingredients:
- 4 large eggs
- 1/4 cup diced bell peppers
- 1/4 cup diced zucchini
- 1/4 cup diced mushrooms
- 1/4 cup chopped spinach
- 2 tablespoons diced onion
- 2 tablespoons shredded low-fat cheese (optional)
- Salt and pepper to taste
- Cooking spray

Instructions:
1. Preheat the oven to 350°F (175°C) and lightly coat a muffin tin with cooking spray.
2. In a bowl, whisk the eggs until well beaten. Season with salt and pepper to taste.
3. Add the diced bell peppers, zucchini, mushrooms, spinach, and onion to the bowl. Mix well to combine the vegetables with the eggs.
4. Divide the egg and vegetable mixture evenly among the muffin cups, filling each about three-quarters full. If desired, sprinkle a little shredded low-fat cheese on top of each muffin.
5. Place the muffin tin in the preheated oven and bake for approximately 20-25 minutes, or until the muffins are set and lightly golden on top.
6. Once cooked, remove the muffins from the oven and let them cool for a few minutes. Use a knife to gently loosen the edges of the muffins, then transfer them to a serving plate.
7. Serve the bariatric Veggie Egg Muffins warm. They can be enjoyed on their own or paired with a side of fresh salad or a slice of whole grain bread.

GREEK YOGURT PARFAIT

Nutrition: Cal 200;Fat 6 g;Carb 18 g;Protein 15 g
Serving 2; Cook time 10 min

Ingredients:
- 1 cup Greek yogurt, plain or flavored (low-fat or non-fat)
- 1/2 cup fresh berries (such as strawberries, blueberries, or raspberries)
- 2 tablespoons chopped nuts (such as almonds or walnuts)
- 2 tablespoons unsweetened granola
- 1 teaspoon honey (optional)
- Fresh mint leaves for garnish (optional)

Instructions:
1. In two serving glasses or bowls, start by layering half of the Greek yogurt at the bottom of each glass.
2. Add a layer of fresh berries on top of the yogurt. You can use one type of berry or a mixture of different berries.
3. Sprinkle a tablespoon of chopped nuts over the berries in each glass.
4. Add another layer of Greek yogurt on top of the nuts.
5. Sprinkle a tablespoon of unsweetened granola over the second layer of yogurt.
6. If desired, drizzle a teaspoon of honey over the granola for added sweetness.
7. Repeat the layering process with the remaining ingredients to create a second parfait.
8. Finish each parfait with a garnish of fresh mint leaves, if desired.
9. Serve the bariatric Greek Yogurt Parfaits immediately or refrigerate for later consumption.

COTTAGE CHEESE PANCAKES

Nutrition: Cal 200;Fat 8 g;Carb 10 g;Protein 20 g
Serving 2; Cook time 20 min

Ingredients:
- 1/2 cup cottage cheese (low-fat or non-fat)
- 2 large eggs
- 1/4 cup almond flour
- 1/4 teaspoon baking powder
- 1/2 teaspoon vanilla extract
- Cooking spray or a little oil for the pan
- Fresh berries and a drizzle of sugar-free syrup for serving (optional)

Instructions:
1. In a blender or food processor, combine the cottage cheese, eggs, almond flour, baking powder, and vanilla extract. Blend until the mixture becomes smooth and well combined.
2. Preheat a non-stick skillet or griddle over medium heat. Lightly coat the surface with cooking spray or a little oil.
3. Pour approximately 1/4 cup of the pancake batter onto the skillet for each pancake. You can make smaller or larger pancakes, depending on your preference.
4. Cook the pancakes for about 2-3 minutes on one side, until bubbles start to form on the surface.
5. Flip the pancakes gently and cook for another 2-3 minutes on the other side, until golden brown and cooked through.

6. Repeat the process with the remaining batter, adjusting the heat if necessary, until all the pancakes are cooked.
7. Once cooked, transfer the pancakes to a serving plate.
8. Serve the bariatric Cottage Cheese Pancakes warm. You can top them with fresh berries and a drizzle of sugar-free syrup for added flavor, if desired.

SPINACH AND FETA OMELET

Nutrition: Cal 170;Fat 10 g;Carb 4 g;Protein 15 g
Serving 2; Cook time 20 min

Ingredients:
- 4 large eggs
- 1 cup fresh spinach leaves, roughly chopped
- 1/4 cup crumbled feta cheese
- 1/4 cup diced tomatoes
- 2 tablespoons diced red onion
- Salt and pepper to taste
- Cooking spray or a little oil for the pan

Instructions:
1. In a bowl, whisk the eggs until well beaten. Season with salt and pepper to taste.
2. Heat a non-stick skillet over medium heat. Lightly coat the surface with cooking spray or a little oil.
3. Add the diced red onion to the skillet and sauté for 2-3 minutes until it becomes translucent and slightly softened.
4. Add the chopped spinach leaves to the skillet and cook for an additional 1-2 minutes until wilted.
5. Pour the beaten eggs evenly over the spinach and onion mixture in the skillet.
6. Allow the eggs to cook for a few minutes until they start to set around the edges.
7. Sprinkle the crumbled feta cheese and diced tomatoes evenly over one half of the omelet.
8. Using a spatula, carefully fold the other half of the omelet over the filling to create a half-moon shape.
9. Cook for another 2-3 minutes until the omelet is cooked through and the cheese is melted.
10. Once cooked, transfer the omelet to a serving plate and cut it in half to make two servings.
11. Serve the bariatric Spinach and Feta Omelet warm. You can pair it with a side salad or whole grain toast for a complete meal.

PROTEIN-PACKED SMOOTHIE BOWL

Nutrition: Cal 270;Fat 8 g;Carb 20 g;Protein 25 g
Serving 2; Cook time 10 min

Ingredients:
- 1 cup Greek yogurt, plain or flavored (low-fat or non-fat)
- 1 cup frozen mixed berries (such as strawberries, blueberries, and raspberries)
- 1/2 ripe banana, frozen
- 1 scoop protein powder (choose a low-sugar, bariatric-friendly option)
- 1 tablespoon almond butter or peanut butter
- 1/2 cup unsweetened almond milk (or any preferred milk)
- Toppings of choice (such as sliced fresh fruit, nuts, seeds, coconut flakes)

Instructions:
1. In a blender, combine the Greek yogurt, frozen mixed berries, frozen banana, protein powder, almond butter or peanut butter, and almond milk.
2. Blend on high speed until all the ingredients are well combined and you achieve a smooth and creamy consistency. If the mixture is too thick, you can add a little more almond milk to reach the desired consistency.
3. Once blended, pour the smoothie mixture into two bowls.
4. Top the smoothie bowls with your preferred toppings. You can use sliced fresh fruit, nuts, seeds, or coconut flakes to add texture and flavor.
5. Serve the protein-packed Smoothie Bowls immediately. Enjoy them with a spoon and savor the delicious and nutritious combination.

AVOCADO TOAST WITH POACHED EGG

Nutrition: Cal 300;Fat 12 g;Carb 22 g;Protein 12 g
Serving 2; Cook time 15 min

Ingredients:
- 2 slices whole grain bread, toasted
- 1 ripe avocado
- 1 teaspoon lemon juice
- Salt and pepper to taste
- 2 large eggs
- 1 teaspoon white vinegar (for poaching)
- Fresh herbs (such as parsley or cilantro) for garnish (optional)

Instructions:

1. In a small bowl, scoop out the flesh of the ripe avocado. Mash it with a fork until you achieve a smooth consistency.
2. Add lemon juice to the mashed avocado and mix well. Season with salt and pepper to taste.
3. Poach the eggs: Fill a medium-sized saucepan with water and bring it to a gentle simmer. Add the white vinegar to the water. Crack one egg into a small bowl or ramekin. Create a gentle whirlpool in the simmering water with a spoon, then carefully slide the egg into the center of the whirlpool. Repeat the process with the second egg. Cook the eggs for about 3-4 minutes for a soft, runny yolk, or longer if desired.
4. While the eggs are poaching, spread the mashed avocado evenly on the toasted whole grain bread slices.
5. Once the eggs are cooked to your liking, use a slotted spoon to carefully remove them from the water, allowing any excess water to drain off.
6. Place one poached egg on top of each slice of avocado toast.
7. Sprinkle some salt and pepper on the poached eggs, and garnish with fresh herbs if desired.
8. Serve the bariatric Avocado Toast with Poached Egg immediately. Enjoy the combination of creamy avocado, perfectly cooked egg, and whole grain toast.

CHIA SEED PUDDING

Nutrition: Cal 150;Fat 7 g;Carb 12 g;Protein 5 g
Serving 2; Cook time 120 min

Ingredients:

- 1 cup unsweetened almond milk (or any preferred milk)
- 1/4 cup chia seeds
- 1-2 tablespoons low-calorie sweetener (such as stevia or erythritol), optional
- 1/2 teaspoon vanilla extract
- Fresh berries or sliced fruit for topping

Instructions:

1. In a bowl, combine the unsweetened almond milk, chia seeds, low-calorie sweetener (if using), and vanilla extract. Stir well to ensure the chia seeds are evenly distributed in the mixture.
2. Let the mixture sit for about 5 minutes, stirring occasionally. This will prevent clumping and allow the chia seeds to absorb the liquid.
3. After 5 minutes, give the mixture a final stir, making sure there are no clumps of chia seeds.
4. Cover the bowl and refrigerate for at least 2 hours, or overnight if possible. This will allow the chia seeds to absorb the liquid and thicken into a pudding-like consistency.
5. Once chilled and set, give the chia seed pudding a stir to break up any clumps that may have formed.
6. Divide the pudding into two serving bowls or jars.
7. Top the chia seed pudding with fresh berries or sliced fruit of your choice.
8. Serve the bariatric Chia Seed Pudding chilled. Enjoy the creamy and nutritious dessert-like treat.

TURKEY SAUSAGE BREAKFAST BURRITO

Nutrition: Cal 285;Fat 16 g;Carb 6 g;Protein 20 g
Serving 2; Cook time 25 min

Ingredients:

- 4 large lettuce leaves (such as romaine or iceberg), washed and dried
- 4 turkey sausage links, casings removed
- 4 large eggs
- 1/4 cup diced bell peppers (any color)
- 1/4 cup diced onions
- Salt and pepper to taste
- Hot sauce or salsa for serving (optional)

Instructions:

1. Heat a non-stick skillet over medium heat. Add the turkey sausage links and cook, breaking them into small pieces with a spatula, until browned and cooked through. Remove the cooked sausage from the skillet and set aside.
2. In the same skillet, add the diced bell peppers and onions. Sauté for 2-3 minutes until they start to soften.
3. In a bowl, whisk the eggs until well beaten. Season with salt and pepper to taste.
4. Push the sautéed peppers and onions to one side of the skillet. Pour the beaten eggs into the empty side of the skillet. Cook, stirring occasionally, until the eggs are scrambled and cooked to your desired consistency.
5. Add the cooked turkey sausage back to the skillet and stir to combine the ingredients.
6. Take two lettuce leaves and place them on a plate. Spoon half of the turkey sausage and scrambled egg mixture onto each lettuce leaf.

7. Roll up the lettuce leaves tightly, tucking in the sides as you go, to create a burrito shape.
8. Repeat the same process with the remaining lettuce leaves and filling to make the second burrito.
9. Serve the bariatric Turkey Sausage Breakfast Burritos with hot sauce or salsa on the side, if desired.

QUINOA BREAKFAST BOWL

Nutrition: Cal 250;Fat 10 g;Carb 35 g;Protein 8 g
Serving 2; Cook time 30 min

Ingredients:
- 1/2 cup quinoa, rinsed
- 1 cup water
- 1 cup unsweetened almond milk (or any preferred milk)
- 1 tablespoon honey or maple syrup
- 1/2 teaspoon vanilla extract
- 1/2 teaspoon ground cinnamon
- 1/4 cup chopped nuts (such as almonds, walnuts, or pecans)
- 1/4 cup fresh berries or sliced fruit
- 1 tablespoon chia seeds or flaxseeds (optional)

Instructions:
1. In a saucepan, combine the quinoa and water. Bring to a boil over medium-high heat. Once boiling, reduce the heat to low, cover, and simmer for about 10-12 minutes or until the quinoa is tender and the water is absorbed.
2. In a separate small saucepan, heat the unsweetened almond milk over medium heat. Add the honey or maple syrup, vanilla extract, and ground cinnamon. Stir well until the sweetener is dissolved and the mixture is heated through.
3. Once the quinoa is cooked, fluff it with a fork and transfer it to a bowl.
4. Pour the warm sweetened almond milk mixture over the cooked quinoa. Stir well to combine, ensuring the quinoa is evenly coated with the mixture.
5. Divide the quinoa mixture into two serving bowls.
6. Top each bowl with chopped nuts, fresh berries or sliced fruit, and chia seeds or flaxseeds (if using).
7. Serve the bariatric Quinoa Breakfast Bowl immediately. Enjoy the warm, comforting, and protein-rich breakfast to start your day.

BREAKFAST CASSEROLE

Nutrition: Cal 265;Fat 10 g;Carb 35 g;Protein 8 g
Serving 2; Cook time 30 min

Ingredients:
- 1/2 cup quinoa, rinsed
- 1 cup water
- 1 cup unsweetened almond milk (or any preferred milk)
- 1 tablespoon honey or maple syrup
- 1/2 teaspoon vanilla extract
- 1/2 teaspoon ground cinnamon
- 1/4 cup chopped nuts (such as almonds, walnuts, or pecans)
- 1/4 cup fresh berries or sliced fruit
- 1 tablespoon chia seeds or flaxseeds (optional)

Instructions:
1. In a saucepan, combine the quinoa and water. Bring to a boil over medium-high heat. Once boiling, reduce the heat to low, cover, and simmer for about 10-12 minutes or until the quinoa is tender and the water is absorbed.
2. In a separate small saucepan, heat the unsweetened almond milk over medium heat. Add the honey or maple syrup, vanilla extract, and ground cinnamon. Stir well until the sweetener is dissolved and the mixture is heated through.
3. Once the quinoa is cooked, fluff it with a fork and transfer it to a bowl.
4. Pour the warm sweetened almond milk mixture over the cooked quinoa. Stir well to combine, ensuring the quinoa is evenly coated with the mixture.
5. Divide the quinoa mixture into two serving bowls.
6. Top each bowl with chopped nuts, fresh berries or sliced fruit, and chia seeds or flaxseeds (if using).
7. Serve the bariatric Quinoa Breakfast Bowl immediately. Enjoy the warm, comforting, and protein-rich breakfast to start your day.
1.
2. In a bowl, whisk together the almond flour, coconut flour, baking powder, and salt until well combined.
3. In a separate bowl, beat the eggs. Add the almond milk, melted coconut oil, and vanilla extract. Mix well.

4. Gradually add the wet ingredients to the dry ingredients, stirring until you have a smooth batter. If the batter appears too thick, you can add a little more almond milk, one tablespoon at a time, until you achieve the desired consistency.
5. Lightly grease the waffle iron with cooking spray or melted coconut oil.
6. Pour half of the batter onto the center of the waffle iron. Use a spatula to spread the batter evenly. Close the waffle iron and cook according to its instructions, usually about 4-5 minutes or until the waffle is golden brown and crisp.
7. Carefully remove the cooked waffle from the iron and transfer it to a plate. Repeat the process with the remaining batter to make the second waffle.
8. Serve the bariatric Almond Flour Waffles warm with your favorite toppings such as fresh berries, sugar-free syrup, or a sprinkle of powdered sugar.

SMOKED SALMON AND CREAM CHEESE ROLL-UPS

Nutrition: Cal 190;Fat 10 g;Carb 2 g;Protein 14 g
Serving 2; Cook time 10 min

Ingredients:
- 4 slices of smoked salmon
- 2 tablespoons cream cheese (reduced-fat or Greek yogurt cream cheese)
- 2 teaspoons capers, drained
- 2 teaspoons fresh dill, chopped
- Juice of half a lemon
- Freshly ground black pepper, to taste

Instructions:
1. Lay out the smoked salmon slices on a clean surface.
2. In a small bowl, mix together the cream cheese, capers, fresh dill, lemon juice, and black pepper until well combined.
3. Spread half of the cream cheese mixture evenly onto each slice of smoked salmon.
4. Starting from one end, roll up each slice of salmon tightly.
5. Use a sharp knife to cut each roll-up into bite-sized pieces.
6. Arrange the Smoked Salmon and Cream Cheese Roll-Ups on a serving platter.
7. Serve immediately and enjoy as a delicious and protein-rich snack or appetizer.

VEGETABLE FRITTATA

Nutrition: Cal 260;Fat 12 g;Carb 8 g;Protein 15 g
Serving 2; Cook time 30 min

Ingredients:
- 4 large eggs
- 2 tablespoons milk (preferably unsweetened almond milk)
- 1/4 cup diced bell peppers (any color)
- 1/4 cup diced zucchini
- 1/4 cup diced mushrooms
- 1/4 cup diced onions
- 1/4 cup shredded low-fat cheese (such as mozzarella or cheddar)
- 1 tablespoon olive oil
- Salt and pepper to taste
- Fresh herbs (such as parsley or chives) for garnish (optional)

Instructions:
1. Preheat your oven to 350°F (175°C).
2. In a bowl, whisk together the eggs, milk, salt, and pepper until well beaten.
3. Heat the olive oil in an oven-safe skillet over medium heat.
4. Add the diced bell peppers, zucchini, mushrooms, and onions to the skillet. Sauté for about 5 minutes or until the vegetables have softened.
5. Pour the beaten egg mixture over the sautéed vegetables in the skillet. Stir gently to evenly distribute the vegetables.
6. Sprinkle the shredded cheese on top of the frittata mixture.
7. Transfer the skillet to the preheated oven and bake for 15 minutes or until the eggs are set and the cheese is melted and lightly golden.
8. Once cooked, remove the skillet from the oven and let it cool for a few minutes.
9. Carefully slide a spatula around the edges of the frittata to loosen it. Slide the frittata onto a cutting board or serving plate.
10. Slice the Vegetable Frittata into wedges and garnish with fresh herbs, if desired.
11. Serve the bariatric Vegetable Frittata warm and enjoy as a nutritious and protein-packed breakfast or brunch option.

CINNAMON APPLE OATMEAL

Nutrition: Cal 190;Fat 10 g;Carb 2 g;Protein 14 g
Serving 2; Cook time 15 min

Ingredients:
- 1 cup rolled oats

- 2 cups water (or low-fat milk for creamier oatmeal)
- 1 medium apple, peeled, cored, and diced
- 1 tablespoon honey (optional)
- 1/2 teaspoon ground cinnamon
- Pinch of salt
- Chopped nuts or seeds for garnish (optional)

Instructions:
1. In a saucepan, bring the water (or milk) to a boil.
2. Add the rolled oats, diced apple, honey (if using), ground cinnamon, and a pinch of salt to the boiling liquid.
3. Reduce the heat to low and simmer for about 5-7 minutes, stirring occasionally, until the oats are cooked and the apples are tender.
4. Remove the saucepan from the heat and let it sit for a minute to thicken.
5. Divide the Bariatric Cinnamon Apple Oatmeal into two serving bowls.
6. Garnish with chopped nuts or seeds if desired, for added texture and flavor.

EGG AND VEGETABLE BREAKFAST WRAP

Nutrition: Cal 210;Fat 8 g;Carb 20 g;Protein 12 g
Serving 2; Cook time 25 min

Ingredients:
- 4 large eggs
- 1/4 cup diced bell peppers (any color)
- 1/4 cup diced zucchini
- 1/4 cup diced mushrooms
- 1/4 cup diced onions
- 2 tablespoons shredded low-fat cheese (such as mozzarella or cheddar)
- 2 whole-wheat or low-carb tortillas (8 inches in diameter)
- Salt and pepper to taste
- Cooking spray or a little olive oil for cooking

Instructions:
1. In a bowl, beat the eggs until well mixed. Season with salt and pepper.
2. Heat a non-stick skillet over medium heat and lightly coat it with cooking spray or a little olive oil.
3. Add the diced bell peppers, zucchini, mushrooms, and onions to the skillet. Sauté for about 3-4 minutes or until the vegetables have softened.
4. Pour the beaten eggs over the sautéed vegetables in the skillet. Stir gently to combine the eggs and vegetables.

5. Continue to cook the eggs, stirring occasionally, until they are fully cooked and scrambled.
6. Once the eggs are cooked, sprinkle the shredded cheese on top and let it melt.
7. Warm the tortillas in a dry skillet or microwave according to the package instructions.
8. Divide the scrambled eggs and vegetable mixture evenly between the two tortillas.
9. Roll up the tortillas, tucking in the sides as you go, to form a wrap.
10. Cut each wrap in half diagonally to create two servings.

BLUEBERRY PROTEIN PANCAKES

Nutrition: Cal 180;Fat 6 g;Carb 15 g;Protein 12 g
Serving 2; Cook time 20 min

Ingredients:
- 1/2 cup oat flour (you can make it by blending rolled oats)
- 1/2 cup low-fat cottage cheese
- 2 large eggs
- 1/2 teaspoon baking powder
- 1/2 teaspoon vanilla extract
- 1/4 cup blueberries (fresh or frozen)
- Cooking spray or a little olive oil for cooking
- Sugar-free syrup or fresh berries for serving (optional)

Instructions:
1. In a blender or food processor, blend the oat flour, cottage cheese, eggs, baking powder, and vanilla extract until smooth and well combined.
2. Heat a non-stick skillet or griddle over medium heat and lightly coat it with cooking spray or a little olive oil.
3. Pour 1/4 cup of the pancake batter onto the skillet to form a pancake.
4. Sprinkle a few blueberries on top of the pancake.
5. Cook for 2-3 minutes or until bubbles start to form on the surface of the pancake.
6. Flip the pancake and cook for an additional 1-2 minutes until golden brown.
7. Repeat the process with the remaining batter, adding more cooking spray or oil as needed.
8. Once all the pancakes are cooked, stack them on a serving plate.
9. Serve the Bariatric Blueberry Protein Pancakes warm, topped with sugar-free syrup or fresh berries if desired.

QUICHE WITH SPINACH AND MUSHROOMS

Nutrition: Cal 170;Fat 6 g;Carb 8 g;Protein 14 g
Serving 2; Cook time 20 min

Ingredients:
- 4 large eggs
- 1/2 cup skim milk
- 1/2 cup low-fat cottage cheese
- 1 cup fresh spinach, chopped
- 1 cup mushrooms, sliced
- 1/4 cup grated Parmesan cheese
- 1/4 teaspoon salt
- 1/4 teaspoon black pepper
- Cooking spray

Instructions:
1. Preheat your oven to 375°F (190°C).
2. In a medium-sized bowl, whisk together the eggs, skim milk, and low-fat cottage cheese until well combined. Set aside.
3. Heat a non-stick skillet over medium heat and lightly coat it with cooking spray. Add the mushrooms and sauté until they release their moisture and become tender, about 5 minutes. Remove the mushrooms from the skillet and set aside.
4. In the same skillet, add the chopped spinach and cook until wilted, about 2-3 minutes. Remove from heat and set aside.
5. Lightly coat a 9-inch pie dish with cooking spray. Pour the egg mixture into the dish.
6. Add the sautéed mushrooms and cooked spinach on top of the egg mixture. Spread them evenly in the dish.
7. Sprinkle the grated Parmesan cheese, salt, and black pepper over the mixture.
8. Place the quiche in the preheated oven and bake for 25-30 minutes or until the center is set and the edges are golden brown.
9. Remove from the oven and let it cool for a few minutes before slicing and serving.

GREEK YOGURT WITH BERRIES AND ALMONDS

Nutrition: Cal 150;Fat 3 g;Carb 18 g;Protein 15 g
Serving 2; Cook time 5 min

Ingredients:
- 1 cup plain non-fat Greek yogurt
- 1 cup mixed berries (such as strawberries, blueberries, raspberries)
- 2 tablespoons sliced almonds
- 1 tablespoon honey (optional, for sweetness)

Instructions:
1. In two serving bowls, divide the Greek yogurt evenly.
2. Wash the mixed berries and remove any stems or hulls. Slice the strawberries if desired.
3. Add the mixed berries on top of the Greek yogurt in each bowl.
4. Sprinkle the sliced almonds over the berries.
5. If desired, drizzle a tablespoon of honey over the yogurt and berries for added sweetness.
6. Serve immediately and enjoy!

SCRAMBLED EGG STUFFED BELL PEPPERS

Nutrition: Cal 150;Fat 8 g;Carb 9 g;Protein 13 g
Serving 2; Cook time 30 min

Ingredients:
- 2 medium-sized bell peppers (any color)
- 4 large eggs
- 1/4 cup low-fat milk
- 1/4 cup shredded reduced-fat cheddar cheese
- 1/4 cup diced onion
- 1/4 cup diced tomato
- 1/4 teaspoon salt
- 1/4 teaspoon black pepper
- Cooking spray

Instructions:
1. Preheat your oven to 375°F (190°C).
2. Cut off the tops of the bell peppers and remove the seeds and membranes from the inside. Rinse the peppers thoroughly.
3. In a small bowl, whisk together the eggs, low-fat milk, salt, and black pepper until well combined.
4. Heat a non-stick skillet over medium heat and lightly coat it with cooking spray. Add the diced onion and cook until softened, about 2-3 minutes.
5. Pour the egg mixture into the skillet with the onions. Stir continuously until the eggs are scrambled and cooked to your desired consistency.
6. Remove the skillet from heat and stir in the diced tomato and shredded cheddar cheese.
7. Spoon the scrambled egg mixture into the hollowed-out bell peppers, dividing it evenly between the two peppers.
8. Place the stuffed bell peppers on a baking sheet and bake in the preheated oven for approximately 20-25 minutes or until the peppers are tender and the filling is cooked through.

9. Remove from the oven and let them cool for a few minutes before serving.

TACOS WITH LETTUCE WRAPS

Nutrition: Cal 175;Fat 8 g;Carb 8 g;Protein 14 g
Serving 2; Cook time 35 min

Ingredients:
- 2 medium-sized bell peppers (any color)
- 4 large eggs
- 1/4 cup low-fat milk
- 1/4 cup shredded reduced-fat cheddar cheese
- 1/4 cup diced onion
- 1/4 cup diced tomato
- 1/4 teaspoon salt
- 1/4 teaspoon black pepper
- Cooking spray

Instructions:
1. Preheat your oven to 375°F (190°C).
2. Cut off the tops of the bell peppers and remove the seeds and membranes from the inside. Rinse the peppers thoroughly.
3. In a small bowl, whisk together the eggs, low-fat milk, salt, and black pepper until well combined.
4. Heat a non-stick skillet over medium heat and lightly coat it with cooking spray. Add the diced onion and cook until softened, about 2-3 minutes.
5. Pour the egg mixture into the skillet with the onions. Stir continuously until the eggs are scrambled and cooked to your desired consistency.
6. Remove the skillet from heat and stir in the diced tomato and shredded cheddar cheese.
7. Spoon the scrambled egg mixture into the hollowed-out bell peppers, dividing it evenly between the two peppers.
8. Place the stuffed bell peppers on a baking sheet and bake in the preheated oven for approximately 20-25 minutes or until the peppers are tender and the filling is cooked through.
9. Remove from the oven and let them cool for a few minutes before serving.

BAKED EGG CUPS WITH HAM AND CHEESE

Nutrition: Cal 135;Fat 8 g;Carb 1 g;Protein 15 g
Serving 2; Cook time 15 min

Ingredients:
- 4 slices of lean ham (approximately 2 ounces)
- 4 large eggs
- 1/4 cup shredded reduced-fat cheddar cheese
- 1/4 teaspoon salt
- 1/4 teaspoon black pepper
- Cooking spray
- Fresh parsley or chives (optional, for garnish)

Instructions:
1. Preheat your oven to 375°F (190°C).
2. Lightly coat two ramekins or muffin cups with cooking spray.
3. Line each ramekin or muffin cup with a slice of lean ham, making sure to cover the bottom and sides. The ham should form a cup shape to hold the eggs.
4. Crack an egg into each ham-lined cup. Season with salt and black pepper.
5. Sprinkle the shredded cheddar cheese evenly over the eggs.
6. Place the ramekins or muffin cups on a baking sheet and transfer to the preheated oven.
7. Bake for approximately 12-15 minutes or until the egg whites are set, but the yolks are still slightly runny. If you prefer a more well-done egg, bake for a few more minutes.
8. Remove from the oven and let them cool for a few minutes before serving.
9. Optional: Garnish with fresh parsley or chives for added flavor and presentation.

SWEET POTATO HASH WITH TURKEY BACON

Nutrition: Cal 200;Fat 6 g;Carb 30 g;Protein 8 g
Serving 2; Cook time 25 min

Ingredients:
- 2 medium-sized sweet potatoes, peeled and diced
- 4 slices of turkey bacon, chopped
- 1/2 cup diced onion
- 1/2 cup diced bell pepper (any color)
- 1/2 teaspoon garlic powder
- 1/2 teaspoon paprika
- 1/4 teaspoon salt
- 1/4 teaspoon black pepper
- Cooking spray

Instructions:
1. In a large non-stick skillet, heat over medium heat and lightly coat it with cooking spray.
2. Add the chopped turkey bacon to the skillet and cook until crispy. Remove the bacon from the skillet and set aside.

3. In the same skillet, add the diced sweet potatoes, onion, and bell pepper. Cook, stirring occasionally, until the sweet potatoes are tender and slightly browned, about 10-12 minutes.
4. Add the cooked turkey bacon back to the skillet with the sweet potato mixture.
5. Sprinkle the garlic powder, paprika, salt, and black pepper over the mixture. Stir well to combine and cook for an additional 2-3 minutes.
6. Remove from heat and divide the sweet potato hash into two servings.
7. Optional: Serve with a side of eggs or a protein of your choice for a more complete meal.

RICOTTA AND BERRY STUFFED FRENCH

Nutrition: Cal 240;Fat 8 g;Carb 25 g;Protein 16 g
Serving 2; Cook time 10 min

Ingredients:
- 4 slices of whole wheat bread
- 1/2 cup low-fat ricotta cheese
- 1/2 cup mixed berries (such as strawberries, blueberries, raspberries)
- 2 large eggs
- 1/4 cup unsweetened almond milk
- 1/2 teaspoon vanilla extract
- Cooking spray
- Optional toppings: Powdered sugar, additional berries, or a drizzle of sugar-free syrup

Instructions:
1. In a small bowl, mix the ricotta cheese and mixed berries together until well combined.
2. Lay out two slices of bread and spread the ricotta and berry mixture evenly on top of each slice. Place the remaining two slices of bread on top to make two sandwiches.
3. In a shallow dish, whisk together the eggs, almond milk, and vanilla extract.
4. Heat a non-stick skillet or griddle over medium heat and lightly coat it with cooking spray.
5. Dip each sandwich into the egg mixture, making sure to coat both sides.
6. Place the dipped sandwiches on the skillet or griddle and cook until golden brown on each side, about 2-3 minutes per side.
7. Remove from heat and let them cool for a few minutes before serving.
8. Optional: Top with powdered sugar, additional berries, or a drizzle of sugar-free syrup.

OMELET MUFFINS WITH HAM AND CHEESE

Nutrition: Cal 150;Fat 9 g;Carb 3 g;Protein 14 g
Serving 2; Cook time 25 min

Ingredients:
- 4 large eggs
- 1/4 cup diced cooked ham
- 1/4 cup shredded reduced-fat cheddar cheese
- 1/4 cup diced onion
- 1/4 cup diced bell pepper (any color)
- 1/4 teaspoon salt
- 1/4 teaspoon black pepper
- Cooking spray

Instructions:
1. Preheat your oven to 375°F (190°C). Lightly coat a muffin tin with cooking spray.
2. In a bowl, beat the eggs until well combined. Season with salt and black pepper.
3. Divide the diced ham, shredded cheddar cheese, diced onion, and diced bell pepper evenly among the muffin cups.
4. Pour the beaten eggs over the ingredients in each muffin cup, filling them about 3/4 full.
5. Gently stir the ingredients in each muffin cup with a fork to ensure even distribution.
6. Place the muffin tin in the preheated oven and bake for approximately 15-20 minutes or until the omelet muffins are set and slightly golden on top.
7. Remove from the oven and let them cool for a few minutes before serving.

BREAKFAST SALAD WITH POACHED EGG

Nutrition: Cal 200;Fat 14 g;Carb 8 g;Protein 12 g
Serving 2; Cook time 15 min

Ingredients:
- 4 cups mixed salad greens
- 2 large eggs
- 1/2 avocado, sliced
- 4 cherry tomatoes, halved
- 2 slices turkey bacon, cooked and crumbled
- 2 tablespoons balsamic vinegar
- 1 tablespoon extra virgin olive oil
- Salt and pepper to taste

Instructions:
1. Divide the mixed salad greens between two plates or bowls.

2. In a small saucepan, bring water to a gentle simmer. Add a splash of vinegar to the water to help the eggs hold their shape.
3. Crack one egg into a small bowl or cup. Create a gentle whirlpool in the simmering water using a spoon, and carefully slide the egg into the center of the whirlpool. Repeat with the second egg. Poach the eggs for about 3-4 minutes for a soft, runny yolk.
4. While the eggs are poaching, arrange the sliced avocado, cherry tomatoes, and crumbled turkey bacon over the salad greens.
5. In a small bowl, whisk together the balsamic vinegar, extra virgin olive oil, salt, and pepper to make the dressing.
6. Once the eggs are cooked to your liking, carefully remove them from the water using a slotted spoon and place them on top of the salad.
7. Drizzle the dressing over the salad, and season with additional salt and pepper if desired.

COCONUT FLOUR PANCAKES

Nutrition: Cal 180;Fat 10 g;Carb 10 g;Protein 10 g
Serving 2; Cook time 15 min

Ingredients:
- 1/4 cup coconut flour
- 4 large eggs
- 1/4 cup unsweetened almond milk
- 1 tablespoon melted coconut oil
- 1 tablespoon honey or a sugar substitute (optional, for added sweetness)
- 1/2 teaspoon baking powder
- 1/2 teaspoon vanilla extract
- Pinch of salt
- Cooking spray or additional coconut oil for greasing the pan

Instructions:
1. In a mixing bowl, whisk together the coconut flour, baking powder, and salt until well combined.
2. In a separate bowl, whisk the eggs until well beaten. Add the almond milk, melted coconut oil, honey (or sugar substitute), and vanilla extract. Mix until smooth.
3. Gradually add the wet ingredients to the dry ingredients, stirring well to ensure there are no lumps. Let the batter sit for a few minutes to allow the coconut flour to absorb the liquid.
4. Heat a non-stick skillet or griddle over medium heat. Lightly coat it with cooking spray or use a small amount of coconut oil to grease the surface.
5. Spoon the pancake batter onto the heated skillet, forming small circles (about 3-4 inches in diameter).
6. Cook for 2-3 minutes on one side until small bubbles form on the surface, then flip and cook for an additional 1-2 minutes on the other side until golden brown.
7. Repeat the process with the remaining batter, greasing the pan as needed.
8. Serve the coconut flour pancakes warm and top with your choice of low-sugar syrup, fresh berries, or a dollop of Greek yogurt.

SMOKED SALMON AND AVOCADO TOAST

Nutrition: Cal 240;Fat 12 g;Carb 18 g;Protein 15 g
Serving 2; Cook time 15 min

Ingredients:
- 2 slices of whole grain bread (preferably low-carb or high-fiber bread)
- 4 ounces smoked salmon
- 1 ripe avocado
- Juice of 1/2 lemon
- 1 tablespoon chopped fresh dill
- Salt and pepper to taste

Instructions:
1. Toast the slices of bread until golden brown and crispy.
2. In a small bowl, mash the ripe avocado with a fork. Add the lemon juice, chopped fresh dill, salt, and pepper. Mix well to combine.
3. Spread a generous amount of the avocado mixture onto each slice of toasted bread.
4. Top the avocado mixture with equal amounts of smoked salmon on each slice of bread.
5. Optional: Garnish with additional fresh dill or a squeeze of lemon juice for added flavor.
6. Serve the smoked salmon and avocado toast immediately.

ZUCCHINI AND CHEESE BREAKFAST CASSEROLE

Nutrition: Cal 150;Fat 9 g;Carb 7 g;Protein 10 g
Serving 2; Cook time 30 min

Ingredients:
- 1 medium zucchini, grated
- 2 large eggs
- 1/4 cup shredded reduced-fat cheddar cheese
- 1/4 cup shredded Parmesan cheese
- 1/4 cup almond flour
- 2 tablespoons chopped fresh parsley
- 1/4 teaspoon garlic powder
- 1/4 teaspoon onion powder
- 1/4 teaspoon salt
- 1/4 teaspoon black pepper
- Cooking spray

Instructions:
1. Preheat your oven to 350°F (175°C).
2. In a large bowl, combine the grated zucchini, eggs, shredded cheddar cheese, shredded Parmesan cheese, almond flour, chopped parsley, garlic powder, onion powder, salt, and black pepper. Mix well to combine.
3. Lightly coat a small baking dish or casserole dish with cooking spray.
4. Transfer the zucchini mixture to the prepared baking dish, spreading it out evenly.
5. Bake in the preheated oven for approximately 25-30 minutes or until the top is golden brown and the center is set.
6. Remove from the oven and let it cool for a few minutes before serving.

EGG WHITE SCRAMBLE WITH VEGETABLES

Nutrition: Cal 80;Fat 0 g;Carb 7 g;Protein 12 g
Serving 2; Cook time 10 min

Ingredients:
- 4 large egg whites
- 1/2 cup diced bell peppers (any color)
- 1/2 cup diced zucchini
- 1/4 cup diced onion
- 1/4 cup diced tomatoes
- 1/4 cup chopped spinach
- 1/4 teaspoon garlic powder
- 1/4 teaspoon onion powder
- Salt and pepper to taste
- Cooking spray

Instructions:
1. Heat a non-stick skillet over medium heat and lightly coat it with cooking spray.
2. Add the diced bell peppers, zucchini, and onion to the skillet. Sauté for 3-4 minutes until the vegetables begin to soften.
3. In a separate bowl, whisk the egg whites until frothy. Season with garlic powder, onion powder, salt, and pepper.
4. Add the egg whites to the skillet with the sautéed vegetables. Stir gently to combine.
5. Cook the mixture for 3-4 minutes, stirring occasionally, until the egg whites are fully cooked and scrambled.
6. Add the diced tomatoes and chopped spinach to the skillet. Cook for an additional 1-2 minutes until the spinach wilts.
7. Remove from heat and divide the egg white scramble with vegetables into two servings.

TURKEY BACON AND EGG BREAKFAST BURRITO

Nutrition: Cal 250;Fat 10 g;Carb 20 g;Protein 20 g
Serving 2; Cook time 15 min

Ingredients:
- 4 large eggs
- 4 slices turkey bacon
- 2 whole wheat or low-carb tortillas
- 1/4 cup shredded reduced-fat cheddar cheese
- 1/4 cup diced bell peppers (any color)
- 1/4 cup diced onion
- Salt and pepper to taste
- Cooking spray

Instructions:
1. In a non-stick skillet, cook the turkey bacon until crispy. Remove from the skillet and crumble into small pieces. Set aside.
2. In the same skillet, lightly coat it with cooking spray and add the diced bell peppers and onion. Sauté for 3-4 minutes until the vegetables begin to soften.
3. In a bowl, beat the eggs until well combined. Season with salt and pepper.
4. Push the sautéed vegetables to one side of the skillet and pour the beaten eggs into the other side. Cook, stirring occasionally, until the eggs are scrambled and fully cooked.

5. Warm the tortillas in a separate skillet or microwave according to package instructions.
6. Divide the scrambled eggs, crumbled turkey bacon, and shredded cheddar cheese evenly between the tortillas.
7. Fold the sides of the tortillas inward, then roll them up tightly to form burritos.
8. Serve the Turkey Bacon and Egg Breakfast Burritos immediately.

GREEK YOGURT WITH GRANOLA AND FRESH FRUIT

Nutrition: Cal 200;Fat 4 g;Carb 30 g;Protein 15 g
Serving 2; Соок time 5 min

Ingredients:
- 1 cup Greek yogurt (preferably low-fat or non-fat)
- 1/2 cup granola (choose a low-sugar or homemade version)
- 1 cup mixed fresh fruit (such as berries, sliced banana, or diced mango)
- Optional: Honey or a sugar substitute (for added sweetness)

Instructions:
1. In two bowls or serving glasses, divide the Greek yogurt evenly.
2. Top each portion of Greek yogurt with 1/4 cup of granola.
3. Add half of the mixed fresh fruit to each bowl or glass, arranging it on top of the granola.
4. Optional: Drizzle with honey or sprinkle with a sugar substitute for added sweetness, if desired.
5. Serve the Greek Yogurt with Granola and Fresh Fruit immediately.

CAULIFLOWER HASH BROWNS

Nutrition: Cal 90;Fat 5 g;Carb 7 g;Protein 6 g
Serving 2; Соок time 15 min

Ingredients:
- 2 cups grated cauliflower (raw or lightly steamed)
- 1 large egg
- 2 tablespoons almond flour
- 2 tablespoons grated Parmesan cheese
- 1/4 teaspoon garlic powder
- 1/4 teaspoon onion powder
- Salt and pepper to taste
- Cooking spray or olive oil for frying

Instructions:
1. Place the grated cauliflower in a clean kitchen towel or cheesecloth. Squeeze out any excess moisture from the cauliflower.
2. In a mixing bowl, combine the grated cauliflower, egg, almond flour, grated Parmesan cheese, garlic powder, onion powder, salt, and pepper. Mix well to combine and form a sticky mixture.
3. Divide the mixture into four equal portions and shape them into patties, pressing firmly to remove any excess moisture.
4. Heat a non-stick skillet over medium heat and lightly coat it with cooking spray or olive oil.
5. Place the cauliflower hash brown patties in the skillet and cook for 3-4 minutes on each side, or until golden brown and crispy.
6. Remove from the skillet and place on a paper towel-lined plate to absorb any excess oil.
7. Serve the cauliflower hash browns hot, with a side of Greek yogurt or a low-sugar dipping sauce, if desired.

SPINACH AND MUSHROOM BREAKFAST WRAP

Nutrition: Cal 230;Fat 10 g;Carb 20 g;Protein 17 g
Serving 2; Соок time 15 min

Ingredients:
- 4 large eggs
- 1 cup fresh spinach leaves
- 1 cup sliced mushrooms
- 1/4 cup diced onion
- 1/4 cup shredded reduced-fat cheddar cheese
- 2 whole wheat or low-carb tortillas
- Salt and pepper to taste
- Cooking spray

Instructions:
1. Heat a non-stick skillet over medium heat and lightly coat it with cooking spray.
2. Add the diced onion and sliced mushrooms to the skillet. Sauté for 3-4 minutes until the vegetables begin to soften.
3. Add the fresh spinach leaves to the skillet and cook for an additional 1-2 minutes until the spinach wilts.
4. In a separate bowl, beat the eggs until well combined. Season with salt and pepper.

5. Push the sautéed vegetables to one side of the skillet and pour the beaten eggs into the other side. Cook, stirring occasionally, until the eggs are scrambled and fully cooked.
6. Warm the tortillas in a separate skillet or microwave according to package instructions.
7. Divide the scrambled eggs and sautéed vegetables evenly between the tortillas.
8. Sprinkle each wrap with shredded cheddar cheese.
9. Roll up the tortillas tightly to form wraps.
10. Serve the Spinach and Mushroom Breakfast Wraps immediately.

QUINOA PORRIDGE WITH BERRIES

Nutrition: Cal 250;Fat 7 g;Carb 40 g;Protein 9 g
Serving 2; Cook time 30 min

Ingredients:
- 1/2 cup quinoa
- 1 cup water
- 1 cup unsweetened almond milk (or your preferred milk substitute)
- 1/2 teaspoon vanilla extract
- 1/2 cup mixed berries (such as blueberries, strawberries, or raspberries)
- 1 tablespoon chopped nuts (such as almonds or walnuts)
- 1 tablespoon honey or a sugar substitute (optional, for added sweetness)

Instructions:
1. Rinse the quinoa thoroughly under cold water to remove any bitterness.
2. In a medium-sized saucepan, bring the water to a boil. Add the rinsed quinoa and reduce the heat to low. Cover and simmer for 15-20 minutes, or until the quinoa is tender and the water has been absorbed.
3. Stir in the almond milk and vanilla extract. Cook for an additional 5 minutes, stirring occasionally, until the porridge thickens to your desired consistency.
4. Remove the saucepan from heat and let it sit covered for 5 minutes.
5. Divide the quinoa porridge into two bowls.
6. Top each bowl with mixed berries and chopped nuts.

7. Optional: Drizzle with honey or sprinkle with a sugar substitute for added sweetness, if desired.
8. Serve the Quinoa Porridge with Berries immediately.

MINI EGG AND VEGETABLE QUICHES

Nutrition: Cal 150;Fat 8 g;Carb 8 g;Protein 12 g
Serving 2; Cook time 25 min

Ingredients:
- 4 large eggs
- 1/4 cup diced bell peppers (any color)
- 1/4 cup diced zucchini
- 1/4 cup diced onion
- 1/4 cup diced tomatoes
- 1/4 cup chopped spinach
- 1/4 cup shredded reduced-fat cheddar cheese
- Salt and pepper to taste
- Cooking spray

Instructions:
1. Preheat the oven to 350°F (175°C). Lightly coat a muffin tin with cooking spray.
2. In a bowl, beat the eggs until well combined. Season with salt and pepper.
3. Divide the diced bell peppers, zucchini, onion, tomatoes, and chopped spinach evenly among the muffin tin cups.
4. Pour the beaten eggs over the vegetable mixture in each cup, filling them about 3/4 full.
5. Sprinkle shredded cheddar cheese on top of each mini quiche.
6. Bake in the preheated oven for 15-20 minutes, or until the eggs are set and the cheese is melted and slightly golden.
7. Remove the mini quiches from the muffin tin and let them cool for a few minutes before serving.

BARIATRIC-FRIENDLY BREAKFAST SKILLET

Nutrition: Cal 200;Fat 10 g;Carb 10 g;Protein 16 g
Serving 2; Cook time 15 min

Ingredients:
- 4 slices turkey bacon, chopped
- 4 large eggs
- 1 cup diced bell peppers (any color)
- 1 cup diced zucchini

- 1/2 cup diced onion
- 1/2 cup diced tomatoes
- Salt and pepper to taste
- Cooking spray

Instructions:

1. Heat a non-stick skillet over medium heat. Add the chopped turkey bacon and cook until crispy. Remove the cooked turkey bacon from the skillet and set aside.
2. In the same skillet, lightly coat it with cooking spray. Add the diced bell peppers, zucchini, and onion. Sauté for 3-4 minutes until the vegetables begin to soften.
3. Add the diced tomatoes to the skillet and cook for an additional 1-2 minutes until the tomatoes are heated through.
4. Push the sautéed vegetables to one side of the skillet. Crack the eggs into the other side of the skillet. Cook the eggs to your desired doneness, either scrambled or sunny-side-up.
5. Season the eggs and vegetables with salt and pepper to taste.
6. Divide the cooked turkey bacon, sautéed vegetables, and eggs evenly between two plates.
7. Serve the Bariatric-Friendly Breakfast Skillet immediately.

ALMOND FLOUR BANANA MUFFINS

Nutrition: Cal 200;Fat 15 g;Carb 10 g;Protein 8 g
Serving 2; Cook time 20 min

Ingredients:
- 1 cup almond flour
- 1/4 teaspoon baking soda
- 1/4 teaspoon cinnamon
- Pinch of salt
- 1 ripe banana, mashed
- 2 tablespoons honey or a sugar substitute
- 2 large eggs
- 1/2 teaspoon vanilla extract

Instructions:

1. Preheat the oven to 350°F (175°C). Line a muffin tin with paper liners or lightly grease the cups with cooking spray.
2. In a mixing bowl, whisk together the almond flour, baking soda, cinnamon, and salt.

3. In a separate bowl, mix together the mashed banana, honey or sugar substitute, eggs, and vanilla extract until well combined.
4. Add the wet ingredients to the dry ingredients and stir until just combined. Do not overmix.
5. Divide the batter evenly among the muffin cups, filling them about 2/3 full.
6. Bake in the preheated oven for 18-20 minutes, or until the muffins are golden brown and a toothpick inserted into the center comes out clean.
7. Remove the muffins from the oven and let them cool in the muffin tin for a few minutes. Then transfer them to a wire rack to cool completely.

VEGGIE SANDWICH WITH WHOLE GRAIN BREAD

Nutrition: Cal 220;Fat 4 g;Carb 40 g;Protein 8 g
Serving 2; Cook time 10 min

Ingredients:
- 4 slices whole grain bread
- 4 tablespoons hummus (choose a low-fat or reduced-calorie version)
- 1/2 medium cucumber, thinly sliced
- 1 medium tomato, thinly sliced
- 1/2 medium red onion, thinly sliced
- 1/2 medium bell pepper, thinly sliced
- 1 cup fresh spinach leaves
- Salt and pepper to taste

Instructions:

1. Spread 1 tablespoon of hummus on each slice of whole grain bread.
2. Layer the cucumber slices, tomato slices, red onion slices, bell pepper slices, and spinach leaves on two slices of bread.
3. Sprinkle with salt and pepper to taste.
4. Top with the remaining slices of bread to form two sandwiches.
5. Cut the sandwiches in half or quarters for easier handling.

APPLE CINNAMON PROTEIN PANCAKES

Nutrition: Cal 250;Fat 6 g;Carb 30 g;Protein 20 g
Serving 2; Cook time 10 min

Ingredients:
- 1/2 cup oat flour (made from grinding oats)
- 1 scoop vanilla protein powder (choose a low-carb or bariatric-friendly option)
- 1/2 teaspoon baking powder
- 1/2 teaspoon ground cinnamon
- 1/4 cup unsweetened applesauce
- 1/4 cup unsweetened almond milk (or your preferred milk substitute)
- 1 large egg
- 1/2 medium apple, grated
- Cooking spray or oil for greasing

Instructions:
1. In a mixing bowl, combine the oat flour, protein powder, baking powder, and cinnamon.
2. In a separate bowl, whisk together the applesauce, almond milk, and egg until well combined.
3. Pour the wet ingredients into the dry ingredients and stir until just combined. Gently fold in the grated apple.
4. Heat a non-stick skillet or griddle over medium heat and lightly coat it with cooking spray or oil.
5. Spoon about 1/4 cup of the pancake batter onto the skillet for each pancake. Cook until bubbles form on the surface, then flip and cook the other side until golden brown.
6. Repeat with the remaining batter, adding more cooking spray or oil as needed.
7. Serve the Apple Cinnamon Protein Pancakes warm.

BROCCOLI AND CHEESE OMELET

Nutrition: Cal 170;Fat 11 g;Carb 3 g;Protein 16 g
Serving 2; Cook time 15 min

Ingredients:
- 4 large eggs
- 1 cup chopped broccoli florets
- 1/2 cup shredded reduced-fat cheddar cheese
- Salt and pepper to taste
- Cooking spray or oil for greasing

Instructions:
1. Heat a non-stick skillet over medium heat. Lightly coat it with cooking spray or a small amount of oil.
2. In a bowl, beat the eggs until well combined. Season with salt and pepper.
3. Pour the beaten eggs into the skillet and tilt the skillet to evenly distribute the eggs.
4. Cook the eggs for a couple of minutes until the edges start to set.
5. Sprinkle the chopped broccoli and shredded cheddar cheese over one half of the omelet.
6. Use a spatula to carefully fold the other half of the omelet over the broccoli and cheese.
7. Cook for another minute or two until the cheese is melted and the omelet is cooked through.
8. Slide the omelet onto a plate and cut it in half to make two servings.
9. Serve the Broccoli and Cheese Omelet hot.

GREEK YOGURT PARFAIT WITH NUTS AND SEEDS

Nutrition: Cal 250;Fat 10 g;Carb 20 g;Protein 20 g
Serving 2; Cook time 5 min

Ingredients:
- 1 cup plain Greek yogurt (choose a low-fat or non-fat option)
- 1 tablespoon honey or a sugar substitute
- 1/4 cup chopped mixed nuts (such as almonds, walnuts, or pecans)
- 1 tablespoon mixed seeds (such as chia seeds, flaxseeds, or pumpkin seeds)
- 1/2 cup fresh berries (such as strawberries, blueberries, or raspberries)

Instructions:
1. In a bowl, mix the Greek yogurt and honey until well combined.
2. In serving glasses or bowls, layer half of the Greek yogurt mixture.
3. Sprinkle half of the chopped nuts and seeds over the yogurt layer.
4. Add half of the fresh berries on top of the nuts and seeds.
5. Repeat the layers with the remaining Greek yogurt, nuts, seeds, and berries.
6. Drizzle a little honey on top for extra sweetness if desired.

SPINACH AND TURKEY SAUSAGE EGG BAKE

Nutrition: Cal 200;Fat 10 g;Carb 4 g;Protein 20 g
Serving 2; Cook time 25 min

Ingredients:
- 4 ounces turkey sausage, cooked and crumbled
- 2 cups fresh spinach leaves
- 4 large eggs
- 1/4 cup unsweetened almond milk (or your preferred milk substitute)
- 1/4 cup shredded reduced-fat cheddar cheese
- Salt and pepper to taste
- Cooking spray or oil for greasing

Instructions:
1. Preheat the oven to 375°F (190°C). Grease a small baking dish with cooking spray or a small amount of oil.
2. Spread the cooked and crumbled turkey sausage evenly in the baking dish.
3. Layer the fresh spinach leaves on top of the turkey sausage.
4. In a bowl, whisk together the eggs, almond milk, shredded cheddar cheese, salt, and pepper until well combined.
5. Pour the egg mixture over the spinach and turkey sausage in the baking dish, ensuring even distribution.
6. Bake in the preheated oven for approximately 20-25 minutes, or until the eggs are set and the top is golden brown.
7. Remove the egg bake from the oven and let it cool for a few minutes.
8. Cut the Spinach and Turkey Sausage Egg Bake into two servings and serve warm.

AVOCADO AND TOMATO BREAKFAST WRAP

Nutrition: Cal 300;Fat 15 g;Carb 30 g;Protein 15 g
Serving 2; Cook time 10 min

Ingredients:
- 2 large whole wheat or low-carb tortillas
- 1 medium avocado, peeled and sliced
- 1 medium tomato, sliced
- 4 large eggs
- Salt and pepper to taste
- Cooking spray or oil for greasing

Instructions:
1. Heat a non-stick skillet over medium heat. Lightly coat it with cooking spray or a small amount of oil.
2. In a small bowl, whisk the eggs until well beaten. Season with salt and pepper.
3. Pour the beaten eggs into the skillet and cook, stirring occasionally, until scrambled and cooked through.
4. Warm the tortillas in a separate skillet or in the microwave for a few seconds until pliable.
5. Place half of the scrambled eggs on each tortilla, spreading them evenly across the center.
6. Top the eggs with slices of avocado and tomato.
7. Season with additional salt and pepper if desired.
8. Fold in the sides of the tortilla and roll it up tightly to form a wrap.
9. Slice the wraps in half and serve immediately.

PUMPKIN SPICE CHIA PUDDING

Nutrition: Cal 120;Fat 5 g;Carb 17 g;Protein 3 g
Serving 2; Cook time 4 hours 10 min

Ingredients:
- 1 cup unsweetened almond milk (or your preferred milk substitute)
- 1/4 cup pumpkin puree
- 2 tablespoons chia seeds
- 1 tablespoon maple syrup (or a sugar substitute)
- 1/2 teaspoon pumpkin pie spice
- 1/4 teaspoon vanilla extract
- Optional toppings: crushed nuts, cinnamon, or whipped cream (use sparingly for a bariatric diet)

Instructions:
1. In a mixing bowl, whisk together the almond milk, pumpkin puree, chia seeds, maple syrup, pumpkin pie spice, and vanilla extract until well combined.
2. Let the mixture sit for 5 minutes, then whisk again to prevent the chia seeds from clumping.
3. Cover the bowl and refrigerate for at least 4 hours or overnight. The chia seeds will absorb the liquid and form a pudding-like consistency.
4. Stir the chilled mixture before serving to ensure even distribution.
5. Divide the Pumpkin Spice Chia Pudding into two serving bowls.

6. Add optional toppings such as crushed nuts, a sprinkle of cinnamon, or a dollop of whipped cream if desired (remember to use toppings sparingly for a bariatric diet).
7. Serve the chia pudding chilled.

CHICKEN SAUSAGE BREAKFAST BURRITO

Nutrition: Cal 290;Fat 12 g;Carb 17 g;Protein 26 g
Serving 2; Cook time 20 min

Ingredients:
- 2 low-carb, high-fiber tortillas (8-10 inch diameter)
- 2 chicken sausage links (pre-cooked, low-fat)
- 4 large egg whites
- 1/4 cup diced onion
- 1/4 cup diced green bell pepper
- 1/4 cup shredded low-fat cheddar cheese
- 1 tbsp olive oil
- Salt and pepper to taste

Instructions:
1. Heat the olive oil in a large non-stick skillet over medium heat.
2. Add the diced onion and green bell pepper and sauté for 2-3 minutes until softened.
3. Slice the chicken sausage links into small pieces and add them to the skillet. Cook for 2-3 minutes until heated through.
4. In a separate bowl, whisk together the egg whites with salt and pepper.
5. Add the egg white mixture to the skillet and scramble until cooked through.
6. Warm the tortillas in the microwave for 10-15 seconds.
7. Divide the egg white and sausage mixture between the two tortillas.
8. Top each burrito with shredded low-fat cheddar cheese.
9. Roll up the burritos and serve immediately.

QUINOA AND VEGETABLE STUFFED PEPPERS

Nutrition: Cal 260;Fat 10 g;Carb 32 g;Protein 12 g
Serving 2; Cook time 60 min

Ingredients:
- 2 medium bell peppers (any color)
- 1/2 cup cooked quinoa
- 1/2 cup diced zucchini
- 1/2 cup diced mushrooms
- 1/4 cup diced onion
- 1/4 cup diced tomato
- 1/4 cup shredded low-fat mozzarella cheese
- 1 tbsp olive oil
- 1/4 tsp garlic powder
- Salt and pepper to taste

Instructions:
1. Preheat your oven to 350°F (180°C).
2. Cut the tops off the bell peppers and remove the seeds and membranes. Set aside.
3. In a large non-stick skillet, heat the olive oil over medium heat.
4. Add the diced onion, zucchini, and mushrooms to the skillet, and sauté for 3-4 minutes until softened.
5. Stir in the diced tomato, cooked quinoa, garlic powder, salt, and pepper. Cook for an additional 2-3 minutes.
6. Stuff each bell pepper with the quinoa and vegetable mixture, filling them evenly.
7. Top each stuffed pepper with an equal amount of shredded low-fat mozzarella cheese.
8. Place the stuffed peppers in a baking dish and add a small amount of water to the bottom of the dish (about 1/4 inch deep).
9. Bake for 30-35 minutes, or until the peppers are tender and the cheese is melted and bubbly.

RICOTTA PANCAKES WITH BERRIES

Nutrition: Cal 280;Fat 19 g;Carb 13 g;Protein 17 g
Serving 2; Cook time 25 min

Ingredients:
- 1/2 cup low-fat ricotta cheese
- 1/4 cup almond flour
- 2 large eggs
- 1/2 tsp vanilla extract
- 1/2 tsp baking powder
- 1/4 tsp ground cinnamon
- Pinch of salt

- 1/2 cup mixed berries (blueberries, raspberries, and strawberries)
- 1 tsp honey (optional)
- Non-stick cooking spray

Instructions:

1. In a medium bowl, whisk together the ricotta cheese, almond flour, eggs, vanilla extract, baking powder, ground cinnamon, and a pinch of salt until well combined.
2. Heat a non-stick skillet or griddle over medium-low heat and lightly coat with non-stick cooking spray.
3. Pour 1/4 cup of the pancake batter onto the skillet for each pancake. Cook for 2-3 minutes, or until the edges are set and bubbles appear on the surface.
4. Carefully flip the pancakes and cook for an additional 1-2 minutes, or until golden brown and cooked through.
5. Divide the pancakes between two plates and top with mixed berries. Drizzle with honey if desired.
6. Serve immediately.

MINI VEGETABLE FRITTATAS

Nutrition: Cal 200;Fat 9 g;Carb 10 g;Protein 20 g
Serving 2; Cook time 35 min

Ingredients:
- 4 large eggs
- 1/4 cup low-fat milk
- 1/2 cup chopped spinach
- 1/4 cup diced red bell pepper
- 1/4 cup diced onion
- 1/4 cup shredded low-fat cheddar cheese
- 1/4 tsp garlic powder
- Salt and pepper to taste
- Non-stick cooking spray

Instructions:

1. Preheat your oven to 350°F (180°C). Spray a 6-cup muffin tin with non-stick cooking spray.
2. In a medium bowl, whisk together the eggs, low-fat milk, garlic powder, salt, and pepper.
3. Divide the chopped spinach, diced red bell pepper, and diced onion evenly among the 6 muffin cups.
4. Pour the egg mixture over the vegetables, filling each muffin cup about 2/3 full.
5. Sprinkle each muffin cup with an equal amount of shredded low-fat cheddar cheese.
6. Bake for 20-25 minutes, or until the frittatas are set and a toothpick inserted in the center comes out clean.
7. Remove the mini frittatas from the oven and let them cool in the muffin tin for a few minutes.

SMOKED SALMON AND SPINACH OMELET

Nutrition: Cal 230;Fat 12 g;Carb 10 g;Protein 21 g
Serving 2; Cook time 20 min

Ingredients:
- 4 large egg whites
- 2 oz smoked salmon, thinly sliced
- 1 cup fresh spinach, roughly chopped
- 1/4 cup diced onion
- 1/4 cup diced tomato
- 1/4 cup crumbled low-fat feta cheese
- 1 tbsp olive oil
- Salt and pepper to taste

Instructions:

1. In a medium bowl, whisk together the egg whites with a pinch of salt and pepper.
2. Heat the olive oil in a large non-stick skillet over medium heat.
3. Add the diced onion to the skillet and sauté for 2-3 minutes until softened.
4. Add the chopped spinach and diced tomato to the skillet, and cook for an additional 1-2 minutes until the spinach is wilted.
5. Pour the egg white mixture over the vegetables in the skillet, making sure it is evenly distributed.
6. Cook the omelet for 2-3 minutes, or until the edges are set and the center is almost cooked through.
7. Arrange the smoked salmon slices and crumbled low-fat feta cheese on one half of the omelet.
8. Carefully fold the other half of the omelet over the filling and cook for an additional 1-2 minutes, or until the cheese is slightly melted and the omelet is cooked through.

GREEK YOGURT WITH CHIA SEEDS AND HONEY

Nutrition: Cal 280;Fat 6 g;Carb 19 g;Protein 15 g

Serving 2; Cook time 40 min

Ingredients:
- 1 cup non-fat Greek yogurt
- 2 tbsp chia seeds
- 2 tsp honey
- 1/4 cup mixed berries (blueberries, raspberries, and strawberries)
- 1/4 tsp ground cinnamon (optional)

Instructions:
1. In a small bowl, combine the non-fat Greek yogurt and chia seeds. Mix well.
2. Cover the bowl and refrigerate for at least 30 minutes (or overnight) to allow the chia seeds to absorb some of the yogurt and expand.
3. After the refrigeration time, give the yogurt and chia seed mixture a good stir.
4. Divide the mixture evenly between two serving bowls or glasses.
5. Drizzle each serving with 1 teaspoon of honey.
6. Top each serving with an equal amount of mixed berries.
7. Optionally, sprinkle a pinch of ground cinnamon over each serving.

EGG AND BACON BREAKFAST TACOS

Nutrition: Cal 240;Fat 11 g;Carb 20 g;Protein 20 g
Serving 2; Cook time 20 min

Ingredients:
- 4 large egg whites
- 2 slices turkey bacon
- 1/4 cup diced tomato
- 1/4 cup diced avocado
- 2 tbsp chopped fresh cilantro
- 4 small low-carb, high-fiber tortillas (6-inch)
- Salt and pepper to taste
- Non-stick cooking spray

Instructions:
1. In a medium bowl, whisk together the egg whites with a pinch of salt and pepper. Set aside.
2. Heat a non-stick skillet over medium heat and lightly coat with non-stick cooking spray.
3. Add the turkey bacon slices to the skillet and cook for 2-3 minutes per side, or until crispy. Remove the bacon from the skillet and set aside on a paper towel-lined plate to drain any excess grease.

4. In the same skillet, pour the egg white mixture and cook, stirring occasionally, for 2-3 minutes, or until fully cooked and scrambled. Remove the skillet from the heat.
5. Warm the low-carb tortillas in the microwave for 10-15 seconds, or until pliable.
6. Assemble the tacos by dividing the scrambled egg whites evenly among the 4 tortillas.
7. Crumble the cooked turkey bacon and sprinkle it over the egg whites.
8. Top each taco with an equal amount of diced tomato, diced avocado, and chopped cilantro.
9. Fold the tortillas in half and serve immediately.

CHOCOLATE PROTEIN PANCAKES

Nutrition: Cal 220;Fat 4 g;Carb 22 g;Protein 25 g
Serving 2; Cook time 20 min

Ingredients:
- 1/2 cup rolled oats
- 1 scoop (about 30g) chocolate protein powder (choose a low-carb, low-fat, and low-sugar option)
- 1/2 cup non-fat Greek yogurt
- 1/4 cup egg whites
- 1/2 tsp baking powder
- 1/2 tsp vanilla extract
- Pinch of salt
- Non-stick cooking spray
- Optional toppings: sugar-free syrup, fresh berries, or a dollop of non-fat Greek yogurt

Instructions:
1. In a blender, add the rolled oats and blend until they form a fine flour-like consistency.
2. Add the chocolate protein powder, non-fat Greek yogurt, egg whites, baking powder, vanilla extract, and a pinch of salt to the blender. Blend until the batter is smooth and well combined.
3. Heat a non-stick skillet or griddle over medium heat and lightly coat with non-stick cooking spray.
4. Pour about 1/4 cup of batter onto the skillet for each pancake. Cook for 2-3 minutes, or until bubbles form on the surface and the edges appear set.
5. Flip the pancake and cook for an additional 1-2 minutes, or until fully cooked through.

6. Repeat with the remaining batter, making a total of 4 pancakes (2 pancakes per serving).
7. Serve the pancakes warm with your choice of optional toppings, such as sugar-free syrup, fresh berries, or a dollop of non-fat Greek yogurt.

VEGGIE OMELET ROLL-UPS

Nutrition: Cal 110;Fat 3 g;Carb 6 g;Protein 15 g
Serving 2; Cook time 25 min

Ingredients:
- 4 large egg whites
- 1/4 cup diced red bell pepper
- 1/4 cup diced onion
- 1/4 cup diced zucchini
- 1/4 cup chopped fresh spinach
- 1/4 cup shredded low-fat cheddar cheese
- Salt and pepper to taste
- Non-stick cooking spray

Instructions:
1. In a medium bowl, whisk together the egg whites with a pinch of salt and pepper. Set aside.
2. Heat a non-stick skillet over medium heat and lightly coat with non-stick cooking spray.
3. Add the diced red bell pepper, onion, and zucchini to the skillet, and cook for 3-4 minutes, or until the vegetables are tender.
4. Add the chopped spinach to the skillet and cook for an additional 1-2 minutes, or until the spinach is wilted. Transfer the cooked vegetables to a plate and set aside.
5. Clean the skillet and return it to medium heat. Lightly coat with non-stick cooking spray.
6. Pour half of the egg white mixture into the skillet, swirling the skillet to create a thin, even layer. Cook for 2-3 minutes, or until the egg whites are fully cooked through. Carefully slide a spatula under the omelet and transfer it to a plate.
7. Repeat steps 5 and 6 with the remaining egg white mixture to make a second omelet.
8. Place half of the cooked vegetables on one side of each omelet. Sprinkle half of the shredded low-fat cheddar cheese over the vegetables.
9. Carefully roll up each omelet, enclosing the vegetables and cheese.
10. Slice each omelet roll-up in half and serve immediately.

QUINOA WITH ALMONDS AND RAISINS

Nutrition: Cal 340;Fat 11 g;Carb 52 g;Protein 10 g
Serving 2; Cook time 30 min

Ingredients:
- 1/2 cup uncooked quinoa, rinsed
- 1 cup water or low-sodium vegetable broth
- 1/4 cup slivered almonds
- 1/4 cup raisins
- 1/2 tsp ground cinnamon
- 1/4 tsp ground cumin
- Salt to taste

Instructions:
1. In a medium saucepan, combine the rinsed quinoa and water or low-sodium vegetable broth. Bring to a boil over medium-high heat, then reduce the heat to low, cover, and simmer for 15 minutes, or until the quinoa has absorbed all the liquid and is tender.
2. While the quinoa is cooking, toast the slivered almonds in a small, dry skillet over medium-low heat, stirring frequently, for 3-4 minutes, or until they are golden brown and fragrant. Remove the skillet from the heat and set aside.
3. When the quinoa is cooked, remove the saucepan from the heat and let it stand, covered, for 5 minutes. Fluff the quinoa with a fork.
4. Stir in the toasted almonds, raisins, ground cinnamon, ground cumin, and salt to taste. Mix well to combine all the ingredients.
5. Divide the quinoa mixture between two bowls and serve warm or at room temperature.

EGG WHITE SCRAMBLE WITH TURKEY SAUSAGE

Nutrition: Cal 322;Fat 7 g;Carb 8 g;Protein 30 g
Serving 2; Cook time 20 min

Ingredients:
- 1 cup egg whites (from about 8 large eggs or liquid egg whites)
- 2 turkey sausage links, cooked and diced
- 1/4 cup diced bell pepper (any color)
- 1/4 cup diced onion
- 1/4 cup chopped fresh spinach

- 1/4 cup shredded low-fat cheddar cheese
- Salt and pepper to taste
- Non-stick cooking spray

Instructions:

1. Heat a non-stick skillet over medium heat and coat it with non-stick cooking spray.
2. Add the diced bell pepper and onion to the skillet, and cook for 3-4 minutes, or until the vegetables are softened and slightly browned.
3. Add the cooked and diced turkey sausage to the skillet, and cook for another 1-2 minutes, stirring occasionally to heat the sausage through.
4. Pour the egg whites into the skillet and season with salt and pepper to taste. Cook, stirring frequently, until the egg whites are almost set but still slightly runny.
5. Add the chopped spinach and shredded low-fat cheddar cheese to the skillet, and continue cooking until the egg whites are fully cooked and the cheese has melted.
6. Divide the egg white scramble between two plates and serve immediately.

TURKEY SAUSAGE AND VEGETABLE BREAKFAST SKILLET

Nutrition: Cal 240;Fat 13 g;Carb 15 g;Protein 18 g
Serving 2; Cook time 25 min

Ingredients:

- 2 cooked turkey sausage links, diced
- 1/2 cup diced red bell pepper
- 1/2 cup diced zucchini
- 1/4 cup diced onion
- 1 cup chopped fresh spinach
- 1/2 cup cherry tomatoes, halved
- 1 tbsp olive oil
- Salt and pepper to taste

Instructions:

1. In a large non-stick skillet, heat the olive oil over medium heat.
2. Add the diced onion and cook for 2-3 minutes until it starts to soften.
3. Add the diced red bell pepper and zucchini to the skillet. Cook for 5-7 minutes, stirring occasionally, until the vegetables are tender.
4. Stir in the cooked turkey sausage and cook for another 2-3 minutes to heat through.

5. Add the chopped spinach and cherry tomatoes to the skillet. Cook for 2-3 minutes, stirring occasionally, until the spinach is wilted and the tomatoes are slightly softened.
6. Season the mixture with salt and pepper to taste.
7. Divide the skillet mixture evenly between two plates and serve immediately. Enjoy your Turkey Sausage and Vegetable Breakfast Skillet!

GREEK YOGURT WITH PEANUT BUTTER AND BANANA

Nutrition: Cal 200;Fat 9 g;Carb 16 g;Protein 20 g
Serving 2; Cook time 5 min

Ingredients:

- 1 cup plain Greek yogurt (choose a low-fat or non-fat option)
- 2 tablespoons natural peanut butter (choose a no-added-sugar variety)
- 1 ripe banana, sliced
- Optional toppings: crushed nuts or a sprinkle of cinnamon (use sparingly for a bariatric diet)

Instructions:

1. In two bowls, divide the Greek yogurt evenly.
2. Drizzle 1 tablespoon of peanut butter over each bowl of yogurt.
3. Top each bowl with sliced bananas.
4. If desired, sprinkle with crushed nuts or a sprinkle of cinnamon (remember to use toppings sparingly for a bariatric diet).
5. Serve the Greek Yogurt with Peanut Butter and Banana immediately.

SWEET POTATO AND SPINACH BREAKFAST WRAP

Nutrition: Cal 250;Fat 5 g;Carb 40 g;Protein 12 g
Serving 2; Cook time 30 min

Ingredients:

- 2 small sweet potatoes, peeled and diced
- 1 cup fresh spinach leaves
- 4 large eggs
- Salt and pepper to taste
- 2 whole wheat or low-carb tortillas
- Optional toppings: salsa or hot sauce (use sparingly for a bariatric diet)

Instructions:

1. Preheat the oven to 400°F (200°C). Line a baking sheet with parchment paper.
2. Place the diced sweet potatoes on the prepared baking sheet and season with salt and pepper. Toss to coat evenly.
3. Bake the sweet potatoes in the preheated oven for approximately 20-25 minutes, or until tender and slightly golden.
4. In a non-stick skillet, sauté the spinach over medium heat until wilted. Set aside.
5. In a small bowl, whisk the eggs until well beaten. Season with salt and pepper.
6. Lightly coat the same skillet with cooking spray or a small amount of oil. Pour the beaten eggs into the skillet and cook, stirring occasionally, until scrambled and cooked through.
7. Warm the tortillas in a separate skillet or in the microwave for a few seconds until pliable.
8. Divide the scrambled eggs, roasted sweet potatoes, and sautéed spinach between the two tortillas, placing them in the center.
9. Optional: Add a small amount of salsa or hot sauce for added flavor (use sparingly for a bariatric diet).
10. Fold in the sides of the tortilla and roll it up tightly to form a wrap.
11. Slice the wraps in half and serve immediately.

ALMOND FLOUR WAFFLES WITH BERRIES

Nutrition: Cal 300;Fat 22 g;Carb 12 g;Protein 12 g
Serving 2; Cook time 8 min

Ingredients:
- 1 cup almond flour
- 2 tablespoons coconut flour
- 1 teaspoon baking powder
- 1/4 teaspoon salt
- 2 large eggs
- 1/4 cup unsweetened almond milk (or your preferred milk substitute)
- 1 tablespoon melted coconut oil (or your preferred oil)
- 1 tablespoon maple syrup (or a sugar substitute)
- 1/2 teaspoon vanilla extract
- Fresh berries of your choice for topping
- Optional toppings: additional maple syrup or a dollop of Greek yogurt (use sparingly for a bariatric diet)

Instructions:
1. Preheat your waffle iron according to the manufacturer's instructions.
2. In a mixing bowl, whisk together the almond flour, coconut flour, baking powder, and salt.
3. In a separate bowl, whisk the eggs, almond milk, melted coconut oil, maple syrup, and vanilla extract until well combined.
4. Pour the wet ingredients into the dry ingredients and stir until a thick batter forms. Let the batter rest for a few minutes to allow the coconut flour to absorb the liquid.
5. Lightly grease the waffle iron with non-stick spray or a small amount of oil.
6. Spoon the batter onto the preheated waffle iron, spreading it out evenly. Close the lid and cook according to your waffle iron's instructions, until the waffles are golden brown and cooked through.
7. Carefully remove the waffles from the iron and place them on a wire rack to cool slightly.
8. Divide the waffles into two servings and top with fresh berries.
9. Optional: Drizzle with a small amount of maple syrup or add a dollop of Greek yogurt for additional flavor (use sparingly for a bariatric diet).

EGG MUFFINS WITH BACON AND CHEESE

Nutrition: Cal 180;Fat 11 g;Carb 2 g;Protein 14 g
Serving 2; Cook time 20 min

Ingredients:
- 4 large eggs
- 2 slices of turkey bacon, cooked and crumbled
- 1/4 cup shredded cheddar cheese (use a reduced-fat variety if desired)
- Salt and pepper to taste
- Optional add-ins: diced bell peppers, spinach, or mushrooms (use sparingly for a bariatric diet)

Instructions:
1. Preheat the oven to 350°F (175°C). Grease a muffin tin or line it with silicone muffin liners.
2. In a mixing bowl, beat the eggs until well combined. Season with salt and pepper.
3. Stir in the cooked and crumbled turkey bacon and shredded cheddar cheese. If desired, add

any optional add-ins such as diced bell peppers, spinach, or mushrooms.

4. Pour the egg mixture evenly into the prepared muffin tin, filling each cup about 2/3 full.

5. Bake in the preheated oven for approximately 15-20 minutes, or until the egg muffins are set and lightly golden on top.

6. Remove the muffin tin from the oven and let the egg muffins cool for a few minutes.

7. Carefully remove the egg muffins from the tin and serve warm.

QUINOA AND VEGGIE BREAKFAST BOWL

Nutrition: Cal 300;Fat 12 g;Carb 35 g;Protein 14 g
Serving 2; Cook time 25 min

Ingredients:
- 1/2 cup quinoa
- 1 cup water
- 1 tablespoon olive oil
- 1/2 cup diced bell peppers
- 1/2 cup diced zucchini
- 1/2 cup diced cherry tomatoes
- 2 large eggs
- Salt and pepper to taste
- Optional toppings: chopped fresh herbs, avocado slices

Instructions:
1. Rinse the quinoa under cold water to remove any bitterness.

2. In a small saucepan, bring the water to a boil. Add the rinsed quinoa, reduce the heat to low, cover, and simmer for about 15 minutes, or until the quinoa is cooked and the water is absorbed. Fluff with a fork.

3. In a skillet, heat the olive oil over medium heat. Add the diced bell peppers and zucchini and sauté until slightly tender, about 5 minutes.

4. Add the diced cherry tomatoes to the skillet and cook for an additional 2 minutes. Season with salt and pepper to taste.

5. In a separate non-stick skillet, cook the eggs to your desired doneness (e.g., fried, scrambled, or poached).

6. Divide the cooked quinoa between two bowls. Top each bowl with the sautéed vegetables and a cooked egg.

BLUEBERRY PROTEIN OVERNIGHT CHIA PUDDING

Nutrition: Cal 250;Fat 10 g;Carb 25 g;Protein 20 g
Serving 2; Cook time 4 hours 5 min

Ingredients:
- 1/4 cup chia seeds
- 1 cup unsweetened almond milk (or your preferred milk substitute)
- 1 scoop of vanilla protein powder (choose a bariatric-friendly option)
- 1/2 teaspoon vanilla extract
- 1 cup fresh blueberries (or your preferred berries)
- Optional toppings: additional berries, chopped nuts, or a drizzle of honey

Instructions:
1. In a mixing bowl, combine the chia seeds, unsweetened almond milk, vanilla protein powder, and vanilla extract. Stir well to combine and ensure there are no lumps.

2. Add the fresh blueberries to the mixture and gently stir to evenly distribute them throughout the pudding.

3. Divide the mixture into two individual serving jars or containers with lids.

4. Cover the jars or containers and refrigerate them overnight or for at least 4-6 hours, allowing the chia seeds to absorb the liquid and form a pudding-like consistency.

5. Once the chia pudding has set, give it a stir to incorporate any settled chia seeds.

6. Serve the Blueberry Protein Overnight Chia Pudding chilled. You can enjoy it as is or add additional toppings such as more berries, chopped nuts, or a drizzle of honey

EGG AND VEGGIE BREAKFAST BURRITO

Nutrition: Cal 250;Fat 10 g;Carb 25 g;Protein 15 g
Serving 2; Cook time 15 min

Ingredients:
- 4 large eggs
- 1/4 cup diced bell peppers
- 1/4 cup diced onions

- 1/4 cup diced tomatoes
- 1/4 cup diced mushrooms
- 2 whole wheat tortillas (small size)
- 1/4 cup shredded reduced-fat cheddar cheese
- Salt and pepper to taste
- Optional toppings: salsa, avocado slices

Instructions:

1. In a mixing bowl, beat the eggs until well combined. Season with salt and pepper.
2. In a non-stick skillet, heat a small amount of cooking spray or oil over medium heat. Add the diced bell peppers, onions, tomatoes, and mushrooms. Sauté until the vegetables are tender.
3. Push the sautéed vegetables to one side of the skillet and pour the beaten eggs into the other side. Scramble the eggs until cooked through.
4. Once the eggs are cooked, mix them with the sautéed vegetables in the skillet. Stir well to combine.
5. Warm the whole wheat tortillas in a separate skillet or microwave for a few seconds to make them pliable.
6. Divide the egg and vegetable mixture evenly between the two tortillas. Sprinkle each burrito with shredded cheddar cheese.
7. Fold the sides of the tortillas inward and then roll them tightly to form the burritos.
8. Optional: If desired, lightly toast the burritos in a skillet to give them a crispy exterior.
9. Serve the Egg and Veggie Breakfast Burritos immediately. You can enjoy them as is or add optional toppings such as salsa or avocado slices

GREEK YOGURT WITH CINNAMON AND WALNUTS

Nutrition: Cal 150;Fat 15 g;Carb 10 g;Protein 15 g
Serving 2; Cook time 5 min

Ingredients:

- 1 cup Greek yogurt (non-fat or low-fat)
- 1 teaspoon ground cinnamon
- 2 tablespoons chopped walnuts
- Optional: 1 teaspoon honey

Instructions:

1. In a small bowl, combine the Greek yogurt and ground cinnamon. Stir well to evenly distribute the cinnamon throughout the yogurt.
2. Divide the cinnamon-infused Greek yogurt into two serving bowls.
3. Sprinkle the chopped walnuts evenly over the yogurt in each bowl.
4. Optional: If desired, drizzle a small amount of honey over each serving for added sweetness. Use sparingly for a bariatric diet or omit if preferred.

ZUCCHINI AND FETA EGG BAKE

Nutrition: Cal 180;Fat 10 g;Carb 8 g;Protein 14 g
Serving 2; Cook time 35 min

Ingredients:

- 2 small zucchinis, grated
- 4 large eggs
- 1/4 cup crumbled feta cheese
- 1/4 cup chopped fresh herbs (such as basil or parsley)
- Salt and pepper, to taste
- Cooking spray or oil for greasing the baking dish

Instructions:

1. Preheat your oven to 350°F (175°C).
2. Grease a small baking dish or individual ramekins with cooking spray or oil.
3. Grate the zucchinis using a box grater or food processor. Squeeze out any excess moisture using a clean kitchen towel or paper towels.
4. In a medium-sized bowl, beat the eggs until well combined. Add the grated zucchini, crumbled feta cheese, and chopped fresh herbs. Season with salt and pepper to taste. Mix everything together until evenly distributed.
5. Pour the mixture into the greased baking dish or ramekins, distributing it evenly.
6. Place the baking dish or ramekins in the preheated oven and bake for approximately 25-30 minutes, or until the eggs are set and the top is golden brown.
7. Remove from the oven and let it cool for a few minutes before serving.

SPINACH AND MUSHROOM PROTEIN PANCAKES

Nutrition: Cal 200;Fat 10 g;Carb 7 g;Protein 18 g
Serving 2; Cook time 30 min

Ingredients:
- 1 cup spinach, finely chopped
- 1/2 cup mushrooms, finely chopped
- 4 large eggs
- 1/4 cup protein powder (flavor of your choice)
- 2 tablespoons almond flour
- 1/2 teaspoon baking powder
- Salt and pepper, to taste
- Cooking spray or oil for greasing the pan

Instructions:
1. In a medium-sized bowl, whisk together the eggs, protein powder, almond flour, baking powder, salt, and pepper until well combined.
2. Add the chopped spinach and mushrooms to the bowl, and mix until the vegetables are evenly coated with the batter.
3. Heat a non-stick skillet or griddle over medium heat and lightly grease it with cooking spray or oil.
4. Pour about 1/4 cup of the batter onto the hot skillet for each pancake, spreading it slightly with the back of a spoon to form a round shape.
5. Cook the pancakes for approximately 2-3 minutes on each side, or until they are golden brown and set in the middle. Flip them carefully using a spatula.
6. Once cooked, transfer the pancakes to a plate and repeat the process with the remaining batter, adding more cooking spray or oil to the skillet as needed.
7. Serve the Spinach and Mushroom Protein Pancakes warm and enjoy!

QUESADILLA WITH TURKEY BACON

Nutrition: Cal 250;Fat 10 g;Carb 25 g;Protein 16 g
Serving 2; Cook time 20 min

Ingredients
- 4 small whole wheat tortillas (6-inch diameter)
- 4 slices turkey bacon
- 1 cup shredded reduced-fat cheese (such as cheddar or Monterey Jack)
- 1/4 cup diced tomatoes
- 1/4 cup diced red onion
- Cooking spray or oil for greasing the pan

Instructions:
1. Cook the turkey bacon according to the package instructions until crispy. Once cooked, set it aside to cool, then crumble or chop it into small pieces.
2. Preheat a non-stick skillet or griddle over medium heat.
3. Lay two tortillas flat on a clean surface. Sprinkle half of the shredded cheese evenly over each tortilla.
4. Divide the crumbled turkey bacon, diced tomatoes, and diced red onion equally between the two tortillas, spreading them out over the cheese.
5. Place the remaining tortillas on top of each filled tortilla, creating two quesadillas.
6. Lightly grease the preheated skillet or griddle with cooking spray or oil. Carefully transfer one quesadilla to the skillet and cook for approximately 2-3 minutes on each side, or until the tortilla is golden brown and the cheese has melted.
7. Repeat the process with the second quesadilla.
8. Once cooked, remove the quesadillas from the skillet and let them cool for a minute or two before cutting them into wedges.
9. Serve the Quesadilla with Turkey Bacon warm and enjoy!

BROCCOLI AND CHEDDAR OMELET

Nutrition: Cal 200;Fat 12 g;Carb 5 g;Protein 16 g
Serving 2; Cook time 20 min

Ingredients
- 4 large eggs
- 1 cup chopped broccoli florets
- 1/2 cup shredded reduced-fat cheddar cheese
- 2 tablespoons chopped fresh chives
- Salt and pepper, to taste
- Cooking spray or oil for greasing the pan

Instructions:
1. In a bowl, beat the eggs until well combined. Season with salt and pepper.
2. Preheat a non-stick skillet over medium heat. Lightly grease the skillet with cooking spray or oil.
3. Add the chopped broccoli florets to the skillet and sauté for 2-3 minutes, or until they are

tender-crisp. Remove from the skillet and set aside.

4. Reduce the heat to low and pour half of the beaten eggs into the skillet, spreading them evenly.

5. Cook the eggs for 1-2 minutes, or until the edges are set and the center is slightly runny.

6. Sprinkle half of the sautéed broccoli, shredded cheddar cheese, and chopped chives evenly over one half of the omelet.

7. Using a spatula, fold the other half of the omelet over the filling. Press gently to seal.

8. Cook for an additional 1-2 minutes to melt the cheese and fully cook the eggs.

9. Slide the omelet onto a plate and repeat the process to make the second omelet.

GREEK YOGURT PARFAIT WITH COCONUT FLAKES AND MANGO

Nutrition: Cal 150;Fat 3 g;Carb 21 g;Protein 13 g
Serving 2; Cook time 5 min

Ingredients
- 1 cup Greek yogurt (low-fat or non-fat)
- 1/2 cup fresh mango, diced
- 2 tablespoons unsweetened coconut flakes
- 2 teaspoons honey (optional for added sweetness)

Instructions:
1. In two serving glasses or bowls, layer half of the Greek yogurt at the bottom of each.

2. Top the yogurt with half of the diced mango, spreading it evenly.

3. Sprinkle one tablespoon of unsweetened coconut flakes over each layer of mango.

4. Repeat the layering process with the remaining Greek yogurt, diced mango, and coconut flakes.

5. If desired, drizzle one teaspoon of honey over each parfait for added sweetness.

6. Serve the Greek Yogurt Parfait with Coconut Flakes and Mango immediately or refrigerate until ready to serve.

HAM AND CHEESE EGG CUPS

Nutrition: Cal 180;Fat 9 g;Carb 1 g;Protein 18 g
Serving 2; Cook time 20 min

Ingredients
- 4 slices ham (thinly sliced)
- 4 large eggs
- 1/4 cup shredded reduced-fat cheddar cheese
- Salt and pepper, to taste
- Cooking spray or oil for greasing the muffin tin

Instructions:
1. Preheat your oven to 375°F (190°C).

2. Lightly grease two cups of a muffin tin with cooking spray or oil.

3. Take each slice of ham and press it into a muffin cup, creating a cup shape with the ham slice.

4. Crack an egg into each ham cup, being careful not to break the yolk.

5. Season each egg with salt and pepper to taste.

6. Sprinkle half of the shredded cheddar cheese evenly over each egg cup.

7. Place the muffin tin in the preheated oven and bake for approximately 12-15 minutes, or until the eggs are cooked to your desired level of doneness.

8. Remove the ham and cheese egg cups from the oven and let them cool for a few minutes.

9. Using a spoon or spatula, carefully lift the egg cups out of the muffin tin and transfer them to a plate.

10. Serve the Ham and Cheese Egg Cups warm and enjoy!

CAULIFLOWER HASH WITH TURKEY SAUSAGE

Nutrition: Cal 180;Fat 10 g;Carb 9 g;Protein 15 g
Serving 2; Cook time 25 min

Ingredients
- 2 cups cauliflower florets, riced or finely chopped
- 4 ounces lean turkey sausage, crumbled
- 1/2 small onion, diced
- 1/2 small bell pepper, diced
- 1 clove garlic, minced
- 1 tablespoon olive oil
- Salt and pepper, to taste
- Optional toppings: chopped fresh herbs (such as parsley or chives)

Instructions:
1. Heat a large skillet over medium heat and add the olive oil.

2.Add the diced onion, bell pepper, and minced garlic to the skillet. Sauté for 2-3 minutes until the vegetables are slightly softened.

3.Add the crumbled turkey sausage to the skillet and cook until browned and cooked through, breaking it up into smaller pieces as it cooks.

4.Add the cauliflower rice or finely chopped cauliflower florets to the skillet. Season with salt and pepper to taste.

5.Sauté the cauliflower and sausage mixture for about 5-6 minutes, or until the cauliflower is tender-crisp and slightly browned.

6.Taste and adjust the seasoning if needed.

7.Remove the skillet from the heat and divide the Cauliflower Hash with Turkey Sausage mixture into two serving bowls.

8.If desired, sprinkle with chopped fresh herbs for added flavor and garnish.

BANANA NUT PROTEIN MUFFINS

Nutrition: Cal 230;Fat 12 g;Carb 13 g;Protein 18 g
Serving 2; Cook time 25 min

Ingredients
•1 medium ripe banana, mashed
•2 large eggs
•1/4 cup unsweetened almond milk (or any milk of your choice)
•1/4 cup vanilla protein powder
•1/4 cup almond flour
•2 tablespoons chopped walnuts (or any nuts of your choice)
•1/2 teaspoon baking powder
•1/2 teaspoon cinnamon
•Optional: a pinch of salt and a drizzle of honey for added sweetness

Instructions:
1.Preheat your oven to 350°F (175°C) and line a muffin tin with paper liners or lightly grease it.

2.In a medium-sized bowl, mash the ripe banana with a fork until smooth.

3.Add the eggs and almond milk to the mashed banana, and whisk until well combined.

4.Stir in the vanilla protein powder, almond flour, chopped walnuts, baking powder, cinnamon, and a pinch of salt (if desired). Mix until all the ingredients are incorporated.

5.Divide the batter evenly among the muffin cups, filling each one about three-quarters full.

6.Bake in the preheated oven for approximately 15-20 minutes, or until a toothpick inserted into the center of a muffin comes out clean.

7.Remove the muffins from the oven and allow them to cool in the pan for a few minutes before transferring them to a wire rack to cool completely.

8.If desired, drizzle a small amount of honey over the muffins for added sweetness.

SMOKED SALMON AND AVOCADO OMELET

Nutrition: Cal 220;Fat 13 g;Carb 6 g;Protein 19 g
Serving 2; Cook time 10 min

Ingredients
•4 large eggs
•2 ounces smoked salmon, thinly sliced
•1/2 avocado, sliced
•1/4 cup diced red onion
•1 tablespoon chopped fresh dill
•Salt and pepper, to taste
•Cooking spray or oil for greasing the pan

Instructions:
1.In a bowl, beat the eggs until well combined. Season with salt and pepper.

2.Preheat a non-stick skillet over medium heat. Lightly grease the skillet with cooking spray or oil.

3.Pour half of the beaten eggs into the skillet, spreading them evenly.

4.Cook the eggs for 1-2 minutes, or until the edges are set and the center is slightly runny.

5.Place half of the smoked salmon slices, avocado slices, diced red onion, and chopped fresh dill on one half of the omelet.

6.Using a spatula, fold the other half of the omelet over the filling. Press gently to seal.

7.Cook for an additional 1-2 minutes to warm up the filling and fully cook the eggs.

8.Slide the omelet onto a plate and repeat the process to make the second omelet.

9.Garnish the Smoked Salmon and Avocado Omelets with additional chopped dill, if desired.

10.Serve the omelets warm and enjoy!

GREEK YOGURT WITH BERRIES AND PISTACHIOS

Nutrition: Cal 170;Fat 7 g;Carb 15 g;Protein 15 g
Serving 2; Cook time 5 min

Ingredients
- 1 cup Greek yogurt (low-fat or non-fat)
- 1 cup mixed berries (such as strawberries, blueberries, and raspberries)
- 2 tablespoons crushed pistachios
- Optional: 1 teaspoon honey or sweetener of your choice

Instructions:
1. In two serving bowls or glasses, divide the Greek yogurt evenly.
2. Top each portion of yogurt with half of the mixed berries, arranging them attractively.
3. Sprinkle one tablespoon of crushed pistachios over each portion of berries and yogurt.
4. If desired, drizzle a small amount of honey or sweetener of your choice over each serving for added sweetness.
5. Serve the Greek Yogurt with Berries and Pistachios immediately and enjoy!

SPINACH AND FETA STUFFED BELL PEPPERS

Nutrition: Cal 150;Fat 7 g;Carb 16 g;Protein 5 g
Serving 2; Cook time 30 min

Ingredients
- 2 bell peppers (any color you prefer)
- 1 cup fresh spinach, chopped
- 1/4 cup crumbled feta cheese
- 2 tablespoons diced red onion
- 1 clove garlic, minced
- 1 tablespoon olive oil
- Salt and pepper, to taste

Instructions:
1. Preheat your oven to 375°F (190°C).
2. Cut off the tops of the bell peppers and remove the seeds and membranes from the inside. Rinse the bell peppers under cold water and set them aside.
3. In a skillet, heat the olive oil over medium heat.
4. Add the diced red onion and minced garlic to the skillet and sauté for 2-3 minutes, or until the onion is translucent and fragrant.
5. Add the chopped spinach to the skillet and cook until wilted, about 2-3 minutes.
6. Remove the skillet from the heat and let the spinach mixture cool for a few minutes.
7. Stir in the crumbled feta cheese and season with salt and pepper to taste.
8. Spoon the spinach and feta mixture into the bell peppers, dividing it evenly between the two.
9. Place the stuffed bell peppers in a baking dish and cover the dish with aluminum foil.
10. Bake in the preheated oven for 25-30 minutes, or until the bell peppers are tender and the filling is heated through.
11. Remove the foil and bake for an additional 5 minutes to lightly brown the tops of the bell peppers.
12. Carefully remove the stuffed bell peppers from the oven and let them cool for a few minutes.
13. Serve the Spinach and Feta Stuffed Bell Peppers warm and enjoy!

BLUEBERRY ALMOND FLOUR PANCAKES

Nutrition: Cal 235;Fat 17 g;Carb 9 g;Protein 12 g
Serving 2; Cook time 15 min

Ingredients
- 1/2 cup almond flour
- 2 large eggs
- 1/4 cup unsweetened almond milk (or any milk of your choice)
- 1/2 teaspoon baking powder
- 1/2 teaspoon vanilla extract
- 1/4 cup fresh blueberries
- Cooking spray or oil for greasing the pan

Instructions:
1. In a bowl, combine the almond flour, eggs, almond milk, baking powder, and vanilla extract. Whisk until well combined and smooth.
2. Gently fold in the fresh blueberries, being careful not to overmix.
3. Preheat a non-stick skillet or griddle over medium heat. Lightly grease the surface with cooking spray or oil.
4. Spoon approximately 1/4 cup of batter onto the skillet for each pancake. Spread it out slightly to form a round shape.

5. Cook the pancakes for 2-3 minutes, or until bubbles start to form on the surface.
6. Flip the pancakes and cook for an additional 1-2 minutes, or until they are golden brown and cooked through.
7. Repeat the process with the remaining batter, greasing the skillet as needed.
8. Serve the Blueberry Almond Flour Pancakes warm with your choice of toppings, such as additional fresh blueberries, a drizzle of honey or maple syrup, or a dollop of Greek yogurt.

VEGETABLE AND CHEESE BREAKFAST WRAP

Nutrition: Cal 250;Fat 10 g;Carb 26 g;Protein 18 g
Serving 2; Cook time 15 min

Ingredients
- 2 large whole wheat tortillas (approximately 8-10 inches in diameter)
- 4 large eggs
- 1/2 cup diced bell peppers (any color you prefer)
- 1/2 cup sliced mushrooms
- 1/4 cup diced red onion
- 1/4 cup shredded low-fat cheddar cheese
- Salt and pepper, to taste
- Cooking spray or oil for the pan

Instructions:
1. Preheat a non-stick skillet over medium heat and lightly grease it with cooking spray or oil.
2. In a bowl, whisk the eggs until well beaten. Season with salt and pepper.
3. Pour the beaten eggs into the skillet and add the diced bell peppers, sliced mushrooms, and diced red onion.
4. Cook the egg and vegetable mixture, stirring occasionally, until the eggs are scrambled and the vegetables are cooked through. This should take about 3-4 minutes.
5. Warm the tortillas in a separate skillet or in the microwave according to the package instructions.
6. Divide the scrambled eggs and vegetables evenly between the two tortillas, placing them in the center.
7. Sprinkle the shredded cheddar cheese over the eggs and vegetables.

8. Fold the sides of each tortilla towards the center, then roll them up tightly to form a wrap.
9. Place the wraps back into the skillet for a minute or two to warm them up and melt the cheese, if desired.
10. Remove the wraps from the skillet and let them cool slightly before serving.
11. Cut each wrap in half diagonally, if desired, and serve the Vegetable and Cheese Breakfast Wraps warm.

PROTEIN-PACKED GREEN SMOOTHIE BOWL

Nutrition: Cal 220;Fat 9 g;Carb 25 g;Protein 15 g
Serving 2; Cook time 15 min

Ingredients
- 2 cups fresh spinach
- 1 ripe banana
- 1/2 cup unsweetened almond milk (or any milk of your choice)
- 1/2 cup plain Greek yogurt (low-fat or non-fat)
- 2 tablespoons chia seeds
- 1 tablespoon almond butter or peanut butter
- Optional toppings: sliced fresh fruits, nuts, seeds, shredded coconut

Instructions:
1. In a blender, combine the fresh spinach, ripe banana, almond milk, Greek yogurt, chia seeds, and almond butter.
2. Blend on high speed until all the ingredients are well combined and the mixture is smooth and creamy.
3. If the consistency is too thick, you can add a little more almond milk to achieve the desired texture.
4. Pour the smoothie into two bowls.
5. Top the smoothie bowls with your choice of sliced fresh fruits, nuts, seeds, or shredded coconut.

QUINOA PORRIDGE WITH PECANS AND MAPLE SYRUP

Nutrition: Cal 220;Fat 9 g;Carb 25 g;Protein 15 g
Serving 2; Cook time 30 min

Ingredients
- 1/2 cup quinoa, rinsed
- 1 cup water

- 1 cup unsweetened almond milk (or any milk of your choice)
- 1/4 teaspoon ground cinnamon
- 2 tablespoons chopped pecans
- 1 tablespoon pure maple syrup

Instructions:

1. In a saucepan, combine the rinsed quinoa, water, almond milk, and ground cinnamon.
2. Bring the mixture to a boil over medium heat.
3. Reduce the heat to low, cover the saucepan, and let it simmer for 15-20 minutes, or until the quinoa is tender and the liquid is absorbed. Stir occasionally to prevent sticking.
4. Once the quinoa is cooked, remove the saucepan from the heat and let it sit for a few minutes to cool slightly.
5. Divide the quinoa porridge between two bowls.
6. Sprinkle the chopped pecans over the porridge.
7. Drizzle the pure maple syrup over the porridge and pecans.
8. Stir the porridge gently to combine all the ingredients.
9. Serve the Quinoa Porridge with Pecans and Maple Syrup warm and enjoy!

MINI HAM AND CHEESE QUICHES

Nutrition: Cal 180;Fat 6 g;Carb 7 g;Protein 22 g
Serving 2; Cook time 30 min

Ingredients

- 4 slices of lean ham, diced
- 1/4 cup shredded low-fat cheddar cheese
- 2 large eggs
- 1/4 cup low-fat milk
- 1/4 teaspoon salt
- 1/8 teaspoon black pepper
- 1/4 teaspoon dried parsley (optional)
- Non-stick cooking spray

Instructions:

1. Preheat your oven to 375°F (190°C).
2. Spray two standard-sized muffin tins with non-stick cooking spray.
3. In a bowl, combine the diced ham and shredded cheddar cheese. Mix well.
4. Divide the ham and cheese mixture evenly among the prepared muffin tins.
5. In another bowl, whisk together the eggs, milk, salt, black pepper, and dried parsley (if using) until well combined.

6. Pour the egg mixture evenly over the ham and cheese mixture in the muffin tins.
7. Place the muffin tins in the preheated oven and bake for about 15-20 minutes, or until the quiches are set and slightly golden on top.
8. Remove the quiches from the oven and let them cool in the muffin tins for a few minutes.
9. Using a spoon or small spatula, carefully remove the mini quiches from the muffin tins and transfer them to a serving plate.
10. Serve the mini ham and cheese quiches warm or at room temperature.

BREAKFAST STIR-FRY

Nutrition: Cal 220;Fat 13 g;Carb 9 g;Protein 18 g
Serving 2; Cook time 20 min

Ingredients

- 4 ounces lean turkey sausage, sliced
- 1 cup broccoli florets
- 1/2 bell pepper, thinly sliced
- 1/2 small onion, thinly sliced
- 2 large eggs, beaten
- 1 tablespoon low-sodium soy sauce
- 1/2 teaspoon garlic powder
- 1/4 teaspoon black pepper
- 1 tablespoon olive oil

Instructions:

1. Heat the olive oil in a non-stick skillet or wok over medium heat.
2. Add the sliced turkey sausage to the skillet and cook until browned and cooked through, about 5 minutes. Remove the sausage from the skillet and set aside.
3. In the same skillet, add the broccoli florets, bell pepper, and onion. Stir-fry for about 3-4 minutes until the vegetables are crisp-tender.
4. Push the vegetables to one side of the skillet and add the beaten eggs to the other side. Scramble the eggs until they are fully cooked.
5. Combine the cooked sausage with the stir-fried vegetables and eggs in the skillet.
6. In a small bowl, whisk together the soy sauce, garlic powder, and black pepper. Pour the sauce over the stir-fry mixture in the skillet.
7. Stir-fry everything together for another 1-2 minutes to allow the flavors to meld.
8. Remove the skillet from the heat and divide the breakfast stir-fry between two plates.

9. Serve the breakfast stir-fry hot.

COCONUT FLOUR BANANA BREAD

Nutrition: Cal 230;Fat 12 g;Carb 26 g;Protein 7 g
Serving 2; Cook time 40 min

Ingredients
- 1/2 cup coconut flour
- 1/2 teaspoon baking soda
- 1/4 teaspoon salt
- 1/2 teaspoon ground cinnamon
- 2 ripe bananas, mashed
- 2 large eggs
- 2 tablespoons coconut oil, melted
- 2 tablespoons honey or preferred sweetener
- 1/2 teaspoon vanilla extract

Instructions:
1. Preheat your oven to 350°F (175°C). Grease a small loaf pan or line it with parchment paper.
2. In a bowl, combine the coconut flour, baking soda, salt, and ground cinnamon. Mix well.
3. In a separate bowl, whisk together the mashed bananas, eggs, melted coconut oil, honey (or sweetener of your choice), and vanilla extract until well combined.
4. Gradually add the wet ingredients to the dry ingredients, stirring until a thick batter forms. Let the batter sit for a few minutes to allow the coconut flour to absorb the moisture.
5. Pour the batter into the prepared loaf pan, smoothing the top with a spatula.
6. Bake in the preheated oven for about 35-40 minutes, or until a toothpick inserted into the center comes out clean.
7. Remove the banana bread from the oven and let it cool in the pan for a few minutes.
8. Once slightly cooled, transfer the banana bread to a wire rack to cool completely before slicing.
9. Slice the coconut flour banana bread into two servings and enjoy.

VEGGIE EGG SCRAMBLE WITH PEPPERS AND ONIONS

Nutrition: Cal 180;Fat 12 g;Carb 7 g;Protein 12 g
Serving 2; Cook time 20 min

Ingredients
- 4 large eggs
- 1/2 bell pepper, diced
- 1/2 small onion, diced
- 1/2 cup sliced mushrooms
- 1/2 cup baby spinach leaves
- 1 tablespoon olive oil
- 1/4 teaspoon salt
- 1/8 teaspoon black pepper
- Optional toppings: chopped fresh herbs (such as parsley or chives)

Instructions:
1. Heat the olive oil in a non-stick skillet over medium heat.
2. Add the diced bell pepper and onion to the skillet. Sauté for about 3-4 minutes until the vegetables start to soften.
3. Add the sliced mushrooms to the skillet and cook for an additional 2 minutes until they begin to brown.
4. Stir in the baby spinach leaves and cook until wilted, about 1 minute.
5. Meanwhile, in a bowl, whisk the eggs until well beaten. Season with salt and black pepper.
6. Push the vegetables to one side of the skillet and pour the beaten eggs into the other side.
7. Allow the eggs to cook undisturbed for a few seconds until they start to set around the edges.
8. Using a spatula, gently scramble the eggs, incorporating the cooked vegetables.
9. Continue to cook the eggs and vegetables, stirring occasionally, until the eggs are fully cooked and no longer runny.
10. Remove the skillet from the heat and divide the veggie egg scramble between two plates.
11. Garnish with chopped fresh herbs, if desired.
12. Serve the veggie egg scramble hot.

TURKEY SAUSAGE BREAKFAST TACOS WITH LETTUCE WRAPS

Nutrition: Cal 200;Fat 9 g;Carb 10 g;Protein 18 g
Serving 2; Cook time 20 min

Ingredients
- 4 ounces lean turkey sausage, casings removed
- 4 large lettuce leaves (such as iceberg or romaine)
- 2 large eggs
- 1/2 bell pepper, diced

- 1/4 small onion, diced
- 1/4 cup shredded low-fat cheese
- Salt and black pepper, to taste
- Optional toppings: salsa, avocado slices, cilantro

Instructions:

1. Heat a non-stick skillet over medium heat. Add the turkey sausage and cook, breaking it up with a spatula, until browned and cooked through. Remove the sausage from the skillet and set aside.
2. In the same skillet, add the diced bell pepper and onion. Sauté for about 3-4 minutes until the vegetables start to soften.
3. Push the vegetables to one side of the skillet and crack the eggs into the other side. Scramble the eggs until they are fully cooked.
4. Return the cooked turkey sausage to the skillet and mix it with the vegetables and eggs. Season with salt and black pepper to taste.
5. Wash and dry the lettuce leaves. Use them as the taco shells, placing the turkey sausage and egg mixture inside each lettuce leaf.
6. Top the tacos with shredded low-fat cheese and any optional toppings of your choice, such as salsa, avocado slices, or cilantro.
7. Serve the turkey sausage breakfast tacos immediately.

GREEK YOGURT WITH HONEY AND MIXED NUTS

Nutrition: Cal 210;Fat 9 g;Carb 19 g;Protein 18 g
Serving 2; Cook time 5 min

Ingredients
- 1 cup plain Greek yogurt (low-fat or non-fat)
- 2 tablespoons honey
- 2 tablespoons mixed nuts (such as almonds, walnuts, and pistachios), chopped

Instructions:

1. In two serving bowls, divide the Greek yogurt evenly.
2. Drizzle 1 tablespoon of honey over each bowl of yogurt.
3. Sprinkle 1 tablespoon of mixed nuts over each bowl of yogurt.
4. Serve the Greek yogurt with honey and mixed nuts immediately.

SWEET POTATO AND TURKEY BACON HASH

Nutrition: Cal 220;Fat 9 g;Carb 28 g;Protein 9 g
Serving 2; Cook time 25 min

Ingredients
- 1 medium sweet potato, peeled and diced
- 4 slices lean turkey bacon, chopped
- 1/2 bell pepper, diced
- 1/2 small onion, diced
- 2 cloves garlic, minced
- 1/2 teaspoon smoked paprika
- 1/4 teaspoon dried thyme
- Salt and black pepper, to taste
- 1 tablespoon olive oil

Instructions:

1. Heat the olive oil in a non-stick skillet over medium heat.
2. Add the chopped turkey bacon to the skillet and cook until crispy. Remove the cooked bacon from the skillet and set aside.
3. In the same skillet, add the diced sweet potato. Cook for about 5 minutes, stirring occasionally, until the sweet potato begins to soften.
4. Add the diced bell pepper and onion to the skillet. Continue cooking for another 5 minutes until the vegetables are tender.
5. Stir in the minced garlic, smoked paprika, dried thyme, salt, and black pepper. Cook for an additional minute until the spices are fragrant.
6. Return the cooked turkey bacon to the skillet and mix well with the sweet potato and vegetable mixture.
7. Continue cooking for another 2-3 minutes, or until the sweet potato is cooked through and slightly crispy.
8. Remove the skillet from the heat and divide the sweet potato and turkey bacon hash between two plates.

RICOTTA AND BLUEBERRY STUFFED FRENCH TOAST

Nutrition: Cal 300;Fat 8 g;Carb 42 g;Protein 16 g
Serving 2; Cook time 15 min

Ingredients
- 4 slices whole grain bread
- 1/2 cup low-fat ricotta cheese

- 1/2 cup fresh blueberries
- 2 large eggs
- 1/4 cup unsweetened almond milk (or any milk of your choice)
- 1/2 teaspoon vanilla extract
- 1/2 teaspoon ground cinnamon
- Cooking spray or a small amount of oil for greasing the pan

Instructions:

1. In a small bowl, combine the ricotta cheese and fresh blueberries. Mash the blueberries slightly to release their juices and mix them into the ricotta cheese.
2. Spread the ricotta-blueberry mixture evenly on two slices of bread. Top each with the remaining two slices of bread to create two sandwiches.
3. In a shallow dish, whisk together the eggs, almond milk, vanilla extract, and ground cinnamon until well combined.
4. Heat a non-stick skillet or griddle over medium heat and lightly grease it with cooking spray or a small amount of oil.
5. Dip each stuffed sandwich into the egg mixture, coating both sides.
6. Place the dipped sandwiches onto the preheated skillet or griddle. Cook for about 3-4 minutes per side, or until golden brown and crispy.
7. Remove the French toast from the skillet or griddle and let it cool for a minute.
8. Slice the stuffed French toast diagonally into halves or quarters and serve immediately.

SPINACH AND FETA EGG MUFFINS

Nutrition: Cal 210;Fat 14 g;Carb 3 g;Protein 18 g
Serving 2; Cook time 25 min

Ingredients
- 6 large eggs
- 1 cup fresh spinach, chopped
- 1/4 cup crumbled feta cheese
- 1/4 cup diced tomatoes
- 2 tablespoons diced red onion
- Salt and black pepper, to taste
- Cooking spray or a small amount of oil for greasing the muffin tin

Instructions:

1. Preheat your oven to 375°F (190°C). Grease a muffin tin with cooking spray or a small amount of oil.
2. In a bowl, beat the eggs until well blended. Season with salt and black pepper to taste.
3. Stir in the chopped spinach, crumbled feta cheese, diced tomatoes, and diced red onion into the egg mixture. Mix well to ensure all ingredients are evenly distributed.
4. Pour the egg mixture into the greased muffin tin, dividing it evenly among the cups.
5. Bake in the preheated oven for about 15-20 minutes, or until the egg muffins are set and slightly golden on top.
6. Remove the muffin tin from the oven and let the egg muffins cool for a few minutes.
7. Gently remove the egg muffins from the muffin tin and serve them warm.

SALAD WITH HARD-BOILED EGG AND AVOCADO

Nutrition: Cal 250;Fat 18 g;Carb 16 g;Protein 9 g
Serving 2; Cook time 15 min

Ingredients
- 4 cups mixed salad greens
- 2 hard-boiled eggs, sliced
- 1 ripe avocado, sliced
- 1 cup cherry tomatoes, halved
- 1/4 cup sliced red onion
- 2 tablespoons balsamic vinegar
- 1 tablespoon extra-virgin olive oil
- Salt and black pepper, to taste

Instructions:

1. In a large bowl, combine the mixed salad greens, sliced hard-boiled eggs, avocado slices, cherry tomatoes, and sliced red onion.
2. In a small bowl, whisk together the balsamic vinegar, extra-virgin olive oil, salt, and black pepper to create the dressing.
3. Drizzle the dressing over the salad mixture and toss gently to coat all ingredients evenly.
4. Divide the salad into two serving bowls.

5. Serve the salad with hard-boiled egg and avocado immediately.

ALMOND FLOUR PUMPKIN PANCAKES

Nutrition: Cal 260;Fat 20 g;Carb 10 g;Protein 11 g
Serving 2; Cook time 25 min

Ingredients
- 1/2 cup almond flour
- 1/4 cup pumpkin puree
- 2 large eggs
- 1 tablespoon coconut oil, melted
- 1 tablespoon unsweetened almond milk (or any milk of your choice)
- 1 tablespoon pure maple syrup or sweetener of your choice
- 1/2 teaspoon baking powder
- 1/2 teaspoon pumpkin pie spice
- 1/4 teaspoon vanilla extract
- Pinch of salt
- Cooking spray or a small amount of oil for greasing the pan

Instructions:
1. In a mixing bowl, whisk together the almond flour, pumpkin puree, eggs, melted coconut oil, almond milk, maple syrup, baking powder, pumpkin pie spice, vanilla extract, and salt. Mix until well combined and smooth.
2. Heat a non-stick skillet or griddle over medium heat and lightly grease it with cooking spray or a small amount of oil.
3. Spoon about 2 tablespoons of the pancake batter onto the skillet for each pancake. Use the back of the spoon to spread the batter into a small circle.
4. Cook the pancakes for about 2-3 minutes on each side, or until they are golden brown and cooked through.
5. Remove the pancakes from the skillet and repeat the process with the remaining batter.
6. Serve the almond flour pumpkin pancakes warm, topped with your choice of toppings such as sugar-free syrup, fresh berries, or a dollop of Greek yogurt.

SMOKED SALMON AND DILL CREAM CHEESE ROLL-UPS

Nutrition: Cal 180;Fat 11 g;Carb 6 g;Protein 14 g
Serving 2; Cook time 15 min

Ingredients
- 6 slices smoked salmon
- 4 ounces cream cheese, softened (choose a low-fat or reduced-fat version if desired)
- 1 tablespoon fresh dill, chopped
- 1 tablespoon lemon juice
- 1/4 teaspoon black pepper
- 1/4 teaspoon garlic powder
- 2 large cucumber, sliced lengthwise into thin strips (use a vegetable peeler or mandoline slicer)
- Fresh dill sprigs for garnish (optional)

Instructions:
1. In a small bowl, mix the softened cream cheese, chopped dill, lemon juice, black pepper, and garlic powder until well combined.
2. Lay out a slice of smoked salmon and spread a thin layer of the dill cream cheese mixture on top.
3. Place a cucumber strip at one end of the salmon slice and roll it up tightly.
4. Repeat steps 2 and 3 with the remaining salmon slices, cream cheese mixture, and cucumber strips.
5. Place the roll-ups on a serving platter or plate, seam side down.
6. Garnish with fresh dill sprigs, if desired.
7. Serve the smoked salmon and dill cream cheese roll-ups chilled.

VEGGIE FRITTATA WITH GOAT CHEESE

Nutrition: Cal 180;Fat 12 g;Carb 5 g;Protein 12 g
Serving 2; Cook time 30 min

Ingredients
- 4 large eggs
- 1/4 cup diced bell peppers
- 1/4 cup diced zucchini
- 1/4 cup diced mushrooms
- 1/4 cup diced onions
- 2 tablespoons crumbled goat cheese
- 1 tablespoon olive oil
- Salt and black pepper, to taste
- Fresh herbs (such as parsley or basil) for garnish (optional)

Instructions:
1. Preheat your oven to 375°F (190°C).

2. In a medium-sized bowl, whisk the eggs until well beaten. Season with salt and black pepper.

3. Heat the olive oil in an oven-safe skillet over medium heat. Add the diced bell peppers, zucchini, mushrooms, and onions. Sauté for about 5 minutes, or until the vegetables are slightly softened.

4. Pour the beaten eggs over the sautéed vegetables in the skillet, making sure they are evenly distributed.

5. Sprinkle the crumbled goat cheese on top of the egg and vegetable mixture.

6. Transfer the skillet to the preheated oven and bake for about 12-15 minutes, or until the frittata is set and lightly golden on top.

7. Remove the skillet from the oven and let the frittata cool for a few minutes.

8. Slice the frittata into wedges and serve warm. Garnish with fresh herbs, if desired.

GREEK YOGURT WITH GRANOLA AND MIXED BERRIES

Nutrition: Cal 220;Fat 6 g;Carb 28 g;Protein 18 g
Serving 2; Cook time 5 min

Ingredients
- 1 cup Greek yogurt (choose a low-fat or non-fat version if desired)
- 1/2 cup granola (choose a low-sugar or sugar-free option if desired)
- 1/2 cup mixed berries (such as strawberries, blueberries, raspberries)
- 1 tablespoon honey (optional, for added sweetness)
- Fresh mint leaves for garnish (optional)

Instructions:
1. In two serving bowls, divide the Greek yogurt equally.

2. Top each bowl of Greek yogurt with half of the granola.

3. Add the mixed berries on top of the granola.

4. Drizzle honey over the yogurt and berries, if desired, for added sweetness.

5. Garnish with fresh mint leaves, if desired, for a fresh and vibrant touch.

6. Serve the Greek yogurt with granola and mixed berries immediately.

CAULIFLOWER AND CHEESE BREAKFAST CASSEROLE

Nutrition: Cal 180;Fat 10 g;Carb 8 g;Protein 15 g
Serving 2; Cook time 45 min

Ingredients
- 2 cups cauliflower florets
- 2 large eggs
- 1/2 cup shredded cheddar cheese (choose a low-fat or reduced-fat version if desired)
- 1/4 cup milk (choose a low-fat or non-fat version if desired)
- 2 tablespoons grated Parmesan cheese
- 1/4 teaspoon garlic powder
- Salt and black pepper, to taste
- Fresh chives or parsley for garnish (optional)

Instructions:
1. Preheat your oven to 375°F (190°C).

2. Steam the cauliflower florets until they are tender but still slightly firm. Drain any excess water.

3. In a mixing bowl, whisk together the eggs, shredded cheddar cheese, milk, grated Parmesan cheese, garlic powder, salt, and black pepper.

4. Add the steamed cauliflower florets to the egg and cheese mixture. Stir gently to combine.

5. Grease a small baking dish or individual ramekins with cooking spray or a small amount of oil.

6. Pour the cauliflower and cheese mixture into the greased baking dish or ramekins.

7. Bake in the preheated oven for approximately 20-25 minutes, or until the casserole is set and lightly golden on top.

8. Remove from the oven and let it cool for a few minutes.

9. Garnish with fresh chives or parsley, if desired.

10. Serve the cauliflower and cheese breakfast casserole warm.

TOFU SCRAMBLE

Nutrition: Cal 153;Fat 10 g;Carb 5 g;Protein 12 g
Serving 2; Cook time 20 min

Ingredients
- 16 ounces of extra-firm tofu
- 1 tablespoons of olive oil
- half of red onion, chopped
- half of bell pepper, chopped

- 2 cups of spinach, chopped
- salt and pepper to taste

Instructions:

1. Drain the tofu and press it dry by setting it on a plate covered with a paper towel and placing a heavy object on top to press it for 10–15 minutes.
2. Crumble the tofu into small pieces in a bowl and set aside.
3. Add the olive oil to a pan over medium heat and then sauté the onions and garlic for 2–3 minutes.
4. Add the bell pepper and spinach. Sauté until the spinach is dark green and wilted.
5. Add the crumbled tofu to the pan and cook for 3–4 minutes, occasionally stirring to break up large clumps.
6. Season with salt and pepper before serving.

COTTAGE CHEESE AND FRUIT BOWL

Nutrition: Cal 200;Fat 7 g;Carb 20 g;Protein 18 g
Serving 2; Cook time 5 min

Ingredients

- 1 cup low-fat cottage cheese
- 1 cup mixed fresh fruits (such as berries, sliced banana, or diced melon)
- 2 tablespoons chopped nuts (such as almonds or walnuts)
- 1 teaspoon honey or maple syrup (optional, for added sweetness)

Instructions:

1. In two bowls, divide the low-fat cottage cheese equally.
2. Top each bowl of cottage cheese with half of the mixed fresh fruits.
3. Sprinkle the chopped nuts on top of the fruit and cottage cheese mixture.
4. Drizzle honey or maple syrup over the bowl, if desired, for added sweetness.
5. Serve the cottage cheese and fruit bowl immediately.

BAKED EGGS IN HAM CUPS

Nutrition: Cal 180;Fat 10 g;Carb 2 g;Protein 24 g
Serving 2; Cook time 20 min

Ingredients

- 4 slices of lean ham
- 4 large eggs
- Salt and black pepper, to taste
- Fresh herbs (such as chives or parsley) for garnish (optional)

Instructions:

1. Preheat your oven to 375°F (190°C).
2. Lightly grease a muffin tin or use silicone muffin cups to prevent sticking.
3. Line each muffin cup with a slice of lean ham, pressing it against the sides to form a cup shape.
4. Crack one egg into each ham cup.
5. Season with salt and black pepper to taste.
6. Place the muffin tin in the preheated oven and bake for approximately 12-15 minutes, or until the egg whites are set and the yolks are still slightly runny.
7. Remove from the oven and let it cool for a few minutes.
8. Garnish with fresh herbs, if desired, for added flavor and presentation.
9. Serve the baked eggs in ham cups warm.

SPINACH AND FETA LETTUCE WRAP

Nutrition: Cal 290;Fat 10 g;Carb 7 g;Protein 7 g
Serving 2; Cook time 20 min

Ingredients

- 2 egg large
- 2 egg white large
- 1 cup baby spinach torn into small pieces
- 4 tablespoons feta crumbles fat-free
- 2 roma tomato diced
- pinch of kosher or sea salt
- 0.5 teaspoon black pepper
- 2 lettuce leaf large

Instructions:

1. Add all ingredients, except lettuce, to a mixing bowl and whisk to combine. Heat nonstick skillet to medium heat, add egg mixture and cook to desired consistency.
2. Add cooked egg to the edge of lettuce leaf and fold over.
3. Best if eaten immediately.

HIGH-PROTEIN GREEK SALAD OMELET WRAP

Nutrition: Cal 290;Fat 10 g;Carb 7 g;Protein 7 g
Serving 2; Cook time 20 min

Ingredients
SALAD
- 1 tablespoon extra-virgin olive oil
- 1 tablespoon lemon juice
- 1 teaspoon red-wine vinegar
- ½ teaspoon dried oregano
- ½ teaspoon ground pepper
- ⅛ teaspoon salt
- ½ cup crumbled or diced feta cheese (about 2 ounces)
- ½ English cucumber or 2 baby cucumbers, halved and thinly sliced
- ½ cup grape tomatoes, halved lengthwise
- ¼ cup diced green bell pepper
- ¼ cup thinly sliced red onion
- 4 Kalamata olives, pitted and sliced

OMELET WRAPS
- 6 egg whites
- 1 tablespoon blanched almond flour
- 1 teaspoon za'atar
- 1 tablespoon finely chopped fresh parsley

Instructions:
TO PREPARE SALAD:

1. Whisk oil, lemon juice, vinegar, oregano, pepper and salt together in a large bowl.
2. Add feta, cucumber, tomatoes, bell pepper, onion and olives to the bowl with the dressing and toss to combine.

TO PREPARE WRAPS:

3. Whisk egg whites, almond flour, za'atar and parsley together in a medium bowl until well combined.
4. Coat a medium nonstick skillet with cooking spray; place over medium heat for 1 minute. Pour half of the egg-white mixture (about 1/2 cup) into the pan; swirl to coat the bottom fully. Cook, lifting the dry edges gently with a spatula so the liquid egg from the center flows to the sides, until the top is almost set, 1 to 2 minutes. Cover the pan and continue cooking until the egg is completely set, about 1 minute more. Use a large flexible spatula to carefully transfer the omelet to a plate. Repeat to make a second omelet.

TO ASSEMBLE WRAPS:

5. Spoon half the salad into the center of each omelet. Fold the bottom and sides to make a wrap. Use a 12-by-6-inch sheet of foil to wrap the bottom half of each wrap to hold it together.

LUNCH

CAULIFLOWER FRIED RICE WITH SHRIMP

Nutrition: Cal 250;Fat 10 g;Carb 20 g;Protein 20 g
Serving 2; Cook time 25 min

Ingredients
- 1 small head of cauliflower
- 8 oz shrimp, peeled and deveined
- 1 cup mixed vegetables (such as peas, carrots, and bell peppers), diced
- 2 cloves garlic, minced
- 2 tablespoons low-sodium soy sauce
- 1 tablespoon sesame oil
- 2 green onions, chopped
- 2 eggs, beaten
- Salt and pepper to taste

Instructions:
1. Cut the cauliflower into florets and place them in a food processor. Pulse until the cauliflower resembles rice-like grains. Be careful not to overprocess it into a mush. Set aside.
2. In a large non-stick skillet or wok, heat the sesame oil over medium-high heat. Add the shrimp and cook for about 2-3 minutes until they turn pink and are cooked through. Remove the shrimp from the skillet and set aside.
3. In the same skillet, add the mixed vegetables and minced garlic. Stir-fry for about 2-3 minutes until the vegetables are tender-crisp.
4. Push the vegetables to one side of the skillet and pour the beaten eggs onto the other side. Scramble the eggs until they are fully cooked.
5. Add the cauliflower rice to the skillet and stir-fry for about 3-4 minutes until it becomes tender.
6. Return the cooked shrimp to the skillet. Add the low-sodium soy sauce, chopped green onions, salt, and pepper. Stir-fry for an additional 1-2 minutes to combine the flavors and heat the shrimp through.
7. Remove from heat and divide the cauliflower fried rice between two plates. Serve hot and enjoy!

TURKEY LETTUCE WRAPS WITH AVOCADO

Nutrition: Cal 250;Fat 15 g;Carb 10 g;Protein 20 g
Serving 2; Cook time 20 min

Ingredients
- 8 oz ground turkey
- 1 tablespoon olive oil
- 1/2 onion, diced
- 2 cloves garlic, minced
- 1/2 teaspoon ground cumin
- 1/2 teaspoon chili powder
- Salt and pepper to taste
- 4 large lettuce leaves (such as romaine or butter lettuce)
- 1/2 avocado, sliced
- 1/4 cup diced tomatoes
- 1/4 cup diced bell peppers
- Fresh cilantro, for garnish

Instructions:
1. Heat the olive oil in a skillet over medium heat. Add the diced onion and minced garlic, and cook until the onion becomes translucent and the garlic is fragrant.
2. Add the ground turkey to the skillet and cook until it is browned and cooked through, breaking it up into crumbles with a spatula.
3. Stir in the ground cumin, chili powder, salt, and pepper. Cook for an additional 2-3 minutes to allow the flavors to blend.
4. Wash and dry the lettuce leaves. Place a spoonful of the cooked turkey mixture onto each lettuce leaf.
5. Top the turkey with sliced avocado, diced tomatoes, and diced bell peppers.
6. Garnish with fresh cilantro.
7. Carefully roll up the lettuce leaves, securing the filling inside like a wrap.
8. Serve the turkey lettuce wraps immediately. Enjoy!

GREEK SALAD WITH GRILLED SALMON

Nutrition: Cal 350;Fat 20 g;Carb 15 g;Protein 25 g
Serving 2; Cook time 20 min

Ingredients
- 8 oz salmon fillets
- 8 cups mixed salad greens

- 1 cup cherry tomatoes, halved
- 1 cucumber, sliced
- 1/4 red onion, thinly sliced
- 1/4 cup Kalamata olives
- 2 tablespoons crumbled feta cheese
- Juice of 1 lemon
- 2 tablespoons extra virgin olive oil
- 1 teaspoon dried oregano
- Salt and pepper to taste

Instructions:

1. Preheat the grill or grill pan over medium heat. Season the salmon fillets with salt, pepper, and dried oregano. Grill the salmon for about 4-5 minutes on each side, or until it is cooked through and flakes easily with a fork. Remove from heat and set aside.
2. In a large bowl, combine the mixed salad greens, cherry tomatoes, cucumber slices, red onion, and Kalamata olives.
3. In a small bowl, whisk together the lemon juice, extra virgin olive oil, dried oregano, salt, and pepper to make the dressing.
4. Pour the dressing over the salad mixture and toss to combine.
5. Divide the salad between two plates. Top each plate with half of the grilled salmon fillet.
6. Sprinkle crumbled feta cheese over the salads.
7. Serve the Greek salad with grilled salmon immediately. Enjoy!

ZUCCHINI NOODLES WITH TOMATO SAUCE AND TURKEY MEATBALLS

Nutrition: Cal 300;Fat 15 g;Carb 15 g;Protein 25 g
Serving 2; Cook time 40 min

Ingredients
FOR THE TURKEY MEATBALLS:
- 8 oz lean ground turkey
- 1/4 cup almond flour
- 1/4 cup grated Parmesan cheese
- 1/4 cup finely chopped fresh parsley
- 1/2 teaspoon dried oregano
- 1/2 teaspoon garlic powder
- Salt and pepper to taste

FOR THE TOMATO SAUCE:
- 1 tablespoon olive oil
- 2 cloves garlic, minced
- 1 can (14 oz) crushed tomatoes

- 1 teaspoon dried basil
- 1/2 teaspoon dried oregano
- Salt and pepper to taste

FOR THE ZUCCHINI NOODLES:
- 2 medium-sized zucchini
- 1 tablespoon olive oil
- Salt and pepper to taste

Instructions:

1. In a mixing bowl, combine the ground turkey, almond flour, grated Parmesan cheese, chopped parsley, dried oregano, garlic powder, salt, and pepper. Mix well until all the ingredients are evenly incorporated.
2. Shape the turkey mixture into small meatballs, about 1 inch in diameter.
3. Heat the olive oil in a skillet over medium heat. Add the minced garlic and cook until fragrant, about 1 minute.
4. Add the crushed tomatoes, dried basil, dried oregano, salt, and pepper to the skillet. Stir well and bring the sauce to a simmer. Reduce the heat to low and let it simmer for about 15 minutes, stirring occasionally.
5. While the tomato sauce is simmering, prepare the zucchini noodles. Use a spiralizer or a julienne peeler to create noodles from the zucchini.
6. Heat the olive oil in a separate skillet over medium heat. Add the zucchini noodles and cook for about 2-3 minutes until they are tender-crisp. Season with salt and pepper.
7. In another skillet, cook the turkey meatballs over medium heat until they are browned and cooked through, about 8-10 minutes.
8. Serve the zucchini noodles topped with the tomato sauce and turkey meatballs.

QUINOA SALAD WITH ROASTED VEGETABLES

Nutrition: Cal 300;Fat 10 g;Carb 45 g;Protein 10 g
Serving 2; Cook time 35 min

Ingredients
- 1 cup quinoa
- 2 cups mixed vegetables (such as bell peppers, zucchini, and carrots), diced
- 1 tablespoon olive oil
- 1/2 teaspoon dried oregano
- Salt and pepper to taste

- 2 cups mixed salad greens
- 1/4 cup crumbled feta cheese
- 2 tablespoons chopped fresh parsley
- Juice of 1 lemon
- 2 tablespoons extra virgin olive oil

Instructions:

1. Preheat the oven to 400°F (200°C).
2. Rinse the quinoa under cold water to remove any bitter residue. In a saucepan, combine the quinoa with 2 cups of water. Bring to a boil, then reduce the heat to low, cover, and simmer for about 15-20 minutes or until the quinoa is tender and the water is absorbed. Remove from heat and let it cool.
3. Place the diced mixed vegetables on a baking sheet. Drizzle with olive oil, sprinkle with dried oregano, salt, and pepper. Toss to coat the vegetables evenly. Roast in the preheated oven for about 15-20 minutes or until the vegetables are tender and slightly caramelized. Remove from the oven and let them cool.
4. In a large bowl, combine the cooked quinoa, roasted vegetables, mixed salad greens, crumbled feta cheese, and chopped fresh parsley.
5. In a small bowl, whisk together the lemon juice, extra virgin olive oil, salt, and pepper to make the dressing.
6. Drizzle the dressing over the quinoa salad and toss to combine all the ingredients.
7. Divide the salad between two plates and serve.

CHICKEN AND VEGETABLE STIR-FRY WITH BROWN RICE

Nutrition: Cal 350;Fat 10 g;Carb 40 g;Protein 25 g
Serving 2; Cook time 25 min

Ingredients

- 2 boneless, skinless chicken breasts (about 4 oz each), thinly sliced
- 2 cups mixed vegetables (such as bell peppers, broccoli, and snap peas), sliced
- 1 tablespoon olive oil
- 2 cloves garlic, minced
- 2 tablespoons low-sodium soy sauce
- 1 tablespoon hoisin sauce
- 1/2 teaspoon sesame oil
- 2 cups cooked brown rice
- Fresh cilantro, for garnish (optional)

- Sesame seeds, for garnish (optional)

Instructions:

1. Heat the olive oil in a large skillet or wok over medium-high heat. Add the sliced chicken and cook for about 4-5 minutes until it is cooked through and no longer pink. Remove the chicken from the skillet and set aside.
2. In the same skillet, add the minced garlic and cook for about 1 minute until it becomes fragrant.
3. Add the mixed vegetables to the skillet and stir-fry for about 3-4 minutes until they are tender-crisp.
4. In a small bowl, whisk together the low-sodium soy sauce, hoisin sauce, and sesame oil. Pour the sauce over the vegetables in the skillet.
5. Return the cooked chicken to the skillet and toss to coat the chicken and vegetables in the sauce. Cook for an additional 1-2 minutes to heat everything through.
6. Divide the cooked brown rice between two plates. Top each plate with half of the chicken and vegetable stir-fry.
7. Garnish with fresh cilantro and sesame seeds, if desired.
8. Serve the chicken and vegetable stir-fry with brown rice immediately. Enjoy!

TUNA SALAD LETTUCE WRAPS

Nutrition: Cal 200;Fat 8 g;Carb 5 g;Protein 25 g
Serving 2; Cook time 10 min

Ingredients

- 2 cans (5 oz each) tuna in water, drained
- 1/4 cup diced celery
- 1/4 cup diced red onion
- 2 tablespoons light mayonnaise
- 1 tablespoon Dijon mustard
- Juice of 1/2 lemon
- Salt and pepper to taste
- 4 large lettuce leaves (such as romaine or butter lettuce)

Instructions:

1. In a bowl, flake the drained tuna with a fork.
2. Add the diced celery, diced red onion, light mayonnaise, Dijon mustard, lemon juice, salt, and pepper to the bowl. Mix well to combine all the ingredients.

3. Wash and dry the lettuce leaves. Place a spoonful of the tuna salad mixture onto each lettuce leaf.
4. Carefully roll up the lettuce leaves, securing the filling inside like a wrap.
5. Serve the tuna salad lettuce wraps immediately. Enjoy!

GRILLED SHRIMP SKEWERS WITH QUINOA TABOULI

Nutrition: Cal 300;Fat 12 g;Carb 25 g;Protein 25 g
Serving 2; Cook time 25 min

Ingredients
FOR THE GRILLED SHRIMP SKEWERS:
- 8 oz shrimp, peeled and deveined
- 1 tablespoon olive oil
- 1 clove garlic, minced
- 1 teaspoon lemon zest
- 1/2 teaspoon paprika
- Salt and pepper to taste

FOR THE QUINOA TABOULI:
- 1 cup cooked quinoa
- 1/2 cucumber, diced
- 1/2 cup cherry tomatoes, halved
- 1/4 cup chopped fresh parsley
- 1/4 cup chopped fresh mint
- Juice of 1 lemon
- 2 tablespoons extra virgin olive oil
- Salt and pepper to taste

Instructions:
1. Preheat the grill or grill pan over medium-high heat.
2. In a bowl, combine the shrimp, olive oil, minced garlic, lemon zest, paprika, salt, and pepper. Toss to coat the shrimp evenly.
3. Thread the shrimp onto skewers.
4. Grill the shrimp skewers for about 2-3 minutes on each side until they are pink and cooked through. Remove from heat and set aside.
5. In a separate bowl, combine the cooked quinoa, diced cucumber, cherry tomatoes, chopped parsley, chopped mint, lemon juice, extra virgin olive oil, salt, and pepper. Mix well to combine all the ingredients.
6. Serve the grilled shrimp skewers alongside the quinoa tabouli.

SPINACH AND FETA STUFFED CHICKEN BREAST WITH STEAMED BROCCOLI

Nutrition: Cal 250;Fat 8 g;Carb 28 g;Protein 35 g
Serving 2; Cook time 30 min

Ingredients
- 2 boneless, skinless chicken breasts (about 4 oz each)
- 1 cup fresh spinach leaves
- 1/4 cup crumbled feta cheese
- 1 clove garlic, minced
- 1/2 teaspoon dried oregano
- Salt and pepper to taste
- 2 cups broccoli florets

Instructions:
1. Preheat the oven to 400°F (200°C).
2. Butterfly the chicken breasts by making a horizontal cut in the thickest part of each breast, being careful not to cut all the way through. Open the chicken breasts like a book.
3. In a bowl, combine the fresh spinach leaves, crumbled feta cheese, minced garlic, dried oregano, salt, and pepper.
4. Spread the spinach and feta mixture evenly on one side of each opened chicken breast. Close the chicken breasts and secure with toothpicks if needed.
5. Place the stuffed chicken breasts on a baking sheet lined with parchment paper. Season the outside of the chicken breasts with salt, pepper, and dried oregano.
6. Bake the stuffed chicken breasts in the preheated oven for about 20-25 minutes or until the chicken is cooked through and no longer pink in the center.
7. While the chicken is baking, steam the broccoli florets until they are tender-crisp, about 5-7 minutes.
8. Serve the spinach and feta stuffed chicken breasts with steamed broccoli.

GRILLED CHICKEN BREAST SALAD WITH MIXED GREENS AND BALSAMIC VINAIGRETTE

Nutrition: Cal 300;Fat 15 g;Carb 10 g;Protein 30 g
Serving 2; Cook time 20 min

Ingredients

FOR THE GRILLED CHICKEN BREAST:
- 2 boneless, skinless chicken breasts (about 4 oz each)
- 1 tablespoon olive oil
- 1 clove garlic, minced
- 1/2 teaspoon dried oregano
- Salt and pepper to taste

FOR THE SALAD:
- 4 cups mixed salad greens
- 1 cup cherry tomatoes, halved
- 1/2 cucumber, sliced
- 1/4 red onion, thinly sliced
- 2 tablespoons chopped fresh basil

FOR THE BALSAMIC VINAIGRETTE:
- 2 tablespoons balsamic vinegar
- 1 tablespoon extra virgin olive oil
- 1/2 teaspoon Dijon mustard
- 1/2 teaspoon honey (optional)
- Salt and pepper to taste

Instructions:
1. Preheat the grill or grill pan over medium-high heat.
2. In a bowl, combine the olive oil, minced garlic, dried oregano, salt, and pepper. Brush the mixture evenly over the chicken breasts.
3. Grill the chicken breasts for about 5-6 minutes on each side or until they are cooked through and reach an internal temperature of 165°F (74°C). Remove from heat and let them rest for a few minutes before slicing.
4. In a large salad bowl, combine the mixed salad greens, cherry tomatoes, sliced cucumber, red onion, and chopped fresh basil.
5. In a small bowl, whisk together the balsamic vinegar, extra virgin olive oil, Dijon mustard, honey (if using), salt, and pepper to make the vinaigrette.
6. Slice the grilled chicken breasts into thin strips.
7. Drizzle the balsamic vinaigrette over the salad and toss to coat the ingredients.
8. Divide the salad between two plates and top each plate with sliced grilled chicken breast.

GREEK YOGURT CHICKEN SALAD LETTUCE WRAPS

Nutrition: Cal 200;Fat 4 g;Carb 6 g;Protein 30 g
Serving 2; Cook time 20 min

Ingredients

- 2 boneless, skinless chicken breasts (about 4 oz each)
- 1/2 cup plain Greek yogurt
- 1/4 cup diced cucumber
- 1/4 cup diced red bell pepper
- 1/4 cup diced red onion
- 2 tablespoons chopped fresh dill
- 1 tablespoon lemon juice
- Salt and pepper to taste
- 4 large lettuce leaves (such as romaine or butter lettuce)

Instructions:
1. Preheat the grill or grill pan over medium-high heat.
2. Season the chicken breasts with salt and pepper. Grill the chicken breasts for about 5-6 minutes on each side or until they are cooked through and reach an internal temperature of 165°F (74°C). Remove from heat and let them cool.
3. In a bowl, combine the plain Greek yogurt, diced cucumber, diced red bell pepper, diced red onion, chopped fresh dill, lemon juice, salt, and pepper. Mix well to combine all the ingredients.
4. Once the grilled chicken breasts have cooled, dice them into small pieces.
5. Add the diced chicken to the Greek yogurt mixture and stir until the chicken is well coated.
6. Wash and dry the lettuce leaves. Place a spoonful of the Greek yogurt chicken salad mixture onto each lettuce leaf.
7. Carefully roll up the lettuce leaves, securing the filling inside like a wrap.
8. Serve the Greek yogurt chicken salad lettuce wraps immediately. Enjoy!

QUINOA-STUFFED BELL PEPPERS

Nutrition: Cal 150;Fat 2 g;Carb 30 g;Protein 5 g
Serving 2; Cook time 45 min

Ingredients

- 2 large bell peppers (any color)
- 1/2 cup cooked quinoa
- 1/4 cup diced zucchini
- 1/4 cup diced yellow squash
- 1/4 cup diced red onion
- 1/4 cup diced tomato
- 2 tablespoons grated Parmesan cheese

- 1 tablespoon chopped fresh parsley
- 1/2 teaspoon dried oregano
- Salt and pepper to taste

Instructions:

1. Preheat the oven to 375°F (190°C).
2. Cut off the tops of the bell peppers and remove the seeds and membranes. Rinse the bell peppers under cold water.
3. In a bowl, combine the cooked quinoa, diced zucchini, diced yellow squash, diced red onion, diced tomato, grated Parmesan cheese, chopped fresh parsley, dried oregano, salt, and pepper. Mix well to combine all the ingredients.
4. Stuff the bell peppers with the quinoa mixture, pressing it down gently.
5. Place the stuffed bell peppers in a baking dish. Cover the dish with aluminum foil.
6. Bake in the preheated oven for about 25-30 minutes or until the bell peppers are tender.
7. Remove the foil and continue baking for an additional 5-10 minutes to lightly brown the tops.
8. Serve the quinoa-stuffed bell peppers as a main dish. Enjoy!

ZUCCHINI NOODLES WITH MARINARA SAUCE AND LEAN GROUND TURKEY

Nutrition: Cal 250;Fat 8 g;Carb 20 g;Protein 25 g
Serving 2; Cook time 25 min

Ingredients

- 2 medium-sized zucchini
- 8 oz lean ground turkey
- 1 cup marinara sauce (low-sodium, no sugar added)
- 1 clove garlic, minced
- 1/4 teaspoon dried basil
- 1/4 teaspoon dried oregano
- Salt and pepper to taste
- Optional toppings: grated Parmesan cheese, chopped fresh basil

Instructions:

1. Use a spiralizer or julienne peeler to create zucchini noodles from the zucchini. Set aside.
2. In a non-stick skillet, cook the lean ground turkey over medium heat until it is browned and cooked through. Break it into small

crumbles while cooking. Drain any excess fat if necessary.

3. Add the minced garlic to the skillet with the ground turkey and sauté for about 1 minute until fragrant.
4. Pour the marinara sauce into the skillet with the turkey. Add the dried basil, dried oregano, salt, and pepper. Stir well to combine. Simmer for about 5 minutes to allow the flavors to meld.
5. In a separate large non-stick skillet, heat a small amount of olive oil or cooking spray over medium heat. Add the zucchini noodles and sauté for about 2-3 minutes until they are tender but still slightly crisp.
6. Divide the zucchini noodles between two plates or bowls. Top with the turkey marinara sauce.
7. If desired, garnish with grated Parmesan cheese and chopped fresh basil.
8. Serve the zucchini noodles with marinara sauce and lean ground turkey immediately. Enjoy!

TURKEY AND AVOCADO LETTUCE WRAPS

Nutrition: Cal 200;Fat 10 g;Carb 10 g;Protein 20 g
Serving 2; Cook time 20 min

Ingredients

- 8 oz lean ground turkey
- 1/2 teaspoon olive oil
- 1/4 cup diced red onion
- 1 clove garlic, minced
- 1/2 teaspoon ground cumin
- 1/2 teaspoon paprika
- Salt and pepper to taste
- 4 large lettuce leaves (such as romaine or butter lettuce)
- 1 ripe avocado, sliced
- 1/4 cup diced tomatoes
- 2 tablespoons chopped fresh cilantro
- Juice of 1/2 lime

Instructions:

1. Heat the olive oil in a non-stick skillet over medium heat.
2. Add the diced red onion and minced garlic to the skillet. Sauté for about 2 minutes until the onion becomes translucent.

3. Add the lean ground turkey to the skillet. Cook, breaking it into small crumbles, until it is browned and cooked through.

4. Stir in the ground cumin, paprika, salt, and pepper. Cook for another minute to allow the flavors to blend.

5. In a small bowl, combine the diced tomatoes, chopped fresh cilantro, and lime juice. Mix well.

6. Wash and dry the lettuce leaves. Lay them flat on a clean surface.

7. Divide the cooked ground turkey mixture evenly among the lettuce leaves, placing it in the center of each leaf.

8. Top each lettuce wrap with avocado slices and spoonfuls of the tomato-cilantro mixture.

9. Gently fold the sides of the lettuce leaves over the filling, rolling them up like a wrap.

BROCCOLI AND CHEESE SOUP WITH LOW-FAT CHEDDAR

Nutrition: Cal 150;Fat 5 g;Carb 19 g;Protein 90 g
Serving 2; Cook time 30 min

Ingredients
• 2 cups broccoli florets
• 1 small onion, chopped
• 1 clove garlic, minced
• 2 cups low-sodium vegetable or chicken broth
• 1 cup low-fat milk
• 1/2 cup shredded low-fat cheddar cheese
• 1 tablespoon olive oil
• Salt and pepper to taste

Instructions:
1. Heat the olive oil in a large pot over medium heat.

2. Add the chopped onion and minced garlic to the pot. Sauté for about 2-3 minutes until the onion becomes translucent.

3. Add the broccoli florets to the pot and stir well to coat them with the onion and garlic mixture.

4. Pour the vegetable or chicken broth into the pot. Bring the mixture to a boil, then reduce the heat to low and simmer for about 10-12 minutes until the broccoli is tender.

5. Use an immersion blender or transfer the mixture to a blender to puree the soup until smooth. If using a blender, be sure to allow the mixture to cool slightly before blending and blend in batches if needed.

6. Return the pureed soup to the pot over low heat. Stir in the low-fat milk and shredded low-fat cheddar cheese. Continue cooking and stirring until the cheese is melted and the soup is heated through. Season with salt and pepper to taste.

7. Serve the broccoli and cheese soup hot. Enjoy!

GRILLED SHRIMP AND VEGETABLE KEBABS

Nutrition: Cal 200;Fat 10 g;Carb 8 g;Protein 20 g
Serving 2; Cook time 20 min

Ingredients
• 12 large shrimp, peeled and deveined
• 1 medium zucchini, sliced into rounds
• 1 medium yellow bell pepper, cut into chunks
• 1 medium red onion, cut into chunks
• 8 cherry tomatoes
• 2 tablespoons olive oil
• 1 tablespoon lemon juice
• 1 clove garlic, minced
• 1/2 teaspoon dried oregano
• Salt and pepper to taste
• Skewers (if using wooden skewers, soak them in water for 30 minutes before grillin

Instructions:
1. Preheat the grill to medium-high heat.

2. In a bowl, combine the olive oil, lemon juice, minced garlic, dried oregano, salt, and pepper. Mix well to make the marinade.

3. Thread the shrimp, zucchini slices, bell pepper chunks, red onion chunks, and cherry tomatoes onto the skewers, alternating the ingredients.

4. Brush the marinade over the shrimp and vegetables, coating them evenly.

5. Place the kebabs on the preheated grill. Cook for about 2-3 minutes on each side, or until the shrimp is opaque and cooked through.

6. Remove the kebabs from the grill and let them rest for a few minutes.
7. Serve the grilled shrimp and vegetable kebabs hot. Enjoy!

CHICKEN LETTUCE WRAPS WITH WATER CHESTNUTS AND SESAME SEEDS

Nutrition: Cal 200;Fat 6 g;Carb 10 g;Protein 25 g
Serving 2; Cook time 20 min

Ingredients
- 8 oz boneless, skinless chicken breast, diced
- 1 tablespoon low-sodium soy sauce
- 1 tablespoon hoisin sauce
- 1 tablespoon rice vinegar
- 1 teaspoon sesame oil
- 1 clove garlic, minced
- 1/2 teaspoon grated fresh ginger
- 1/2 cup diced water chestnuts
- 2 green onions, chopped
- 1 tablespoon sesame seeds
- 4 large lettuce leaves (such as iceberg or butter lettuce)
- Optional toppings: chopped cilantro, lime wedges

Instructions:
1. In a small bowl, combine the low-sodium soy sauce, hoisin sauce, rice vinegar, sesame oil, minced garlic, and grated fresh ginger. Mix well to create the sauce.
2. Heat a non-stick skillet over medium-high heat. Add the diced chicken breast to the skillet and cook until it is no longer pink in the center.
3. Reduce the heat to medium and pour the sauce mixture over the cooked chicken. Stir to coat the chicken evenly and cook for an additional 2-3 minutes to allow the flavors to meld.
4. Add the diced water chestnuts, chopped green onions, and sesame seeds to the skillet. Stir well to incorporate the ingredients.
5. Wash and dry the lettuce leaves. Lay them flat on a clean surface.
6. Spoon the chicken mixture onto the lettuce leaves, dividing it evenly among them.
7. If desired, garnish the wraps with chopped cilantro and squeeze a lime wedge over each wrap.

8. Serve the chicken lettuce wraps immediately. Enjoy!

SPINACH AND FETA STUFFED CHICKEN BREAST

Nutrition: Cal 200;Fat 8 g;Carb 2 g;Protein 30 g
Serving 2; Cook time 35 min

Ingredients
- 2 boneless, skinless chicken breasts
- 1 cup fresh spinach leaves
- 1/4 cup crumbled feta cheese
- 1 clove garlic, minced
- 1/2 teaspoon dried oregano
- Salt and pepper to taste
- 1 tablespoon olive oil

Instructions:
1. Preheat the oven to 375°F (190°C).
2. Using a sharp knife, make a horizontal slit in each chicken breast to create a pocket. Be careful not to cut all the way through.
3. In a small bowl, mix together the spinach, feta cheese, minced garlic, dried oregano, salt, and pepper.
4. Stuff the spinach and feta mixture into the pockets of the chicken breasts, dividing it evenly between them.
5. Heat the olive oil in an oven-safe skillet over medium-high heat.
6. Place the stuffed chicken breasts in the skillet and cook for about 3-4 minutes on each side until they are browned.
7. Transfer the skillet to the preheated oven and bake for 20-25 minutes, or until the chicken is cooked through and reaches an internal temperature of 165°F (74°C).
8. Remove the skillet from the oven and let the chicken rest for a few minutes before serving.
9. Serve the spinach and feta stuffed chicken breasts hot. Enjoy!

TOMATO AND MOZZARELLA SALAD WITH FRESH BASIL

Nutrition: Cal 150;Fat 11 g;Carb 5 g;Protein 8 g
Serving 2; Cook time 10 min

Ingredients
- 2 medium tomatoes, sliced
- 4 oz fresh mozzarella cheese, sliced

- 1/4 cup fresh basil leaves
- 1 tablespoon extra-virgin olive oil
- 1 tablespoon balsamic vinegar
- Salt and pepper to taste

Instructions:

1. Arrange the tomato slices and mozzarella slices on a serving platter.
2. Tear the fresh basil leaves into smaller pieces and sprinkle them over the tomatoes and mozzarella.
3. In a small bowl, whisk together the extra-virgin olive oil and balsamic vinegar.
4. Drizzle the dressing over the tomato and mozzarella salad.
5. Season with salt and pepper to taste.
6. Serve the tomato and mozzarella salad immediately. Enjoy!

CAULIFLOWER FRIED RICE WITH DICED CHICKEN BREAST

Nutrition: Cal 250;Fat 10 g;Carb 15 g;Protein 25 g
Serving 2; Cook time 20 min

Ingredients
- 2 cups cauliflower rice
- 8 oz boneless, skinless chicken breast, diced
- 1/2 cup diced carrots
- 1/2 cup frozen peas
- 1/2 cup diced bell peppers
- 2 green onions, chopped
- 2 cloves garlic, minced
- 2 tablespoons low-sodium soy sauce
- 1 tablespoon sesame oil
- 1 tablespoon olive oil
- Salt and pepper to taste
- Optional toppings: chopped cilantro, sliced green onions

Instructions:

1. Heat the olive oil in a large skillet or wok over medium heat.
2. Add the diced chicken breast to the skillet and cook until it is no longer pink in the center. Remove the chicken from the skillet and set it aside.
3. In the same skillet, add the minced garlic and diced vegetables (carrots, peas, bell peppers). Stir-fry for about 3-4 minutes until the vegetables are tender.
4. Push the vegetables to one side of the skillet and add the cauliflower rice to the other side. Cook for about 2 minutes until the cauliflower rice is heated through.
5. Return the cooked chicken breast to the skillet and mix it with the vegetables and cauliflower rice.
6. In a small bowl, whisk together the low-sodium soy sauce and sesame oil. Pour the sauce over the skillet mixture and stir well to coat everything evenly. Cook for an additional 2 minutes to allow the flavors to combine.
7. Season with salt and pepper to taste. Stir in the chopped green onions.
8. Remove the skillet from the heat.
9. Serve the cauliflower fried rice with diced chicken breast hot. Top with optional toppings such as chopped cilantro or sliced green onions if desired. Enjoy!

BLACK BEAN AND CORN SALAD WITH LIME VINAIGRETTE

Nutrition: Cal 150;Fat 4 g;Carb 25 g;Protein 7 g
Serving 2; Cook time 10 min

Ingredients
- 1 can (15 oz) black beans, drained and rinsed
- 1 cup corn kernels (fresh or frozen)
- 1/2 cup diced bell peppers (any color)
- 1/4 cup diced red onion
- 1/4 cup chopped fresh cilantro
- 1 tablespoon lime juice
- 1 tablespoon extra-virgin olive oil
- 1 clove garlic, minced
- 1/2 teaspoon ground cumin
- Salt and pepper to taste

Instructions:

1. In a large bowl, combine the black beans, corn kernels, diced bell peppers, red onion, and chopped cilantro.
2. In a small bowl, whisk together the lime juice, extra-virgin olive oil, minced garlic, ground cumin, salt, and pepper to make the lime vinaigrette.
3. Pour the lime vinaigrette over the black bean and corn salad. Toss well to coat all the ingredients.
4. Adjust the seasoning with additional salt and pepper if needed.

5. Let the salad sit for about 10 minutes to allow the flavors to meld together.
6. Serve the black bean and corn salad cold or at room temperature. Enjoy!

TUNA AND WHITE BEAN SALAD

Nutrition: Cal 250;Fat 6 g;Carb 30 g;Protein 20 g
Serving 2; Cook time 10 min

Ingredients
- 1 can (5 oz) tuna in water, drained
- 1 can (15 oz) white beans, drained and rinsed
- 1/2 cup diced cucumber
- 1/4 cup diced red onion
- 1/4 cup chopped fresh parsley
- 2 tablespoons lemon juice
- 1 tablespoon extra-virgin olive oil
- 1 clove garlic, minced
- Salt and pepper to taste

Instructions:
1. In a large bowl, combine the drained tuna, white beans, diced cucumber, red onion, and chopped parsley.
2. In a small bowl, whisk together the lemon juice, extra-virgin olive oil, minced garlic, salt, and pepper to make the dressing.
3. Pour the dressing over the tuna and white bean salad. Toss well to coat all the ingredients.
4. Adjust the seasoning with additional salt and pepper if needed.
5. Let the salad sit for a few minutes to allow the flavors to meld together.
6. Serve the tuna and white bean salad cold or at room temperature. Enjoy!

GRILLED SALMON WITH ROASTED ASPARAGUS

Nutrition: Cal 300;Fat 18 g;Carb 6 g;Protein 30 g
Serving 2; Cook time 20 min

Ingredients
- 2 salmon fillets (4-6 oz each)
- 1 bunch asparagus, trimmed
- 1 tablespoon olive oil
- 1 clove garlic, minced
- 1/2 teaspoon lemon zest
- Salt and pepper to taste
- Lemon wedges, for serving

Instructions:
1. Preheat the grill to medium-high heat.

2. In a small bowl, mix together the olive oil, minced garlic, lemon zest, salt, and pepper.
3. Brush the salmon fillets and asparagus spears with the olive oil mixture, coating them evenly.
4. Place the salmon fillets on the grill, skin-side down, and the asparagus spears directly on the grill grates. Cook for about 4-6 minutes per side, or until the salmon is opaque and flakes easily with a fork, and the asparagus is tender and lightly charred.
5. Remove the salmon and asparagus from the grill.
6. Serve the grilled salmon with roasted asparagus hot, with lemon wedges on the side for squeezing over the salmon.

SHRIMP AND AVOCADO SALAD WITH CILANTRO LIME DRESSING

Nutrition: Cal 250;Fat 12 g;Carb 15 g;Protein 20 g
Serving 2; Cook time 15 min

Ingredients
FOR THE SALAD:
- 8 oz shrimp, peeled and deveined
- 2 cups mixed salad greens
- 1 ripe avocado, diced
- 1/4 cup cherry tomatoes, halved
- 1/4 cup diced cucumber
- 1/4 cup diced red onion

FOR THE CILANTRO LIME DRESSING:
- 1/4 cup fresh cilantro, chopped
- 2 tablespoons lime juice
- 1 tablespoon olive oil
- 1 clove garlic, minced
- Salt and pepper to taste

Instructions:
1. Heat a non-stick skillet over medium heat. Add the shrimp and cook for 2-3 minutes on each side until they are pink and cooked through. Set aside.
2. In a large bowl, combine the mixed salad greens, diced avocado, cherry tomatoes, diced cucumber, and diced red onion.
3. In a separate small bowl, whisk together the chopped cilantro, lime juice, olive oil, minced garlic, salt, and pepper to make the cilantro lime dressing.

4. Pour the dressing over the salad mixture and toss gently to coat all the ingredients.
5. Divide the salad onto two plates and top each with cooked shrimp.
6. Serve the shrimp and avocado salad with cilantro lime dressing immediately. Enjoy!

SPAGHETTI SQUASH WITH TURKEY MEATBALLS AND MARINARA SAUCE

Nutrition: Cal 300;Fat 10 g;Carb 30 g;Protein 25 g
Serving 2; Cook time 60 min

Ingredients
FOR THE SPAGHETTI SQUASH:
• 1 medium-sized spaghetti squash
• Salt and pepper to taste
FOR THE TURKEY MEATBALLS:
• 8 oz lean ground turkey
• 1/4 cup whole wheat breadcrumbs
• 1/4 cup grated Parmesan cheese
• 1/4 cup chopped fresh parsley
• 1 clove garlic, minced
• 1/4 teaspoon dried oregano
• 1/4 teaspoon dried basil
• 1/4 teaspoon salt
• 1/4 teaspoon black pepper
FOR THE MARINARA SAUCE:
• 1 cup low-sodium marinara sauce
Instructions:
1. Preheat the oven to 400°F (200°C).
2. Cut the spaghetti squash in half lengthwise. Scoop out the seeds and pulp. Season the inside of the squash halves with salt and pepper.
3. Place the squash halves, cut side down, on a baking sheet. Roast in the oven for about 40-45 minutes, or until the flesh is tender and easily scraped with a fork. Remove from the oven and set aside.
4. In a mixing bowl, combine the ground turkey, breadcrumbs, grated Parmesan cheese, chopped parsley, minced garlic, dried oregano, dried basil, salt, and black pepper. Mix well until all ingredients are evenly incorporated.
5. Shape the turkey mixture into small meatballs, about 1 inch in diameter.

6. In a non-stick skillet, heat a small amount of olive oil over medium heat. Add the turkey meatballs and cook for about 8-10 minutes, turning occasionally, until they are cooked through and browned on all sides. Remove from the skillet and set aside.
7. In the same skillet, heat the marinara sauce over medium heat until warmed through.
8. Use a fork to scrape the flesh of the roasted spaghetti squash into strands.
9. Divide the spaghetti squash strands onto two plates. Top with the turkey meatballs and marinara sauce.
10. Serve the spaghetti squash with turkey meatballs and marinara sauce hot. Enjoy!

CAPRESE SKEWERS WITH CHERRY TOMATOES, MOZZARELLA, AND FRESH BASIL

Nutrition: Cal 120;Fat 6 g;Carb 6 g;Protein 8 g
Serving 2; Cook time 10 min

Ingredients
• 12 cherry tomatoes
• 12 small mozzarella balls (bocconcini)
• Fresh basil leaves
• Balsamic glaze (optional)
• Salt and pepper to taste
Instructions:
1. Wash the cherry tomatoes and basil leaves.
2. Skewer one cherry tomato, one mozzarella ball, and one basil leaf onto each toothpick or skewer. Repeat until all ingredients are used.
3. Arrange the skewers on a serving platter.
4. Drizzle the caprese skewers with balsamic glaze, if desired.
5. Season with salt and pepper to taste.
6. Serve the caprese skewers with cherry tomatoes, mozzarella, and fresh basil as a light and refreshing appetizer or snack.

LENTIL AND VEGETABLE SOUP

Nutrition: Cal 250;Fat 5 g;Carb 40 g;Protein 15 g
Serving 2; Cook time 40 min

Ingredients
• 1 cup dry lentils, rinsed
• 1 tablespoon olive oil
• 1 small onion, diced

- 2 cloves garlic, minced
- 2 carrots, diced
- 2 celery stalks, diced
- 1 zucchini, diced
- 4 cups low-sodium vegetable broth
- 1 bay leaf
- 1 teaspoon dried thyme
- Salt and pepper to taste
- Fresh parsley, chopped (for garnish)

Instructions:
1. Heat the olive oil in a large pot over medium heat. Add the onion and garlic and sauté until fragrant and translucent.
2. Add the carrots, celery, and zucchini to the pot and sauté for a few more minutes until slightly softened.
3. Add the rinsed lentils, vegetable broth, bay leaf, dried thyme, salt, and pepper to the pot. Stir well to combine.
4. Bring the soup to a boil, then reduce the heat to low. Cover the pot and let it simmer for about 30 minutes, or until the lentils are tender.
5. Taste the soup and adjust the seasonings as needed.
6. Remove the bay leaf from the soup.
7. Serve the lentil and vegetable soup hot, garnished with fresh parsley.

GRILLED FLANK STEAK SALAD

Nutrition: Cal 300;Fat 15 g;Carb 10 g;Protein 25 g
Serving 2; Cook time 15 min

Ingredients
- 8 oz flank steak
- 4 cups mixed salad greens
- 1/2 cup cherry tomatoes, halved
- 1/4 cup sliced red onion
- 1/4 cup sliced cucumber
- 1/4 cup sliced bell peppers (any color)
- 1 tablespoon olive oil
- 1 tablespoon balsamic vinegar
- Salt and pepper to taste

Instructions:
1. Preheat a grill or grill pan over medium-high heat.
2. Season the flank steak with salt and pepper on both sides.
3. Grill the flank steak for about 4-5 minutes per side, or until desired doneness. Cooking time

may vary depending on the thickness of the steak. Remove from the grill and let it rest for a few minutes.
4. While the steak is resting, prepare the salad. In a large bowl, combine the mixed salad greens, cherry tomatoes, sliced red onion, sliced cucumber, and sliced bell peppers.
5. In a small bowl, whisk together the olive oil and balsamic vinegar to make the dressing. Season with salt and pepper to taste.
6. Thinly slice the grilled flank steak against the grain.
7. Add the sliced steak to the salad bowl and drizzle with the dressing.
8. Toss the salad gently to coat all the ingredients.
9. Divide the grilled flank steak salad onto two plates.
10. Serve the grilled flank steak salad immediately.

BAKED CHICKEN TENDERS WITH ALMOND CRUST

Nutrition: Cal 250;Fat 12 g;Carb 6 g;Protein 30 g
Serving 2; Cook time 25 min

Ingredients
- 8 oz boneless, skinless chicken breast tenders
- 1/2 cup almond flour
- 1/4 cup grated Parmesan cheese
- 1 teaspoon paprika
- 1/2 teaspoon garlic powder
- 1/2 teaspoon dried thyme
- 1/2 teaspoon salt
- 1/4 teaspoon black pepper
- 1 egg, beaten
- Cooking spray

Instructions:
1. Preheat the oven to 425°F (220°C). Line a baking sheet with parchment paper and set aside.
2. In a shallow bowl, combine the almond flour, grated Parmesan cheese, paprika, garlic powder, dried thyme, salt, and black pepper. Mix well to combine.
3. Dip each chicken tender into the beaten egg, allowing any excess to drip off.
4. Press the chicken tender into the almond flour mixture, coating it evenly on all sides. Place the coated chicken tender on the prepared

baking sheet. Repeat for the remaining chicken tenders.

5. Lightly spray the tops of the chicken tenders with cooking spray. This will help them brown and crisp up in the oven.

6. Bake the chicken tenders for 15-18 minutes, or until they are golden brown and cooked through. The internal temperature should reach 165°F (74°C).

7. Remove the chicken tenders from the oven and let them cool for a few minutes before serving.

8. Serve the baked chicken tenders with almond crust as a main dish alongside your choice of low-carb dipping sauce or with a side of mixed greens.

CUCUMBER AND CARROT SUSHI ROLLS WITH SMOKED SALMON

Nutrition: Cal 180;Fat 8 g;Carb 14 g;Protein 12 g
Serving 2; Cook time 30 min

Ingredients
- 2 large cucumbers
- 2 medium carrots
- 4 oz smoked salmon
- 2 tablespoons low-sodium soy sauce
- 1 tablespoon rice vinegar
- 1 teaspoon sesame oil
- 1/2 teaspoon grated ginger (optional)
- Nori sheets (seaweed sheets)
- Wasabi and pickled ginger (optional, for serving)

Instructions:
1. Peel the cucumbers and carrots. Cut them into thin, long strips or use a julienne peeler to create "noodles."

2. In a small bowl, whisk together the soy sauce, rice vinegar, sesame oil, and grated ginger (if using). This will be the dipping sauce for the sushi rolls.

3. Lay a nori sheet on a clean, flat surface.

4. Arrange a layer of cucumber and carrot strips on the bottom half of the nori sheet, leaving a small border at the bottom.

5. Place a layer of smoked salmon on top of the cucumber and carrot.

6. Moisten the top border of the nori sheet with water. This will help seal the sushi roll.

7. Starting from the bottom, tightly roll the nori sheet, enclosing the fillings. Use gentle pressure to keep the roll compact.

8. Repeat the process with the remaining ingredients to make another roll.

9. Use a sharp knife to slice each roll into bite-sized pieces.

10. Serve the cucumber and carrot sushi rolls with smoked salmon with the prepared dipping sauce, wasabi, and pickled ginger if desired.

TURKEY CHILI WITH KIDNEY BEANS AND BELL PEPPERS

Nutrition: Cal 220;Fat 5 g;Carb 25 g;Protein 20 g
Serving 2; Cook time 30 min

Ingredients
- 8 oz lean ground turkey
- 1/2 cup diced onion
- 1/2 cup diced bell peppers (any color)
- 1 garlic clove, minced
- 1 can (14 oz) diced tomatoes, no salt added
- 1 can (14 oz) kidney beans, drained and rinsed
- 1 cup low-sodium chicken broth
- 1 teaspoon chili powder
- 1/2 teaspoon cumin
- 1/2 teaspoon paprika
- Salt and pepper to taste
- Optional toppings: chopped fresh cilantro, low-fat Greek yogurt, grated low-fat cheddar cheese

Instructions:
1. Heat a large pot or Dutch oven over medium heat. Add the ground turkey and cook until browned and cooked through, breaking it up with a spoon. Drain any excess fat if necessary.

2. Add the diced onion, bell peppers, and minced garlic to the pot. Cook for 3-4 minutes, or until the vegetables are slightly softened.

3. Add the diced tomatoes (with their juices), kidney beans, chicken broth, chili powder, cumin, paprika, salt, and pepper to the pot. Stir well to combine.

4. Bring the mixture to a boil, then reduce the heat to low. Cover the pot and let the chili simmer for about 15-20 minutes, stirring occasionally.

5. Taste the chili and adjust the seasoning if needed.

6. Ladle the turkey chili into bowls and top with optional toppings such as chopped fresh cilantro, low-fat Greek yogurt, or grated low-fat cheddar cheese.
7. Serve the turkey chili hot and enjoy!

STUFFED PORTOBELLO MUSHROOMS WITH SPINACH AND FETA

Nutrition: Cal 150;Fat 10 g;Carb 8 g;Protein 9 g
Serving 2; Cook time 30 min

Ingredients
- 4 large Portobello mushrooms
- 2 cups fresh spinach, chopped
- 1/2 cup crumbled feta cheese
- 2 tablespoons olive oil
- 2 cloves garlic, minced
- Salt and pepper to taste

Instructions:
1. Preheat the oven to 375°F (190°C). Line a baking sheet with parchment paper and set aside.
2. Remove the stems from the Portobello mushrooms and gently scrape out the gills using a spoon. This will create space for the filling.
3. In a skillet, heat 1 tablespoon of olive oil over medium heat. Add the minced garlic and cook for 1 minute until fragrant.
4. Add the chopped spinach to the skillet and sauté until wilted, about 2-3 minutes. Season with salt and pepper to taste.
5. Remove the skillet from heat and let the spinach cool slightly. Once cooled, stir in the crumbled feta cheese.
6. Brush the remaining tablespoon of olive oil over the tops and bottoms of the Portobello mushrooms. Season with salt and pepper.
7. Spoon the spinach and feta mixture into the cavity of each mushroom, distributing it evenly among the four.
8. Place the stuffed Portobello mushrooms on the prepared baking sheet and bake for approximately 20 minutes, or until the mushrooms are tender and the filling is heated through.
9. Remove the mushrooms from the oven and let them cool for a few minutes before serving.
10. Serve the stuffed Portobello mushrooms as a main dish, accompanied by a side salad or steamed vegetables, if desired.

TOFU AND VEGETABLE STIR-FRY

Nutrition: Cal 200;Fat 10 g;Carb 15 g;Protein 14 g
Serving 2; Cook time 25 min

Ingredients
- 8 oz extra-firm tofu, drained and cubed
- 1 cup broccoli florets
- 1 small carrot, julienned
- 1/2 red bell pepper, sliced
- 1/2 yellow bell pepper, sliced
- 1/2 zucchini, sliced
- 1/2 cup snap peas
- 2 cloves garlic, minced
- 2 tablespoons low-sodium soy sauce
- 1 tablespoon sesame oil
- 1 tablespoon cornstarch
- 1/4 cup vegetable broth or water
- Salt and pepper to taste
- Optional garnish: sliced green onions, sesame seeds

Instructions:
1. In a small bowl, whisk together the soy sauce, sesame oil, cornstarch, and vegetable broth (or water). Set aside.
2. Heat a non-stick skillet or wok over medium heat. Add the tofu cubes and cook until lightly browned on all sides. Remove the tofu from the skillet and set aside.
3. In the same skillet, add the minced garlic and stir-fry for about 30 seconds, until fragrant.
4. Add the broccoli florets, julienned carrot, bell peppers, zucchini, and snap peas to the skillet. Stir-fry for 4-5 minutes, or until the vegetables are tender-crisp.
5. Return the tofu to the skillet and pour the prepared sauce over the tofu and vegetables. Stir well to coat everything evenly.
6. Continue cooking for another 2-3 minutes, or until the sauce has thickened.
7. Season with salt and pepper to taste.
8. Remove from heat and garnish with sliced green onions and sesame seeds if desired.

9. Serve the tofu and vegetable stir-fry hot over steamed brown rice or cauliflower rice, if desired.

GREEK SALAD WITH GRILLED SHRIMP

Nutrition: Cal 250;Fat 12 g;Carb 15 g;Protein 20 g
Serving 2; Cook time 15 min

Ingredients
- 8 oz shrimp, peeled and deveined
- 4 cups mixed salad greens
- 1 cup cherry tomatoes, halved
- 1/2 cucumber, sliced
- 1/4 red onion, thinly sliced
- 1/4 cup Kalamata olives, pitted
- 1/4 cup crumbled feta cheese
- 2 tablespoons extra virgin olive oil
- 1 tablespoon lemon juice
- 1 teaspoon dried oregano
- Salt and pepper to taste

Instructions:
1. Preheat the grill or grill pan over medium heat.
2. In a bowl, toss the shrimp with 1 tablespoon of olive oil, lemon juice, dried oregano, salt, and pepper.
3. Grill the shrimp for 2-3 minutes per side, or until they are pink and cooked through. Remove from the grill and set aside.
4. In a large salad bowl, combine the mixed salad greens, cherry tomatoes, cucumber slices, red onion slices, Kalamata olives, and crumbled feta cheese.
5. In a small bowl, whisk together the remaining tablespoon of olive oil, lemon juice, dried oregano, salt, and pepper. This will be the dressing for the salad.
6. Pour the dressing over the salad and toss to combine.
7. Divide the salad into two plates and top each with grilled shrimp.
8. Serve immediately and enjoy.

CHICKEN AND VEGETABLE KABOBS

Nutrition: Cal 220;Fat 8 g;Carb 13 g;Protein 25 g
Serving 2; Cook time 20 min

Ingredients

- 8 oz boneless, skinless chicken breast, cut into 1-inch cubes
- 1 red bell pepper, cut into 1-inch pieces
- 1 green bell pepper, cut into 1-inch pieces
- 1 small red onion, cut into 1-inch pieces
- 8 cherry tomatoes
- 2 tablespoons olive oil
- 1 tablespoon lemon juice
- 2 cloves garlic, minced
- 1 teaspoon dried oregano
- Salt and pepper to taste

Instructions:
1. In a bowl, whisk together the olive oil, lemon juice, minced garlic, dried oregano, salt, and pepper to create the marinade.
2. Add the chicken cubes to the marinade and toss to coat. Let it marinate in the refrigerator for at least 30 minutes, or up to 4 hours for more flavor.
3. Preheat the grill or grill pan over medium heat.
4. Thread the marinated chicken cubes, bell pepper pieces, onion pieces, and cherry tomatoes onto skewers, alternating the ingredients.
5. Place the skewers on the grill and cook for about 10 minutes, turning occasionally, until the chicken is cooked through and the vegetables are tender.
6. Remove the skewers from the grill and let them rest for a few minutes before serving.
7. Serve the chicken and vegetable kabobs as a main dish or with a side of salad, rice, or quinoa.

QUINOA AND BLACK BEAN STUFFED TOMATOES

Nutrition: Cal 180;Fat 4 g;Carb 30 g;Protein 7 g
Serving 2; Cook time 30 min

Ingredients
- 2 large tomatoes
- 1/2 cup cooked quinoa
- 1/2 cup canned black beans, rinsed and drained
- 1/4 cup diced red bell pepper
- 1/4 cup diced green bell pepper
- 1/4 cup diced red onion
- 1/4 cup chopped fresh cilantro
- 2 tablespoons lime juice
- 1 tablespoon olive oil

- 1/2 teaspoon ground cumin
- Salt and pepper to taste

Instructions:

1. Preheat the oven to 375°F (190°C).
2. Cut off the tops of the tomatoes and scoop out the seeds and pulp, creating a hollow space inside each tomato. Set aside.
3. In a bowl, combine the cooked quinoa, black beans, diced red bell pepper, diced green bell pepper, diced red onion, chopped cilantro, lime juice, olive oil, ground cumin, salt, and pepper. Mix well to combine.
4. Stuff each tomato with the quinoa and black bean mixture, pressing it down gently.
5. Place the stuffed tomatoes on a baking sheet and bake in the preheated oven for 20 minutes, or until the tomatoes are tender and the filling is heated through.
6. Remove from the oven and let them cool for a few minutes before serving.
7. Serve the quinoa and black bean stuffed tomatoes as a main dish or with a side salad for a complete meal.

ROASTED VEGETABLE AND HUMMUS WRAP

Nutrition: Cal 250;Fat 8 g;Carb 37 g;Protein 9 g
Serving 2; Cook time 30 min

Ingredients

- 2 whole wheat or low-carb tortilla wraps
- 1 cup mixed roasted vegetables (such as bell peppers, zucchini, eggplant, and onion)
- 4 tablespoons hummus
- 1/4 cup crumbled feta cheese
- 1/4 cup chopped fresh parsley

Instructions:

1. Preheat the oven to 400°F (200°C). Line a baking sheet with parchment paper.
2. Toss the mixed vegetables with a drizzle of olive oil and season with salt and pepper. Spread them out on the prepared baking sheet and roast in the preheated oven for about 20 minutes, or until the vegetables are tender and slightly charred.
3. Warm the tortilla wraps in a dry skillet over medium heat for about 30 seconds on each side to make them more pliable.

4. Spread 2 tablespoons of hummus on each tortilla, leaving a border around the edges.
5. Place half of the roasted vegetables on each tortilla, spreading them evenly.
6. Sprinkle half of the crumbled feta cheese and chopped parsley over the vegetables.
7. Roll up the tortilla tightly, tucking in the sides as you go.
8. Cut each wrap in half diagonally and serve immediately.
9. Optional: You can lightly grill or toast the wraps in a panini press for a warm and crispy texture.

SPICY THAI CHICKEN LETTUCE WRAPS

Nutrition: Cal 240;Fat 8 g;Carb 14 g;Protein 26 g
Serving 2; Cook time 25 min

Ingredients

- 2 boneless, skinless chicken breasts (approximately 8 oz total)
- 1 tablespoon low-sodium soy sauce
- 1 tablespoon fish sauce
- 1 tablespoon lime juice
- 1 tablespoon Sriracha sauce (adjust according to spice preference)
- 1 tablespoon olive oil
- 1 teaspoon grated ginger
- 2 cloves garlic, minced
- 1/2 cup diced red bell pepper
- 1/2 cup diced water chestnuts
- 1/4 cup chopped fresh cilantro
- 8 large lettuce leaves (such as butter lettuce or romaine)
- Optional toppings: chopped peanuts, lime wedges, extra cilantro

Instructions:

1. In a small bowl, whisk together the soy sauce, fish sauce, lime juice, Sriracha sauce, and set aside.
2. Heat the olive oil in a large skillet over medium heat. Add the grated ginger and minced garlic, and sauté for about 1 minute until fragrant.
3. Add the diced red bell pepper and water chestnuts to the skillet and cook for another 2-3 minutes until the vegetables start to soften.
4. Push the vegetables to one side of the skillet and add the chicken breasts. Cook for about 5-6

minutes per side until cooked through. Remove from the skillet and let the chicken rest for a few minutes.

5. Slice the cooked chicken into thin strips and return them to the skillet with the cooked vegetables.

6. Pour the prepared sauce over the chicken and vegetables in the skillet. Stir well to coat everything evenly and cook for an additional 1-2 minutes until heated through.

7. Remove from heat and stir in the chopped cilantro.

8. To serve, spoon the chicken mixture onto the lettuce leaves and roll them up like a burrito.

9. Optional: Garnish with chopped peanuts, extra cilantro, and serve with lime wedges for squeezing over the wraps.

GREEK TURKEY BURGER

Nutrition: Cal 160;Fat 7 g;Carb 4 g;Protein 19 g
Serving 2; Cook time 20 min

Ingredients
- 8 oz lean ground turkey
- 1/4 cup crumbled feta cheese
- 1/4 cup diced red onion
- 2 tablespoons chopped fresh parsley
- 1 clove garlic, minced
- 1/2 teaspoon dried oregano
- 1/4 teaspoon salt
- 1/4 teaspoon black pepper
- 2 whole wheat or low-carb burger buns
- Toppings: sliced cucumber, sliced tomato, lettuce

FOR THE GREEK YOGURT SAUCE:
- 1/4 cup plain Greek yogurt
- 1 tablespoon lemon juice
- 1 tablespoon chopped fresh dill
- 1/4 teaspoon garlic powder
- Salt and pepper to taste

Instructions:
1. Preheat a grill or skillet over medium heat.

2. In a mixing bowl, combine the ground turkey, crumbled feta cheese, diced red onion, chopped parsley, minced garlic, dried oregano, salt, and black pepper. Mix well until all ingredients are evenly incorporated.

3. Divide the mixture into two equal portions and shape them into burger patties.

4. Place the turkey patties on the preheated grill or skillet. Cook for about 5-6 minutes on each side, or until the internal temperature reaches 165°F (74°C) and the burgers are cooked through.

5. While the burgers are cooking, prepare the Greek yogurt sauce by combining the Greek yogurt, lemon juice, chopped dill, garlic powder, salt, and pepper in a small bowl. Stir well to combine.

6. Toast the burger buns, if desired.

7. Once the burgers are cooked, remove them from the heat and let them rest for a few minutes.

8. Assemble the burgers by spreading the Greek yogurt sauce on the bottom half of each bun. Place a turkey burger patty on top, followed by sliced cucumber, sliced tomato, and lettuce. Top with the other half of the bun.

9. Serve the Greek turkey burgers immediately.

ROASTED VEGETABLE AND QUINOA SALAD

Nutrition: Cal 250;Fat 11 g;Carb 34 g;Protein 6 g
Serving 2; Cook time 30 min

Ingredients
- 1 cup cooked quinoa
- 1 small zucchini, diced
- 1 small yellow squash, diced
- 1 red bell pepper, diced
- 1 yellow bell pepper, diced
- 1 small red onion, thinly sliced
- 2 tablespoons olive oil
- 1 teaspoon dried Italian seasoning
- Salt and pepper to taste
- 2 cups mixed salad greens
- 2 tablespoons crumbled feta cheese (optional)
- Balsamic vinaigrette dressing (to taste)

Instructions:
1. Preheat the oven to 400°F (200°C).

2. In a large baking sheet, spread out the diced zucchini, yellow squash, red bell pepper, yellow bell pepper, and red onion.

3. Drizzle the olive oil over the vegetables and sprinkle with the dried Italian seasoning, salt, and pepper. Toss well to coat the vegetables evenly.

4. Roast the vegetables in the preheated oven for about 20-25 minutes, or until they are tender

and slightly caramelized, stirring halfway through.

5. While the vegetables are roasting, prepare the quinoa according to the package instructions. Once cooked, let it cool slightly.

6. In a large mixing bowl, combine the cooked quinoa and roasted vegetables. Toss gently to combine.

7. To serve, divide the mixed salad greens between two plates. Top with the roasted vegetable and quinoa mixture.

8. Optional: Sprinkle crumbled feta cheese over the salad for added flavor.

9. Drizzle balsamic vinaigrette dressing over the salad according to taste.

10. Serve the roasted vegetable and quinoa salad immediately.

BAKED COD WITH ROASTED ASPARAGUS

Nutrition: Cal 250;Fat 11 g;Carb 34 g;Protein 6 g
Serving 2; Cook time 30 min

Ingredients
- 1 cup cooked quinoa
- 1 small zucchini, diced
- 1 small yellow squash, diced
- 1 red bell pepper, diced
- 1 yellow bell pepper, diced
- 1 small red onion, thinly sliced
- 2 tablespoons olive oil
- 1 teaspoon dried Italian seasoning
- Salt and pepper to taste
- 2 cups mixed salad greens
- 2 tablespoons crumbled feta cheese (optional)
- Balsamic vinaigrette dressing (to taste)

Instructions:
1. Preheat the oven to 400°F (200°C).

2. In a large baking sheet, spread out the diced zucchini, yellow squash, red bell pepper, yellow bell pepper, and red onion.

3. Drizzle the olive oil over the vegetables and sprinkle with the dried Italian seasoning, salt, and pepper. Toss well to coat the vegetables evenly.

4. Roast the vegetables in the preheated oven for about 20-25 minutes, or until they are tender and slightly caramelized, stirring halfway through.

5. While the vegetables are roasting, prepare the quinoa according to the package instructions. Once cooked, let it cool slightly.

6. In a large mixing bowl, combine the cooked quinoa and roasted vegetables. Toss gently to combine.

7. To serve, divide the mixed salad greens between two plates. Top with the roasted vegetable and quinoa mixture.

8. Optional: Sprinkle crumbled feta cheese over the salad for added flavor.

9. Drizzle balsamic vinaigrette dressing over the salad according to taste.

10. Serve the roasted vegetable and quinoa salad immediately.

CHICKEN AND VEGETABLE STIR-FRY

Nutrition: Cal 250;Fat 9 g;Carb 16 g;Protein 25 g
Serving 2; Cook time 20 min

Ingredients
- 2 boneless, skinless chicken breasts, thinly sliced
- 1 tablespoon vegetable oil
- 2 cloves garlic, minced
- 1 teaspoon grated ginger
- 1 cup broccoli florets
- 1 medium bell pepper, thinly sliced
- 1 medium carrot, thinly sliced
- 1 cup snap peas
- 2 tablespoons low-sodium soy sauce
- 1 tablespoon oyster sauce (optional)
- Salt and pepper to taste
- Sesame seeds (for garnish)

Instructions:
1. Heat the vegetable oil in a large skillet or wok over medium-high heat.

2. Add the minced garlic and grated ginger to the skillet and cook for about 1 minute until fragrant.

3. Add the sliced chicken to the skillet and cook until it is no longer pink and cooked through, about 5-7 minutes. Remove the chicken from the skillet and set aside.

4. In the same skillet, add the broccoli florets, bell pepper, carrot, and snap peas. Stir-fry the vegetables for about 4-5 minutes until they are crisp-tender.

5. Return the cooked chicken to the skillet with the vegetables.
6. In a small bowl, whisk together the low-sodium soy sauce and oyster sauce. Pour the sauce over the chicken and vegetables. Stir well to coat everything evenly. Cook for an additional 1-2 minutes.
7. Season with salt and pepper to taste.
8. Serve the chicken and vegetable stir-fry hot, garnished with sesame seeds.

TURKEY AND BLACK BEAN LETTUCE WRAPS WITH AVOCADO AND SALSA

Nutrition: Cal 250;Fat 8 g;Carb 26 g;Protein 20 g
Serving 2; Cook time 20 min

Ingredients
- 1 tablespoon olive oil
- 1 small onion, diced
- 2 cloves garlic, minced
- 1/2 pound lean ground turkey
- 1 teaspoon chili powder
- 1/2 teaspoon cumin
- 1/2 teaspoon paprika
- 1/4 teaspoon salt
- 1/4 teaspoon black pepper
- 1 can (15 ounces) black beans, rinsed and drained
- 1/4 cup salsa
- 8 large lettuce leaves (such as romaine or butter lettuce)
- Optional toppings: diced tomatoes, diced avocado, chopped cilantro

Instructions:
1. Heat olive oil in a large skillet over medium heat. Add the diced onion and minced garlic, and sauté until they are softened and fragrant, about 3-4 minutes.
2. Add the ground turkey to the skillet and cook until it is browned and cooked through, breaking it up into small crumbles with a spatula or spoon.
3. Stir in the chili powder, cumin, paprika, salt, and black pepper. Cook for an additional 1-2 minutes to allow the spices to blend.
4. Add the black beans and salsa to the skillet, and stir well to combine. Cook for another 2-3 minutes until the mixture is heated through.

5. Remove the skillet from the heat and allow the mixture to cool slightly.
6. Assemble the lettuce wraps by placing a spoonful of the turkey and black bean mixture onto each lettuce leaf. Top with diced tomatoes, diced avocado, and chopped cilantro if desired.
7. Serve the turkey and black bean lettuce wraps immediately.

SPINACH AND MUSHROOM FRITTATA WITH A SIDE OF MIXED GREENS

Nutrition: Cal 200;Fat 12 g;Carb 8 g;Protein 14 g
Serving 2; Cook time 20 min

Ingredients
- 4 large eggs
- 1/4 cup milk (low-fat or skim)
- 1/4 teaspoon salt
- 1/4 teaspoon black pepper
- 1 tablespoon olive oil
- 1 small onion, diced
- 2 cups fresh spinach leaves, chopped
- 1 cup sliced mushrooms
- 1/4 cup shredded reduced-fat cheese (such as cheddar or mozzarella)
- Fresh parsley for garnish (optional)

Instructions:
1. Preheat the oven to 350°F (175°C).
2. In a mixing bowl, whisk together the eggs, milk, salt, and black pepper until well combined.
3. Heat the olive oil in an oven-safe skillet over medium heat. Add the diced onion and sauté until it becomes translucent, about 2-3 minutes.
4. Add the chopped spinach and sliced mushrooms to the skillet. Cook until the spinach wilts and the mushrooms are tender, about 3-4 minutes.
5. Pour the egg mixture over the vegetables in the skillet. Stir gently to distribute the vegetables evenly.
6. Sprinkle the shredded cheese over the top of the frittata.
7. Transfer the skillet to the preheated oven and bake for 10-12 minutes, or until the eggs are set and the cheese is melted and lightly browned.

8. Remove the frittata from the oven and let it cool for a few minutes. Cut it into wedges and garnish with fresh parsley, if desired.

GRILLED SHRIMP AND AVOCADO SALAD

Nutrition: Cal 300;Fat 82 g;Carb 12 g;Protein 25 g
Serving 2; Cook time 15 min

Ingredients
- 8 oz (225g) shrimp, peeled and deveined
- 1 tablespoon olive oil
- 1/2 teaspoon smoked paprika
- 1/4 teaspoon garlic powder
- Salt and pepper to taste
- 4 cups mixed salad greens
- 1 ripe avocado, sliced
- 1/2 cup cherry tomatoes, halved
- 1/4 cup red onion, thinly sliced
- 2 tablespoons chopped fresh cilantro

Instructions:
1. Preheat the grill or grill pan over medium-high heat.
2. In a bowl, toss the shrimp with olive oil, smoked paprika, garlic powder, salt, and pepper until evenly coated.
3. Grill the shrimp for 2-3 minutes per side until they turn pink and opaque. Remove from the heat and set aside.
4. In a large salad bowl, combine the mixed salad greens, avocado slices, cherry tomatoes, red onion, and chopped cilantro.
5. In a small bowl, whisk together the lemon juice, olive oil, Dijon mustard, salt, and pepper to make the dressing.
6. Pour the dressing over the salad ingredients and toss gently to combine.
7. Divide the salad mixture onto two plates. Top each plate with the grilled shrimp.
8. Serve the grilled shrimp and avocado salad immediately as a light and refreshing meal.

STUFFED CHICKEN BREAST WITH SPINACH AND RICOTTA CHEESE

Nutrition: Cal 220;Fat 6 g;Carb 4 g;Protein 35 g
Serving 2; Cook time 35 min

Ingredients
- 2 boneless, skinless chicken breasts
- 1 cup fresh spinach, chopped
- 1/2 cup low-fat ricotta cheese
- 1/4 cup grated Parmesan cheese
- 1 garlic clove, minced
- 1/2 teaspoon dried basil
- Salt and pepper to taste
- Cooking spray

Instructions:
1. Preheat the oven to 375°F (190°C).
2. Using a sharp knife, make a slit horizontally along the thickest part of each chicken breast, creating a pocket for stuffing. Be careful not to cut all the way through.
3. In a bowl, combine the chopped spinach, ricotta cheese, Parmesan cheese, minced garlic, dried basil, salt, and pepper. Mix well to create the stuffing mixture.
4. Stuff each chicken breast with an equal amount of the spinach and ricotta stuffing mixture. Use toothpicks to secure the openings if necessary.
5. Lightly coat a baking dish with cooking spray. Place the stuffed chicken breasts in the dish.
6. Bake the chicken in the preheated oven for about 25-30 minutes or until the chicken is cooked through and reaches an internal temperature of 165°F (74°C).
7. Once cooked, remove the chicken from the oven and let it rest for a few minutes before serving.
8. Serve the stuffed chicken breast with a side of steamed vegetables or a green salad for a complete and balanced meal.

ROASTED BUTTERNUT SQUASH AND QUINOA SALAD

Nutrition: Cal 280;Fat 8 g;Carb 49 g;Protein 7 g
Serving 2; Cook time 40 min

Ingredients
- 1 small butternut squash, peeled, seeded, and cut into cubes
- 1 cup cooked quinoa
- 2 cups mixed salad greens
- 1/4 cup dried cranberries
- 1/4 cup pumpkin seeds
- 2 tablespoons crumbled feta cheese
- 2 tablespoons balsamic vinegar
- 1 tablespoon olive oil
- Salt and pepper to taste

Instructions:

1. Preheat the oven to 400°F (200°C).
2. Place the butternut squash cubes on a baking sheet. Drizzle with olive oil and sprinkle with salt and pepper. Toss to coat the squash evenly.
3. Roast the butternut squash in the preheated oven for about 25-30 minutes, or until it is tender and lightly browned. Stir occasionally during cooking to ensure even roasting.
4. In a large bowl, combine the cooked quinoa, mixed salad greens, dried cranberries, pumpkin seeds, and crumbled feta cheese.
5. In a small bowl, whisk together the balsamic vinegar, olive oil, salt, and pepper to make the dressing.
6. Add the roasted butternut squash to the salad bowl and drizzle the dressing over the salad. Toss well to combine all the ingredients.
7. Divide the salad into two portions and serve immediately.

LEMON GARLIC GRILLED CHICKEN SKEWERS WITH ROASTED BRUSSELS SPROUTS

Nutrition: Cal 250;Fat 10 g;Carb 21 g;Protein 30 g
Serving 2; Cook time 30 min

Ingredients
FOR THE LEMON GARLIC GRILLED CHICKEN SKEWERS:
- 2 boneless, skinless chicken breasts, cut into cubes
- Juice of 1 lemon
- 2 cloves of garlic, minced
- 1 tablespoon olive oil
- Salt and pepper to taste

FOR THE ROASTED BRUSSELS SPROUTS:
- 2 cups Brussels sprouts, trimmed and halved
- 1 tablespoon olive oil
- Salt and pepper to taste

Instructions:
1. Preheat the grill to medium-high heat.

2. In a bowl, combine the lemon juice, minced garlic, olive oil, salt, and pepper. Add the chicken cubes and toss to coat them evenly with the marinade. Let it marinate for about 15 minutes.
3. While the chicken is marinating, preheat the oven to 400°F (200°C) for the Brussels sprouts.
4. Thread the marinated chicken cubes onto skewers. If using wooden skewers, soak them in water for about 10 minutes before threading the chicken to prevent them from burning on the grill.
5. Place the chicken skewers on the preheated grill and cook for about 8-10 minutes, turning them occasionally, until the chicken is cooked through and slightly charred.
6. While the chicken is grilling, prepare the roasted Brussels sprouts. Toss the Brussels sprouts with olive oil, salt, and pepper in a baking dish.
7. Roast the Brussels sprouts in the preheated oven for about 15-20 minutes, or until they are tender and browned, stirring once or twice during cooking.
8. Once the chicken skewers and Brussels sprouts are cooked, remove them from the heat.
9. Serve the lemon garlic grilled chicken skewers alongside the roasted Brussels sprouts. You can garnish with fresh herbs like parsley or basil if desired.

MEDITERRANEAN TUNA SALAD WITH OLIVES, TOMATOES, AND FETA CHEESE

Nutrition: Cal 250;Fat 12 g;Carb 6 g;Protein 30 g
Serving 2; Cook time 10 min

Ingredients
- 2 cans of tuna, drained
- 1 cup cherry tomatoes, halved
- 1/4 cup Kalamata olives, pitted and sliced
- 1/4 cup crumbled feta cheese
- 2 tablespoons extra virgin olive oil
- Juice of 1 lemon
- 2 tablespoons chopped fresh parsley
- Salt and pepper to taste
- Lettuce leaves for serving

Instructions:

1. In a mixing bowl, combine the drained tuna, cherry tomatoes, Kalamata olives, and crumbled feta cheese.
2. In a small bowl, whisk together the extra virgin olive oil, lemon juice, chopped parsley, salt, and pepper.
3. Pour the dressing over the tuna mixture and gently toss to combine, ensuring all ingredients are coated with the dressing.
4. Taste and adjust the seasoning if needed.
5. Serve the Mediterranean tuna salad on a bed of lettuce leaves or in lettuce wraps for a low-carb option.

CAULIFLOWER CRUST MINI PIZZAS WITH TURKEY SAUSAGE AND VEGGIES

Nutrition: Cal 300;Fat 15 g;Carb 19 g;Protein 23 g
Serving 2; Cook time 45 min

Ingredients
- 1 medium head of cauliflower
- 1/2 cup shredded mozzarella cheese
- 1/4 cup grated Parmesan cheese
- 1 large egg
- 1/2 teaspoon dried oregano
- 1/2 teaspoon dried basil
- 1/4 teaspoon garlic powder
- 1/4 teaspoon salt
- 1/4 teaspoon black pepper
- 1/2 cup marinara sauce
- 4 ounces cooked turkey sausage, crumbled
- Assorted diced vegetables (e.g., bell peppers, mushrooms, onions)
- 1/2 cup shredded mozzarella cheese (additional)
- Fresh basil leaves (optional garnish)

Instructions:

1. Preheat the oven to 425°F (220°C). Line a baking sheet with parchment paper.
2. Cut the cauliflower into florets and transfer them to a food processor. Pulse until the cauliflower resembles rice-like grains.
3. Place the cauliflower rice in a microwave-safe bowl and microwave on high for 5 minutes. Let it cool for a few minutes.
4. Transfer the cooked cauliflower rice to a clean kitchen towel or cheesecloth. Squeeze out as much moisture as possible.
5. In a mixing bowl, combine the cauliflower rice, shredded mozzarella cheese, grated Parmesan cheese, egg, dried oregano, dried basil, garlic powder, salt, and black pepper. Mix well to form a dough-like consistency.
6. Divide the dough into two equal portions. Place each portion on the prepared baking sheet and shape into mini pizza crusts, about 1/4 inch thick.
7. Bake the cauliflower crusts in the preheated oven for 20 minutes or until golden brown and firm.
8. Remove the crusts from the oven and let them cool slightly. Leave the oven on.
9. Spread marinara sauce evenly over each cauliflower crust. Top with crumbled turkey sausage, diced vegetables, and additional shredded mozzarella cheese.
10. Place the topped pizzas back in the oven and bake for an additional 10-12 minutes or until the cheese is melted and bubbly.
11. Garnish with fresh basil leaves, if desired.
12. Allow the mini pizzas to cool slightly before serving.

SHRIMP AND VEGETABLE SPRING ROLLS

Nutrition: Cal 250;Fat 15 g;Carb 35 g;Protein 20 g
Serving 2; Cook time 30 min

Ingredients
- 8 rice paper wrappers
- 16 cooked shrimp, peeled and deveined
- 1 cup shredded lettuce
- 1 cup julienned carrots
- 1 cup julienned cucumbers
- 1/2 cup fresh cilantro leaves
- 1/2 cup fresh mint leaves
- 1/4 cup chopped peanuts (optional)
- Water for soaking the rice paper wrappers

FOR THE DIPPING SAUCE:
- 2 tablespoons low-sodium soy sauce
- 1 tablespoon lime juice
- 1 tablespoon rice vinegar
- 1 teaspoon honey
- 1/2 teaspoon grated ginger
- 1/2 teaspoon minced garlic

Instructions:

1. Prepare all the ingredients by washing and cutting them into thin strips.
2. Fill a shallow dish with warm water. Dip one rice paper wrapper into the water for a few seconds until it softens.
3. Place the softened rice paper wrapper on a clean surface. Arrange 2 shrimp in the center of the wrapper.
4. Add a small handful of shredded lettuce, julienned carrots, cucumbers, cilantro leaves, and mint leaves on top of the shrimp.
5. Fold the bottom edge of the wrapper over the filling, then fold the sides inward. Roll tightly to enclose the filling, similar to a burrito. Repeat with the remaining wrappers and filling.
6. In a small bowl, whisk together the soy sauce, lime juice, rice vinegar, honey, grated ginger, and minced garlic to make the dipping sauce.
7. Serve the shrimp and vegetable spring rolls with the dipping sauce on the side. You can also sprinkle chopped peanuts on top for added crunch and flavor.

ZUCCHINI AND CARROT FRITTERS WITH GREEK YOGURT SAUCE

Nutrition: Cal 210;Fat 12 g;Carb 16 g;Protein 11 g
Serving 2; Cook time 30 min

Ingredients
FOR THE FRITTERS:
- 2 medium zucchinis, grated
- 2 medium carrots, grated
- 1/4 cup almond flour
- 1/4 cup grated Parmesan cheese
- 2 green onions, finely chopped
- 2 cloves garlic, minced
- 2 eggs, beaten
- 1/2 teaspoon salt
- 1/4 teaspoon black pepper
- 2 tablespoons olive oil
FOR THE GREEK YOGURT SAUCE:
- 1/2 cup Greek yogurt
- 1 tablespoon lemon juice
- 1 tablespoon chopped fresh dill
- 1/2 teaspoon minced garlic
- Salt and pepper to taste
Instructions:

1. Place the grated zucchini and carrots in a colander and sprinkle with salt. Let them sit for 10 minutes to release excess moisture. Squeeze out any remaining moisture using a clean kitchen towel or paper towels.
2. In a large bowl, combine the grated zucchini, carrots, almond flour, Parmesan cheese, green onions, minced garlic, beaten eggs, salt, and black pepper. Mix well until everything is evenly combined.
3. Heat olive oil in a non-stick skillet over medium heat.
4. Take a heaping tablespoon of the zucchini-carrot mixture and shape it into a fritter. Place it in the skillet and flatten it slightly with a spatula. Repeat with the remaining mixture, leaving some space between the fritters in the skillet.
5. Cook the fritters for 3-4 minutes on each side, until they are golden brown and crispy. You may need to cook them in batches depending on the size of your skillet. Transfer the cooked fritters to a plate lined with paper towels to remove any excess oil.
6. In a small bowl, whisk together Greek yogurt, lemon juice, chopped dill, minced garlic, salt, and pepper to make the yogurt sauce.
7. Serve the zucchini and carrot fritters with the Greek yogurt sauce on the side as a dipping sauce.

CHICKEN AND BLACK BEAN CHILI

Nutrition: Cal 350;Fat 7 g;Carb 35 g;Protein 35 g
Serving 2; Cook time 30 min

Ingredients
- 2 boneless, skinless chicken breasts, diced
- 1 tablespoon olive oil
- 1 small onion, chopped
- 2 cloves garlic, minced
- 1 bell pepper, chopped
- 1 can (14 oz) diced tomatoes
- 1 can (14 oz) black beans, rinsed and drained
- 1 cup low-sodium chicken broth
- 1 tablespoon chili powder
- 1 teaspoon cumin
- 1/2 teaspoon paprika

- Salt and pepper to taste
- Optional toppings: chopped green onions, shredded cheese, Greek yogurt

Instructions:

1. Heat olive oil in a large pot or Dutch oven over medium heat. Add the diced chicken and cook until browned and cooked through. Remove the chicken from the pot and set aside.
2. In the same pot, add the chopped onion, minced garlic, and bell pepper. Sauté until the vegetables are softened, about 5 minutes.
3. Add the diced tomatoes, black beans, chicken broth, chili powder, cumin, paprika, salt, and pepper to the pot. Stir well to combine.
4. Bring the mixture to a boil, then reduce the heat and simmer for 15-20 minutes, allowing the flavors to meld together.
5. Return the cooked chicken to the pot and stir to combine. Cook for an additional 5 minutes to heat the chicken through.
6. Taste and adjust the seasonings if needed.
7. Serve the chicken and black bean chili hot, garnished with chopped green onions, shredded cheese, and a dollop of Greek yogurt if desired.

SPINACH AND MUSHROOM STUFFED BELL PEPPERS WITH QUINOA

Nutrition: Cal 200;Fat 6 g;Carb 30 g;Protein 7 g
Serving 2; Cook time 40 min

Ingredients
- 2 large bell peppers (any color), halved and seeds removed
- 1 cup cooked quinoa
- 1 cup baby spinach, chopped
- 1 cup mushrooms, finely chopped
- 1 small onion, finely chopped
- 2 cloves garlic, minced
- 1 tablespoon olive oil
- 1/4 teaspoon dried oregano
- 1/4 teaspoon dried basil
- Salt and pepper to taste
- Optional toppings: grated Parmesan cheese, chopped fresh parsley

Instructions:

1. Preheat your oven to 375°F (190°C).
2. Heat olive oil in a pan over medium heat. Add the chopped onion and minced garlic, and sauté until the onion is translucent and fragrant.
3. Add the chopped mushrooms to the pan and cook until they release their moisture and become tender.
4. Add the chopped spinach to the pan and cook until wilted. Season with salt, pepper, dried oregano, and dried basil. Stir to combine.
5. In a mixing bowl, combine the cooked quinoa with the spinach and mushroom mixture. Mix well to ensure the ingredients are evenly distributed.
6. Stuff each bell pepper half with the quinoa, spinach, and mushroom mixture, pressing it down gently to fill the cavity.
7. Place the stuffed bell peppers in a baking dish, cut side up. If the bell peppers are wobbly, you can trim a little off the bottom to make them stable.
8. Cover the baking dish with aluminum foil and bake in the preheated oven for 20-25 minutes, or until the bell peppers are tender.
9. Remove the foil and sprinkle grated Parmesan cheese on top of each stuffed bell pepper. Return to the oven and bake for an additional 5 minutes, or until the cheese is melted and lightly browned.
10. Remove from the oven and let the stuffed bell peppers cool slightly before serving. Garnish with chopped fresh parsley if desired.

GRILLED CHICKEN SKEWERS WITH LEMON-HERB YOGURT SAUCE

Nutrition: Cal 250;Fat 10 g;Carb 6 g;Protein 32 g
Serving 2; Cook time 30 min

Ingredients
- 2 boneless, skinless chicken breasts, cut into cubes
- 1 tablespoon olive oil
- 1 teaspoon lemon zest
- 1 tablespoon fresh lemon juice
- 1 teaspoon dried oregano
- Salt and pepper to taste

FOR THE LEMON-HERB YOGURT SAUCE:

- 1/2 cup plain Greek yogurt
- 1 tablespoon fresh lemon juice
- 1 tablespoon chopped fresh herbs (such as parsley, dill, or basil)
- 1 clove garlic, minced
- Salt and pepper to taste

Instructions:

1. In a mixing bowl, combine the olive oil, lemon zest, lemon juice, dried oregano, salt, and pepper. Add the chicken cubes to the bowl and toss to coat them well with the marinade. Let it marinate for at least 15 minutes, or up to 1 hour in the refrigerator.
2. Preheat a grill or grill pan over medium-high heat.
3. Thread the marinated chicken cubes onto skewers, evenly dividing them between the skewers.
4. Place the chicken skewers on the preheated grill and cook for about 8-10 minutes, turning occasionally, until the chicken is cooked through and lightly charred on the outside.
5. While the chicken is grilling, prepare the lemon-herb yogurt sauce. In a small bowl, combine the Greek yogurt, lemon juice, chopped fresh herbs, minced garlic, salt, and pepper. Stir well to combine.
6. Remove the grilled chicken skewers from the heat and let them rest for a few minutes.
7. Serve the grilled chicken skewers with the lemon-herb yogurt sauce on the side for dipping.

BROCCOLI AND CHEDDAR SOUP WITH LEAN HAM

Nutrition: Cal 250;Fat 10 g;Carb 20 g;Protein 20 g
Serving 2; Cook time 30 min

Ingredients
- 2 cups broccoli florets
- 1 small onion, chopped
- 2 cloves garlic, minced
- 2 cups low-sodium chicken or vegetable broth
- 1 cup low-fat milk
- 1 cup shredded low-fat cheddar cheese
- 4 ounces lean ham, diced
- Salt and pepper to taste

Instructions:

1. In a large pot, heat a little bit of olive oil over medium heat. Add the chopped onion and minced garlic and sauté until fragrant and translucent.
2. Add the broccoli florets to the pot and stir to combine with the onion and garlic. Cook for about 5 minutes, until the broccoli is slightly tender.
3. Pour in the chicken or vegetable broth and bring to a boil. Reduce the heat to low and let it simmer for about 10 minutes, until the broccoli is fully cooked.
4. Using an immersion blender or regular blender, puree the soup until smooth. If using a regular blender, be sure to let the soup cool slightly before blending and blend in batches if needed.
5. Return the soup to the pot and stir in the low-fat milk and shredded cheddar cheese. Continue stirring until the cheese is melted and well incorporated into the soup.
6. Add the diced lean ham to the soup and stir to combine. Cook for an additional 2-3 minutes until the ham is heated through.
7. Season with salt and pepper to taste.
8. Ladle the soup into bowls and serve hot.

QUINOA AND BLACK BEAN SALAD

Nutrition: Cal 320;Fat 8 g;Carb 52 g;Protein 12 g
Serving 2; Cook time 20 min

Ingredients
- 1 cup cooked quinoa
- 1 cup canned black beans, rinsed and drained
- 1 cup cherry tomatoes, halved
- 1/2 cup diced red bell pepper
- 1/4 cup chopped red onion
- 1/4 cup chopped fresh cilantro
- 2 tablespoons lime juice
- 1 tablespoon extra-virgin olive oil
- 1/2 teaspoon ground cumin
- Salt and pepper to taste

Instructions:

1. In a large mixing bowl, combine the cooked quinoa, black beans, cherry tomatoes, red bell pepper, red onion, and cilantro.
2. In a small bowl, whisk together the lime juice, olive oil, ground cumin, salt, and pepper.

3. Pour the dressing over the quinoa and black bean mixture and toss well to combine.

4. Adjust the seasoning to taste with additional salt and pepper if needed.

5. Let the salad sit for about 10 minutes to allow the flavors to meld together.

6. Serve the quinoa and black bean salad as a side dish or a main course. It can be enjoyed warm, at room temperature, or chilled.

GRILLED CHICKEN AND VEGETABLE SKEWERS WITH QUINOA SALAD

Nutrition: Cal 400;Fat 14 g;Carb 38 g;Protein 30 g
Serving 2; Cook time 30 min

Ingredients
FOR THE GRILLED CHICKEN AND VEGETABLE SKEWERS :
- 2 boneless, skinless chicken breasts, cut into bite-sized pieces
- 1 red bell pepper, cut into chunks
- 1 zucchini, sliced
- 1 red onion, cut into chunks
- 8 cherry tomatoes
- 2 tablespoons olive oil
- 1 tablespoon lemon juice
- 1 teaspoon dried oregano
- Salt and pepper to taste

FOR THE QUINOA SALAD:
- 1 cup cooked quinoa
- 1 cup mixed salad greens
- 1/2 cucumber, diced
- 1/4 cup diced red onion
- 2 tablespoons chopped fresh parsley
- 2 tablespoons lemon juice
- 1 tablespoon extra-virgin olive oil
- Salt and pepper to taste

Instructions:
1. Preheat the grill to medium-high heat.

2. In a bowl, combine the olive oil, lemon juice, dried oregano, salt, and pepper. Add the chicken pieces and toss to coat them evenly. Let the chicken marinate for 10 minutes.

3. Thread the marinated chicken, bell pepper, zucchini, red onion, and cherry tomatoes onto skewers, alternating the ingredients.

4. Place the skewers on the preheated grill and cook for about 12-15 minutes, turning

occasionally, until the chicken is cooked through and the vegetables are tender.

5. While the skewers are grilling, prepare the quinoa salad. In a bowl, combine the cooked quinoa, mixed salad greens, diced cucumber, diced red onion, chopped parsley, lemon juice, olive oil, salt, and pepper. Toss everything together until well combined.

6. Once the skewers are cooked, remove them from the grill and let them rest for a few minutes.

7. Serve the grilled chicken and vegetable skewers alongside the quinoa salad. Enjoy!

MEDITERRANEAN QUINOA SALAD

Nutrition: Cal 300;Fat 11 g;Carb 42 g;Protein 8 g
Serving 2; Cook time 15 min

Ingredients
- 1 cup cooked quinoa
- 1 cup diced cucumber
- 1 cup cherry tomatoes, halved
- 1/2 cup diced red bell pepper
- 1/4 cup diced red onion
- 1/4 cup sliced Kalamata olives
- 2 tablespoons crumbled feta cheese
- 2 tablespoons chopped fresh parsley
- 2 tablespoons lemon juice
- 1 tablespoon extra-virgin olive oil
- Salt and pepper to taste

Instructions:
1. In a large bowl, combine the cooked quinoa, diced cucumber, cherry tomatoes, red bell pepper, red onion, Kalamata olives, crumbled feta cheese, and chopped parsley.

2. In a small bowl, whisk together the lemon juice, olive oil, salt, and pepper.

3. Pour the dressing over the quinoa salad and toss everything together until well combined.

4. Taste and adjust the seasoning if needed.

5. Let the salad sit for a few minutes to allow the flavors to meld together.

6. Serve the Mediterranean quinoa salad as a refreshing and nutritious side dish or a light main course.

BAKED COD WITH LEMON AND HERB QUINOA

Nutrition: Cal 280;Fat 8 g;Carb 27 g;Protein 27 g
Serving 2; Cook time 25 min

Ingredients
•2 cod fillets (about 4-6 ounces each)
•1 lemon, sliced
•2 tablespoons fresh lemon juice
•2 tablespoons chopped fresh herbs (such as parsley, dill, or basil)
•1 tablespoon olive oil
•Salt and pepper to taste

FOR THE LEMON AND HERB QUINOA:
•1 cup cooked quinoa
•1 tablespoon fresh lemon juice
•1 tablespoon chopped fresh herbs
•Salt and pepper to taste

Instructions:
1. Preheat the oven to 375°F (190°C). Line a baking sheet with parchment paper.
2. Place the cod fillets on the prepared baking sheet. Season them with salt and pepper.
3. Arrange the lemon slices on top of the cod fillets. Drizzle the fresh lemon juice and olive oil over the fish.
4. Sprinkle the chopped herbs evenly over the cod fillets.
5. Bake in the preheated oven for about 15-20 minutes or until the fish is opaque and flakes easily with a fork.
6. While the cod is baking, prepare the lemon and herb quinoa. In a separate bowl, combine the cooked quinoa, fresh lemon juice, chopped herbs, salt, and pepper. Toss well to combine.
7. Once the cod is cooked, remove it from the oven and let it rest for a few minutes.
8. Serve the baked cod alongside the lemon and herb quinoa. Garnish with additional fresh herbs if desired.

CAPRESE STUFFED CHICKEN BREAST WITH ROASTED VEGETABLES

Nutrition: Cal 320;Fat 36 g;Carb 12 g;Protein 40 g
Serving 2; Cook time 50 min

Ingredients
•2 boneless, skinless chicken breasts
•4 slices mozzarella cheese
•2 large tomatoes, sliced
•1/4 cup fresh basil leaves
•Salt and pepper to taste

FOR THE ROASTED VEGETABLES:
•2 cups mixed vegetables (such as bell peppers, zucchini, and eggplant), chopped
•1 tablespoon olive oil
•Salt and pepper to taste

Instructions:
1. Preheat the oven to 375°F (190°C). Line a baking sheet with parchment paper.
2. Butterfly each chicken breast by slicing horizontally through the thickest part of the breast, but not cutting all the way through. Open the chicken breast like a book.
3. Place 2 slices of mozzarella cheese inside each chicken breast. Top with tomato slices and fresh basil leaves. Season with salt and pepper.
4. Fold the chicken breast over the filling, securing it with toothpicks if needed. Season the outside of the chicken with additional salt and pepper.
5. Place the stuffed chicken breasts on the prepared baking sheet. Bake in the preheated oven for about 25-30 minutes or until the chicken is cooked through and the cheese is melted and bubbly.
6. While the chicken is baking, prepare the roasted vegetables. Toss the chopped vegetables with olive oil, salt, and pepper. Spread them out on another baking sheet and roast in the oven for about 15-20 minutes or until they are tender and slightly browned.
7. Once the chicken and vegetables are cooked, remove them from the oven and let them rest for a few minutes.
8. Serve the Caprese stuffed chicken breast alongside the roasted vegetables. You can garnish with additional fresh basil if desired.

CUCUMBER AND SMOKED SALMON ROLL-UPS WITH CREAM CHEESE

Nutrition: Cal 320;Fat 36 g;Carb 12 g;Protein 40 g
Serving 2; Cook time 50 min

Ingredients
- 1 large cucumber
- 4 ounces (115g) smoked salmon
- 4 tablespoons cream cheese
- Fresh dill, chopped (for garnish)

Instructions:
1. Using a vegetable peeler or a mandoline slicer, slice the cucumber lengthwise into thin, long strips.
2. Lay the cucumber slices flat on a clean surface. Spread about 1 tablespoon of cream cheese evenly on each cucumber slice.
3. Lay a slice of smoked salmon over the cream cheese on each cucumber slice.
4. Carefully roll up each cucumber slice with the cream cheese and smoked salmon inside. Secure the rolls with toothpicks if needed.
5. Place the cucumber and smoked salmon roll-ups on a serving platter. Garnish with fresh dill.
6. Serve immediately and enjoy!

TURKEY AND VEGETABLE LETTUCE CUPS

Nutrition: Cal 180;Fat 6 g;Carb 12 g;Protein 20 g
Serving 2; Cook time 20 min

Ingredients
- 8 large lettuce leaves (such as romaine or iceberg)
- 1/2 pound ground turkey
- 1/2 cup diced bell peppers (any color)
- 1/2 cup diced zucchini
- 1/2 cup diced carrots
- 1/4 cup diced onion
- 2 cloves garlic, minced
- 1 tablespoon low-sodium soy sauce
- 1 tablespoon hoisin sauce
- 1 teaspoon sesame oil
- 1/2 teaspoon ground ginger
- Salt and pepper to taste
- Optional toppings: chopped green onions, sesame seeds

Instructions:
1. Heat a non-stick skillet over medium heat and spray with cooking spray.
2. Add the ground turkey to the skillet and cook until browned and cooked through. Remove from heat and set aside.
3. In the same skillet, add the diced bell peppers, zucchini, carrots, onion, and minced garlic. Cook for 3-4 minutes until the vegetables are slightly softened.
4. In a small bowl, whisk together the low-sodium soy sauce, hoisin sauce, sesame oil, ground ginger, salt, and pepper.
5. Add the cooked ground turkey back to the skillet with the vegetables. Pour the sauce over the mixture and stir to combine. Cook for an additional 1-2 minutes until everything is heated through.
6. Arrange the lettuce leaves on a serving platter.
7. Spoon the turkey and vegetable mixture onto each lettuce leaf, dividing it evenly.
8. Top with optional toppings such as chopped green onions and sesame seeds.
9. Serve immediately and enjoy!

LENTIL AND VEGETABLE CURRY WITH CAULIFLOWER RICE

Nutrition: Cal 320;Fat 6 g;Carb 50 g;Protein 15 g
Serving 2; Cook time 40 min

Ingredients
- 1 cup dry lentils (green or brown)
- 1 tablespoon olive oil
- 1 onion, diced
- 2 cloves garlic, minced
- 1 tablespoon curry powder
- 1 teaspoon ground cumin
- 1 teaspoon ground turmeric
- 1/2 teaspoon ground ginger
- 1/4 teaspoon cayenne pepper (optional, for heat)
- 1 carrot, diced
- 1 bell pepper, diced
- 1 zucchini, diced
- 1 cup vegetable broth
- 1 can diced tomatoes
- Salt and pepper to taste
- Fresh cilantro, for garnish
- 2 cups cauliflower rice (store-bought or homemade)

Instructions:
1. Cook the lentils according to the package instructions. Drain and set aside.
2. In a large skillet, heat the olive oil over medium heat. Add the diced onion and minced garlic, and sauté until softened and fragrant.

3. Add the curry powder, cumin, turmeric, ginger, and cayenne pepper (if using) to the skillet. Stir well to coat the onions and garlic with the spices.
4. Add the diced carrot, bell pepper, and zucchini to the skillet. Sauté for a few minutes until the vegetables start to soften.
5. Pour in the vegetable broth and diced tomatoes (with their juices) into the skillet. Stir to combine.
6. Reduce the heat to low, cover the skillet, and let the curry simmer for about 15-20 minutes, or until the vegetables are tender.
7. Season with salt and pepper to taste.
8. While the curry is simmering, prepare the cauliflower rice by pulsing the cauliflower florets in a food processor until they resemble rice grains.
9. Heat a separate non-stick skillet over medium heat and add the cauliflower rice. Cook for 5-7 minutes, stirring occasionally, until the cauliflower is tender.
10. Divide the cauliflower rice into two bowls or plates.
11. Spoon the lentil and vegetable curry over the cauliflower rice.
12. Garnish with fresh cilantro.

GRILLED SHRIMP AND AVOCADO LETTUCE CUPS

Nutrition: Cal 250;Fat 15 g;Carb 15 g;Protein 18 g
Serving 2; Cook time 15 min

Ingredients
- 12 large shrimp, peeled and deveined
- 1 tablespoon olive oil
- 1 clove garlic, minced
- 1 teaspoon paprika
- Salt and pepper to taste
- 2 avocados, diced
- Juice of 1 lime
- 2 tablespoons chopped fresh cilantro
- 1/4 cup diced red onion
- 1/4 cup diced cucumber
- 1/4 cup diced tomato
- 2 tablespoons Greek yogurt
- 1 tablespoon lime juice
- Lettuce leaves (such as butter lettuce or romaine) for serving

Instructions:
1. Preheat the grill to medium-high heat.
2. In a bowl, combine the olive oil, minced garlic, paprika, salt, and pepper. Add the shrimp and toss to coat.
3. Grill the shrimp for 2-3 minutes per side, or until they turn pink and opaque. Remove from the grill and set aside.
4. In a separate bowl, combine the diced avocados, lime juice, chopped cilantro, diced red onion, diced cucumber, and diced tomato. Gently mix until well combined.
5. In a small bowl, whisk together the Greek yogurt and lime juice to make the dressing.
6. To serve, arrange lettuce leaves on plates or a platter. Spoon the avocado mixture onto the lettuce leaves.
7. Place the grilled shrimp on top of the avocado mixture.
8. Drizzle the Greek yogurt dressing over the shrimp and avocado.
9. Garnish with additional cilantro if desired.
10. Serve immediately and enjoy!

STUFFED ZUCCHINI BOATS WITH LEAN GROUND BEEF AND BLACK BEANS

Nutrition: Cal 250;Fat 9 g;Carb 20 g;Protein 22 g
Serving 2; Cook time 40 min

Ingredients
- 2 medium zucchini
- 1/2 pound lean ground beef
- 1/2 cup black beans, drained and rinsed
- 1/4 cup diced onion
- 1/4 cup diced bell pepper
- 2 cloves garlic, minced
- 1/2 teaspoon ground cumin
- 1/2 teaspoon paprika
- Salt and pepper to taste
- 1/2 cup shredded low-fat cheese (such as cheddar or mozzarella)
- Fresh cilantro, chopped (for garnish)

Instructions:
1. Preheat the oven to 375°F (190°C).
2. Slice the zucchini in half lengthwise and scoop out the seeds and flesh, leaving a hollow boat-shaped shell. Reserve the scooped-out flesh for later use.

3. In a skillet, cook the lean ground beef over medium heat until browned. Drain any excess fat.
4. Add the diced onion, bell pepper, and minced garlic to the skillet with the ground beef. Cook for 2-3 minutes until the vegetables are tender.
5. Add the reserved zucchini flesh, black beans, cumin, paprika, salt, and pepper to the skillet. Stir to combine and cook for an additional 2-3 minutes.
6. Fill each zucchini boat with the ground beef and vegetable mixture.
7. Place the stuffed zucchini boats on a baking sheet and sprinkle the shredded cheese over the top.
8. Bake in the preheated oven for 20-25 minutes, or until the zucchini is tender and the cheese is melted and bubbly.
9. Remove from the oven and let cool for a few minutes.
10. Garnish with chopped cilantro and serve.

LEMON GARLIC ROASTED CHICKEN THIGHS WITH SAUTTED SPINACH

Nutrition: Cal 300;Fat 18 g;Carb 30 g;Protein 30 g
Serving 2; Cook time 40 min

Ingredients
- 4 boneless, skinless chicken thighs
- 2 tablespoons olive oil
- 2 cloves garlic, minced
- 1 lemon, zest and juice
- 1 teaspoon dried thyme
- Salt and pepper to taste
- 4 cups fresh spinach leaves
- 1 tablespoon butter

Instructions:
1. Preheat the oven to 400°F (200°C).
2. In a small bowl, mix together the olive oil, minced garlic, lemon zest, lemon juice, dried thyme, salt, and pepper.
3. Place the chicken thighs in a baking dish and pour the lemon garlic mixture over them, ensuring they are well coated.

4. Bake the chicken thighs in the preheated oven for 25-30 minutes, or until they reach an internal temperature of 165°F (74°C).
5. While the chicken is baking, heat the butter in a skillet over medium heat.
6. Add the spinach leaves to the skillet and sauté for 2-3 minutes until wilted.
7. Season the spinach with salt and pepper to taste.
8. Once the chicken thighs are cooked, remove them from the oven and let them rest for a few minutes.
9. Serve the chicken thighs with the sautéed spinach on the side.

TUNA SALAD LETTUCE WRAPS WITH CELERY AND RED ONION

Nutrition: Cal 150;Fat 4 g;Carb 7 g;Protein 20 g
Serving 2; Cook time 10 min

Ingredients
- 2 cans of tuna in water, drained
- 2 tablespoons light mayonnaise
- 1 stalk of celery, finely diced
- 1/4 cup red onion, finely diced
- 1 tablespoon lemon juice
- Salt and pepper to taste
- 4 large lettuce leaves (such as romaine or butter lettuce)

Instructions:
1. In a bowl, combine the drained tuna, light mayonnaise, diced celery, diced red onion, lemon juice, salt, and pepper. Mix well to combine.
2. Taste and adjust the seasoning if needed.
3. Place a scoop of the tuna salad mixture onto each lettuce leaf.
4. Roll up the lettuce leaf tightly, enclosing the tuna salad filling.
5. Serve immediately as a refreshing and light meal.

QUINOA AND BLACK BEAN STUFFED BELL PEPPERS

Nutrition: Cal 250;Fat 8 g;Carb 37 g;Protein 15 g
Serving 2; Cook time 45 min

Ingredients
- 4 bell peppers (choose your preferred color)
- 1 cup cooked quinoa

- 1 cup cooked black beans
- 1/2 cup diced tomatoes
- 1/2 cup diced red onion
- 1/2 cup diced zucchini
- 1/2 cup diced yellow squash
- 1/4 cup chopped fresh cilantro
- 1 teaspoon cumin
- 1/2 teaspoon chili powder
- Salt and pepper to taste
- 1/2 cup shredded reduced-fat cheddar cheese (optional)

Instructions:
1. Preheat your oven to 375°F (190°C).
2. Cut the tops off the bell peppers and remove the seeds and membranes. Set aside.
3. In a large mixing bowl, combine the cooked quinoa, black beans, diced tomatoes, red onion, zucchini, yellow squash, cilantro, cumin, chili powder, salt, and pepper. Mix well to combine all the ingredients.
4. Stuff each bell pepper with the quinoa and black bean mixture, pressing it down gently.
5. Place the stuffed bell peppers in a baking dish or on a baking sheet. If desired, sprinkle shredded cheddar cheese on top of each pepper.
6. Bake in the preheated oven for 30-35 minutes or until the peppers are tender and slightly browned.
7. Once cooked, remove from the oven and let them cool for a few minutes before serving.

GRILLED TURKEY BURGERS WITH TZATZIKI SAUCE

Nutrition: Cal 330;Fat 12 g;Carb 25 g;Protein 35 g
Serving 2; Cook time 25 min

Ingredients
FOR THE TURKEY BURGERS:
- 1 lb (450g) lean ground turkey
- 1/4 cup finely chopped red onion
- 2 cloves garlic, minced
- 1 tablespoon chopped fresh parsley
- 1 teaspoon dried oregano
- 1/2 teaspoon salt
- 1/4 teaspoon black pepper

FOR THE TZATZIKI SAUCE:
- 1 cup Greek yogurt (low-fat or non-fat)
- 1/2 cup grated cucumber, squeezed to remove excess moisture

- 1 clove garlic, minced
- 1 tablespoon lemon juice
- 1 tablespoon chopped fresh dill
- Salt and pepper to taste

FOR SERVING:
- Whole wheat burger buns (optional)
- Lettuce leaves
- Sliced tomatoes
- Sliced red onion

Instructions:
1. Preheat your grill or stovetop grill pan to medium-high heat.
2. In a mixing bowl, combine the ground turkey, chopped red onion, minced garlic, parsley, oregano, salt, and black pepper. Mix well until all the ingredients are evenly incorporated.
3. Divide the turkey mixture into two equal portions and shape them into burger patties.
4. Place the turkey burgers on the preheated grill or grill pan and cook for about 4-5 minutes per side or until the internal temperature reaches 165°F (74°C) and the burgers are cooked through.
5. While the burgers are cooking, prepare the tzatziki sauce. In a separate bowl, combine the Greek yogurt, grated cucumber, minced garlic, lemon juice, chopped dill, salt, and pepper. Stir well to combine.
6. Once the turkey burgers are cooked, remove them from the grill and let them rest for a few minutes.
7. If desired, lightly toast the whole wheat burger buns on the grill.
8. Assemble the burgers by placing a turkey patty on the bottom half of each bun. Top with tzatziki sauce, lettuce leaves, sliced tomatoes, and sliced red onion. Cover with the top bun.
9. Serve the grilled turkey burgers with a side salad or steamed vegetables for a complete meal.

EGGPLANT AND ZUCCHINI LASAGNA WITH LEAN GROUND TURKEY

Nutrition: Cal 350;Fat 12 g;Carb 25 g;Protein 25 g
Serving 2; Cook time 1 hour 15 min

Ingredients
- 1 large eggplant, sliced lengthwise into thin strips
- 2 medium zucchini, sliced lengthwise into thin strips
- 1 lb (450g) lean ground turkey
- 1 cup low-sodium marinara sauce
- 1 cup part-skim ricotta cheese
- 1/2 cup grated Parmesan cheese
- 1/2 cup shredded part-skim mozzarella cheese
- 2 cloves garlic, minced
- 1 teaspoon dried basil
- 1 teaspoon dried oregano
- Salt and pepper to taste
- Cooking spray

Instructions:
1. Preheat your oven to 375°F (190°C).
2. Lay the sliced eggplant and zucchini on a baking sheet lined with parchment paper. Lightly sprinkle them with salt and let them sit for about 10 minutes to remove excess moisture.
3. In a large skillet, cook the lean ground turkey over medium heat until browned and cooked through. Add minced garlic, dried basil, dried oregano, salt, and pepper. Stir well to combine the flavors. Remove from heat.
4. In a separate bowl, combine the ricotta cheese and grated Parmesan cheese.
5. Lightly spray a baking dish with cooking spray. Spread a thin layer of marinara sauce on the bottom of the dish.
6. Layer half of the eggplant slices on top of the marinara sauce. Spread half of the ground turkey mixture evenly over the eggplant.
7. Next, layer half of the zucchini slices over the turkey mixture. Spread half of the ricotta cheese mixture over the zucchini.
8. Repeat the layers with the remaining ingredients, starting with marinara sauce, followed by eggplant, ground turkey, zucchini, and ricotta cheese.
9. Top the lasagna with shredded mozzarella cheese.
10. Cover the baking dish with foil and bake in the preheated oven for 40 minutes.
11. Remove the foil and bake for an additional 10-15 minutes or until the cheese is golden and bubbly.
12. Let the lasagna cool for a few minutes before serving.

SHRIMP AND VEGETABLE STIR-FRY WITH COCONUT AMINOS

Nutrition: Cal 300;Fat 12 g;Carb 20 g;Protein 25 g
Serving 2; Cook time 20 min

Ingredients
- 1 lb (450g) shrimp, peeled and deveined
- 2 cups mixed vegetables (such as bell peppers, broccoli, carrots, snap peas)
- 2 cloves garlic, minced
- 1 tablespoon grated ginger
- 2 tablespoons coconut aminos (a soy sauce alternative)
- 1 tablespoon sesame oil
- 1 tablespoon olive oil
- Salt and pepper to taste
- Optional: chopped green onions and sesame seeds for garnish

Instructions:
1. Heat the olive oil and sesame oil in a large skillet or wok over medium-high heat.
2. Add the minced garlic and grated ginger to the skillet and cook for 1-2 minutes until fragrant.
3. Add the mixed vegetables to the skillet and stir-fry for about 4-5 minutes until they are crisp-tender.
4. Push the vegetables to one side of the skillet and add the shrimp to the other side. Cook the shrimp for 2-3 minutes on each side until they are pink and cooked through.
5. Combine the shrimp and vegetables in the skillet and pour the coconut aminos over the mixture. Stir well to coat everything evenly.
6. Season with salt and pepper to taste.
7. Cook for an additional 1-2 minutes to allow the flavors to blend together.
8. Remove from heat and garnish with chopped green onions and sesame seeds if desired.
9. Serve the shrimp and vegetable stir-fry as is or over cauliflower rice for a low-carb option.

BAKED CHICKEN BREAST WITH ROASTED BRUSSELS SPROUTS

Nutrition: Cal 300;Fat 12 g;Carb 20 g;Protein 25 g
Serving 2; Cook time 40 min

Ingredients
FOR THE BAKED CHICKEN BREAST:
- 2 boneless, skinless chicken breasts
- 1 tablespoon olive oil
- 1 teaspoon garlic powder
- 1 teaspoon paprika
- 1/2 teaspoon dried thyme
- Salt and pepper to taste

FOR THE ROASTED BRUSSELS SPROUTS:
- 2 cups Brussels sprouts, halved
- 1 tablespoon olive oil
- Salt and pepper to taste

Instructions:
1. Preheat your oven to 400°F (200°C).
2. Place the chicken breasts on a baking sheet lined with parchment paper or aluminum foil.
3. Drizzle olive oil over the chicken breasts, then sprinkle them with garlic powder, paprika, dried thyme, salt, and pepper. Use your hands to rub the seasonings into the chicken, coating them evenly.
4. In a separate bowl, toss the halved Brussels sprouts with olive oil, salt, and pepper.
5. Arrange the Brussels sprouts on the same baking sheet, surrounding the chicken breasts.
6. Place the baking sheet in the preheated oven and bake for 20-25 minutes or until the chicken is cooked through, reaching an internal temperature of 165°F (74°C), and the Brussels sprouts are tender and slightly caramelized.
7. Remove from the oven and let the chicken rest for a few minutes before slicing.
8. Serve the baked chicken breast with the roasted Brussels sprouts.

TERIYAKI TURKEY LETTUCE WRAPS WITH PINEAPPLE AND BELL PEPPERS

Nutrition: Cal 250;Fat 8 g;Carb 20 g;Protein 25 g
Serving 2; Cook time 25 min

Ingredients
- 1 lb (450g) lean ground turkey
- 1 cup diced pineapple
- 1 bell pepper, diced
- 2 tablespoons low-sodium teriyaki sauce
- 2 tablespoons reduced-sodium soy sauce
- 1 tablespoon honey or a sugar substitute
- 1 tablespoon rice vinegar
- 1 teaspoon grated ginger
- 1 clove garlic, minced
- 8 large lettuce leaves (such as iceberg or butter lettuce)
- Optional toppings: chopped green onions, sesame seeds

Instructions:
1. In a small bowl, whisk together the teriyaki sauce, soy sauce, honey or sugar substitute, rice vinegar, grated ginger, and minced garlic. Set aside.
2. Heat a large skillet or wok over medium-high heat.
3. Add the ground turkey to the skillet and cook, breaking it up with a spoon, until it is browned and cooked through.
4. Pour the teriyaki sauce mixture into the skillet with the cooked turkey. Stir well to coat the turkey evenly with the sauce.
5. Add the diced pineapple and bell pepper to the skillet. Stir-fry for an additional 3-4 minutes until the pineapple is heated through and the bell pepper is slightly softened.
6. Remove the skillet from heat.
7. Spoon the teriyaki turkey mixture onto each lettuce leaf, dividing it evenly.
8. Garnish with chopped green onions and sesame seeds if desired.
9. Serve the teriyaki turkey lettuce wraps immediately.

QUINOA AND BLACK BEAN STUFFED SWEET POTATOES WITH SALSA

Nutrition: Cal 350;Fat 2 g;Carb 65 g;Protein 12 g
Serving 2; Cook time 60 min

Ingredients
- 2 medium-sized sweet potatoes
- 1/2 cup cooked quinoa
- 1/2 cup cooked black beans
- 1/4 cup diced red onion
- 1/4 cup diced bell pepper (any color)

- 1/4 cup diced tomato
- 2 tablespoons chopped fresh cilantro
- Juice of 1/2 lime
- Salt and pepper to taste
- Salsa for topping

Instructions:
1. Preheat your oven to 400°F (200°C).
2. Pierce the sweet potatoes several times with a fork or knife to allow steam to escape while baking.
3. Place the sweet potatoes on a baking sheet lined with parchment paper or aluminum foil. Bake for about 45-60 minutes or until the sweet potatoes are tender and easily pierced with a fork.
4. While the sweet potatoes are baking, prepare the filling. In a mixing bowl, combine the cooked quinoa, black beans, diced red onion, diced bell pepper, diced tomato, chopped cilantro, lime juice, salt, and pepper. Mix well to combine all the ingredients.
5. Once the sweet potatoes are cooked, remove them from the oven and let them cool slightly.
6. Cut a lengthwise slit in the top of each sweet potato and gently push the ends towards the center to create an opening.
7. Spoon the quinoa and black bean filling into the opening of each sweet potato, dividing it evenly.
8. Top each stuffed sweet potato with salsa.
9. Serve the quinoa and black bean stuffed sweet potatoes as a complete meal or with a side salad.

GRILLED CHICKEN AND VEGETABLE QUESADILLAS

Nutrition: Cal 350;Fat 8 g;Carb 25 g;Protein 30 g
Serving 2; Cook time 25 min

Ingredients
- 2 small boneless, skinless chicken breasts
- 1 bell pepper, thinly sliced
- 1 small onion, thinly sliced
- 1 cup sliced mushrooms
- 2 whole wheat or low-carb tortillas
- 1/2 cup shredded reduced-fat cheese (such as cheddar or Monterey Jack)
- Cooking spray

- Optional toppings: salsa, guacamole, Greek yogurt

Instructions:
1. Preheat your grill or stovetop grill pan over medium heat.
2. Season the chicken breasts with salt, pepper, and any other desired seasonings.
3. Grill the chicken breasts for about 5-6 minutes per side or until they are cooked through and reach an internal temperature of 165°F (74°C). Remove from heat and let them rest for a few minutes before slicing.
4. In the meantime, coat a separate skillet with cooking spray and place it over medium heat.
5. Add the bell pepper, onion, and mushrooms to the skillet. Sauté for 4-5 minutes until the vegetables are tender and slightly caramelized.
6. Remove the vegetables from the skillet and set them aside.
7. Wipe the skillet clean and lightly coat it with cooking spray.
8. Place one tortilla in the skillet and sprinkle half of the shredded cheese evenly over the tortilla.
9. Arrange half of the sliced chicken and sautéed vegetables over the cheese.
10. Sprinkle the remaining cheese on top and cover with the second tortilla.
11. Cook the quesadilla for 2-3 minutes per side until the tortillas are golden brown and the cheese is melted.
12. Remove the quesadilla from the skillet and let it cool for a minute before slicing into wedges.
13. Repeat the process with the remaining ingredients to make the second quesadilla.
14. Serve the grilled chicken and vegetable quesadillas with salsa, guacamole, Greek yogurt, or any other desired toppings.

GREEK CUCUMBER SALAD WITH CHERRY TOMATOES

Nutrition: Cal 120;Fat 8 g;Carb 8 g;Protein 4 g
Serving 2; Cook time 15 min

Ingredients
- 2 medium cucumbers, peeled and diced
- 1 cup cherry tomatoes, halved
- 1/2 cup diced red onion
- 1/2 cup crumbled feta cheese

- 2 tablespoons chopped fresh dill
- Juice of 1 lemon
- 2 tablespoons extra-virgin olive oil
- Salt and pepper to taste

Instructions:

1. In a large bowl, combine the diced cucumbers, halved cherry tomatoes, diced red onion, crumbled feta cheese, and chopped fresh dill.
2. In a separate small bowl, whisk together the lemon juice, extra-virgin olive oil, salt, and pepper to make the dressing.
3. Pour the dressing over the cucumber mixture and toss well to coat all the ingredients evenly.
4. Adjust the seasoning with salt and pepper according to your taste.
5. Let the Greek cucumber salad sit at room temperature for about 10 minutes to allow the flavors to meld together.
6. Serve the salad as a side dish or as a light main course.

TURKEY AND VEGETABLE LETTUCE WRAPS

Nutrition: Cal 250;Fat 12 g;Carb 14 g;Protein 27 g
Serving 2; Cook time 25 min

Ingredients
- 1 lb (450g) lean ground turkey
- 1 tablespoon olive oil
- 1 small onion, finely chopped
- 2 cloves garlic, minced
- 1 bell pepper, finely chopped
- 1 medium carrot, grated
- 1 cup sliced mushrooms
- 2 tablespoons low-sodium soy sauce
- 1 tablespoon hoisin sauce
- 1 teaspoon grated ginger
- 1/2 teaspoon sesame oil
- 8 large lettuce leaves (such as iceberg or butter lettuce)
- Optional toppings: chopped green onions, sesame seeds

Instructions:

1. Heat the olive oil in a large skillet or wok over medium-high heat.
2. Add the chopped onion and minced garlic to the skillet and sauté for 2-3 minutes until they become fragrant and slightly softened.
3. Add the ground turkey to the skillet and cook, breaking it up with a spoon, until it is browned and cooked through.
4. Push the cooked turkey to one side of the skillet and add the chopped bell pepper, grated carrot, and sliced mushrooms to the other side. Cook for 3-4 minutes until the vegetables are tender-crisp.
5. Combine the cooked turkey and vegetables in the skillet and add the low-sodium soy sauce, hoisin sauce, grated ginger, and sesame oil. Stir well to coat everything evenly.
6. Cook for an additional 1-2 minutes to allow the flavors to blend together.
7. Remove from heat.
8. Spoon the turkey and vegetable mixture onto each lettuce leaf, dividing it evenly.
9. Garnish with chopped green onions and sesame seeds if desired.
10. Serve the turkey and vegetable lettuce wraps immediately.

ROASTED BUTTERNUT SQUASH SOUP WITH

Nutrition: Cal 160;Fat 5 g;Carb 26 g;Protein 5 g
Serving 2; Cook time 60 min

Ingredients
- 1 small butternut squash, peeled, seeded, and cut into cubes
- 1 tablespoon olive oil
- 1 small onion, chopped
- 2 cloves garlic, minced
- 3 cups low-sodium vegetable broth
- 1 teaspoon dried thyme
- 1/2 teaspoon ground cumin
- Salt and pepper to taste
- 2 cups fresh spinach leaves
- Optional toppings: Greek yogurt, pumpkin seeds, chopped fresh parsley

Instructions:

1. Preheat your oven to 400°F (200°C).
2. Place the cubed butternut squash on a baking sheet. Drizzle with olive oil and sprinkle with salt and pepper. Toss to coat the squash evenly.
3. Roast the butternut squash in the preheated oven for about 30-40 minutes or until it is tender and lightly browned.

4. In the meantime, heat a large pot over medium heat. Add the chopped onion and minced garlic to the pot and sauté for 2-3 minutes until they become fragrant and slightly softened.
5. Add the roasted butternut squash cubes to the pot, along with the low-sodium vegetable broth, dried thyme, and ground cumin. Stir well to combine.
6. Bring the mixture to a boil, then reduce the heat to low and let it simmer for about 15-20 minutes to allow the flavors to meld together.
7. Use an immersion blender or transfer the soup to a countertop blender to puree until smooth.
8. Season with salt and pepper to taste.
9. Add the fresh spinach leaves to the soup and stir until they wilt and become incorporated.
10. Cook for an additional 1-2 minutes until the spinach is tender.
11. Remove from heat.
12. Ladle the roasted butternut squash soup into bowls and garnish with optional toppings such as a dollop of Greek yogurt, pumpkin seeds, or chopped fresh parsley.

LEMON GARLIC SHRIMP AND BROCCOLI

Nutrition: Cal 220;Fat 9 g;Carb 7 g;Protein 27 g
Serving 2; Cook time 15 min

Ingredient
- 1 lb (450g) medium-sized shrimp, peeled and deveined
- 2 cups broccoli florets
- 2 cloves garlic, minced
- Juice of 1 lemon
- 2 tablespoons olive oil
- Salt and pepper to taste
- Optional garnish: chopped fresh parsley, lemon wedges

Instructions:
1. In a small bowl, whisk together the minced garlic, lemon juice, olive oil, salt, and pepper to make the marinade.
2. Place the shrimp in a ziplock bag or a shallow dish and pour the marinade over them. Toss well to coat the shrimp evenly. Let them marinate for 5-10 minutes.
3. Heat a large skillet over medium heat.
4. Add the marinated shrimp to the skillet and cook for 2-3 minutes on each side until they turn pink and opaque. Remove the cooked shrimp from the skillet and set them aside.
5. In the same skillet, add the broccoli florets and cook for 4-5 minutes until they are crisp-tender. You can cover the skillet with a lid to steam the broccoli slightly, if desired.
6. Return the cooked shrimp to the skillet with the broccoli and toss them together for another minute to heat through.
7. Remove from heat.
8. Serve the lemon garlic shrimp and broccoli as a main dish or over a bed of cauliflower rice or quinoa, if desired.
9. Garnish with chopped fresh parsley and lemon wedges, if desired.

CAULIFLOWER CRUST MINI QUICHES

Nutrition: Cal 150;Fat 8 g;Carb 8 g;Protein 12 g
Serving 2; Cook time 35 min

Ingredients
FOR THE CAULIFLOWER CRUST:
- 2 cups cauliflower rice
- 1/4 cup grated Parmesan cheese
- 1 egg, beaten
- Salt and pepper to taste
FOR THE FILLING:
- 1/2 cup diced bell peppers
- 1/2 cup diced mushrooms
- 1/4 cup diced red onion
- 1/4 cup chopped spinach
- 4 large eggs
- 1/4 cup milk (you can use low-fat or plant-based milk for a bariatric diet)
- Salt and pepper to taste
- Optional: shredded cheese (such as low-fat cheddar) for topping

Instructions:
1. Preheat your oven to 375°F (190°C) and grease a muffin tin or line it with paper liners.

2. In a microwave-safe bowl, steam the cauliflower rice by microwaving it for 4-5 minutes until it is tender. Allow it to cool slightly.

3. Once the cauliflower rice has cooled, place it in a clean kitchen towel and squeeze out as much moisture as possible.

4. In a bowl, combine the cauliflower rice, grated Parmesan cheese, beaten egg, salt, and pepper. Mix well to form a dough-like consistency.

5. Divide the cauliflower dough among the muffin tin cups and press it into the bottom and sides to form crusts. Set aside.

6. In a separate bowl, whisk together the eggs and milk. Season with salt and pepper.

7. Distribute the diced bell peppers, mushrooms, red onion, and chopped spinach evenly among the cauliflower crusts in the muffin tin.

8. Pour the egg mixture over the vegetable fillings, dividing it evenly.

9. If desired, sprinkle some shredded cheese on top of each quiche.

10. Place the muffin tin in the preheated oven and bake for approximately 20-25 minutes until the quiches are set and lightly golden.

11. Remove from the oven and let them cool slightly before serving.

LENTIL AND VEGETABLE CURRY

Nutrition: Cal 250;Fat 4 g;Carb 45 g;Protein 18 g
Serving 2; Cook time 40 min

Ingredients
- 1 cup dried lentils (any variety), rinsed and drained
- 1 tablespoon olive oil
- 1 small onion, chopped
- 2 cloves garlic, minced
- 1 tablespoon curry powder
- 1 teaspoon ground cumin
- 1/2 teaspoon ground turmeric
- 1/2 teaspoon ground coriander
- 1 cup chopped mixed vegetables (such as carrots, bell peppers, zucchini)
- 1 can (14 oz) diced tomatoes
- 1 cup vegetable broth
- Salt and pepper to taste
- Optional toppings: chopped fresh cilantro, Greek yogurt

Instructions:
1. In a large pot, heat the olive oil over medium heat.

2. Add the chopped onion and minced garlic to the pot and sauté for 2-3 minutes until they become fragrant and slightly softened.

3. Add the curry powder, cumin, turmeric, and coriander to the pot. Stir well to coat the onions and garlic with the spices. Cook for an additional minute to toast the spices.

4. Add the chopped mixed vegetables to the pot and cook for 3-4 minutes until they begin to soften.

5. Stir in the rinsed lentils, diced tomatoes (with their juices), and vegetable broth. Season with salt and pepper to taste.

6. Bring the mixture to a boil, then reduce the heat to low and let it simmer, covered, for approximately 25-30 minutes or until the lentils are tender and the flavors are well combined. Stir occasionally.

7. If the curry appears too thick, you can add a bit more vegetable broth or water to achieve your desired consistency.

8. Remove from heat.

9. Serve the lentil and vegetable curry in bowls. Garnish with chopped fresh cilantro and a dollop of Greek yogurt, if desired.

10. Enjoy the flavorful and hearty Lentil and Vegetable Curry with a side of steamed brown rice or cauliflower rice, if desired.

GREEK-STYLE TURKEY MEATBALL

Nutrition: Cal 220;Fat 9 g;Carb 11 g;Protein 27 g
Serving 2; Cook time 30 min

Ingredients
FOR THE MEATBALLS:
- 1 lb (450g) lean ground turkey
- 1/4 cup breadcrumbs (you can use whole wheat or gluten-free breadcrumbs)
- 1/4 cup grated Parmesan cheese
- 1/4 cup chopped fresh parsley
- 2 cloves garlic, minced
- 1 teaspoon dried oregano
- 1/2 teaspoon dried thyme
- 1/2 teaspoon ground cumin
- Salt and pepper to taste

•Optional: 1 egg (to help bind the meatballs)

FOR THE TZATZIKI SAUCE:

•1/2 cup Greek yogurt (low-fat or non-fat)

•1/4 cup grated cucumber, squeezed to remove excess moisture

•1 clove garlic, minced

•1 tablespoon lemon juice

•1 tablespoon chopped fresh dill

•Salt and pepper to taste

Instructions:

1. Preheat your oven to 375°F (190°C) and line a baking sheet with parchment paper.

2. In a mixing bowl, combine the ground turkey, breadcrumbs, grated Parmesan cheese, chopped parsley, minced garlic, dried oregano, dried thyme, ground cumin, salt, and pepper. Optionally, you can add an egg to help bind the meatballs together. Mix well until all ingredients are evenly incorporated.

3. Shape the mixture into small meatballs, about 1-2 tablespoons each, and place them on the prepared baking sheet.

4. Bake the meatballs in the preheated oven for approximately 15-20 minutes until they are cooked through and golden brown.

5. While the meatballs are baking, prepare the tzatziki sauce. In a small bowl, combine the Greek yogurt, grated cucumber, minced garlic, lemon juice, chopped fresh dill, salt, and pepper. Mix well until everything is well combined.

6. Once the meatballs are cooked, remove them from the oven and let them cool slightly.

7. Serve the Greek-style turkey meatballs with the tzatziki sauce on the side. You can also serve them with a side salad or whole grain pita bread, if desired.

CAPRESE QUINOA SALAD

Nutrition: Cal 250;Fat 12 g;Carb 20 g;Protein 13 g
Serving 2; Cook time 20 min

Ingredients

•1 cup cooked quinoa

•1 cup cherry tomatoes, halved

•4 ounces fresh mozzarella cheese, diced

•1/4 cup fresh basil leaves, chopped

•1 tablespoon extra virgin olive oil

•1 tablespoon balsamic vinegar

•Salt and pepper to taste

Instructions:

1. Cook quinoa according to package instructions. Let it cool completely.

2. In a mixing bowl, combine the cooked quinoa, cherry tomatoes, fresh mozzarella cheese, and chopped basil leaves.

3. Drizzle the extra virgin olive oil and balsamic vinegar over the salad. Season with salt and pepper to taste.

4. Toss everything together until all ingredients are well coated with the dressing.

5. Serve the Caprese quinoa salad immediately or refrigerate for about 30 minutes to allow the flavors to meld together.

6. Enjoy the refreshing and protein-rich Caprese Quinoa Salad as a light and satisfying meal!

ZUCCHINI AND CORN CHOWDER

Nutrition: Cal 180;Fat 6 g;Carb 22 g;Protein 62 g
Serving 2; Cook time 30 min

Ingredients

•2 medium zucchini, diced

•1 cup corn kernels (fresh or frozen)

•1 small onion, chopped

•2 cloves garlic, minced

•2 cups low-sodium vegetable broth

•1 cup unsweetened almond milk (or any low-fat milk of your choice)

•1 tablespoon olive oil

•1/2 teaspoon dried thyme

•Salt and pepper to taste

•Optional toppings: chopped fresh parsley, grated Parmesan cheese

Instructions:

1. In a large pot, heat the olive oil over medium heat.

2. Add the chopped onion and minced garlic to the pot and sauté for 2-3 minutes until they become fragrant and slightly softened.

3. Add the diced zucchini to the pot and cook for another 3-4 minutes until they begin to soften.

4. Stir in the corn kernels and dried thyme. Cook for an additional 2 minutes.

5. Pour in the vegetable broth and bring the mixture to a boil. Reduce the heat to low and let it simmer for about 10-15 minutes until the vegetables are tender.

6. Using an immersion blender or a regular blender, puree about half of the soup until smooth. This will help thicken the chowder while still leaving some texture.

7. Pour the almond milk into the pot and stir well to combine. Season with salt and pepper to taste.

8. Simmer the chowder for another 5 minutes, stirring occasionally.

9. Remove from heat.

10. Serve the Zucchini and Corn Chowder in bowls. Garnish with chopped fresh parsley and grated Parmesan cheese, if desired.

11. Enjoy the creamy and comforting Zucchini and Corn Chowder as a satisfying meal!

TUNA AND AVOCADO SALAD WITH LEMON VINAIGRETTE

Nutrition: Cal 250;Fat 16 g;Carb 12 g;Protein 25 g
Serving 2; Cook time 30 min

Ingredients
FOR THE SALAD:
- 2 cans (5 oz each) tuna in water, drained
- 1 large avocado, diced
- 1 cup cherry tomatoes, halved
- 1/4 cup red onion, thinly sliced
- 2 cups mixed salad greens

FOR THE LEMON VINAIGRETTE:
- 2 tablespoons freshly squeezed lemon juice
- 1 tablespoon extra virgin olive oil
- 1 teaspoon Dijon mustard
- Salt and pepper to taste

Instructions:
1. In a large bowl, combine the drained tuna, diced avocado, cherry tomatoes, red onion, and mixed salad greens.

2. In a separate small bowl, whisk together the lemon juice, extra virgin olive oil, Dijon mustard, salt, and pepper to make the lemon vinaigrette.

3. Pour the lemon vinaigrette over the salad ingredients and toss gently to coat everything evenly.

4. Divide the tuna and avocado salad into two serving plates or bowls.

5. Serve the salad immediately and enjoy the fresh and nutritious Tuna and Avocado Salad with Lemon Vinaigrette!

STUFFED CHICKEN BREASTS WITH SPINACH

Nutrition: Cal 250;Fat 12 g;Carb 6 g;Protein 35 g
Serving 2; Cook time 30 min

Ingredients
- 2 boneless, skinless chicken breasts
- 2 cups fresh spinach leaves
- 1/4 cup low-fat feta cheese, crumbled
- 1/4 cup sun-dried tomatoes, chopped
- 1 clove garlic, minced
- 1/2 teaspoon dried oregano
- Salt and pepper to taste
- 1 tablespoon olive oil

Instructions:
1. Preheat your oven to 375°F (190°C).

2. Slice each chicken breast horizontally, almost but not completely through, to create a pocket for the stuffing.

3. In a small bowl, combine the fresh spinach, feta cheese, sun-dried tomatoes, minced garlic, dried oregano, salt, and pepper. Mix well.

4. Stuff each chicken breast with half of the spinach mixture, pressing the edges together to seal the filling inside.

5. Heat the olive oil in an oven-safe skillet over medium-high heat.

6. Add the stuffed chicken breasts to the skillet and sear for about 2-3 minutes on each side until they develop a golden brown crust.

7. Transfer the skillet with the chicken to the preheated oven and bake for about 15-20 minutes or until the chicken is cooked through and no longer pink in the center.

8. Remove the skillet from the oven and let the chicken rest for a few minutes before slicing.

9. Serve the Stuffed Chicken Breasts with Spinach as a main dish. You can pair it with steamed vegetables or a side salad for a complete meal.

GRILLED SHRIMP AND VEGETABLE WRAPS WITH HUMMUS

Nutrition: Cal 270;Fat 8 g;Carb 27 g;Protein 22 g
Serving 2; Cook time 20 min

Ingredients
- 8 large shrimp, peeled and deveined
- 1 medium zucchini, sliced into thin strips

- 1 red bell pepper, sliced into thin strips
- 1 yellow bell pepper, sliced into thin strips
- 1 tablespoon olive oil
- Salt and pepper to taste
- 4 whole wheat or low-carb tortillas
- 1/4 cup hummus (choose a low-fat or reduced-calorie version)

Instructions:
1. Preheat the grill or a grill pan over medium-high heat.
2. In a bowl, toss the shrimp, zucchini strips, red bell pepper strips, and yellow bell pepper strips with olive oil, salt, and pepper.
3. Grill the shrimp and vegetables for about 2-3 minutes on each side until the shrimp are cooked through and the vegetables are slightly charred and tender.
4. Remove the shrimp and vegetables from the grill and set aside.
5. Warm the tortillas on the grill for about 10-20 seconds on each side until they are pliable.
6. Spread about 1 tablespoon of hummus on each tortilla.
7. Divide the grilled shrimp and vegetables evenly among the tortillas.
8. Roll up the tortillas tightly, tucking in the sides as you go, to form wraps.
9. Cut each wrap in half diagonally, if desired.

MOROCCAN-SPICED LENTIL SOUP

Nutrition: Cal 250;Fat 8 g;Carb 30 g;Protein 12 g
Serving 2; Cook time 40 min

Ingredients
- 1 cup dried red lentils
- 1 onion, chopped
- 2 cloves garlic, minced
- 1 carrot, diced
- 1 celery stalk, diced
- 1 tablespoon olive oil
- 1 teaspoon ground cumin
- 1 teaspoon ground coriander
- 1/2 teaspoon ground turmeric
- 1/2 teaspoon ground cinnamon
- 4 cups low-sodium vegetable broth
- 1 cup canned diced tomatoes
- Salt and pepper to taste
- Fresh cilantro or parsley, chopped (for garnish)

Instructions:
1. Rinse the dried red lentils under cold water and drain.
2. In a large pot, heat the olive oil over medium heat.
3. Add the chopped onion, minced garlic, diced carrot, and diced celery to the pot. Sauté for about 5 minutes until the vegetables begin to soften.
4. Stir in the ground cumin, ground coriander, ground turmeric, and ground cinnamon. Cook for another minute until the spices become fragrant.
5. Add the rinsed lentils, vegetable broth, and canned diced tomatoes to the pot. Season with salt and pepper to taste.
6. Bring the soup to a boil, then reduce the heat to low and let it simmer for about 30 minutes or until the lentils are tender.
7. Using an immersion blender or a regular blender, puree about half of the soup until smooth. This will help thicken the soup while still leaving some texture.
8. If needed, adjust the consistency of the soup by adding more vegetable broth or water.
9. Serve the Moroccan-Spiced Lentil Soup hot, garnished with fresh cilantro or parsley.

TURKEY TACO SALAD WITH BLACK BEANS

Nutrition: Cal 320;Fat 12 g;Carb 28 g;Protein 28 g
Serving 2; Cook time 20 min

Ingredients
- 8 oz lean ground turkey
- 1 teaspoon olive oil
- 1/2 teaspoon chili powder
- 1/2 teaspoon ground cumin
- 1/2 teaspoon paprika
- 1/4 teaspoon garlic powder
- Salt and pepper to taste
- 4 cups mixed salad greens
- 1 cup canned black beans, rinsed and drained
- 1/2 cup cherry tomatoes, halved
- 1/4 cup red onion, thinly sliced
- 1/4 cup shredded reduced-fat cheddar cheese
- 2 tablespoons non-fat Greek yogurt (optional, for topping)
- Fresh cilantro, chopped (for garnish)

FOR THE DRESSING:
- 2 tablespoons lime juice
- 1 tablespoon olive oil
- 1/2 teaspoon honey
- Salt and pepper to taste

Instructions:
1. In a skillet, heat the olive oil over medium heat. Add the ground turkey and cook until browned and cooked through, breaking it up with a spoon.
2. Stir in the chili powder, ground cumin, paprika, garlic powder, salt, and pepper. Cook for an additional 1-2 minutes to allow the spices to blend in.
3. In a large salad bowl, assemble the mixed salad greens, black beans, cherry tomatoes, red onion, and shredded cheddar cheese.
4. In a small bowl, whisk together the lime juice, olive oil, honey, salt, and pepper to make the dressing.
5. Add the cooked ground turkey to the salad bowl and drizzle the dressing over the ingredients. Toss gently to combine.
6. Divide the Turkey Taco Salad into two serving bowls or plates.
7. Top with a dollop of non-fat Greek yogurt (if desired) and garnish with fresh cilantro.
8. Serve the Turkey Taco Salad immediately and enjoy the flavorsome and nutritious meal!

BROCCOLI AND CHEDDAR QUICHE WITH A SIDE SALAD

Nutrition: Cal 300;Fat 17 g;Carb 25 g;Protein 16 g
Serving 2; Cook time 45 min

Ingredients
FOR THE QUICHE:
- 4 large eggs
- 1/2 cup low-fat milk
- 1 cup broccoli florets, steamed and chopped
- 1/2 cup shredded reduced-fat cheddar cheese
- 1/4 cup diced onion
- Salt and pepper to taste

FOR THE CRUST:
- 1 pre-made low-carb or whole wheat pie crust (or use a crustless version)

FOR THE SIDE SALAD:
- 4 cups mixed salad greens
- 1/2 cup cherry tomatoes, halved
- 1/4 cup sliced cucumber
- 1/4 cup sliced red onion
- 2 tablespoons balsamic vinegar
- 1 tablespoon olive oil
- Salt and pepper to taste

Instructions:
1. Preheat your oven to 375°F (190°C).
2. In a mixing bowl, whisk together the eggs and low-fat milk. Season with salt and pepper.
3. Stir in the chopped steamed broccoli, shredded cheddar cheese, and diced onion.
4. If using a pre-made pie crust, place it in a pie dish. If using a crustless version, lightly grease a pie dish.
5. Pour the quiche mixture into the prepared pie crust or directly into the greased pie dish.
6. Bake the quiche in the preheated oven for approximately 25-30 minutes, or until the eggs are set and the top is golden brown.
7. While the quiche is baking, prepare the side salad. In a bowl, combine the mixed salad greens, cherry tomatoes, sliced cucumber, and sliced red onion.
8. In a small bowl, whisk together the balsamic vinegar, olive oil, salt, and pepper to make the dressing for the side salad.
9. Drizzle the dressing over the salad and toss gently to coat.
10. Once the quiche is cooked, remove it from the oven and let it cool slightly before slicing.
11. Serve the Broccoli and Cheddar Quiche with a side of the mixed green salad.

TERIYAKI GLAZED TOFU STIR-FRY

Nutrition: Cal 270;Fat 8 g;Carb 27 g;Protein 22 g
Serving 2; Cook time 20 min

Ingredients
FOR THE TERIYAKI SAUCE:
- 2 tablespoons low-sodium soy sauce
- 1 tablespoon honey or maple syrup
- 1 tablespoon rice vinegar
- 1 garlic clove, minced
- 1/2 teaspoon grated ginger
- 1/2 teaspoon cornstarch

FOR THE STIR-FRY:
- 8 oz firm tofu, drained and cut into cubes
- 1 tablespoon sesame oil

- 1 cup mixed vegetables (such as bell peppers, broccoli, carrots, and snap peas), sliced
- 2 cups cooked brown rice

Instructions:

1. In a small bowl, whisk together the low-sodium soy sauce, honey (or maple syrup), rice vinegar, minced garlic, grated ginger, and cornstarch to make the teriyaki sauce. Set aside.
2. Heat the sesame oil in a large skillet or wok over medium heat.
3. Add the tofu cubes to the skillet and cook for about 5 minutes, stirring occasionally, until the tofu is lightly browned on all sides.
4. Push the tofu to one side of the skillet and add the sliced mixed vegetables to the other side. Stir-fry the vegetables for about 3-4 minutes until they are tender-crisp.
5. Pour the teriyaki sauce over the tofu and vegetables. Stir everything together to coat the tofu and vegetables evenly with the sauce.
6. Continue cooking for another 2-3 minutes until the sauce thickens slightly.
7. Divide the cooked brown rice between two plates or bowls.
8. Spoon the teriyaki glazed tofu and vegetables over the brown rice.

ASIAN-STYLE LETTUCE WRAPS WITH GROUND TURKEY

Nutrition: Cal 270;Fat 11 g;Carb 17 g;Protein 23 g
Serving 2; Cook time 20 min

Ingredients
FOR THE LETTUCE WRAPS:

- 8 large lettuce leaves (such as iceberg or butter lettuce)
- 8 oz lean ground turkey
- 1 tablespoon olive oil
- 1/2 cup diced onion
- 2 cloves garlic, minced
- 1/2 cup diced water chestnuts
- 1/4 cup low-sodium soy sauce
- 2 tablespoons hoisin sauce
- 1 tablespoon rice vinegar
- 1 teaspoon sesame oil
- 1/2 teaspoon grated ginger
- Optional toppings: sliced green onions, chopped cilantro, and lime wedges

Instructions:

1. Rinse the lettuce leaves and pat them dry. Set them aside.
2. Heat the olive oil in a skillet over medium heat.
3. Add the diced onion and minced garlic to the skillet and sauté for 2-3 minutes until softened.
4. Add the ground turkey to the skillet and cook until browned, breaking it up with a spoon.
5. Stir in the diced water chestnuts, low-sodium soy sauce, hoisin sauce, rice vinegar, sesame oil, and grated ginger. Cook for an additional 2-3 minutes to allow the flavors to meld.
6. Remove the skillet from heat and let the mixture cool slightly.
7. To assemble the lettuce wraps, place a spoonful of the turkey mixture onto each lettuce leaf.
8. Optional: Top the wraps with sliced green onions, chopped cilantro, and a squeeze of lime juice.
9. Serve the Asian-Style Lettuce Wraps immediately, either as a main dish or as an appetizer.

GRILLED CHICKEN CAESAR SALAD

Nutrition: Cal 270;Fat 11 g;Carb 10 g;Protein 33 g
Serving 2; Cook time 20 min

Ingredients
FOR THE SALAD:

- 2 boneless, skinless chicken breasts (4-6 oz each)
- 6 cups romaine lettuce, chopped
- 1/4 cup grated Parmesan cheese
- 1/4 cup croutons (optional)
- Salt and pepper to taste

FOR THE CAESAR DRESSING:

- 2 tablespoons plain Greek yogurt
- 1 tablespoon lemon juice
- 1 tablespoon grated Parmesan cheese
- 1 teaspoon Dijon mustard
- 1 garlic clove, minced
- 1/2 teaspoon Worcestershire sauce
- Salt and pepper to taste

Instructions:

1. Preheat the grill to medium-high heat.
2. Season the chicken breasts with salt and pepper.

3. Grill the chicken breasts for about 6-8 minutes per side, or until cooked through with an internal temperature of 165°F (75°C).

4. Remove the chicken from the grill and let it rest for a few minutes. Then, slice it into thin strips.

5. In a large salad bowl, combine the chopped romaine lettuce, grated Parmesan cheese, and croutons (if using).

6. In a separate small bowl, whisk together the Greek yogurt, lemon juice, grated Parmesan cheese, Dijon mustard, minced garlic, Worcestershire sauce, salt, and pepper to make the Caesar dressing.

7. Pour the Caesar dressing over the salad and toss well to coat the lettuce evenly.

8. Divide the dressed salad between two plates and top each with the sliced grilled chicken.

9. Optional: Garnish with additional grated Parmesan cheese and cracked black pepper.

CAPRESE SKEWERS WITH GRILLED SHRIMP AND BALSAMIC GLAZE

Nutrition: Cal 250;Fat 12 g;Carb 12 g;Protein 16 g
Serving 2; Cook time 20 min

Ingredients
FOR THE SKEWERS:
• 10 large shrimp, peeled and deveined
• 10 small fresh mozzarella balls (bocconcini)
• 10 cherry tomatoes
• Fresh basil leaves
• Salt and pepper to taste
FOR THE BALSAMIC GLAZE:
• 1/4 cup balsamic vinegar
• 1 tablespoon honey or maple syrup
Instructions:
1. Preheat the grill to medium-high heat.
2. Season the shrimp with salt and pepper.
3. Thread the shrimp onto skewers, alternating with mozzarella balls, cherry tomatoes, and basil leaves.
4. In a small saucepan, combine the balsamic vinegar and honey (or maple syrup) for the glaze. Bring to a simmer over medium heat and cook for about 5 minutes until the mixture thickens slightly.

5. Grill the skewers for about 2-3 minutes per side until the shrimp are cooked through and the cheese has softened.

6. Remove the skewers from the grill and place them on a serving platter.

7. Drizzle the balsamic glaze over the skewers.

8. Optional: Garnish with additional fresh basil leaves.

9. Serve the Caprese Skewers with Grilled Shrimp and Balsamic Glaze immediately, and enjoy the delightful flavors!

BLACK BEAN AND QUINOA STUFFED BELL PEPPERS WITH SALSA VERDE

Nutrition: Cal 270;Fat 7 g;Carb 43 g;Protein 12 g
Serving 2; Cook time 40 min

Ingredients
FOR THE STUFFED BELL PEPPERS:
• 2 large bell peppers (any color)
• 1/2 cup cooked quinoa
• 1/2 cup canned black beans, rinsed and drained
• 1/4 cup diced onion
• 1/4 cup diced tomatoes
• 1/4 cup diced bell peppers (from the tops)
• 1/4 cup shredded low-fat cheese (such as reduced-fat cheddar or Mexican blend)
• 1/2 teaspoon cumin
• 1/2 teaspoon paprika
• Salt and pepper to taste
FOR THE SALSA VERDE:
• 1/2 cup fresh cilantro leaves
• 1/4 cup diced onion
• 1 jalapeño pepper, seeded and chopped
• 1 clove garlic, minced
• 1 tablespoon lime juice
• 1 tablespoon olive oil
• Salt and pepper to taste
Instructions:
1. Preheat the oven to 375°F (190°C).
2. Cut off the tops of the bell peppers and remove the seeds and membranes. Dice the tops and set aside.
3. In a bowl, combine cooked quinoa, black beans, diced onion, diced tomatoes, diced bell peppers (from the tops), shredded cheese, cumin, paprika, salt, and pepper. Mix well.

4. Spoon the quinoa and black bean mixture into the hollowed-out bell peppers.

5. Place the stuffed bell peppers in a baking dish and cover with foil.

6. Bake in the preheated oven for about 25-30 minutes until the peppers are tender and the filling is heated through.

7. While the peppers are baking, prepare the salsa verde by combining cilantro, diced onion, jalapeño pepper, minced garlic, lime juice, olive oil, salt, and pepper in a blender or food processor. Blend until smooth.

8. Once the stuffed bell peppers are cooked, remove them from the oven and let them cool slightly.

9. Drizzle the salsa verde over the stuffed bell peppers.

TURKEY AND VEGETABLE LETTUCE WRAPS WITH THAI PEANUT SAUCE

Nutrition: Cal 270;Fat 14 g;Carb 13 g;Protein 22 g
Serving 2; Cook time 20 min

Ingredients
FOR THE LETTUCE WRAPS:
- 8 large lettuce leaves (such as iceberg or butter lettuce)
- 1/2 pound lean ground turkey
- 1/2 cup shredded carrots
- 1/2 cup shredded cabbage
- 1/4 cup diced red bell pepper
- 2 green onions, sliced
- 2 cloves garlic, minced
- 1 tablespoon low-sodium soy sauce
- 1 tablespoon sesame oil
- 1/2 teaspoon ground ginger
- Salt and pepper to taste

FOR THE THAI PEANUT SAUCE:
- 2 tablespoons natural peanut butter
- 1 tablespoon low-sodium soy sauce
- 1 tablespoon lime juice
- 1 tablespoon honey or maple syrup
- 1 teaspoon sriracha or hot sauce (optional)
- Water (as needed to adjust consistency)

Instructions:
1. In a small bowl, whisk together all the ingredients for the Thai peanut sauce until

well combined. Add water gradually to adjust the consistency, if needed. Set aside.

2. Heat sesame oil in a large skillet or wok over medium heat.

3. Add ground turkey to the skillet and cook until browned, breaking it up into crumbles with a spatula.

4. Add minced garlic, shredded carrots, shredded cabbage, diced red bell pepper, sliced green onions, soy sauce, ground ginger, salt, and pepper to the skillet. Stir-fry for about 5-7 minutes, or until the vegetables are tender.

5. Remove the skillet from the heat and let the mixture cool slightly.

6. Arrange the lettuce leaves on a serving platter.

7. Spoon the turkey and vegetable mixture onto each lettuce leaf, dividing it equally.

8. Drizzle the Thai peanut sauce over the filling in each lettuce wrap.

9. Optional: Garnish with additional sliced green onions and chopped peanuts for added flavor and texture.

LEMON GARLIC ROASTED SALMON WITH ROASTED BRUSSELS SPROUTS

Nutrition: Cal 310;Fat 18 g;Carb 12 g;Protein 33 g
Serving 2; Cook time 30 min

Ingredients
FOR THE SALMON:
- 2 salmon fillets (approximately 4-6 ounces each)
- 2 tablespoons lemon juice
- 2 cloves garlic, minced
- 1 tablespoon olive oil
- Salt and pepper to taste

FOR THE BRUSSELS SPROUTS:
- 2 cups Brussels sprouts, trimmed and halved
- 1 tablespoon olive oil
- Salt and pepper to taste

Instructions:
1. Preheat the oven to 400°F (200°C).

2. In a small bowl, combine the lemon juice, minced garlic, olive oil, salt, and pepper. Stir well.

3. Place the salmon fillets in a baking dish and pour the lemon garlic mixture over them. Make sure the fillets are evenly coated.

4. In a separate baking dish, toss the halved Brussels sprouts with olive oil, salt, and pepper.
5. Place both baking dishes in the preheated oven. Roast the salmon for about 15-20 minutes, or until it flakes easily with a fork. Roast the Brussels sprouts for about 15-20 minutes, or until they are tender and slightly browned.
6. Remove the baking dishes from the oven.
7. Serve the roasted salmon with the roasted Brussels sprouts as a side dish.
8. Optional: Garnish with fresh lemon slices and chopped parsley for added flavor and presentation.

BROCCOLI AND CHEESE STUFFED CHICKEN BREAST

Nutrition: Cal 270;Fat 10 g;Carb 6 g;Protein 36 g
Serving 2; Cook time 40 min

Ingredients
- 2 boneless, skinless chicken breasts (approximately 4-6 ounces each)
- 1 cup steamed broccoli florets, chopped
- 1/2 cup shredded low-fat cheddar cheese
- 1/4 cup plain Greek yogurt
- 1/4 teaspoon garlic powder
- 1/4 teaspoon onion powder
- Salt and pepper to taste

Instructions:
1. Preheat the oven to 375°F (190°C).
2. Butterfly the chicken breasts by cutting them horizontally, but not all the way through, creating a pocket for the filling.
3. In a bowl, mix together the chopped broccoli, shredded cheddar cheese, Greek yogurt, garlic powder, onion powder, salt, and pepper.
4. Stuff each chicken breast with the broccoli and cheese mixture, pressing it gently to fill the pocket.
5. Secure the chicken breasts with toothpicks to hold the filling in place.
6. Heat a non-stick skillet over medium heat and lightly spray it with cooking spray.
7. Sear the stuffed chicken breasts in the skillet for about 2-3 minutes on each side until lightly browned.
8. Transfer the chicken breasts to a baking dish and place them in the preheated oven.

9. Bake for approximately 25-30 minutes or until the chicken is cooked through and no longer pink in the center.
10. Remove the toothpicks before serving.
11. Serve the broccoli and cheese stuffed chicken breast with a side of steamed vegetables or a fresh salad.

GREEK YOGURT TUNA SALAD WITH CELERY AND DILL

Nutrition: Cal 200;Fat 4 g;Carb 6 g;Protein 28 g
Serving 2; Cook time 10 min

Ingredients
- 2 cans of tuna (in water), drained
- 1/2 cup plain Greek yogurt
- 2 tablespoons lemon juice
- 1/4 cup diced celery
- 1/4 cup chopped fresh dill
- Salt and pepper to taste

Instructions:
1. In a medium-sized bowl, combine the drained tuna, plain Greek yogurt, lemon juice, diced celery, and chopped fresh dill.
2. Mix well until all the ingredients are thoroughly combined.
3. Season with salt and pepper to taste.
4. Serve the Greek yogurt tuna salad on its own, or use it as a filling for lettuce wraps or whole-grain bread.
5. Enjoy your light and flavorful Greek yogurt tuna salad with the freshness of celery and dill!

SHRIMP AND AVOCADO CEVICHE WITH LIME DRESSING

Nutrition: Cal 200;Fat 10 g;Carb 10 g;Protein 20 g
Serving 2; Cook time 20 min

Ingredients
- 1/2 pound shrimp, cooked and peeled
- 1 ripe avocado, diced
- 1/4 cup red onion, finely chopped
- 1/4 cup cucumber, diced
- 1/4 cup cherry tomatoes, halved
- 2 tablespoons fresh cilantro, chopped
- Juice of 2 limes
- 1 tablespoon extra-virgin olive oil
- Salt and pepper to taste

Instructions:

1. In a medium bowl, combine the cooked shrimp, diced avocado, red onion, cucumber, cherry tomatoes, and chopped cilantro.
2. In a small bowl, whisk together the lime juice, extra-virgin olive oil, salt, and pepper.
3. Pour the lime dressing over the shrimp and avocado mixture and gently toss to coat.
4. Let the ceviche sit for about 10 minutes to allow the flavors to meld together.
5. Serve the shrimp and avocado ceviche chilled.
6. You can enjoy it as is or serve it with lettuce leaves, whole-grain crackers, or baked tortilla chips for a light and refreshing meal.

ZUCCHINI NOODLES WITH PESTO AND GRILLED CHICKEN

Nutrition: Cal 300;Fat 15 g;Carb 10 g;Protein 30 g
Serving 2; Cook time 30 min

Ingredients
- 2 medium-sized zucchini
- 2 boneless, skinless chicken breasts
- 2 tablespoons pesto sauce
- 1 tablespoon olive oil
- Salt and pepper to taste

FOR THE PESTO SAUCE:
- 1 cup fresh basil leaves
- 1/4 cup grated Parmesan cheese
- 1/4 cup pine nuts
- 1 clove garlic
- 2 tablespoons olive oil
- Salt and pepper to taste

Instructions:
1. Preheat the grill to medium-high heat.
2. In a food processor or blender, combine the basil leaves, grated Parmesan cheese, pine nuts, garlic, olive oil, salt, and pepper. Blend until smooth to make the pesto sauce.
3. Spiralize the zucchini to create zucchini noodles.
4. Season the chicken breasts with salt and pepper, then brush them with olive oil.
5. Grill the chicken breasts for about 6-8 minutes per side or until cooked through. Allow them to rest for a few minutes before slicing.
6. In a large skillet, heat the olive oil over medium heat. Add the zucchini noodles and sauté for 3-4 minutes or until they are slightly softened.
7. Remove the skillet from heat and toss the zucchini noodles with the pesto sauce until well coated.
8. Divide the zucchini noodles onto plates and top with sliced grilled chicken.
9. Garnish with additional Parmesan cheese and fresh basil, if desired.

LENTIL AND VEGETABLE STIR-FRY

Nutrition: Cal 250;Fat 6 g;Carb 40 g;Protein 12 g
Serving 2; Cook time 20 min

Ingredients
- 1 cup cooked lentils
- 1 cup mixed vegetables (such as bell peppers, carrots, snap peas, broccoli)
- 1/2 onion, thinly sliced
- 2 cloves garlic, minced
- 1 tablespoon low-sodium soy sauce
- 1 tablespoon sesame oil
- 1 teaspoon grated ginger
- Salt and pepper to taste
- Optional toppings: chopped green onions, sesame seeds

Instructions:
1. Heat the sesame oil in a large skillet or wok over medium heat.
2. Add the onion and garlic to the skillet and sauté until the onion becomes translucent.
3. Add the mixed vegetables to the skillet and stir-fry for about 5-7 minutes until they are tender-crisp.
4. Add the cooked lentils to the skillet and stir to combine with the vegetables.
5. In a small bowl, whisk together the low-sodium soy sauce and grated ginger.
6. Pour the soy sauce mixture over the lentils and vegetables, and stir to coat evenly.
7. Cook for an additional 2-3 minutes, until everything is heated through.
8. Season with salt and pepper to taste.
9. Remove from heat and garnish with chopped green onions and sesame seeds, if desired.

GREEK SALAD WITH GRILLED CHICKEN

Nutrition: Cal 300;Fat 15 g;Carb 12 g;Protein 31 g

Serving 2; Cook time 25 min

Ingredients
- 2 boneless, skinless chicken breasts
- 4 cups mixed salad greens
- 1 cup cherry tomatoes, halved
- 1 cucumber, sliced
- 1/2 red onion, thinly sliced
- 1/2 cup Kalamata olives, pitted
- 1/2 cup crumbled feta cheese
- 2 tablespoons extra virgin olive oil
- 1 tablespoon lemon juice
- 1 teaspoon dried oregano
- Salt and pepper to taste

Instructions:
1. Preheat the grill to medium-high heat.
2. Season the chicken breasts with salt, pepper, and dried oregano.
3. Grill the chicken breasts for about 6-8 minutes per side or until cooked through. Allow them to rest for a few minutes before slicing.
4. In a large salad bowl, combine the mixed salad greens, cherry tomatoes, cucumber, red onion, Kalamata olives, and crumbled feta cheese.
5. In a small bowl, whisk together the extra virgin olive oil, lemon juice, salt, and pepper to make the dressing.
6. Pour the dressing over the salad ingredients and toss to coat evenly.
7. Slice the grilled chicken breasts into thin strips.
8. Divide the salad onto plates and top with the grilled chicken slices.

QUINOA AND ROASTED VEGETABLE SALAD WITH FETA CHEESE AND LEMON DRESSING

Nutrition: Cal 350;Fat 12 g;Carb 35 g;Protein 10 g
Serving 2; Cook time 35 min

Ingredients
- 1 cup quinoa
- 2 cups water or low-sodium vegetable broth
- 1 small zucchini, diced
- 1 red bell pepper, diced
- 1 yellow bell pepper, diced
- 1 small red onion, thinly sliced
- 1 tablespoon olive oil
- Salt and pepper to taste
- 1/4 cup crumbled feta cheese
- Fresh parsley or basil for garnish

FOR THE DRESSING:
- 2 tablespoons olive oil
- 2 tablespoons lemon juice
- 1 clove garlic, minced
- 1 teaspoon Dijon mustard
- Salt and pepper to taste

Instructions:
1. Preheat the oven to 400°F (200°C).
2. Rinse the quinoa under cold water to remove any bitterness.
3. In a medium saucepan, bring the water or vegetable broth to a boil. Add the rinsed quinoa, reduce the heat to low, cover, and simmer for about 15 minutes or until the quinoa is tender and the water is absorbed. Remove from heat and let it cool.
4. While the quinoa is cooking, prepare the roasted vegetables. In a baking sheet, toss the diced zucchini, red bell pepper, yellow bell pepper, and red onion with olive oil, salt, and pepper. Spread them in a single layer and roast in the preheated oven for about 15-20 minutes or until the vegetables are tender and slightly caramelized. Remove from the oven and let them cool.
5. In a small bowl, whisk together the olive oil, lemon juice, minced garlic, Dijon mustard, salt, and pepper to make the dressing.
6. In a large mixing bowl, combine the cooked quinoa, roasted vegetables, and crumbled feta cheese.
7. Pour the dressing over the quinoa and vegetable mixture and toss gently to coat everything evenly.
8. Taste and adjust the seasoning if needed.
9. Let the salad sit for about 10-15 minutes to allow the flavors to meld together.
10. Garnish with fresh parsley or basil before serving.

TUNA AND WHITE BEAN WRAP WITH LETTUCE

Nutrition: Cal 250;Fat 6 g;Carb 20 g;Protein 20 g
Serving 2; Cook time 15 min

Ingredients
- 1 can of tuna in water, drained
- 1/2 cup white beans, drained and rinsed
- 2 tablespoons low-fat mayonnaise
- 1 tablespoon Dijon mustard
- 1 tablespoon lemon juice
- Salt and pepper to taste
- 4 large lettuce leaves (such as romaine or iceberg)
- Optional toppings: sliced tomatoes, cucumber, red onion

Instructions:
1. In a medium bowl, combine the drained tuna, white beans, low-fat mayonnaise, Dijon mustard, lemon juice, salt, and pepper. Mix well to combine all the ingredients.
2. Taste the mixture and adjust the seasoning if needed.
3. Lay out the lettuce leaves on a clean surface or plate.
4. Divide the tuna and white bean mixture evenly among the lettuce leaves, placing it in the center of each leaf.
5. If desired, add additional toppings such as sliced tomatoes, cucumber, or red onion.
6. Fold the sides of the lettuce leaves over the filling, then roll up tightly to form a wrap.
7. Secure the wraps with toothpicks if necessary.
8. Serve immediately or wrap in foil or parchment paper for later consumption.

SHRIMP AND BROCCOLI STIR-FRY WITH GARLIC

Nutrition: Cal 250;Fat 9 g;Carb 12 g;Protein 25 g

Serving 2; Cook time 20 min

Ingredients
- 8 oz (225g) shrimp, peeled and deveined
- 2 cups broccoli florets
- 2 cloves garlic, minced
- 2 tablespoons low-sodium soy sauce
- 1 tablespoon olive oil
- 1/2 teaspoon sesame oil (optional)
- Salt and pepper to taste

Instructions:
1. Heat the olive oil in a large skillet or wok over medium heat.
2. Add the minced garlic and sauté for about 1 minute until fragrant.
3. Add the broccoli florets to the skillet and stir-fry for 3-4 minutes until slightly tender.
4. Push the broccoli to one side of the skillet and add the shrimp to the other side.
5. Cook the shrimp for 2-3 minutes on each side until they turn pink and opaque.
6. Mix the shrimp and broccoli together in the skillet.
7. Drizzle the low-sodium soy sauce and sesame oil (if using) over the shrimp and broccoli.
8. Season with salt and pepper to taste.
9. Continue to stir-fry for another 1-2 minutes until everything is well-coated and heated through.
10. Remove from heat and serve the shrimp and broccoli stir-fry hot.

GRILLED CHICKEN AND VEGETABLE SKEWERS

Nutrition: Cal 250;Fat 9 g;Carb 12 g;Protein 35 g
Serving 2; Cook time 25 min

Ingredients
- 2 boneless, skinless chicken breasts, cut into cubes
- 1 zucchini, sliced into rounds
- 1 red bell pepper, cut into chunks
- 1 red onion, cut into chunks
- 8 cherry tomatoes
- 2 tablespoons olive oil
- 2 cloves garlic, minced
- 1 teaspoon dried herbs (such as oregano, basil, or thyme)
- Salt and pepper to taste

FOR THE MARINADE:
- 2 tablespoons lemon juice
- 1 tablespoon low-sodium soy sauce
- 1 tablespoon olive oil
- 1 teaspoon Dijon mustard

Instructions:
1. In a bowl, whisk together the ingredients for the marinade: lemon juice, low-sodium soy sauce, olive oil, and Dijon mustard.
2. Add the chicken cubes to the marinade and toss to coat. Allow the chicken to marinate in the refrigerator for at least 15 minutes.
3. Preheat the grill or grill pan over medium-high heat.
4. In a separate bowl, combine the olive oil, minced garlic, dried herbs, salt, and pepper.
5. Thread the marinated chicken cubes onto skewers, alternating with the zucchini rounds, red bell pepper chunks, red onion chunks, and cherry tomatoes.
6. Brush the olive oil and herb mixture onto the skewered chicken and vegetables.
7. Place the skewers on the preheated grill and cook for 10-12 minutes, turning occasionally, until the chicken is cooked through and the vegetables are tender.
8. Remove the skewers from the grill and let them rest for a few minutes before serving.
9. Serve the grilled chicken and vegetable skewers hot.

STUFFED BELL PEPPERS WITH LEAN GROUND TURKEY, QUINOA, AND SALSA

Nutrition: Cal 250;Fat 6 g;Carb 20 g;Protein 25 g
Serving 2; Cook time 45 min

Ingredients
- 2 large bell peppers (any color)
- 1/2 pound lean ground turkey
- 1/2 cup cooked quinoa
- 1/4 cup salsa (choose a low-sodium or sugar-free option)
- 1/4 cup diced onion
- 1/4 cup diced bell pepper (from the tops of the bell peppers)
- 1 clove garlic, minced
- 1/2 teaspoon ground cumin
- 1/2 teaspoon chili powder
- Salt and pepper to taste

- Optional toppings: shredded low-fat cheese, chopped fresh cilantro

Instructions:

1. Preheat the oven to 375°F (190°C).
2. Cut the tops off the bell peppers and remove the seeds and membranes. Reserve the diced bell pepper from the tops for later use.
3. In a skillet, cook the lean ground turkey over medium heat until browned. Drain any excess fat.
4. In the same skillet, add the diced onion, diced bell pepper, and minced garlic. Sauté for a few minutes until the vegetables are tender.
5. Add the cooked quinoa, salsa, ground cumin, chili powder, salt, and pepper to the skillet. Stir well to combine.
6. Spoon the turkey and quinoa mixture into the hollowed-out bell peppers, filling them evenly.
7. Place the stuffed bell peppers in a baking dish and cover with foil.
8. Bake in the preheated oven for 25-30 minutes or until the bell peppers are tender.
9. If desired, remove the foil, sprinkle shredded low-fat cheese on top of the stuffed bell peppers, and return to the oven for an additional 5 minutes or until the cheese is melted and bubbly.
10. Remove from the oven and let cool for a few minutes.
11. Serve the stuffed bell peppers hot, garnished with chopped fresh cilantro if desired.

SPINACH AND FETA STUFFED MUSHROOMS

Nutrition: Cal 180;Fat 12 g;Carb 12 g;Protein 10 g
Serving 2; Cook time 25 min

Ingredients
FOR SPINACH AND FETA STUFFED MUSHROOMS   :
- 8 large white mushrooms
- 1 cup fresh spinach, chopped
- 1/4 cup crumbled feta cheese
- 1 clove garlic, minced
- 1 tablespoon olive oil
- Salt and pepper to taste
FOR MIXED GREENS SALAD:
- 4 cups mixed salad greens
- 1/2 cup cherry tomatoes, halved

- 1/4 cup sliced cucumber
- 1/4 cup sliced red onion
- 1 tablespoon balsamic vinegar
- 1 tablespoon extra virgin olive oil
- Salt and pepper to taste

Instructions:

1. Preheat the oven to 375°F (190°C).
2. Clean the mushrooms and remove the stems. Set the mushroom caps aside.
3. Finely chop the mushroom stems.
4. Heat the olive oil in a skillet over medium heat. Add the chopped mushroom stems and minced garlic. Sauté for 2-3 minutes until the mushrooms are tender.
5. Add the chopped spinach to the skillet and cook for another 2 minutes until the spinach is wilted.
6. Remove the skillet from heat and let it cool for a few minutes.
7. Stir in the crumbled feta cheese and season with salt and pepper to taste.
8. Stuff the mushroom caps with the spinach and feta mixture, pressing it down gently.
9. Place the stuffed mushrooms on a baking sheet lined with parchment paper.
10. Bake in the preheated oven for 15-20 minutes, or until the mushrooms are tender and the cheese is slightly browned.
11. While the mushrooms are baking, prepare the mixed greens salad. In a large bowl, combine the mixed salad greens, cherry tomatoes, sliced cucumber, and sliced red onion.
12. In a small bowl, whisk together the balsamic vinegar, extra virgin olive oil, salt, and pepper to make the dressing.
13. Drizzle the dressing over the salad and toss to coat evenly.
14. Serve the spinach and feta stuffed mushrooms alongside the mixed greens salad.

LENTIL SOUP WITH VEGETABLES AND HERBS

Nutrition: Cal 250;Fat 5 g;Carb 40 g;Protein 15 g
Serving 2; Cook time 45 min

Ingredients
- 1 cup dry green or brown lentils
- 4 cups low-sodium vegetable broth

- 1 tablespoon olive oil
- 1 onion, chopped
- 2 carrots, diced
- 2 celery stalks, diced
- 2 cloves garlic, minced
- 1 teaspoon ground cumin
- 1 teaspoon dried thyme
- 1 bay leaf
- 1 cup diced tomatoes (canned or fresh)
- 2 cups chopped vegetables (such as zucchini, bell peppers, or spinach)
- Salt and pepper to taste
- Fresh herbs for garnish (such as parsley or cilantro)

Instructions:

1. Rinse the lentils under cold water and drain.
2. In a large pot, heat the olive oil over medium heat. Add the chopped onion, carrots, and celery. Sauté for about 5 minutes until the vegetables start to soften.
3. Add the minced garlic, ground cumin, dried thyme, and bay leaf to the pot. Stir and cook for another minute until fragrant.
4. Add the lentils and vegetable broth to the pot. Bring to a boil, then reduce the heat to low and cover the pot. Simmer for about 20-25 minutes until the lentils are tender.
5. Add the diced tomatoes and chopped vegetables to the pot. Cook for an additional 10 minutes until the vegetables are cooked to your desired tenderness.
6. Season the soup with salt and pepper to taste.
7. Remove the bay leaf from the pot before serving.
8. Ladle the lentil soup into bowls and garnish with fresh herbs.

GREEK YOGURT CHICKEN SALAD WITH GRAPES AND ALMONDS

Nutrition: Cal 230;Fat 10 g;Carb 10 g;Protein 30 g
Serving 2; Cook time 10 min

Ingredients

- 2 cups cooked chicken breast, diced
- 1/2 cup plain Greek yogurt
- 1/4 cup diced red onion
- 1/4 cup diced celery
- 1/2 cup halved seedless grapes
- 1/4 cup sliced almonds
- 1 tablespoon lemon juice
- 1 tablespoon chopped fresh dill (optional)
- Salt and pepper to taste
- Lettuce leaves for serving

Instructions:

1. In a large bowl, combine the diced chicken breast, Greek yogurt, red onion, celery, grapes, sliced almonds, lemon juice, and chopped fresh dill (if using). Mix well to combine.
2. Season the chicken salad with salt and pepper to taste. Adjust the seasoning according to your preference.
3. Refrigerate the chicken salad for at least 30 minutes to allow the flavors to meld together.
4. When ready to serve, place a scoop of the Greek yogurt chicken salad onto each lettuce leaf.
5. Serve chilled and enjoy!

ZUCCHINI NOODLES WITH MARINARA SAUCE AND LEAN GROUND BEEF

Nutrition: Cal 250;Fat 10 g;Carb 15 g;Protein 22 g
Serving 2; Cook time 20 min

Ingredients

- 2 medium zucchini
- 1/2 pound lean ground beef
- 1 cup marinara sauce (low-sodium and sugar-free)
- 1 garlic clove, minced
- 1/4 teaspoon dried oregano
- 1/4 teaspoon dried basil
- Salt and pepper to taste
- Fresh basil leaves for garnish (optional)

Instructions:

1. Spiralize the zucchini into noodles using a spiralizer or julienne peeler. Set aside.
2. In a large non-stick skillet, cook the lean ground beef over medium heat until browned. Break it up into crumbles using a spatula.
3. Add the minced garlic, dried oregano, dried basil, salt, and pepper to the skillet. Stir well to combine.
4. Pour the marinara sauce into the skillet with the ground beef. Stir to coat the beef with the sauce. Simmer for 5-7 minutes until heated through.
5. In a separate non-stick skillet, lightly sauté the zucchini noodles for 2-3 minutes until they are

just tender. Avoid overcooking to maintain a slight crunch.

6.Divide the zucchini noodles between two plates and top with the marinara sauce and ground beef mixture.

7.Garnish with fresh basil leaves if desired

TURKEY AND AVOCADO ROLL-UPS WITH LETTUCE AND MUSTARD

Nutrition: Cal 205;Fat 9 g;Carb 9 g;Protein 22 g
Serving 2; Cook time 10 min

Ingredients
•6 slices of low-sodium turkey breast
•1 ripe avocado, sliced
•6 large lettuce leaves
•2 tablespoons mustard (choose a low-sodium variety)

Instructions:
1.Lay out the turkey slices on a clean surface.

2.Spread a thin layer of mustard on each slice of turkey.

3.Place a lettuce leaf on top of each turkey slice.

4.Lay a few slices of avocado on each lettuce leaf.

5.Roll up the turkey slices tightly around the avocado and lettuce, starting from one end. Secure with toothpicks if necessary.

6.Repeat the process with the remaining turkey slices, avocado, and lettuce leaves.

7.Serve the turkey and avocado roll-ups as a light meal or snack.

QUINOA AND BLACK BEAN STUFFED TOMATOES WITH CILANTRO

Nutrition: Cal 190;Fat 3 g;Carb 33 g;Protein 7 g
Serving 2; Cook time 20 min

Ingredients
•2 large tomatoes
•1/2 cup cooked quinoa
•1/2 cup canned black beans, rinsed and drained
•1/4 cup chopped fresh cilantro
•1/4 cup diced red onion
•1/4 cup diced bell pepper
•1 tablespoon lime juice
•Salt and pepper to taste

Instructions:
1.Preheat the oven to 350°F (175°C).

2.Slice off the tops of the tomatoes and scoop out the pulp and seeds, creating a hollow space for stuffing. Reserve the pulp for other use or discard.

3.In a mixing bowl, combine the cooked quinoa, black beans, cilantro, red onion, bell pepper, lime juice, salt, and pepper. Mix well to combine.

4.Stuff each tomato with the quinoa and black bean mixture, pressing gently to fill the hollow space completely.

5.Place the stuffed tomatoes on a baking sheet and bake in the preheated oven for about 15 minutes, or until the tomatoes are tender.

6.Remove from the oven and let the stuffed tomatoes cool for a few minutes.

7.Serve the quinoa and black bean stuffed tomatoes as a light and healthy meal option.

BAKED SALMON WITH LEMON DILL SAUCE AND STEAMED ASPARAGUS

Nutrition: Cal 300;Fat 17 g;Carb 6 g;Protein 33 g
Serving 2; Cook time 30 min

Ingredients
•2 salmon fillets (4-6 ounces each)
•Salt and pepper to taste
•1 lemon, sliced
•Fresh dill sprigs for garnish

FOR THE LEMON DILL SAUCE:
•1/4 cup plain Greek yogurt
•1 tablespoon fresh lemon juice
•1 teaspoon Dijon mustard
•1 tablespoon chopped fresh dill
•Salt and pepper to taste

FOR THE STEAMED ASPARAGUS:
•1 bunch of asparagus, trimmed
•Salt to taste

Instructions:
1.Preheat the oven to 400°F (200°C).

2.Season the salmon fillets with salt and pepper on both sides. Place them on a baking sheet lined with parchment paper.

3.Arrange lemon slices on top of the salmon fillets.

4.Bake the salmon in the preheated oven for about 15-20 minutes, or until it is cooked through and flakes easily with a fork.

5. While the salmon is baking, prepare the lemon dill sauce. In a small bowl, whisk together the Greek yogurt, lemon juice, Dijon mustard, chopped dill, salt, and pepper.

6. Steam the asparagus by placing it in a steamer basket over boiling water for about 5-7 minutes, or until tender. Alternatively, you can microwave the asparagus with a small amount of water for 3-4 minutes.

7. Arrange the cooked salmon and steamed asparagus on serving plates. Drizzle the lemon dill sauce over the salmon fillets.

8. Garnish with fresh dill sprigs.

9. Serve the baked salmon with lemon dill sauce and steamed asparagus as a nutritious and satisfying meal.

CAPRESE SKEWERS WITH CHERRY TOMATOES, MOZZARELLA, AND BASIL

Nutrition: Cal 150;Fat 8 g;Carb 14 g;Protein 8 g
Serving 2; Cook time 15 min

Ingredients
- 1 cup cherry tomatoes
- 8 small mozzarella balls (about 1-inch in diameter)
- Fresh basil leaves
- Balsamic glaze for drizzling
- Salt and pepper to taste
- Wooden skewers

Instructions:
1. Rinse the cherry tomatoes and pat them dry with a paper towel. Set aside.
2. Thread one cherry tomato onto a wooden skewer, followed by a small mozzarella ball and a fresh basil leaf. Repeat this pattern until the skewer is filled.
3. Repeat the process with the remaining ingredients to make more skewers.
4. Season the skewers with salt and pepper to taste.
5. Arrange the Caprese skewers on a serving platter.
6. Drizzle balsamic glaze over the skewers.
7. Serve the Caprese skewers as a light and flavorful appetizer or snack.

GREEK-STYLE STUFFED PEPPERS WITH GROUND CHICKEN AND QUINOA

Nutrition: Cal 300;Fat 10 g;Carb 22 g;Protein 27 g
Serving 2; Cook time 45 min

Ingredients
- 2 large bell peppers (any color)
- 8 oz ground chicken
- 1/2 cup cooked quinoa
- 1/4 cup diced red onion
- 1/4 cup diced cucumber
- 1/4 cup diced tomatoes
- 2 tbsp crumbled feta cheese
- 1 tbsp chopped fresh parsley
- 1 tbsp lemon juice
- 1 tsp dried oregano
- Salt and pepper to taste

Instructions:
1. Preheat the oven to 375°F (190°C).
2. Cut the tops off the bell peppers and remove the seeds and membranes. Rinse them and set aside.
3. In a skillet, cook the ground chicken over medium heat until no longer pink. Season with salt, pepper, and dried oregano.
4. In a mixing bowl, combine the cooked ground chicken, cooked quinoa, red onion, cucumber, tomatoes, feta cheese, parsley, and lemon juice. Mix well.
5. Stuff the mixture into the hollowed-out bell peppers, pressing it down gently.
6. Place the stuffed peppers in a baking dish and cover with foil.
7. Bake in the preheated oven for 30 minutes.
8. Remove the foil and bake for an additional 10-15 minutes, or until the peppers are tender and the filling is heated through.
9. Serve the Greek-style stuffed peppers as a nutritious and satisfying meal.

TURKEY AND BLACK BEAN LETTUCE WRAPS WITH SALSA AND AVOCADO

Nutrition: Cal 250;Fat 10 g;Carb 15 g;Protein 20 g
Serving 2; Cook time 20 min

Ingredients

- 8 large lettuce leaves (such as romaine or butter lettuce)
- 8 oz lean ground turkey
- 1/2 cup canned black beans, rinsed and drained
- 1/4 cup diced red onion
- 1/4 cup diced bell pepper
- 2 cloves garlic, minced
- 1 tsp cumin
- 1/2 tsp chili powder
- Salt and pepper to taste
- 1/2 cup salsa
- 1 small avocado, diced

Instructions:

1. Heat a non-stick skillet over medium heat.
2. Add the ground turkey, red onion, bell pepper, and garlic to the skillet. Cook until the turkey is browned and cooked through, breaking it up into small pieces with a spoon.
3. Season the turkey mixture with cumin, chili powder, salt, and pepper. Stir well to combine.
4. Add the black beans to the skillet and cook for an additional 2-3 minutes to heat through.
5. Remove the skillet from heat and set aside.
6. Wash and dry the lettuce leaves. Arrange them on a serving platter.
7. Spoon the turkey and black bean mixture onto each lettuce leaf.
8. Top each lettuce wrap with salsa and diced avocado.
9. Serve the turkey and black bean lettuce wraps as a light and flavorful meal.

DINNER

GRILLED LEMON HERB CHICKEN BREAST

Nutrition: Cal 200;Fat 5 g;Carb 1 g;Protein 25 g
Serving 2; Cook time 20 min

Ingredients
- 2 boneless, skinless chicken breasts
- 1 lemon, juiced and zested
- 2 cloves garlic, minced
- 1 tsp dried oregano
- 1 tsp dried thyme
- Salt and pepper to taste
- Cooking spray

Instructions:
1. In a small bowl, combine the lemon juice, lemon zest, minced garlic, dried oregano, dried thyme, salt, and pepper to create the marinade.
2. Place the chicken breasts in a shallow dish or resealable plastic bag. Pour the marinade over the chicken, ensuring it is well coated. Let it marinate in the refrigerator for at least 30 minutes (or up to 4 hours for more flavor).
3. Preheat the grill to medium-high heat.
4. Remove the chicken breasts from the marinade and discard the excess marinade.
5. Lightly coat the grill grates with cooking spray to prevent sticking.
6. Place the chicken breasts on the preheated grill and cook for about 6-8 minutes per side, or until the internal temperature reaches 165°F (75°C) using a meat thermometer.
7. Remove the chicken from the grill and let it rest for a few minutes before serving.
8. Slice the grilled lemon herb chicken breast and serve it with your choice of side dishes, such as steamed vegetables or a mixed green salad.

BAKED COD WITH LEMON AND DILL

Nutrition: Cal 200;Fat 5 g;Carb 1 g;Protein 25 g
Serving 2; Cook time 25 min

Ingredients
- 2 cod fillets (approximately 4-6 ounces each)
- 1 lemon, sliced
- 2 tablespoons fresh dill, chopped
- 1 tablespoon olive oil
- Salt and pepper to taste

Instructions:
1. Preheat the oven to 400°F (200°C) and lightly grease a baking dish with olive oil or cooking spray.
2. Rinse the cod fillets and pat them dry with paper towels.
3. Place the cod fillets in the prepared baking dish and season them with salt and pepper to taste.
4. Drizzle the olive oil over the fillets, ensuring they are coated evenly.
5. Sprinkle the fresh dill over the cod fillets, pressing it lightly to adhere.
6. Arrange the lemon slices on top of the fillets.
7. Cover the baking dish with aluminum foil and bake in the preheated oven for approximately 15-20 minutes, or until the fish is opaque and easily flakes with a fork.
8. Remove the foil and broil for an additional 2-3 minutes to lightly brown the top.
9. Carefully transfer the baked cod fillets to serving plates and garnish with additional fresh dill if desired.
10. Serve the baked cod with steamed vegetables or a side salad for a complete and nutritious meal.

TURKEY MEATLOAF MUFFINS WITH CAULIFLOWER MASH

Nutrition: Cal 270;Fat 12 g;Carb 12 g;Protein 25 g
Serving 2; Cook time 45 min

Ingredients
FOR TURKEY MEATLOAF MUFFINS:
- 1 pound ground turkey (lean)
- 1/2 cup finely chopped onion
- 1/2 cup grated zucchini
- 1/4 cup grated carrot
- 1/4 cup almond flour
- 1/4 cup low-sodium tomato sauce
- 1 large egg
- 1 teaspoon Worcestershire sauce
- 1/2 teaspoon garlic powder
- 1/2 teaspoon dried thyme
- Salt and pepper to taste
FOR CAULIFLOWER MASH:
- 1 small head cauliflower, cut into florets
- 2 tablespoons unsalted butter
- 1/4 cup low-fat milk
- Salt and pepper to taste

Instructions:

1. Preheat the oven to 375°F (190°C) and lightly grease a muffin tin with olive oil or cooking spray.

2. In a large mixing bowl, combine the ground turkey, chopped onion, grated zucchini, grated carrot, almond flour, tomato sauce, egg, Worcestershire sauce, garlic powder, dried thyme, salt, and pepper. Mix well until all ingredients are evenly incorporated.

3. Divide the turkey mixture evenly among the muffin tin cups, filling them to the top.

4. Place the muffin tin in the preheated oven and bake for approximately 25-30 minutes, or until the turkey meatloaf muffins are cooked through and reach an internal temperature of 165°F (74°C).

5. While the meatloaf muffins are baking, prepare the cauliflower mash. Steam or boil the cauliflower florets until they are tender. Drain the cauliflower and transfer it to a food processor.

6. Add the butter, milk, salt, and pepper to the food processor with the cauliflower. Process until the mixture is smooth and creamy.

7. Taste the cauliflower mash and adjust the seasoning if needed.

8. Once the turkey meatloaf muffins are cooked, remove them from the oven and let them cool slightly before removing them from the muffin tin.

9. Serve the turkey meatloaf muffins with a side of cauliflower mash, and enjoy a nutritious and satisfying meal.

ZUCCHINI NOODLES WITH SHRIMP SCAMPI

Nutrition: Cal 200;Fat 11 g;Carb 11 g;Protein 20 g
Serving 2; Cook time 20 min

Ingredients
- 2 medium zucchini
- 8 ounces shrimp, peeled and deveined
- 2 tablespoons olive oil
- 3 cloves garlic, minced
- 1/4 teaspoon red pepper flakes (optional)
- 2 tablespoons lemon juice
- Salt and pepper to taste
- 2 tablespoons chopped fresh parsley
- Grated Parmesan cheese for garnish (optional)

Instructions:

1. Using a spiralizer or julienne peeler, create zucchini noodles from the two zucchini. Set aside.

2. In a large skillet, heat the olive oil over medium heat. Add the minced garlic and red pepper flakes (if using) and sauté for about 1 minute until fragrant.

3. Add the shrimp to the skillet and cook for about 2-3 minutes per side until pink and cooked through. Remove the shrimp from the skillet and set aside.

4. In the same skillet, add the zucchini noodles and lemon juice. Sauté for about 3-4 minutes until the zucchini noodles are slightly softened but still crisp.

5. Return the cooked shrimp to the skillet with the zucchini noodles. Season with salt and pepper to taste. Toss everything together to coat the zucchini noodles and shrimp with the flavors.

6. Remove the skillet from heat and sprinkle chopped parsley over the dish.

7. Serve the zucchini noodles with shrimp scampi immediately. If desired, garnish with grated Parmesan cheese.

CAPRESE CHICKEN WITH ROASTED ASPARAGUS

Nutrition: Cal 370;Fat 19 g;Carb 12 g;Protein 36 g
Serving 2; Cook time 30 min

Ingredients
- 2 boneless, skinless chicken breasts
- 2 tablespoons olive oil
- 2 cloves garlic, minced
- 4 slices fresh mozzarella cheese
- 2 medium tomatoes, sliced
- 1/4 cup fresh basil leaves
- Salt and pepper to taste
- 1 bunch asparagus
- 1 tablespoon balsamic glaze (optional)

Instructions:

1. Preheat the oven to 400°F (200°C). Line a baking sheet with parchment paper.

2. Place the chicken breasts on the prepared baking sheet. Drizzle with olive oil and minced garlic. Season with salt and pepper.

3. Bake the chicken breasts in the preheated oven for about 20-25 minutes or until they reach an internal temperature of 165°F (74°C).
4. While the chicken is baking, prepare the asparagus. Trim off the woody ends and place the asparagus on a separate baking sheet. Drizzle with olive oil and sprinkle with salt and pepper. Toss to coat evenly.
5. After the chicken has baked for about 10 minutes, add the asparagus to the oven. Roast the asparagus for about 10-12 minutes or until tender and slightly crispy.
6. Remove the chicken and asparagus from the oven. Top each chicken breast with a slice of fresh mozzarella cheese. Return to the oven for an additional 2-3 minutes or until the cheese is melted and bubbly.
7. To serve, place a chicken breast on each plate. Top with sliced tomatoes and fresh basil leaves. Arrange the roasted asparagus on the side. Drizzle with balsamic glaze, if desired.

CAULIFLOWER CRUST PIZZA WITH TURKEY PEPPERONI AND VEGGIES

Nutrition: Cal 300;Fat 10 g;Carb 22 g;Protein 25 g
Serving 2; Cook time 45 min

Ingredients
FOR THE CAULIFLOWER CRUST:
• 1 medium head cauliflower
• 1/4 cup grated Parmesan cheese
• 1/4 cup mozzarella cheese, shredded
• 1/2 teaspoon dried oregano
• 1/2 teaspoon garlic powder
• 1/4 teaspoon salt
• 1/4 teaspoon black pepper
• 1 large egg, beaten
FOR THE TOPPINGS:
• 1/2 cup tomato sauce (low-sodium)
• 1/2 cup mozzarella cheese, shredded
• Turkey pepperoni slices
• Assorted vegetables of your choice (such as bell peppers, onions, mushrooms, etc.)
Instructions:
1. Preheat the oven to 425°F (220°C). Line a baking sheet or pizza stone with parchment paper.

2. Cut the cauliflower into florets and transfer them to a food processor. Pulse until the cauliflower is finely ground and resembles rice.
3. Transfer the cauliflower rice to a microwave-safe bowl. Microwave on high for 5-6 minutes until the cauliflower is cooked and softened. Allow it to cool slightly.
4. Place the cooked cauliflower rice on a clean kitchen towel or cheesecloth. Squeeze out as much moisture as possible. This will help create a crispier crust.
5. In a mixing bowl, combine the cauliflower rice, grated Parmesan cheese, shredded mozzarella cheese, dried oregano, garlic powder, salt, black pepper, and beaten egg. Mix well until a dough-like consistency forms.
6. Transfer the cauliflower dough to the prepared baking sheet or pizza stone. Spread it out and shape it into a round pizza crust of desired thickness.
7. Bake the cauliflower crust in the preheated oven for about 20-25 minutes or until golden brown and firm.
8. Remove the crust from the oven and let it cool for a few minutes. Leave the oven on.
9. Once the crust has cooled slightly, spread the tomato sauce evenly over the crust. Sprinkle with shredded mozzarella cheese.
10. Add your desired toppings such as turkey pepperoni slices and assorted vegetables.
11. Return the pizza to the oven and bake for an additional 10-15 minutes, or until the cheese is melted and bubbly.
12. Remove the pizza from the oven and let it cool for a few minutes before slicing.
13. Serve the cauliflower crust pizza hot and enjoy!

GRILLED SALMON WITH QUINOA AND STEAMED GREEN BEANS

Nutrition: Cal 370;Fat 20 g;Carb 22 g;Protein 31 g
Serving 2; Cook time 25 min

Ingredients
• 2 salmon fillets (approximately 4-6 ounces each)
• 1 cup cooked quinoa
• 2 cups green beans, trimmed
• 1 tablespoon olive oil
• 1 tablespoon lemon juice
• Salt and pepper to taste
• Fresh dill or parsley for garnish (optional)
Instructions:

1. Preheat the grill to medium heat. If you don't have a grill, you can use a grill pan or skillet on the stovetop.
2. Season the salmon fillets with salt, pepper, and a drizzle of olive oil. Let them sit for a few minutes to marinate.
3. In the meantime, cook the quinoa according to package instructions if you haven't already. Set aside.
4. Place the green beans in a steamer basket and steam them for about 5-7 minutes until tender-crisp. Remove from heat and set aside.
5. Once the grill is hot, place the salmon fillets skin-side down on the grill grates. Grill for approximately 4-5 minutes per side, or until the salmon is cooked through and easily flakes with a fork. Cooking time may vary depending on the thickness of the fillets.
6. While the salmon is grilling, prepare the lemon dressing by combining the olive oil, lemon juice, salt, and pepper in a small bowl. Whisk until well combined.
7. Once the salmon is cooked, remove it from the grill and let it rest for a few minutes.
8. To serve, divide the cooked quinoa between two plates. Place a grilled salmon fillet on top of each bed of quinoa.
9. Arrange the steamed green beans alongside the salmon.
10. Drizzle the lemon dressing over the salmon and quinoa.
11. Garnish with fresh dill or parsley, if desired.
12. Serve the grilled salmon with quinoa and steamed green beans immediately while still warm.

BEEF AND VEGETABLE STIR-FRY WITH BROWN RICE

Nutrition: Cal 370;Fat 15 g;Carb 35 g;Protein 30 g
Serving 2; Cook time 25 min

Ingredients
- 8 ounces lean beef (such as sirloin or flank steak), thinly sliced
- 2 cups mixed vegetables (such as bell peppers, broccoli, carrots, snap peas), sliced
- 1 tablespoon low-sodium soy sauce
- 1 tablespoon oyster sauce (optional)
- 1 tablespoon sesame oil
- 1 tablespoon olive oil
- 2 cloves garlic, minced
- 1 teaspoon grated ginger
- Salt and pepper to taste

- 1 cup cooked brown rice

Instructions:
1. Heat the olive oil and sesame oil in a large skillet or wok over medium-high heat.
2. Add the minced garlic and grated ginger to the hot oil and sauté for about 1 minute until fragrant.
3. Add the sliced beef to the skillet and stir-fry for 2-3 minutes until browned and cooked through. Remove the beef from the skillet and set aside.
4. In the same skillet, add the mixed vegetables and stir-fry for 3-4 minutes until they are tender-crisp.
5. Return the cooked beef to the skillet with the vegetables.
6. Add the soy sauce and oyster sauce (if using) to the skillet and toss to coat the beef and vegetables evenly. Season with salt and pepper to taste.
7. Cook for an additional 1-2 minutes until everything is heated through.
8. Divide the cooked brown rice between two plates or bowls.
9. Top the rice with the beef and vegetable stir-fry.
10. Garnish with chopped green onions or sesame seeds if desired.
11. Serve the beef and vegetable stir-fry with brown rice immediately.

SPINACH AND FETA STUFFED PORK TENDERLOIN

Nutrition: Cal 280;Fat 14 g;Carb 3 g;Protein 36 g
Serving 2; Cook time 45 min

Ingredients
- 1 pound pork tenderloin
- 2 cups fresh spinach, chopped
- 1/4 cup crumbled feta cheese
- 2 cloves garlic, minced
- 1 tablespoon olive oil
- Salt and pepper to taste

Instructions:
1. Preheat your oven to 375°F (190°C).
2. Cut a slit lengthwise down the center of the pork tenderloin, being careful not to cut all the way through. Open up the slit to create a pocket for the stuffing.
3. In a skillet, heat the olive oil over medium heat. Add the minced garlic and sauté for 1-2 minutes until fragrant.

4. Add the chopped spinach to the skillet and cook until wilted, about 2-3 minutes. Remove from heat.
5. Stir in the crumbled feta cheese into the cooked spinach mixture until well combined.
6. Season the pork tenderloin with salt and pepper to taste.
7. Stuff the spinach and feta mixture into the pocket of the pork tenderloin, pressing it in evenly.
8. Secure the opening of the pork tenderloin with kitchen twine or toothpicks to hold the stuffing inside.
9. Place the stuffed pork tenderloin on a baking sheet or in a roasting pan.
10. Bake in the preheated oven for 25-30 minutes, or until the internal temperature of the pork reaches 145°F (63°C) for medium doneness.
11. Remove the pork tenderloin from the oven and let it rest for a few minutes before slicing.
12. Slice the stuffed pork tenderloin into medallions and serve with your choice of side dishes such as steamed vegetables or a green salad.

BAKED TILAPIA WITH ROASTED SWEET POTATOES AND ASPARAGUS

Nutrition: Cal 330;Fat 10 g;Carb 33 g;Protein 30 g
Serving 2; Cook time 35 min

Ingredients
- 2 tilapia fillets (about 4-6 ounces each)
- 2 small sweet potatoes, peeled and cut into cubes
- 1 bunch asparagus, trimmed
- 1 tablespoon olive oil
- 1 teaspoon garlic powder
- 1 teaspoon paprika
- Salt and pepper to taste
- Fresh lemon wedges for serving

Instructions:
1. Preheat your oven to 400°F (200°C).
2. Place the sweet potato cubes on a baking sheet and drizzle with half of the olive oil. Sprinkle with garlic powder, paprika, salt, and pepper. Toss to coat the sweet potatoes evenly. Roast in the preheated oven for about 15-20 minutes, or until the sweet potatoes are tender and lightly browned.
3. While the sweet potatoes are roasting, prepare the asparagus. Place the trimmed asparagus on another baking sheet and drizzle with the remaining olive oil. Season with salt and pepper to taste. Toss to coat the asparagus evenly. Add the asparagus to the oven during the last 10 minutes of cooking time for the sweet potatoes.
4. Season the tilapia fillets with salt, pepper, and a sprinkle of garlic powder. Place the seasoned tilapia fillets on a separate baking sheet lined with parchment paper.
5. Once the sweet potatoes and asparagus have roasted for the allotted time, remove them from the oven and set aside. Place the baking sheet with the tilapia fillets in the oven and bake for about 10-12 minutes, or until the fish is cooked through and flakes easily with a fork.
6. Divide the baked tilapia fillets, roasted sweet potatoes, and asparagus between two plates.
7. Serve with fresh lemon wedges for squeezing over the fish, if desired.

CHICKEN FAJITA BOWL WITH BROWN RICE, BLACK BEANS, AND SALSA

Nutrition: Cal 400;Fat 10 g;Carb 47 g;Protein 33 g
Serving 2; Cook time 30 min

Ingredients
FOR THE CHICKEN FAJITAS:
- 2 boneless, skinless chicken breasts (about 4-6 ounces each), sliced into thin strips
- 1 red bell pepper, sliced
- 1 green bell pepper, sliced
- 1 small onion, sliced
- 1 tablespoon olive oil
- 1 teaspoon chili powder
- 1/2 teaspoon cumin
- 1/2 teaspoon paprika
- Salt and pepper to taste

FOR THE BROWN RICE AND BLACK BEANS:
- 1 cup cooked brown rice
- 1 cup canned black beans, rinsed and drained

FOR THE SALSA:
- 1/2 cup diced tomatoes
- 1/4 cup diced red onion
- 1/4 cup chopped cilantro
- 1 tablespoon lime juice
- Salt and pepper to taste

OPTIONAL TOPPINGS:
- Greek yogurt or low-fat sour cream
- Sliced avocado
- Lime wedges

Instructions:
1. In a small bowl, combine the chili powder, cumin, paprika, salt, and pepper. Set aside.
2. Heat the olive oil in a large skillet over medium-high heat. Add the sliced chicken and cook for about 4-6 minutes, or until cooked through. Remove the chicken from the skillet and set aside.
3. In the same skillet, add the sliced bell peppers and onion. Sprinkle the spice mixture over the vegetables and sauté for about 5-7 minutes, or until the vegetables are tender and lightly charred.
4. While the vegetables are cooking, prepare the salsa. In a small bowl, combine the diced tomatoes, diced red onion, chopped cilantro, lime juice, salt, and pepper. Mix well.
5. To assemble the bowls, divide the cooked brown rice and black beans between two bowls. Top with the sautéed chicken fajitas and the cooked bell peppers and onions. Spoon the salsa over the bowls.
6. If desired, garnish the bowls with Greek yogurt or low-fat sour cream, sliced avocado, and a squeeze of fresh lime juice.

TURKEY AND VEGETABLE KEBABS WITH QUINOA SALAD

Nutrition: Cal 350;Fat 15 g;Carb 25 g;Protein 25 g
Serving 2; Cook time 25 min

Ingredients
FOR THE TURKEY AND VEGETABLE KEBABS:
- 8 oz lean ground turkey
- 1 small zucchini, sliced into rounds
- 1 small red bell pepper, cut into chunks
- 1 small red onion, cut into chunks
- 8 cherry tomatoes
- 2 tablespoons olive oil
- 1 tablespoon lemon juice
- 1 teaspoon dried oregano
- Salt and pepper to taste

FOR THE QUINOA SALAD:
- 1/2 cup cooked quinoa
- 1 cup mixed salad greens
- 1/4 cup diced cucumber
- 1/4 cup diced cherry tomatoes
- 1/4 cup diced red onion
- 1 tablespoon chopped fresh parsley
- 1 tablespoon lemon juice
- 1 tablespoon olive oil
- Salt and pepper to taste

Instructions:
1. Preheat the grill or preheat the oven to 400°F (200°C).
2. In a mixing bowl, combine the ground turkey, olive oil, lemon juice, dried oregano, salt, and pepper. Mix well until all the ingredients are evenly incorporated.
3. Divide the turkey mixture into four equal portions and shape each portion into a small log shape. Thread the turkey logs onto skewers, alternating with the zucchini rounds, bell pepper chunks, red onion chunks, and cherry tomatoes.
4. Place the kebabs on the preheated grill or on a baking sheet if using the oven. Grill or bake for about 12-15 minutes, or until the turkey is cooked through and the vegetables are tender.
5. While the kebabs are cooking, prepare the quinoa salad. In a bowl, combine the cooked quinoa, mixed salad greens, diced cucumber, diced cherry tomatoes, diced red onion, chopped parsley, lemon juice, olive oil, salt, and pepper. Toss well to combine.
6. Serve the turkey and vegetable kebabs alongside the quinoa salad.

EGGPLANT PARMESAN WITH SIDE SALAD

Nutrition: Cal 400;Fat 20 g;Carb 30 g;Protein 20 g
Serving 2; Cook time 45 min

Ingredients
FOR EGGPLANT PARMESAN:
- 1 medium eggplant, sliced into 1/2-inch rounds
- 1 cup whole wheat bread crumbs
- 1/4 cup grated Parmesan cheese
- 1 teaspoon dried oregano
- 1 teaspoon dried basil
- 1/2 teaspoon garlic powder
- 2 large eggs, beaten
- 1 cup marinara sauce (low-sodium)

- 1 cup shredded mozzarella cheese (part-skim)
- Olive oil cooking spray
- Fresh basil leaves for garnish (optional)

FOR SIDE SALAD:
- 4 cups mixed greens (spinach, arugula, or lettuce)
- 1/2 cucumber, sliced
- 1/2 cup cherry tomatoes, halved
- 1/4 red onion, thinly sliced
- 1 tablespoon extra-virgin olive oil
- 1 tablespoon balsamic vinegar
- Salt and pepper to taste

Instructions:
1. Preheat the oven to 400°F (200°C). Line a baking sheet with parchment paper.
2. In a shallow bowl, combine whole wheat bread crumbs, grated Parmesan cheese, dried oregano, dried basil, and garlic powder.
3. Dip each eggplant slice into the beaten eggs, allowing the excess to drip off, then coat it with the breadcrumb mixture. Place the coated slices on the prepared baking sheet.
4. Spray the tops of the coated eggplant slices with olive oil cooking spray. This will help them become crispy when baked.
5. Bake the eggplant slices in the preheated oven for about 20-25 minutes, flipping them halfway through, until they are golden and crispy.
6. While the eggplant is baking, prepare the side salad. In a large bowl, combine mixed greens, cucumber, cherry tomatoes, and red onion.
7. In a small bowl, whisk together extra-virgin olive oil, balsamic vinegar, salt, and pepper to make the salad dressing. Drizzle the dressing over the salad and toss to coat.
8. Once the eggplant slices are done, remove them from the oven and reduce the oven temperature to 375°F (190°C).
9. In a baking dish, spread a thin layer of marinara sauce, then place half of the baked eggplant slices on top. Add another layer of marinara sauce and half of the shredded mozzarella cheese.
10. Place the remaining eggplant slices on top, followed by the remaining marinara sauce and shredded mozzarella cheese.

TERIYAKI SALMON WITH BOK CHOY AND BROWN RICE

Nutrition: Cal 350;Fat 10 g;Carb 30 g;Protein 30 g
Serving 2; Cook time 30 min

Ingredients
- 2 salmon fillets (approximately 4-6 ounces each)
- 1/4 cup low-sodium soy sauce
- 2 tablespoons honey
- 1 tablespoon rice vinegar
- 1 teaspoon minced garlic
- 1 teaspoon grated ginger
- 2 heads of baby bok choy, halved lengthwise
- 1 cup cooked brown rice
- Sesame seeds for garnish (optional)
- Sliced green onions for garnish (optional)

Instructions:
1. In a small bowl, whisk together soy sauce, honey, rice vinegar, minced garlic, and grated ginger to make the teriyaki sauce.
2. Place the salmon fillets in a shallow dish and pour half of the teriyaki sauce over them. Reserve the remaining sauce for later.
3. Allow the salmon to marinate in the sauce for about 10 minutes.
4. While the salmon is marinating, prepare the bok choy. Heat a non-stick skillet over medium heat and lightly spray it with cooking oil.
5. Place the bok choy halves cut-side down in the skillet and cook for about 3-4 minutes, or until they are lightly browned. Flip the bok choy and cook for an additional 3-4 minutes until tender.
6. Remove the bok choy from the skillet and set aside.
7. In the same skillet, add the marinated salmon fillets, reserving the marinade. Cook the salmon for about 3-4 minutes on each side, or until it reaches your desired level of doneness.
8. While the salmon is cooking, pour the reserved marinade into a small saucepan and bring it to a boil over medium-high heat. Reduce the heat and simmer for a few minutes until the sauce thickens slightly.
9. Once the salmon is cooked, remove it from the skillet and brush it with the thickened teriyaki sauce.

10. Serve the teriyaki salmon alongside the bok choy and cooked brown rice.
11. Garnish with sesame seeds and sliced green onions if desired.

STUFFED ZUCCHINI BOATS WITH LEAN GROUND TURKEY

Nutrition: Cal 250;Fat 10 g;Carb 15 g;Protein 20 g
Serving 2; Cook time 40 min

Ingredients
- 2 medium-sized zucchini
- 1/2 pound lean ground turkey
- 1/4 cup diced onion
- 1/4 cup diced bell pepper
- 1 clove garlic, minced
- 1/2 teaspoon dried oregano
- 1/2 teaspoon dried basil
- 1/4 teaspoon salt
- 1/4 teaspoon black pepper
- 1/2 cup marinara sauce (low-sugar or homemade)
- 1/4 cup shredded mozzarella cheese (part-skim)
- Fresh parsley for garnish (optional)

Instructions:
1. Preheat your oven to 375°F (190°C).
2. Slice each zucchini in half lengthwise, then scoop out the seeds and flesh from the center, creating hollow "boats." Set aside.
3. In a skillet over medium heat, cook the lean ground turkey until browned and cooked through. Drain any excess fat if necessary.
4. Add the diced onion, bell pepper, minced garlic, dried oregano, dried basil, salt, and black pepper to the skillet with the cooked turkey. Sauté for 3-4 minutes, or until the vegetables are tender.
5. Stir in the marinara sauce and cook for an additional 2 minutes, allowing the flavors to combine.
6. Place the zucchini boats in a baking dish, then spoon the turkey mixture evenly into each boat.
7. Cover the baking dish with foil and bake in the preheated oven for 20 minutes.
8. Remove the foil and sprinkle the shredded mozzarella cheese over the top of each zucchini boat.

9. Return the baking dish to the oven and bake for an additional 5-7 minutes, or until the cheese is melted and lightly browned.
10. Remove from the oven and let the zucchini boats cool for a few minutes.
11. Garnish with fresh parsley if desired and serve.

GARLIC AND HERB ROASTED PORK TENDERLOIN

Nutrition: Cal 250;Fat 8 g;Carb 8 g;Protein 30 g
Serving 2; Cook time 40 min

Ingredients
- 1 pound pork tenderloin
- 2 cloves garlic, minced
- 1 teaspoon dried thyme
- 1 teaspoon dried rosemary
- 1/2 teaspoon salt
- 1/4 teaspoon black pepper
- 1 tablespoon olive oil
- 2 cups broccoli florets
- Lemon wedges for serving (optional)

Instructions:
1. Preheat your oven to 375°F (190°C).
2. In a small bowl, combine the minced garlic, dried thyme, dried rosemary, salt, black pepper, and olive oil to make a herb rub.
3. Pat the pork tenderloin dry with paper towels, then rub the herb mixture all over the pork, ensuring it is evenly coated.
4. Place the pork tenderloin on a baking sheet lined with parchment paper or a lightly greased roasting pan.
5. Roast the pork in the preheated oven for 25-30 minutes, or until the internal temperature reaches 145°F (63°C) when measured with a meat thermometer.
6. While the pork is roasting, steam the broccoli florets. Place the broccoli in a steamer basket over a pot of boiling water and steam for about 5-7 minutes, or until tender-crisp. Alternatively, you can microwave the broccoli with a little water for 2-3 minutes.
7. Once the pork is cooked, remove it from the oven and let it rest for a few minutes before slicing.
8. Slice the pork tenderloin into medallions and serve alongside the steamed broccoli.

9. Optionally, squeeze fresh lemon juice over the pork and broccoli for added flavor.

TURKEY AND VEGETABLE CHILI

Nutrition: Cal 300;Fat 10 g;Carb 25 g;Protein 25 g
Serving 2; Cook time 30 min

Ingredients
- 1 pound ground turkey
- 1 tablespoon olive oil
- 1 onion, diced
- 2 cloves garlic, minced
- 1 bell pepper, diced
- 1 zucchini, diced
- 1 can (14.5 ounces) diced tomatoes
- 1 can (15 ounces) kidney beans, drained and rinsed
- 1 cup low-sodium chicken broth
- 2 tablespoons chili powder
- 1 teaspoon cumin
- 1/2 teaspoon paprika
- 1/2 teaspoon oregano
- Salt and pepper to taste
- Optional toppings: Greek yogurt, shredded cheese, chopped cilantro

Instructions:
1. Heat the olive oil in a large pot or Dutch oven over medium heat. Add the ground turkey and cook until browned, breaking it up with a spoon.
2. Add the diced onion and minced garlic to the pot and cook for 2-3 minutes until the onion is softened.
3. Add the diced bell pepper and zucchini to the pot and cook for another 3-4 minutes until the vegetables are slightly tender.
4. Stir in the diced tomatoes, kidney beans, chicken broth, chili powder, cumin, paprika, oregano, salt, and pepper. Bring the mixture to a simmer.
5. Reduce the heat to low, cover the pot, and let the chili simmer for 15-20 minutes, stirring occasionally.
6. Taste and adjust the seasonings as needed. If you prefer a spicier chili, you can add a pinch of cayenne pepper or red pepper flakes.
7. Serve the turkey and vegetable chili hot, garnished with optional toppings like Greek yogurt, shredded cheese, or chopped cilantro.

GRILLED SHRIMP SKEWERS WITH QUINOA

Nutrition: Cal 350;Fat 10 g;Carb 30 g;Protein 25 g
Serving 2; Cook time 30 min

Ingredients
- 1 pound shrimp, peeled and deveined
- 2 tablespoons olive oil
- 2 cloves garlic, minced
- 1 teaspoon paprika
- Salt and pepper to taste
- 1 cup quinoa
- 2 cups water or low-sodium chicken broth
- 2 cups mixed vegetables (such as bell peppers, zucchini, and cherry tomatoes)
- Cooking spray

Instructions:
1. Preheat your grill to medium heat.
2. In a bowl, combine the shrimp, olive oil, minced garlic, paprika, salt, and pepper. Toss to coat the shrimp evenly with the seasonings.
3. Thread the shrimp onto skewers, dividing them evenly.
4. In a saucepan, rinse the quinoa under cold water. Drain and add it to the saucepan along with the water or chicken broth. Bring to a boil, then reduce the heat to low, cover, and simmer for about 15 minutes or until the quinoa is cooked and the liquid is absorbed. Fluff with a fork.
5. Meanwhile, spread the mixed vegetables on a baking sheet lined with parchment paper. Spray them lightly with cooking spray and season with salt and pepper.
6. Place the baking sheet in the oven and roast the vegetables at 400°F (200°C) for about 15-20 minutes or until they are tender and slightly browned.
7. While the vegetables are roasting, grill the shrimp skewers for about 2-3 minutes per side or until they are opaque and cooked through.
8. Divide the cooked quinoa and roasted vegetables among two plates. Top with the grilled shrimp skewers.

ASIAN-STYLE BEEF LETTUCE WRAPS WITH MUSHROOMS

Nutrition: Cal 250;Fat 10 g;Carb 8 g;Protein 25 g

Serving 2; Cook time 20 min

Ingredients

- 1 pound lean ground beef
- 2 cups mushrooms, finely chopped
- 2 cloves garlic, minced
- 1 tablespoon ginger, grated
- 2 tablespoons low-sodium soy sauce
- 1 tablespoon hoisin sauce
- 1 tablespoon rice vinegar
- 1 tablespoon sesame oil
- 1 teaspoon sriracha sauce (optional, for spicy kick)
- 1 head iceberg or butter lettuce, leaves separated
- Optional toppings: sliced green onions, chopped cilantro, sesame seeds

Instructions:

1. Heat a large skillet or wok over medium heat. Add the ground beef and cook until browned, breaking it up into small crumbles.
2. Add the chopped mushrooms, minced garlic, and grated ginger to the skillet. Stir-fry for about 3-4 minutes or until the mushrooms have softened.
3. In a small bowl, whisk together the soy sauce, hoisin sauce, rice vinegar, sesame oil, and sriracha sauce (if using). Pour the sauce over the beef and mushroom mixture. Stir well to coat everything evenly. Cook for an additional 2-3 minutes to allow the flavors to meld together.
4. Arrange the lettuce leaves on a serving platter. Spoon the beef and mushroom mixture into each lettuce leaf.
5. Garnish the lettuce wraps with sliced green onions, chopped cilantro, and sesame seeds, if desired.

BAKED CHICKEN WITH ROASTED ROOT VEGETABLES

Nutrition: Cal 300;Fat 10 g;Carb 20 g;Protein 35 g
Serving 2; Cook time 35 min

Ingredients

- 2 boneless, skinless chicken breasts
- 2 cups mixed root vegetables (such as carrots, parsnips, and sweet potatoes), peeled and chopped into small cubes
- 1 tablespoon olive oil
- 1 teaspoon dried thyme
- 1/2 teaspoon garlic powder

- 1/2 teaspoon paprika
- Salt and pepper, to taste

Instructions:

1. Preheat the oven to 400°F (200°C).
2. Season the chicken breasts with salt, pepper, dried thyme, garlic powder, and paprika. Rub the seasonings onto the chicken to evenly coat.
3. In a separate bowl, toss the chopped root vegetables with olive oil, salt, and pepper. Spread them out in a single layer on a baking sheet.
4. Place the seasoned chicken breasts on top of the root vegetables on the baking sheet.
5. Bake in the preheated oven for 25-30 minutes or until the chicken is cooked through and the vegetables are tender. The internal temperature of the chicken should reach 165°F (74°C).
6. Remove the baking sheet from the oven and let the chicken rest for a few minutes before slicing.
7. Serve the baked chicken with the roasted root vegetables. Optionally, you can add a side of steamed greens or a simple salad for added nutrition.

GREEK STUFFED BELL PEPPERS WITH GROUND TURKEY AND FETA

Nutrition: Cal 250;Fat 8 g;Carb 20 g;Protein 20 g
Serving 2; Cook time 40 min

Ingredients

- 2 bell peppers (any color)
- 1/2 pound lean ground turkey
- 1/2 cup cooked quinoa
- 1/4 cup crumbled feta cheese
- 1/4 cup diced tomatoes
- 1/4 cup chopped red onion
- 1/4 cup chopped Kalamata olives
- 1/4 cup chopped fresh parsley
- 1 teaspoon dried oregano
- 1/2 teaspoon garlic powder
- Salt and pepper, to taste
- Olive oil, for drizzling

Instructions:

1. Preheat the oven to 375°F (190°C).

2. Cut the bell peppers in half lengthwise and remove the seeds and membranes. Place the pepper halves on a baking sheet, cut side up.

3. In a skillet, cook the ground turkey over medium heat until browned. Drain any excess fat.

4. In a mixing bowl, combine the cooked ground turkey, cooked quinoa, crumbled feta cheese, diced tomatoes, chopped red onion, chopped Kalamata olives, chopped parsley, dried oregano, garlic powder, salt, and pepper. Mix well to combine.

5. Spoon the turkey and quinoa mixture into each bell pepper half, filling them evenly.

6. Drizzle a little olive oil over the stuffed peppers and sprinkle with some additional dried oregano, if desired.

7. Bake in the preheated oven for 25-30 minutes or until the peppers are tender and the filling is heated through.

8. Remove from the oven and let them cool for a few minutes before serving.

9. Serve the Greek stuffed bell peppers as a main dish for a complete meal. Optionally, you can serve them with a side salad or steamed vegetables.

SPAGHETTI SQUASH WITH TURKEY BOLOGNESE SAUCE

Nutrition: Cal 300;Fat 10 g;Carb 30 g;Protein 20 g
Serving 2; Cook time 60 min

Ingredients
- 1 medium spaghetti squash
- 1/2 pound lean ground turkey
- 1/2 onion, chopped
- 1 clove garlic, minced
- 1/2 cup diced tomatoes
- 1/4 cup tomato paste
- 1/2 teaspoon dried basil
- 1/2 teaspoon dried oregano
- Salt and pepper, to taste
- Fresh basil leaves, for garnish

Instructions:
1. Preheat the oven to 375°F (190°C).
2. Slice the spaghetti squash in half lengthwise and scoop out the seeds and fibers. Place the squash halves on a baking sheet, cut side down.

3. Bake the spaghetti squash in the preheated oven for 30-40 minutes or until the flesh is tender and can be easily scraped with a fork. Remove from the oven and let it cool slightly.

4. While the spaghetti squash is baking, prepare the Bolognese sauce. In a skillet, cook the lean ground turkey over medium heat until browned. Add the chopped onion and minced garlic and cook until the onion is translucent.

5. Stir in the diced tomatoes, tomato paste, dried basil, dried oregano, salt, and pepper. Reduce the heat to low and let the sauce simmer for about 15-20 minutes, allowing the flavors to meld together.

6. Once the spaghetti squash has cooled slightly, use a fork to scrape the flesh, creating spaghetti-like strands.

LEMON HERB GRILLED SHRIMP WITH QUINOA AND ROASTED ASPARAGUS

Nutrition: Cal 300;Fat 10 g;Carb 30 g;Protein 20 g
Serving 2; Cook time 30 min

Ingredients
FOR THE LEMON HERB GRILLED SHRIMP:
- 1/2 pound shrimp, peeled and deveined
- 2 tablespoons lemon juice
- 1 tablespoon olive oil
- 1 clove garlic, minced
- 1/2 teaspoon dried oregano
- Salt and pepper, to taste

FOR THE QUINOA:
- 1 cup cooked quinoa
- 1 tablespoon fresh lemon juice
- 1 tablespoon chopped fresh parsley
- Salt and pepper, to taste

FOR THE ROASTED ASPARAGUS:
- 1 bunch asparagus, trimmed
- 1 tablespoon olive oil
- Salt and pepper, to taste

Instructions:
1. Preheat the grill to medium-high heat.
2. In a bowl, combine the lemon juice, olive oil, minced garlic, dried oregano, salt, and pepper. Add the shrimp and toss to coat. Let it marinate for about 10 minutes.

3. While the shrimp is marinating, preheat the oven to 425°F (220°C).
4. On a baking sheet, arrange the trimmed asparagus in a single layer. Drizzle with olive oil and sprinkle with salt and pepper. Toss to coat. Roast in the preheated oven for about 10-12 minutes or until the asparagus is tender and slightly crispy.
5. Meanwhile, grill the marinated shrimp for about 2-3 minutes per side or until they turn pink and opaque.
6. In a separate bowl, combine the cooked quinoa, fresh lemon juice, chopped parsley, salt, and pepper. Toss to combine.
7. Serve the lemon herb grilled shrimp with a side of quinoa and roasted asparagus.

TURKEY AND VEGETABLE STIR-FRY WITH CAULIFLOWER RICE

Nutrition: Cal 250;Fat 10 g;Carb 15 g;Protein 20 g
Serving 2; Cook time 30 min

Ingredients
FOR THE STIR-FRY:
- 1/2 pound lean ground turkey
- 1 small onion, thinly sliced
- 1 bell pepper, thinly sliced
- 1 zucchini, thinly sliced
- 1 carrot, thinly sliced
- 2 cloves garlic, minced
- 1 tablespoon low-sodium soy sauce
- 1 tablespoon olive oil
- Salt and pepper, to taste
- Optional: Fresh herbs for garnish (e.g., cilantro or green onions)

FOR THE CAULIFLOWER RICE:
- 1 small head cauliflower, riced (approximately 2 cups)
- 1 tablespoon olive oil
- Salt and pepper, to taste

Instructions:
1. Heat olive oil in a large skillet or wok over medium-high heat. Add the ground turkey and cook until browned, breaking it up into small crumbles.
2. Add the sliced onion, bell pepper, zucchini, carrot, and minced garlic to the skillet. Stir-fry for about 5-7 minutes or until the vegetables are tender-crisp.

3. Stir in the low-sodium soy sauce and season with salt and pepper to taste. Cook for an additional 1-2 minutes to allow the flavors to blend.
4. While the stir-fry is cooking, prepare the cauliflower rice. Place the riced cauliflower in a microwave-safe bowl and cook on high for 4-5 minutes, or until the cauliflower is tender. Alternatively, you can sauté the cauliflower rice in a separate pan with olive oil until cooked.
5. Season the cauliflower rice with salt and pepper to taste.
6. Divide the cauliflower rice between two plates and top with the turkey and vegetable stir-fry.

HERB-CRUSTED BAKED SALMON WITH SAUTÉED SPINACH

Nutrition: Cal 300;Fat 15 g;Carb 5 g;Protein 35 g
Serving 2; Cook time 25 min

Ingredients
FOR THE HERB-CRUSTED SALMON:
- 2 salmon fillets (approximately 4-6 ounces each)
- 1 tablespoon olive oil
- 1 tablespoon Dijon mustard
- 1/4 cup whole wheat breadcrumbs
- 1 teaspoon dried herbs (such as thyme, oregano, or parsley)
- Salt and pepper, to taste

FOR THE SAUTÉED SPINACH:
- 4 cups fresh spinach leaves
- 1 clove garlic, minced
- 1 tablespoon olive oil
- Salt and pepper, to taste

Instructions:
1. Preheat the oven to 400°F (200°C). Line a baking sheet with parchment paper or foil.
2. In a small bowl, combine the olive oil, Dijon mustard, breadcrumbs, dried herbs, salt, and pepper. Mix well to form a paste.
3. Place the salmon fillets on the prepared baking sheet. Spread the herb paste evenly over the top of each fillet.
4. Bake the salmon in the preheated oven for 12-15 minutes, or until it flakes easily with a fork and reaches an internal temperature of 145°F (63°C).

5. While the salmon is baking, heat olive oil in a large skillet over medium heat. Add the minced garlic and sauté for about 1 minute, until fragrant.

6. Add the spinach leaves to the skillet and sauté for 2-3 minutes, until wilted. Season with salt and pepper to taste.

7. Divide the sautéed spinach onto two plates. Place a salmon fillet on top of each bed of spinach.

MEXICAN CHICKEN AND BLACK BEAN SKILLET

Nutrition: Cal 300;Fat 8 g;Carb 25 g;Protein 30 g
Serving 2; Cook time 25 min

Ingredients
- 2 boneless, skinless chicken breasts, cut into bite-sized pieces
- 1 tablespoon olive oil
- 1 small onion, diced
- 1 bell pepper, diced
- 1 clove garlic, minced
- 1 can (15 ounces) black beans, drained and rinsed
- 1 can (10 ounces) diced tomatoes with green chilies
- 1 teaspoon chili powder
- 1/2 teaspoon cumin
- Salt and pepper, to taste
- Fresh cilantro, chopped (for garnish, optional)

FOR SERVING:
- Cauliflower rice or cooked brown rice (optional)

Instructions:
1. Heat the olive oil in a large skillet over medium heat. Add the diced onion and bell pepper, and sauté for 3-4 minutes until they start to soften.
2. Add the minced garlic to the skillet and cook for an additional minute until fragrant.
3. Push the vegetables to one side of the skillet and add the chicken pieces. Cook for about 5-6 minutes, stirring occasionally, until the chicken is browned and cooked through.
4. Stir in the black beans, diced tomatoes with green chilies, chili powder, cumin, salt, and

pepper. Mix well to combine all the ingredients.

5. Reduce the heat to low and simmer the mixture for about 10 minutes, allowing the flavors to blend together.
6. Taste and adjust the seasonings as desired.
7. Remove from heat and garnish with fresh chopped cilantro, if desired.
8. Serve the Mexican chicken and black bean skillet as is or with cauliflower rice or cooked brown rice, if desired.

LEMON HERB BAKED SALMON WITH STEAMED BROCCOLI AND QUINOA

Nutrition: Cal 350;Fat 15 g;Carb 25 g;Protein 30 g
Serving 2; Cook time 30 min

Ingredients
- 2 salmon fillets (4-6 ounces each)
- 1 tablespoon olive oil
- Juice of 1 lemon
- 1 teaspoon lemon zest
- 1 teaspoon dried herbs (such as dill, thyme, or parsley)
- Salt and pepper, to taste
- 2 cups broccoli florets
- 1 cup cooked quinoa

Instructions:
1. Preheat the oven to 375°F (190°C).
2. Place the salmon fillets on a baking sheet lined with parchment paper or aluminum foil.
3. In a small bowl, whisk together the olive oil, lemon juice, lemon zest, dried herbs, salt, and pepper.
4. Drizzle the lemon herb mixture over the salmon fillets, ensuring they are evenly coated.
5. Bake the salmon in the preheated oven for about 15-20 minutes or until it flakes easily with a fork and reaches an internal temperature of 145°F (63°C).
6. While the salmon is baking, steam the broccoli florets until they are tender yet still slightly crisp, about 5-7 minutes.
7. Cook the quinoa according to the package instructions or use pre-cooked quinoa for convenience.

8. Once the salmon is cooked, remove it from the oven and let it rest for a few minutes.
9. Divide the steamed broccoli and cooked quinoa between two plates.
10. Place a baked salmon fillet on top of each plate.
11. Serve the lemon herb baked salmon with steamed broccoli and quinoa immediately.

fresh lemon juice over the chicken and vegetables for added flavor, if desired.

GRILLED CHICKEN BREAST WITH ROASTED CAULIFLOWER

Nutrition: Cal 350;Fat 12 g;Carb 12 g;Protein 40 g
Serving 2; Cook time 40 min

Ingredients
- 2 boneless, skinless chicken breasts
- 2 tablespoons olive oil
- 1 teaspoon garlic powder
- 1 teaspoon paprika
- Salt and pepper, to taste
- 1 small head of cauliflower, cut into florets
- 1 cup green beans, trimmed
- Optional: Fresh lemon wedges for serving

Instructions:
1. Preheat your grill to medium-high heat.
2. In a small bowl, mix together the olive oil, garlic powder, paprika, salt, and pepper. Rub the mixture all over the chicken breasts to coat them evenly.
3. Place the seasoned chicken breasts on the grill and cook for about 6-8 minutes per side, or until the internal temperature reaches 165°F (75°C). Cooking times may vary depending on the thickness of the chicken breasts. Remove from the grill and let them rest for a few minutes.
4. While the chicken is grilling, preheat your oven to 425°F (220°C).
5. On a baking sheet, spread out the cauliflower florets and green beans. Drizzle with a little olive oil and season with salt and pepper.
6. Roast the vegetables in the preheated oven for about 15-20 minutes, or until they are tender and lightly browned.
7. Serve the grilled chicken breasts with a side of roasted cauliflower and green beans. Squeeze

STUFFED ZUCCHINI WITH LEAN GROUND BEEF

Nutrition: Cal 350;Fat 12 g;Carb 20 g;Protein 30 g
Serving 2; Cook time 40 min

Ingredients
- 2 medium-sized zucchini
- 250 grams lean ground beef
- 1 small onion, diced
- 2 cloves garlic, minced
- 1 small tomato, diced
- 1 tablespoon tomato paste
- 1 teaspoon dried oregano
- 1 teaspoon dried basil
- Salt and pepper, to taste
- Optional: Grated Parmesan cheese for topping

Instructions:
1. Preheat your oven to 375°F (190°C).
2. Slice the zucchini in half lengthwise. Scoop out the seeds and some of the flesh, creating a hollow center in each zucchini half. Reserve the scooped-out flesh for later use.
3. In a skillet, heat a little olive oil over medium heat. Add the diced onion and minced garlic and cook until they become soft and translucent.
4. Add the lean ground beef to the skillet and cook until it is browned and fully cooked. Break up the beef into small crumbles as it cooks.
5. Add the diced tomato, tomato paste, dried oregano, dried basil, salt, and pepper to the skillet. Stir to combine everything well and let the mixture cook for a few more minutes to allow the flavors to meld together.
6. Take the reserved zucchini flesh and chop it into small pieces. Add it to the skillet with the beef mixture and cook for a couple of minutes until the zucchini softens.
7. Place the hollowed-out zucchini halves in a baking dish. Spoon the beef and vegetable mixture into the zucchini halves, filling them generously.
8. Cover the baking dish with aluminum foil and bake in the preheated oven for about 25-30 minutes, or until the zucchini is tender.
9. Remove the foil, sprinkle the stuffed zucchini with grated Parmesan cheese if desired, and bake for an additional 5 minutes, or until the cheese melts and turns golden.

SHRIMP AND BROCCOLI QUINOA STIR-FRY WITH TERIYAKI SAUCE

Nutrition: Cal 350;Fat 10 g;Carb 35 g;Protein 30 g
Serving 2; Cook time 20 min

Ingredients
- 200 grams shrimp, peeled and deveined
- 2 cups broccoli florets
- 1 cup cooked quinoa
- 1 small onion, thinly sliced
- 2 cloves garlic, minced
- 2 tablespoons low-sodium teriyaki sauce
- 1 tablespoon olive oil
- Salt and pepper, to taste
- Optional toppings: Sesame seeds, chopped green onions

Instructions:
1. In a large skillet or wok, heat the olive oil over medium-high heat.
2. Add the sliced onion and minced garlic to the skillet and sauté until the onion becomes translucent and fragrant.
3. Add the shrimp to the skillet and cook for 2-3 minutes on each side until they turn pink and are cooked through. Remove the cooked shrimp from the skillet and set aside.
4. In the same skillet, add the broccoli florets and cook for 3-4 minutes until they are tender-crisp.
5. Return the cooked shrimp to the skillet with the broccoli. Add the cooked quinoa and teriyaki sauce to the skillet. Toss everything together to coat the ingredients evenly with the sauce.
6. Season with salt and pepper to taste. Cook for an additional 2-3 minutes to heat everything through.
7. Remove the skillet from heat and divide the shrimp and broccoli quinoa stir-fry into two serving bowls or plates.
8. Garnish with sesame seeds and chopped green onions if desired.

BAKED PORK CHOPS WITH ROASTED SWEET POTATOES AND BRUSSELS SPROUTS

Nutrition: Cal 350;Fat 10 g;Carb 30 g;Protein 30 g
Serving 2; Cook time 45 min

Ingredients
- 2 boneless pork chops (approximately 4-6 ounces each)
- 2 medium sweet potatoes, peeled and cubed
- 10-12 Brussels sprouts, halved
- 1 tablespoon olive oil
- 1 teaspoon dried thyme
- 1/2 teaspoon garlic powder
- Salt and pepper, to taste

Instructions:
1. Preheat the oven to 400°F (200°C).
2. Place the sweet potato cubes and halved Brussels sprouts on a baking sheet. Drizzle with olive oil and sprinkle with dried thyme, garlic powder, salt, and pepper. Toss to coat the vegetables evenly with the seasonings.
3. Place the baking sheet in the preheated oven and roast for about 25-30 minutes, or until the sweet potatoes are tender and the Brussels sprouts are browned and crispy.
4. While the vegetables are roasting, season the pork chops with salt and pepper on both sides.
5. Heat a non-stick skillet over medium-high heat. Add the pork chops to the skillet and cook for 3-4 minutes on each side, or until they are browned.
6. Transfer the browned pork chops to a baking dish and place them in the oven for about 10-15 minutes, or until they reach an internal temperature of 145°F (63°C).
7. Remove the pork chops from the oven and let them rest for a few minutes before serving.
8. Divide the baked pork chops, roasted sweet potatoes, and Brussels sprouts onto two plates.

CAULIFLOWER FRIED RICE WITH SHRIMP AND VEGETABLES

Nutrition: Cal 250;Fat 10 g;Carb 20 g;Protein 25 g
Serving 2; Cook time 25 min

Ingredients
- 1 medium head of cauliflower
- 8 ounces shrimp, peeled and deveined
- 1 cup mixed vegetables (such as diced carrots, peas, and bell peppers)
- 2 cloves garlic, minced
- 1 tablespoon low-sodium soy sauce
- 1 tablespoon sesame oil
- 2 green onions, sliced
- Salt and pepper, to taste

Instructions:
1. Cut the cauliflower into florets and place them in a food processor. Pulse until the cauliflower resembles rice-like grains. Alternatively, you can grate the cauliflower using a box grater.
2. Heat a large skillet or wok over medium heat. Add the sesame oil and minced garlic. Cook for about 1 minute until the garlic becomes fragrant.
3. Add the shrimp to the skillet and cook for 2-3 minutes, or until they turn pink and opaque. Remove the shrimp from the skillet and set aside.
4. In the same skillet, add the mixed vegetables and cook for 2-3 minutes until they are slightly tender.
5. Push the vegetables to one side of the skillet and add the riced cauliflower to the other side. Cook for 2-3 minutes, stirring occasionally, until the cauliflower is tender.
6. Return the cooked shrimp to the skillet with the cauliflower and vegetables. Stir to combine.
7. Add the low-sodium soy sauce and season with salt and pepper to taste. Stir well to coat all the ingredients with the sauce.
8. Continue to cook for another 1-2 minutes until everything is heated through.
9. Remove the skillet from heat and garnish with sliced green onions.

GREEK-STYLE STUFFED EGGPLANT WITH GROUND TURKEY

Nutrition: Cal 300;Fat 10 g;Carb 25 g;Protein 25 g
Serving 2; Cook time 50 min

Ingredients
- 2 small eggplants
- 8 ounces lean ground turkey
- 1 small onion, diced
- 2 cloves garlic, minced
- 1 cup diced tomatoes (canned or fresh)
- 1/4 cup chopped fresh parsley
- 1/4 cup crumbled feta cheese
- 1 tablespoon olive oil
- 1 teaspoon dried oregano
- Salt and pepper, to taste

Instructions:
1. Preheat the oven to 375°F (190°C).
2. Slice the eggplants in half lengthwise. Scoop out the flesh from the center, leaving about a 1/4-inch thick shell. Reserve the scooped-out flesh for later use.
3. Place the eggplant halves on a baking sheet, cut side up. Brush them with olive oil and sprinkle with salt and pepper. Bake in the preheated oven for 20 minutes until slightly tender.
4. Meanwhile, heat the olive oil in a large skillet over medium heat. Add the diced onion and minced garlic. Cook for about 2-3 minutes until the onion becomes translucent.
5. Add the ground turkey to the skillet and cook, breaking it up with a spatula, until it is browned and cooked through.
6. Add the reserved eggplant flesh to the skillet along with the diced tomatoes, dried oregano, and salt and pepper to taste. Stir well to combine.
7. Cover the skillet and let the mixture simmer for 10 minutes to allow the flavors to blend.
8. Remove the skillet from heat and stir in the chopped fresh parsley and crumbled feta cheese.
9. Take the partially baked eggplant halves from the oven and carefully fill them with the ground turkey and tomato mixture.
10. Return the stuffed eggplants to the oven and bake for an additional 15-20 minutes until the eggplants are fully cooked and tender.
11. Remove from the oven and let them cool for a few minutes before serving.

GARLIC HERB GRILLED FLANK STEAK WITH GRILLED ASPARAGUS

Nutrition: Cal 270;Fat 12 g;Carb 10 g;Protein 29 g
Serving 2; Cook time 25 min

Ingredients
- 1 pound flank steak
- 2 cloves garlic, minced
- 2 tablespoons fresh herbs (such as rosemary, thyme, or parsley), finely chopped
- 1 tablespoon olive oil
- Salt and pepper, to taste
- 1 bunch asparagus, trimmed
- Cooking spray

Instructions:
1. Preheat the grill to medium-high heat.
2. In a small bowl, mix together the minced garlic, fresh herbs, olive oil, salt, and pepper.
3. Rub the garlic herb mixture all over the flank steak, ensuring it is evenly coated. Let it marinate for about 15 minutes at room temperature.
4. Meanwhile, prepare the asparagus by lightly coating them with cooking spray. Season with salt and pepper.
5. Place the flank steak on the preheated grill and cook for about 4-6 minutes per side for medium-rare, or until it reaches your desired level of doneness. Cooking time may vary depending on the thickness of the steak.
6. While the steak is grilling, place the asparagus on the grill and cook for about 3-4 minutes, turning occasionally, until they are tender and slightly charred.
7. Once the steak is cooked to your liking, remove it from the grill and let it rest for a few minutes before slicing.
8. Slice the flank steak against the grain into thin strips.

MOROCCAN-SPICED CHICKEN SKEWERS WITH CAULIFLOWER COUSCOUS

Nutrition: Cal 300;Fat 10 g;Carb 15 g;Protein 35 g
Serving 2; Cook time 30 min

Ingredients
FOR THE CHICKEN SKEWERS:
- 2 boneless, skinless chicken breasts, cut into cubes
- 2 tablespoons olive oil
- 2 teaspoons ground cumin
- 1 teaspoon ground coriander
- 1 teaspoon paprika
- 1/2 teaspoon ground cinnamon
- Salt and pepper, to taste
- Wooden skewers, soaked in water for 30 minutes

FOR THE CAULIFLOWER COUSCOUS:
- 1 small head of cauliflower, riced (approx. 2 cups)
- 1 tablespoon olive oil
- 2 cloves garlic, minced
- 1/4 cup chopped fresh parsley
- Juice of 1 lemon
- Salt and pepper, to taste

Instructions:
1. Preheat the grill or grill pan to medium-high heat.
2. In a bowl, combine the olive oil, ground cumin, ground coriander, paprika, ground cinnamon, salt, and pepper. Mix well to create a marinade.
3. Add the chicken cubes to the marinade and toss to coat. Let the chicken marinate for at least 10 minutes to allow the flavors to infuse.
4. While the chicken is marinating, prepare the cauliflower couscous. Using a food processor, pulse the cauliflower florets until they resemble a couscous-like texture. Set aside.
5. Heat olive oil in a skillet over medium heat. Add the minced garlic and sauté for about 1 minute until fragrant.
6. Add the riced cauliflower to the skillet and cook for about 5-7 minutes until it becomes tender. Stir occasionally.
7. Remove the skillet from heat and stir in the chopped parsley, lemon juice, salt, and pepper. Set aside.
8. Thread the marinated chicken cubes onto the soaked wooden skewers.
9. Place the chicken skewers on the preheated grill or grill pan and cook for about 10-12 minutes, turning occasionally, until the chicken is cooked through and has grill marks.
10. Serve the Moroccan-spiced chicken skewers over the cauliflower couscous. Garnish with additional fresh herbs if desired.

BAKED TILAPIA WITH QUINOA AND ROASTED VEGETABLES

Nutrition: Cal 300;Fat 10 g;Carb 25 g;Protein 25 g
Serving 2; Cook time 35 min

Ingredients
FOR THE BAKED TILAPIA:
- 2 tilapia fillets (approx. 4-6 ounces each)
- 1 tablespoon olive oil
- 1 tablespoon lemon juice
- 1 teaspoon dried herbs (such as thyme, oregano, or basil)
- Salt and pepper, to taste

FOR THE QUINOA:
- 1/2 cup quinoa
- 1 cup water or low-sodium vegetable broth

FOR THE ROASTED VEGETABLES:
- 2 cups mixed vegetables (such as bell peppers, zucchini, broccoli, or carrots), cut into bite-sized pieces
- 1 tablespoon olive oil
- 1/2 teaspoon garlic powder
- Salt and pepper, to taste

Instructions:
1. Preheat the oven to 400°F (200°C).
2. In a small bowl, mix together olive oil, lemon juice, dried herbs, salt, and pepper to create a marinade.
3. Place the tilapia fillets in a baking dish and brush both sides with the marinade. Let them marinate for about 10 minutes.
4. In a small saucepan, combine quinoa and water (or vegetable broth) and bring to a boil. Reduce the heat to low, cover, and simmer for about 15-20 minutes or until the liquid is absorbed and the quinoa is tender. Remove from heat and let it sit covered for 5 minutes. Fluff with a fork before serving.

5. Meanwhile, in a separate baking dish, toss the mixed vegetables with olive oil, garlic powder, salt, and pepper. Spread them out evenly.

6. Place both the marinated tilapia fillets and the baking dish with the vegetables in the preheated oven. Bake for about 15-20 minutes, or until the tilapia is cooked through and flakes easily with a fork, and the vegetables are tender and slightly browned.

7. Once cooked, serve the baked tilapia on a bed of cooked quinoa and with a side of roasted vegetables.

TURKEY AND VEGETABLE CURRY WITH CAULIFLOWER RICE

Nutrition: Cal 300;Fat 15 g;Carb 15 g;Protein 25 g
Serving 2; Соок time 30 min

Ingredients
FOR THE TURKEY AND VEGETABLE CURRY:
• 8 ounces ground turkey
• 1 tablespoon olive oil
• 1 small onion, diced
• 2 cloves garlic, minced
• 1 tablespoon curry powder
• 1 teaspoon ground cumin
• 1 teaspoon ground turmeric
• 1/2 teaspoon ground ginger
• 1 cup mixed vegetables (such as bell peppers, carrots, and peas)
• 1 cup low-sodium vegetable broth
• 1/2 cup coconut milk (light)
• Salt and pepper, to taste
• Fresh cilantro, for garnish (optional)
FOR THE CAULIFLOWER RICE:
• 1 medium-sized cauliflower head
• 1 tablespoon olive oil
• Salt and pepper, to taste
Instructions:
1. Prepare the cauliflower rice by cutting the cauliflower head into florets. Place the florets in a food processor and pulse until they resemble rice-like grains.
2. In a large skillet, heat the olive oil over medium heat. Add the diced onion and minced garlic, and sauté until they become soft and fragrant.
3. Add the ground turkey to the skillet and cook until it is browned and cooked through.

4. Sprinkle the curry powder, cumin, turmeric, and ginger over the turkey mixture. Stir well to coat the turkey and onions with the spices.

5. Add the mixed vegetables, vegetable broth, and coconut milk to the skillet. Stir to combine. Bring the mixture to a simmer and let it cook for about 10-15 minutes, or until the vegetables are tender and the flavors are well combined. Season with salt and pepper to taste.

6. While the curry is simmering, heat the olive oil in a separate skillet over medium heat. Add the cauliflower rice and sauté for about 5-7 minutes, or until the cauliflower is tender. Season with salt and pepper to taste.

7. Serve the turkey and vegetable curry over the cauliflower rice. Garnish with fresh cilantro, if desired.

STUFFED CABBAGE ROLLS WITH LEAN GROUND BEEF AND BROWN RICE

Nutrition: Cal 250;Fat 8 g;Carb 20 g;Protein 20 g
Serving 2; Соок time 1 hour 20 min

Ingredients
FOR THE STUFFED CABBAGE ROLLS:
• 8 large cabbage leaves
• 8 ounces lean ground beef
• 1/2 cup cooked brown rice
• 1 small onion, diced
• 2 cloves garlic, minced
• 1/2 teaspoon dried thyme
• 1/2 teaspoon dried oregano
• 1/4 teaspoon paprika
• Salt and pepper, to taste
• 1 cup low-sodium tomato sauce
FOR THE TOMATO SAUCE:
• 1 cup low-sodium tomato sauce
• 1/2 teaspoon dried basil
• 1/2 teaspoon dried parsley
• 1/4 teaspoon garlic powder
Instructions:
1. Preheat the oven to 375°F (190°C). Prepare a baking dish by greasing it lightly with cooking spray.
2. In a large pot of boiling water, blanch the cabbage leaves for about 2-3 minutes, or until they are tender. Drain and set aside.

3. In a skillet, cook the ground beef over medium heat until it is browned. Add the diced onion and minced garlic, and cook until they become soft and fragrant.
4. Add the cooked brown rice, dried thyme, dried oregano, paprika, salt, and pepper to the skillet. Stir well to combine all the ingredients.
5. Spoon a portion of the beef and rice mixture onto each cabbage leaf. Roll the leaves tightly, folding in the sides as you go. Place the rolled cabbage rolls seam-side down in the prepared baking dish.
6. In a small bowl, mix together the tomato sauce, dried basil, dried parsley, and garlic powder. Pour the tomato sauce mixture over the cabbage rolls, evenly coating them.
7. Cover the baking dish with foil and bake in the preheated oven for about 45 minutes. Then, remove the foil and bake for an additional 10-15 minutes, or until the cabbage rolls are cooked through and the sauce is bubbly.

GRILLED SHRIMP AND VEGETABLE KABOBS WITH QUINOA SALAD

Nutrition: Cal 260;Fat 9 g;Carb 25 g;Protein 21 g
Serving 2; Cook time 30 min

Ingredients
FOR THE GRILLED SHRIMP AND VEGETABLE KABOBS:
• 12 large shrimp, peeled and deveined
• 1 red bell pepper, cut into chunks
• 1 yellow bell pepper, cut into chunks
• 1 zucchini, sliced into rounds
• 1 red onion, cut into wedges
• 2 tablespoons olive oil
• 1 teaspoon garlic powder
• 1 teaspoon paprika
• Salt and pepper, to taste
• Wooden or metal skewers
FOR THE QUINOA SALAD:
• 1 cup cooked quinoa
• 1 cup cherry tomatoes, halved
• 1/2 cucumber, diced
• 1/4 cup diced red onion
• 2 tablespoons chopped fresh parsley
• 2 tablespoons lemon juice
• 1 tablespoon olive oil

• Salt and pepper, to taste
Instructions:
1. Preheat the grill to medium-high heat.
2. In a bowl, combine the shrimp, bell peppers, zucchini, red onion, olive oil, garlic powder, paprika, salt, and pepper. Toss to coat the ingredients evenly.
3. Thread the shrimp and vegetables onto skewers, alternating between shrimp and vegetables.
4. Place the kabobs on the preheated grill and cook for about 3-4 minutes per side, or until the shrimp are pink and opaque and the vegetables are tender.
5. While the kabobs are grilling, prepare the quinoa salad. In a separate bowl, combine the cooked quinoa, cherry tomatoes, cucumber, red onion, parsley, lemon juice, olive oil, salt, and pepper. Mix well to combine all the ingredients.
6. Remove the kabobs from the grill and serve them alongside the quinoa salad.

SPINACH AND FETA STUFFED TURKEY BREAST WITH ROASTED CARROTS

Nutrition: Cal 300;Fat 10 g;Carb 15 g;Protein 43 g
Serving 2; Cook time 45 min

Ingredients
FOR THE SPINACH AND FETA STUFFED TURKEY BREAST:
• 1 pound turkey breast, boneless and skinless
• 2 cups fresh spinach leaves
• 1/4 cup crumbled feta cheese
• 1 tablespoon olive oil
• 1 teaspoon dried oregano
• 1/2 teaspoon garlic powder
• Salt and pepper, to taste
FOR THE ROASTED CARROTS:
• 4 large carrots, peeled and sliced into sticks
• 1 tablespoon olive oil
• 1/2 teaspoon dried thyme
• Salt and pepper, to taste
Instructions:
1. Preheat the oven to 375°F (190°C).
2. Prepare the stuffing by sautéing the spinach leaves in olive oil until wilted. Remove from heat and let cool. Once cooled, squeeze out any excess liquid.

3. In a small bowl, mix the cooked spinach, feta cheese, dried oregano, garlic powder, salt, and pepper.
4. Butterfly the turkey breast by slicing it horizontally but not all the way through, so it opens like a book. Spread the spinach and feta stuffing evenly on one side of the turkey breast.
5. Fold the other side of the turkey breast over the stuffing and secure with toothpicks or kitchen twine to keep it closed.
6. Place the stuffed turkey breast on a baking sheet lined with parchment paper.
7. In a separate bowl, toss the carrot sticks with olive oil, dried thyme, salt, and pepper.
8. Arrange the seasoned carrots around the stuffed turkey breast on the baking sheet.
9. Roast in the preheated oven for about 35-40 minutes, or until the turkey reaches an internal temperature of 165°F (74°C) and the carrots are tender.
10. Remove from the oven and let the turkey breast rest for a few minutes before slicing.
11. Serve the sliced stuffed turkey breast with the roasted carrots.

BROCCOLI AND MUSHROOM STIR-FRY WITH TOFU AND SOY SAUCE

Nutrition: Cal 240;Fat 12 g;Carb 14 g;Protein 16 g
Serving 2; Cook time 20 min

Ingredients
- 8 ounces tofu, firm or extra firm, drained and cut into cubes
- 2 cups broccoli florets
- 1 cup sliced mushrooms
- 1 tablespoon vegetable oil
- 2 cloves garlic, minced
- 1 tablespoon low-sodium soy sauce
- 1/2 teaspoon sesame oil (optional)
- Salt and pepper, to taste
- Optional toppings: sesame seeds, chopped green onions

Instructions:
1. Heat the vegetable oil in a large skillet or wok over medium-high heat.
2. Add the minced garlic and cook for about 30 seconds until fragrant.

3. Add the tofu cubes to the skillet and cook for about 5 minutes, stirring occasionally, until lightly browned on all sides. Remove the tofu from the skillet and set aside.
4. In the same skillet, add the broccoli florets and sliced mushrooms. Stir-fry for about 5-7 minutes until the vegetables are tender-crisp.
5. Return the tofu to the skillet and add the low-sodium soy sauce and sesame oil (if using). Stir to coat the tofu and vegetables evenly. Cook for an additional 1-2 minutes.
6. Season with salt and pepper to taste.
7. Remove from heat and serve the stir-fry hot.
8. Optional: Sprinkle with sesame seeds and chopped green onions for added flavor and garnish.

ITALIAN-STYLE BAKED CHICKEN WITH ZUCCHINI NOODLES

Nutrition: Cal 270;Fat 12 g;Carb 10 g;Protein 35 g
Serving 2; Cook time 30 min

Ingredients
FOR THE CHICKEN:
- 2 small chicken breasts (about 4-6 ounces each)
- 1 tablespoon olive oil
- 1 teaspoon dried Italian seasoning
- 1/2 teaspoon garlic powder
- Salt and pepper, to taste
FOR THE ZUCCHINI NOODLES:
- 2 medium zucchini, spiralized or cut into thin strips
- 1 tablespoon olive oil
- 2 cloves garlic, minced
- 1/4 teaspoon red pepper flakes (optional)
- Salt and pepper, to taste

Instructions:
1. Preheat the oven to 400°F (200°C).
2. Place the chicken breasts on a baking sheet lined with parchment paper.
3. Drizzle the chicken breasts with olive oil and sprinkle with dried Italian seasoning, garlic powder, salt, and pepper. Rub the seasonings into the chicken to coat it evenly.
4. Bake the chicken in the preheated oven for 20-25 minutes or until cooked through and the internal temperature reaches 165°F (75°C).

5. While the chicken is baking, prepare the zucchini noodles. Heat olive oil in a large skillet over medium heat.

6. Add the minced garlic and red pepper flakes (if using) to the skillet and cook for about 1 minute until fragrant.

7. Add the zucchini noodles to the skillet and sauté for 3-5 minutes until the noodles are tender but still slightly crisp. Season with salt and pepper to taste.

8. Remove the chicken from the oven and let it rest for a few minutes before slicing.

9. Serve the sliced chicken over the zucchini noodles.

QUINOA-STUFFED ACORN SQUASH WITH LEAN GROUND TURKEY

Nutrition: Cal 350;Fat 11 g;Carb 43 g;Protein 30 g
Serving 2; Cook time 46 min

Ingredients
- 2 small acorn squashes
- 1/2 cup quinoa, uncooked
- 1 cup low-sodium chicken broth
- 8 ounces lean ground turkey
- 1/2 onion, finely chopped
- 1 garlic clove, minced
- 1/2 teaspoon dried thyme
- 1/2 teaspoon dried sage
- Salt and pepper, to taste
- 1/4 cup grated Parmesan cheese (optional)
- Fresh parsley, chopped (for garnish)

Instructions:
1. Preheat the oven to 400°F (200°C).
2. Cut the acorn squashes in half lengthwise and scoop out the seeds and fibers. Place the halves on a baking sheet, cut side up.
3. In a medium saucepan, combine the quinoa and chicken broth. Bring to a boil, then reduce heat, cover, and simmer for 15-20 minutes or until the quinoa is cooked and the liquid is absorbed.
4. In a large skillet, cook the lean ground turkey over medium heat until browned. Add the chopped onion, minced garlic, dried thyme, dried sage, salt, and pepper. Cook for an additional 3-5 minutes until the onions are softened.

5. Add the cooked quinoa to the skillet with the turkey mixture. Stir well to combine.

6. Spoon the quinoa and turkey mixture into the hollowed-out acorn squash halves. Press the mixture down gently to fill the squash completely.

7. Optional: Sprinkle grated Parmesan cheese over the stuffed squash halves.

8. Cover the baking sheet with foil and bake in the preheated oven for 25-30 minutes or until the squash is tender.

9. Remove the foil and bake for an additional 5-10 minutes to brown the top slightly.

10. Remove from the oven and let the stuffed squash cool for a few minutes before serving.

11. Garnish with fresh chopped parsley and serve warm.

LEMON GARLIC GRILLED SHRIMP WITH ROASTED ASPARAGUS AND BROWN RICE

Nutrition: Cal 400;Fat 11 g;Carb 43 g;Protein 30 g
Serving 2; Cook time 30 min

Ingredients
FOR THE LEMON GARLIC GRILLED SHRIMP:
- 12 ounces shrimp, peeled and deveined
- 2 cloves garlic, minced
- 1 tablespoon fresh lemon juice
- 1 tablespoon olive oil
- Salt and pepper, to taste

FOR THE ROASTED ASPARAGUS:
- 1 bunch asparagus, trimmed
- 1 tablespoon olive oil
- Salt and pepper, to taste

FOR THE BROWN RICE:
- 1 cup brown rice
- 2 cups water or low-sodium chicken broth

Instructions:
1. Preheat the grill to medium-high heat.
2. In a bowl, combine the minced garlic, lemon juice, olive oil, salt, and pepper. Add the peeled and deveined shrimp to the bowl and toss to coat the shrimp with the marinade. Let it marinate for 10-15 minutes.
3. While the shrimp is marinating, preheat the oven to 425°F (220°C) for the roasted asparagus.

4. Place the trimmed asparagus on a baking sheet and drizzle with olive oil. Season with salt and pepper, then toss to coat evenly. Roast in the preheated oven for 10-12 minutes or until the asparagus is tender.

5. In a medium saucepan, combine the brown rice and water or low-sodium chicken broth. Bring to a boil, then reduce heat, cover, and simmer for 20-25 minutes or until the rice is cooked and the liquid is absorbed. Fluff the rice with a fork before serving.

6. While the rice is cooking, grill the marinated shrimp on the preheated grill for 2-3 minutes per side or until they turn pink and are cooked through. Be careful not to overcook the shrimp as they can become tough.

7. Once the shrimp, roasted asparagus, and brown rice are cooked, divide them equally between two plates.

8. Serve the lemon garlic grilled shrimp on a bed of brown rice with the roasted asparagus on the side.

MEXICAN-STYLE STUFFED BELL

Nutrition: Cal 300;Fat 10 g;Carb 33 g;Protein 28 g
Serving 2; Соок time 45 min

Ingredients
- 2 large bell peppers (any color)
- 8 ounces lean ground turkey
- 1/2 cup cooked quinoa
- 1/4 cup diced onion
- 1/4 cup diced tomatoes
- 1/4 cup canned black beans, rinsed and drained
- 1/4 cup frozen corn kernels
- 1/2 teaspoon chili powder
- 1/2 teaspoon cumin
- 1/4 teaspoon garlic powder
- Salt and pepper, to taste
- 1/4 cup shredded reduced-fat cheese (optional)
- Fresh cilantro, for garnish

Instructions:
1. Preheat the oven to 375°F (190°C).
2. Cut the bell peppers in half lengthwise and remove the seeds and membranes. Place the pepper halves on a baking dish or sheet, cut side up.

3. In a non-stick skillet, cook the ground turkey over medium heat until browned. Drain any excess fat if needed.

4. Add the diced onion, diced tomatoes, black beans, and corn to the skillet with the ground turkey. Cook for a few minutes until the vegetables are slightly softened.

5. Stir in the cooked quinoa, chili powder, cumin, garlic powder, salt, and pepper. Mix everything well until combined.

6. Spoon the turkey and quinoa mixture into the bell pepper halves, dividing it evenly among them.

7. Optional: Sprinkle the shredded cheese on top of the stuffed peppers.

8. Cover the baking dish with foil and bake in the preheated oven for 25-30 minutes or until the bell peppers are tender.

9. Remove the foil and continue baking for an additional 5 minutes, or until the cheese is melted and slightly golden.

10. Garnish with fresh cilantro before serving.

GRILLED SALMON WITH LEMON DILL SAUCE

Nutrition: Cal 350;Fat 20 g;Carb 8 g;Protein 35 g
Serving 2; Соок time 20 min

Ingredients
- 2 salmon fillets (4-6 ounces each)
- Salt and pepper, to taste
- 1 tablespoon olive oil
- 1 bunch asparagus, trimmed
- Lemon wedges, for serving

FOR THE LEMON DILL SAUCE:
- 1/4 cup plain Greek yogurt
- 1 tablespoon fresh lemon juice
- 1 teaspoon lemon zest
- 1 tablespoon chopped fresh dill
- Salt and pepper, to taste

Instructions:
1. Preheat the grill to medium-high heat.
2. Season the salmon fillets with salt and pepper on both sides.
3. Brush the salmon fillets with olive oil to prevent sticking to the grill.
4. Grill the salmon fillets for about 4-6 minutes per side, or until cooked through and flaky.

Cooking time may vary depending on the thickness of the fillets. Set aside.

5. While the salmon is grilling, prepare the Lemon Dill Sauce. In a small bowl, combine the Greek yogurt, lemon juice, lemon zest, chopped dill, salt, and pepper. Mix well to combine.

6. Steam the asparagus until tender-crisp, about 3-5 minutes. You can steam them in a steamer basket or by placing them in a microwave-safe dish with a small amount of water and microwaving on high for a few minutes.

7. Serve the grilled salmon with a dollop of Lemon Dill Sauce on top and steamed asparagus on the side.

8. Garnish with lemon wedges for an extra burst of freshness.

ZUCCHINI NOODLES WITH TURKEY BOLOGNESE SAUCE

Nutrition: Cal 250;Fat 10 g;Carb 17 g;Protein 22 g
Serving 2; Cook time 30 min

Ingredients
- 2 medium-sized zucchini
- 1/2 pound lean ground turkey
- 1/2 small onion, finely chopped
- 2 cloves garlic, minced
- 1/2 cup diced tomatoes
- 1/4 cup tomato sauce
- 1/4 cup low-sodium chicken broth
- 1 teaspoon Italian seasoning
- Salt and pepper, to taste
- Fresh basil, for garnish

Instructions:

1. Using a spiralizer or julienne peeler, create zucchini noodles (zoodles) from the zucchini. Set aside.

2. In a large non-stick skillet, cook the ground turkey over medium heat until browned and cooked through. Break it up into small crumbles as it cooks.

3. Add the chopped onion and minced garlic to the skillet. Sauté for a few minutes until the onion is soft and translucent.

4. Stir in the diced tomatoes, tomato sauce, chicken broth, Italian seasoning, salt, and pepper. Reduce the heat to low and let the sauce simmer for about 15-20 minutes to allow the flavors to meld together.

5. While the sauce is simmering, heat a separate non-stick skillet over medium heat. Add the zucchini noodles and cook for about 3-5 minutes until they are just tender. Be careful not to overcook them to maintain their texture.

6. Once the zucchini noodles are cooked, drain any excess liquid if necessary.

7. Serve the zucchini noodles on plates or bowls, topped with the turkey Bolognese sauce.

8. Garnish with fresh basil leaves for added flavor and freshness.

STUFFED BELL PEPPERS WITH LEAN GROUND CHICKEN AND QUINOA

Nutrition: Cal 270;Fat 9 g;Carb 23 g;Protein 22 g
Serving 2; Cook time 40 min

Ingredients
- 2 large bell peppers (any color)
- 1/2 pound lean ground chicken
- 1/2 small onion, finely chopped
- 1 clove garlic, minced
- 1/2 cup cooked quinoa
- 1/4 cup diced tomatoes
- 1/4 cup low-sodium chicken broth
- 1/2 teaspoon cumin
- 1/2 teaspoon paprika
- Salt and pepper, to taste
- Fresh parsley, for garnish

Instructions:

1. Preheat the oven to 375°F (190°C). Line a baking dish with parchment paper.

2. Cut the tops off the bell peppers and remove the seeds and membranes. Rinse the peppers and set them aside.

3. In a large skillet, cook the ground chicken over medium heat until browned and cooked through. Break it up into small crumbles as it cooks.

4. Add the chopped onion and minced garlic to the skillet. Sauté for a few minutes until the onion is soft and translucent.

5. Stir in the cooked quinoa, diced tomatoes, chicken broth, cumin, paprika, salt, and pepper. Cook for a few minutes until well combined and heated through.

6. Stuff the bell peppers with the chicken and quinoa mixture, filling them to the top. Place the stuffed peppers in the prepared baking dish.
7. Cover the dish with foil and bake for 25-30 minutes until the peppers are tender.
8. Remove the foil and bake for an additional 5-10 minutes to lightly brown the tops of the peppers.
9. Remove from the oven and let the peppers cool slightly before serving.
10. Garnish with fresh parsley for added freshness and flavor.

GARLIC HERB ROASTED PORK TENDERLOIN

Nutrition: Cal 310;Fat 12 g;Carb 13 g;Protein 37 g
Serving 2; Cook time 40 min

Ingredients
- 1 pork tenderloin (approximately 1 pound)
- 2 cloves garlic, minced
- 1 teaspoon dried rosemary
- 1 teaspoon dried thyme
- 1/2 teaspoon salt
- 1/4 teaspoon black pepper
- 2 tablespoons olive oil
- 1 medium head cauliflower, cut into florets
- 1 tablespoon olive oil (for cauliflower)
- Salt and pepper, to taste

Instructions:
1. Preheat the oven to 400°F (200°C).
2. In a small bowl, combine the minced garlic, dried rosemary, dried thyme, salt, black pepper, and olive oil. Mix well to form a paste.
3. Place the pork tenderloin on a baking sheet lined with parchment paper. Rub the garlic herb paste all over the pork, coating it evenly.
4. In a separate bowl, toss the cauliflower florets with olive oil, salt, and pepper until well coated.
5. Arrange the cauliflower around the pork tenderloin on the baking sheet.
6. Roast in the preheated oven for approximately 25-30 minutes, or until the pork reaches an internal temperature of 145°F (63°C) and the cauliflower is golden brown and tender.
7. Remove the baking sheet from the oven and let the pork rest for a few minutes before slicing.

8. Slice the pork tenderloin into thin medallions and serve with the roasted cauliflower.

SPICY SHRIMP AND BROCCOLI STIR-FRY WITH BROWN RICE

Nutrition: Cal 320;Fat 10 g;Carb 30 g;Protein 27 g
Serving 2; Cook time 20 min

Ingredients
- 1 pork tenderloin (approximately 1 pound)
- 2 cloves garlic, minced
- 1 teaspoon dried rosemary
- 1 teaspoon dried thyme
- 1/2 teaspoon salt
- 1/4 teaspoon black pepper
- 2 tablespoons olive oil
- 1 medium head cauliflower, cut into florets
- 1 tablespoon olive oil (for cauliflower)
- Salt and pepper, to taste

Instructions:
1. In a small bowl, whisk together the low-sodium soy sauce, sesame oil, sriracha sauce, red pepper flakes, minced garlic, salt, and pepper.
2. Heat a large skillet or wok over medium-high heat. Add the shrimp and stir-fry for 2-3 minutes until they turn pink and are cooked through. Remove the shrimp from the skillet and set aside.
3. In the same skillet, add the broccoli florets, sliced bell pepper, and sliced onion. Stir-fry for 3-4 minutes until the vegetables are crisp-tender.
4. Return the shrimp to the skillet and pour the sauce over the shrimp and vegetables. Stir well to coat everything evenly. Cook for an additional 1-2 minutes to heat through and allow the flavors to meld.
5. Serve the spicy shrimp and broccoli stir-fry over cooked brown rice.

GREEK-STYLE STUFFED TOMATOES WITH GROUND TURKEY AND QUINOA

Nutrition: Cal 280;Fat 11 g;Carb 22 g;Protein 22 g
Serving 2; Cook time 30 min

Ingredients
- 4 large tomatoes

- 1/2 pound lean ground turkey
- 1/2 cup cooked quinoa
- 1/4 cup chopped red onion
- 1/4 cup chopped bell pepper
- 1/4 cup chopped cucumber
- 1/4 cup crumbled feta cheese
- 2 tablespoons chopped fresh parsley
- 2 tablespoons chopped fresh mint
- 1 tablespoon lemon juice
- 1 tablespoon olive oil
- 2 cloves garlic, minced
- Salt and pepper, to taste

Instructions:
1. Preheat the oven to 375°F (190°C).
2. Slice off the tops of the tomatoes and carefully scoop out the insides, leaving a hollow shell. Reserve the tomato pulp.
3. In a large skillet, heat the olive oil over medium heat. Add the ground turkey and cook until browned, breaking it up into small pieces.
4. Add the chopped red onion, bell pepper, and garlic to the skillet. Sauté for 3-4 minutes until the vegetables are tender.
5. In a mixing bowl, combine the cooked quinoa, cooked ground turkey and vegetables, chopped cucumber, feta cheese, chopped parsley, chopped mint, lemon juice, salt, and pepper. Mix well to combine.
6. Stuff the mixture into the hollowed-out tomatoes, pressing it down gently.
7. Place the stuffed tomatoes in a baking dish and bake in the preheated oven for 15-20 minutes until the tomatoes are tender.
8. Serve the Greek-style stuffed tomatoes as a main dish or with a side salad for a complete meal.

CHICKEN AND VEGETABLE LETTUCE WRAPS WITH PEANUT SAUCE

Nutrition: Cal 270;Fat 10 g;Carb 16 g;Protein 20 g
Serving 2; Cook time 20 min

Ingredients
FOR THE LETTUCE WRAPS:
- 2 boneless, skinless chicken breasts, diced
- 1 tablespoon olive oil
- 1/2 cup diced bell peppers (any color)
- 1/2 cup diced carrots
- 1/2 cup diced zucchini
- 1/2 cup diced mushrooms
- 2 cloves garlic, minced
- 1 teaspoon grated ginger
- 1 tablespoon low-sodium soy sauce
- Salt and pepper, to taste
- 8 large lettuce leaves (such as Bibb or butter lettuce)

FOR THE PEANUT SAUCE:
- 2 tablespoons natural peanut butter
- 1 tablespoon low-sodium soy sauce
- 1 tablespoon lime juice
- 1 tablespoon honey or maple syrup
- 1/2 teaspoon sesame oil
- 1/4 teaspoon red pepper flakes (optional)
- Water, as needed for thinning

Instructions:
1. In a small bowl, whisk together all the ingredients for the peanut sauce until smooth. If the sauce is too thick, add water, 1 tablespoon at a time, until desired consistency is reached. Set aside.
2. Heat olive oil in a large skillet or wok over medium-high heat. Add the diced chicken and cook until browned and cooked through, about 5-6 minutes. Remove the chicken from the skillet and set aside.
3. In the same skillet, add the bell peppers, carrots, zucchini, mushrooms, garlic, and ginger. Sauté for 3-4 minutes until the vegetables are tender-crisp.
4. Return the cooked chicken to the skillet and add the soy sauce. Stir well to combine and cook for an additional 1-2 minutes. Season with salt and pepper to taste.
5. To serve, spoon the chicken and vegetable mixture onto the lettuce leaves, dividing it evenly among them. Drizzle with the peanut sauce and fold the lettuce leaves to create wraps.
6. Enjoy the chicken and vegetable lettuce wraps with peanut sauce as a light and flavorful meal. The crisp lettuce provides a refreshing crunch, while the chicken and vegetables offer protein and fiber. The peanut sauce adds a delicious and creamy touch. Serve any remaining peanut sauce on the side for dipping.

BAKED COD WITH ROASTED VEGETABLES AND QUINOA PILAF

Nutrition: Cal 330;Fat 12 g;Carb 33 g;Protein 29 g
Serving 2; Cook time 30 min

Ingredients
FOR THE BAKED COD:
•2 cod fillets (4-6 ounces each)
•1 tablespoon olive oil
•1 tablespoon lemon juice
•1 teaspoon minced garlic
•1/2 teaspoon dried thyme
•Salt and pepper, to taste
FOR THE ROASTED VEGETABLES:
•1 cup diced bell peppers (any color)
•1 cup diced zucchini
•1 cup diced cherry tomatoes
•1 cup diced red onion
•1 tablespoon olive oil
•1/2 teaspoon dried oregano
•Salt and pepper, to taste
FOR THE QUINOA PILAF:
•1/2 cup quinoa
•1 cup low-sodium chicken or vegetable broth
•1/4 cup diced carrots
•1/4 cup diced celery
•1/4 cup diced bell peppers (any color)
•1/4 cup diced red onion
•1 tablespoon chopped fresh parsley
•Salt and pepper, to taste
Instructions:
1.Preheat the oven to 400°F (200°C).
2.In a small bowl, whisk together olive oil, lemon juice, minced garlic, dried thyme, salt, and pepper. Place the cod fillets in a baking dish and pour the marinade over them, making sure to coat both sides. Let them marinate for about 10 minutes while you prepare the vegetables.
3.In a separate baking dish, toss together the diced bell peppers, zucchini, cherry tomatoes, red onion, olive oil, dried oregano, salt, and pepper. Spread the vegetables evenly in the dish.
4.Place both baking dishes in the preheated oven. Bake the cod fillets for about 12-15 minutes or until they are cooked through and flake easily with a fork. Roast the vegetables for about 20-25 minutes or until they are tender and slightly caramelized.
5.While the cod and vegetables are baking, prepare the quinoa pilaf. Rinse the quinoa under cold water to remove any bitterness. In a small saucepan, bring the chicken or vegetable broth to a boil. Add the quinoa, diced carrots, celery, bell peppers, and red onion. Reduce the heat to low, cover the saucepan, and let it simmer for about 15-20 minutes or until the quinoa is tender and the liquid is absorbed. Fluff the quinoa with a fork and stir in the chopped parsley. Season with salt and pepper to taste.
6.Serve the baked cod on a plate alongside the roasted vegetables and quinoa pilaf. The baked cod is flavorful and moist, while the roasted vegetables provide a variety of textures and flavors. The quinoa pilaf adds a nutritious and satisfying element to the dish.

CAPRESE CHICKEN WITH BALSAMIC GLAZE AND STEAMED GREEN BEANS

Nutrition: Cal 310;Fat 12 g;Carb 11 g;Protein 36 g
Serving 2; Cook time 30 min

Ingredients
FOR THE CAPRESE CHICKEN:
•2 boneless, skinless chicken breasts (4-6 ounces each)
•2 slices of fresh mozzarella cheese
•2 slices of tomato
•4-6 fresh basil leaves
•Salt and pepper, to taste
FOR THE BALSAMIC GLAZE:
•1/4 cup balsamic vinegar
•1 tablespoon honey (optional, for sweetness)
•Salt and pepper, to taste
FOR THE STEAMED GREEN BEANS:
•2 cups fresh green beans, ends trimmed
•Salt, to taste
Instructions:
1.Preheat the oven to 400°F (200°C).
2.Season the chicken breasts with salt and pepper on both sides. Heat a non-stick skillet over medium-high heat and cook the chicken breasts for about 4-6 minutes on each side or

until they are cooked through and no longer pink in the center. Remove the chicken from the skillet and set aside.

3. In the same skillet, reduce the heat to low and add the balsamic vinegar. If desired, add honey for sweetness. Stir the vinegar and honey together and let it simmer for a few minutes until it thickens into a glaze-like consistency. Season with salt and pepper to taste.

4. Place the cooked chicken breasts on a baking sheet lined with parchment paper. Top each chicken breast with a slice of fresh mozzarella cheese, a slice of tomato, and a few basil leaves.

5. Drizzle the balsamic glaze over the top of the chicken breasts. Place the baking sheet in the preheated oven and bake for about 5-7 minutes or until the cheese is melted and bubbly.

6. While the chicken is baking, steam the green beans. Fill a pot with a few inches of water and bring it to a boil. Place the green beans in a steamer basket or a colander and set it over the pot. Cover the pot and steam the green beans for about 4-5 minutes or until they are tender yet still crisp. Remove from heat and season with salt to taste.

7. Serve the Caprese chicken on a plate with a side of steamed green beans. The chicken is juicy and flavorful, topped with melted mozzarella, fresh tomatoes, and fragrant basil. The balsamic glaze adds a tangy and sweet element to the dish, while the steamed green beans provide a nutritious and vibrant side.

CAULIFLOWER CRUST PIZZA WITH GRILLED CHICKEN AND VEGGIES

Nutrition: Cal 290;Fat 10 g;Carb 16 g;Protein 27 g
Serving 2; Cook time 40 min

Ingredients
FOR THE CAULIFLOWER CRUST:
- 2 cups cauliflower rice
- 1 egg
- 1/2 cup grated Parmesan cheese
- 1/2 teaspoon dried oregano
- 1/2 teaspoon garlic powder
- Salt and pepper, to taste

FOR THE TOPPINGS:
- 1/2 cup marinara sauce (sugar-free)
- 1 grilled chicken breast, sliced
- 1/4 cup sliced bell peppers
- 1/4 cup sliced red onions
- 1/4 cup sliced mushrooms
- 1/4 cup shredded mozzarella cheese
- Fresh basil leaves, for garnish

Instructions:
1. Preheat the oven to 425°F (220°C). Line a baking sheet with parchment paper.

2. In a microwave-safe bowl, microwave the cauliflower rice for 4-5 minutes or until soft. Allow it to cool for a few minutes.

3. Place the cooled cauliflower rice in a clean kitchen towel or cheesecloth and squeeze out any excess moisture.

4. In a mixing bowl, combine the cauliflower rice, egg, grated Parmesan cheese, dried oregano, garlic powder, salt, and pepper. Mix well until all the ingredients are combined.

5. Transfer the cauliflower mixture to the prepared baking sheet. Use your hands to shape it into a round pizza crust, about 1/4 inch thick.

6. Bake the cauliflower crust in the preheated oven for 15-20 minutes or until it is firm and golden brown.

7. Remove the crust from the oven and let it cool slightly. Leave the oven on.

8. Spread the marinara sauce evenly over the cauliflower crust, leaving a small border around the edges.

9. Arrange the sliced grilled chicken, bell peppers, red onions, and mushrooms on top of the sauce.

10. Sprinkle the shredded mozzarella cheese over the toppings.

11. Place the pizza back in the oven and bake for an additional 10-15 minutes or until the cheese is melted and bubbly.

12. Once the pizza is done, remove it from the oven and let it cool for a few minutes.

13. Garnish with fresh basil leaves and slice into wedges.

TERIYAKI GLAZED TURKEY MEATBALLS WITH STIR-FRIED VEGETABLES

Nutrition: Cal 340;Fat 12 g;Carb 23 g;Protein 30 g
Serving 2; Соок time 30 min

Ingredients
FOR THE TURKEY MEATBALLS:
- 1 pound lean ground turkey
- 1/4 cup breadcrumbs (whole wheat or gluten-free)
- 1/4 cup finely chopped green onions
- 2 tablespoons low-sodium soy sauce
- 1 teaspoon minced garlic
- 1/2 teaspoon grated ginger
- 1/4 teaspoon black pepper

FOR THE TERIYAKI GLAZE:
- 2 tablespoons low-sodium soy sauce
- 2 tablespoons water
- 1 tablespoon honey or low-calorie sweetener
- 1 teaspoon cornstarch

FOR THE STIR-FRIED VEGETABLES:
- 2 cups mixed vegetables (such as broccoli, bell peppers, snap peas)
- 1 tablespoon olive oil
- 1 tablespoon low-sodium soy sauce

Instructions:
1. Preheat the oven to 400°F (200°C). Line a baking sheet with parchment paper.
2. In a mixing bowl, combine the ground turkey, breadcrumbs, green onions, soy sauce, minced garlic, grated ginger, and black pepper. Mix well until all the ingredients are evenly combined.
3. Shape the mixture into small meatballs, about 1 inch in diameter. Place them on the prepared baking sheet.
4. Bake the turkey meatballs in the preheated oven for 15-20 minutes or until they are cooked through and golden brown.
5. While the meatballs are baking, prepare the teriyaki glaze. In a small saucepan, combine the soy sauce, water, honey (or low-calorie sweetener), and cornstarch. Whisk together until the cornstarch is dissolved.
6. Place the saucepan over medium heat and bring the mixture to a simmer. Cook for 2-3 minutes, stirring constantly, until the sauce thickens and becomes glossy. Remove from heat.
7. In a separate pan, heat the olive oil over medium heat. Add the mixed vegetables and stir-fry for 5-7 minutes or until they are crisp-tender. Drizzle with low-sodium soy sauce and toss to coat.
8. Once the turkey meatballs are cooked, remove them from the oven and brush them with the prepared teriyaki glaze.
9. Serve the teriyaki glazed turkey meatballs alongside the stir-fried vegetables.

LEMON GARLIC GRILLED SHRIMP SKEWERS WITH QUINOA AND ROASTED ASPARAGUS

Nutrition: Cal 330;Fat 12 g;Carb 35 g;Protein 30 g
Serving 2; Соок time 30 min

Ingredients
FOR THE GRILLED SHRIMP SKEWERS:
- 1 pound shrimp, peeled and deveined
- 2 cloves garlic, minced
- 2 tablespoons lemon juice
- 1 tablespoon olive oil
- 1/2 teaspoon lemon zest
- Salt and pepper to taste

FOR THE QUINOA:
- 1 cup quinoa
- 2 cups water or low-sodium broth
- Salt to taste

FOR THE ROASTED ASPARAGUS:
- 1 bunch asparagus, trimmed
- 1 tablespoon olive oil
- Salt and pepper to taste

Instructions:
1. Preheat the grill to medium heat.
2. In a bowl, combine the minced garlic, lemon juice, olive oil, lemon zest, salt, and pepper. Mix well.
3. Thread the shrimp onto skewers and brush them with the lemon garlic marinade. Let them marinate for 10-15 minutes.
4. While the shrimp is marinating, rinse the quinoa under cold water. In a saucepan, bring the water or broth to a boil. Add the quinoa and salt, reduce the heat, cover, and simmer for 15-20 minutes or until the quinoa is tender and the liquid is absorbed. Fluff with a fork.

5. Preheat the oven to 400°F (200°C). Line a baking sheet with parchment paper.
6. Toss the trimmed asparagus with olive oil, salt, and pepper. Place them on the prepared baking sheet in a single layer. Roast for 10-12 minutes or until the asparagus is tender and slightly charred.
7. While the asparagus is roasting, grill the shrimp skewers for about 2-3 minutes per side or until they are pink and opaque.

STUFFED CABBAGE SOUP WITH LEAN GROUND BEEF AND CABBAGE

Nutrition: Cal 250;Fat 12 g;Carb 20 g;Protein 25 g
Serving 2; Cook time 40 min

Ingredients
- 1/2 pound lean ground beef
- 1/2 small onion, diced
- 2 cloves garlic, minced
- 4 cups low-sodium beef broth
- 1 can (14.5 ounces) diced tomatoes
- 2 cups shredded cabbage
- 1/2 cup cooked brown rice
- 1 teaspoon paprika
- 1/2 teaspoon dried thyme
- Salt and pepper to taste
- Fresh parsley for garnish (optional)

Instructions:
1. In a large pot or Dutch oven, brown the lean ground beef over medium heat. Break it up into small pieces using a spoon or spatula.
2. Add the diced onion and minced garlic to the pot and cook until the onion is translucent.
3. Pour in the beef broth and diced tomatoes with their juice. Stir in the shredded cabbage, cooked brown rice, paprika, dried thyme, salt, and pepper.
4. Bring the soup to a boil, then reduce the heat to low and let it simmer for about 25-30 minutes, or until the cabbage is tender.
5. Taste and adjust the seasoning with salt and pepper if needed.
6. Ladle the soup into bowls and garnish with fresh parsley, if desired.

GRILLED CHICKEN BREAST WITH ROASTED ROOT VEGETABLES

Nutrition: Cal 350;Fat 12 g;Carb 25 g;Protein 35 g
Serving 2; Cook time 40 min

Ingredients
- 2 boneless, skinless chicken breasts
- 2 tablespoons olive oil
- 1 teaspoon garlic powder
- 1 teaspoon paprika
- 1/2 teaspoon salt
- 1/4 teaspoon black pepper
- 2 cups mixed root vegetables (such as carrots, parsnips, and sweet potatoes), cut into small cubes
- 1 tablespoon chopped fresh rosemary (optional)
- Cooking spray

Instructions:
1. Preheat the grill to medium-high heat.
2. In a small bowl, mix together the olive oil, garlic powder, paprika, salt, and black pepper.
3. Brush the chicken breasts with the olive oil mixture on both sides.
4. Place the chicken breasts on the grill and cook for about 6-8 minutes per side, or until cooked through and the internal temperature reaches 165°F (75°C). Remove from the grill and let them rest for a few minutes.
5. While the chicken is grilling, preheat the oven to 425°F (220°C).
6. In a large mixing bowl, combine the mixed root vegetables with the remaining olive oil mixture and chopped rosemary (if using). Toss until the vegetables are evenly coated.
7. Spread the vegetables in a single layer on a baking sheet lined with parchment paper or sprayed with cooking spray.
8. Roast the vegetables in the preheated oven for about 20-25 minutes, or until they are tender and lightly browned, stirring once halfway through cooking.
9. Serve the grilled chicken breasts with the roasted root vegetables as a side.

LEMON HERB GRILLED TILAPIA WITH CAULIFLOWER RICE

Nutrition: Cal 250;Fat 9 g;Carb 12 g;Protein 30 g
Serving 2; Cook time 25 min

Ingredients

- 2 tilapia fillets
- 2 tablespoons fresh lemon juice
- 1 tablespoon olive oil
- 1 teaspoon dried oregano
- 1 teaspoon dried thyme
- 1/2 teaspoon garlic powder
- Salt and pepper to taste
- 2 cups cauliflower rice
- 1 tablespoon chopped fresh parsley (optional)

Instructions:

1. Preheat the grill to medium-high heat.
2. In a small bowl, mix together the lemon juice, olive oil, dried oregano, dried thyme, garlic powder, salt, and pepper.
3. Brush both sides of the tilapia fillets with the lemon herb mixture.
4. Place the tilapia fillets on the grill and cook for about 4-5 minutes per side, or until the fish is cooked through and flakes easily with a fork. Remove from the grill and set aside.
5. While the tilapia is grilling, prepare the cauliflower rice. You can use pre-packaged cauliflower rice or make your own by pulsing cauliflower florets in a food processor until they resemble rice grains.
6. Heat a non-stick skillet over medium heat and add the cauliflower rice. Cook for 5-6 minutes, or until the cauliflower rice is tender. You can add a little olive oil or vegetable broth for moisture if needed. Season with salt and pepper to taste.
7. Once the cauliflower rice is cooked, remove from heat and stir in the chopped fresh parsley (if using).
8. Serve the grilled tilapia fillets on top of the cauliflower rice.

SPINACH AND FETA STUFFED CHICKEN THIGHS

Nutrition: Cal 270;Fat 14 g;Carb 6 g;Protein 33 g
Serving 2; Cook time 25 min

Ingredients

FOR THE CHICKEN THIGHS:

- 4 boneless, skinless chicken thighs
- 1 cup fresh spinach, chopped
- 1/4 cup crumbled feta cheese
- 1/2 teaspoon garlic powder
- 1/2 teaspoon dried oregano
- Salt and pepper to taste
- Olive oil for cooking

FOR THE ROASTED BRUSSELS SPROUTS:

- 2 cups Brussels sprouts, halved
- 1 tablespoon olive oil
- Salt and pepper to taste

Instructions:

1. Preheat the oven to 400°F (200°C).
2. Prepare the chicken thighs by making a slit along one side of each thigh to create a pocket for the stuffing.
3. In a small bowl, mix together the chopped spinach, crumbled feta cheese, garlic powder, dried oregano, salt, and pepper.
4. Stuff each chicken thigh with the spinach and feta mixture, using toothpicks to secure the openings if necessary.
5. Heat a non-stick skillet over medium heat and add a drizzle of olive oil. Place the stuffed chicken thighs in the skillet and cook for about 4-5 minutes on each side, or until the chicken is browned. Remove from heat.
6. Transfer the browned chicken thighs to a baking dish and place in the preheated oven. Bake for approximately 20-25 minutes, or until the chicken is cooked through and reaches an internal temperature of 165°F (74°C).
7. While the chicken is baking, prepare the roasted Brussels sprouts. Place the halved Brussels sprouts on a baking sheet, drizzle with olive oil, and season with salt and pepper. Toss to coat evenly.
8. Place the baking sheet with Brussels sprouts in the oven alongside the chicken thighs and roast for approximately 15-20 minutes, or until the Brussels sprouts are tender and lightly browned.
9. Once the chicken thighs and Brussels sprouts are cooked, remove them from the oven.
10. Serve the spinach and feta stuffed chicken thighs with the roasted Brussels sprouts.

TURKEY AND BLACK BEAN CHILI WITH BELL PEPPERS AND SPICES

Nutrition: Cal 250;Fat 5 g;Carb 20 g;Protein 25 g

Serving 2; Cook time 30 min

Ingredients

- 1 pound lean ground turkey
- 1 bell pepper, diced
- 1 can (15 ounces) black beans, rinsed and drained
- 1 can (14 ounces) diced tomatoes
- 1 onion, diced
- 2 cloves garlic, minced
- 1 tablespoon chili powder
- 1 teaspoon cumin
- 1/2 teaspoon paprika
- 1/2 teaspoon oregano
- Salt and pepper to taste
- Optional toppings: chopped green onions, shredded cheese, plain Greek yogurt

Instructions:

1. Heat a large pot or Dutch oven over medium heat. Add the ground turkey and cook until browned, breaking it up with a spoon as it cooks.
2. Add the diced onion, minced garlic, and diced bell pepper to the pot. Cook for about 5 minutes, or until the vegetables have softened.
3. Stir in the chili powder, cumin, paprika, oregano, salt, and pepper. Cook for another minute to toast the spices and enhance their flavors.
4. Add the rinsed and drained black beans, diced tomatoes (with their juice), and about 1 cup of water to the pot. Stir well to combine all the ingredients.
5. Bring the chili to a simmer and let it cook for about 20 minutes, stirring occasionally. If the chili becomes too thick, you can add more water as needed.
6. Taste and adjust the seasoning with salt and pepper if desired.
7. Serve the turkey and black bean chili hot, topped with your choice of optional toppings such as chopped green onions, shredded cheese, or a dollop of plain Greek yogurt.

BAKED ITALIAN CHICKEN WITH ZUCCHINI NOODLES AND MARINARA SAUCE

Nutrition: Cal 300;Fat 10 g;Carb 15 g;Protein 30 g
Serving 2; Cook time 30 min

Ingredients

FOR THE BAKED ITALIAN CHICKEN:

- 2 boneless, skinless chicken breasts
- 1 tablespoon olive oil
- 1 teaspoon dried Italian seasoning
- 1/2 teaspoon garlic powder
- Salt and pepper to taste

FOR THE ZUCCHINI NOODLES:

- 2 medium-sized zucchini
- 1 tablespoon olive oil
- Salt and pepper to taste

FOR THE MARINARA SAUCE:

- 1 cup low-sodium marinara sauce

Instructions:

1. Preheat your oven to 400°F (200°C).
2. Place the chicken breasts on a baking sheet lined with parchment paper. Drizzle the olive oil over the chicken breasts and sprinkle with the dried Italian seasoning, garlic powder, salt, and pepper. Use your hands to rub the seasoning onto the chicken to coat evenly.
3. Bake the chicken in the preheated oven for 20-25 minutes, or until the internal temperature reaches 165°F (74°C). Remove from the oven and let the chicken rest for a few minutes before slicing.
4. While the chicken is baking, prepare the zucchini noodles. Using a spiralizer or a vegetable peeler, create long, thin strips of zucchini noodles. Heat the olive oil in a large skillet over medium heat. Add the zucchini noodles and sauté for 2-3 minutes until tender but still slightly crisp. Season with salt and pepper to taste.
5. In a small saucepan, heat the marinara sauce over low heat until warmed through.
6. To serve, divide the zucchini noodles between two plates. Top with sliced baked Italian chicken and drizzle with marinara sauce. Garnish with grated Parmesan cheese and fresh basil leaves if desired.

GREEK-STYLE STUFFED EGGPLANT BOATS WITH GROUND TURKEY AND TOMATOES

Nutrition: Cal 310;Fat 6 g;Carb 21 g;Protein 26 g
Serving 2; Cook time 45 min

Ingredients

- 2 small eggplants

- 1 tablespoon olive oil
- 1/2 medium onion, finely chopped
- 2 cloves garlic, minced
- 1/2 pound lean ground turkey
- 1/2 cup diced tomatoes
- 2 tablespoons tomato paste
- 1 teaspoon dried oregano
- 1/2 teaspoon dried basil
- Salt and pepper to taste
- 1/4 cup crumbled feta cheese
- Fresh parsley for garnish

Instructions:

1. Preheat your oven to 375°F (190°C).
2. Slice the eggplants in half lengthwise. Use a spoon to scoop out the flesh, leaving about a 1/4-inch thick shell. Chop the scooped-out eggplant flesh into small pieces and set aside.
3. Heat the olive oil in a large skillet over medium heat. Add the onion and garlic and sauté until softened and fragrant, about 3-4 minutes.
4. Add the ground turkey to the skillet and cook until browned, breaking it up into small pieces with a spoon.
5. Add the diced tomatoes, tomato paste, dried oregano, dried basil, salt, and pepper to the skillet. Stir to combine.
6. Add the chopped eggplant flesh to the skillet and cook for an additional 5 minutes, or until the eggplant is tender.
7. Place the hollowed-out eggplant shells on a baking sheet lined with parchment paper. Fill each shell with the turkey and eggplant mixture.
8. Bake in the preheated oven for 20-25 minutes, or until the eggplant boats are tender and slightly browned.
9. Remove from the oven and sprinkle the tops with crumbled feta cheese. Return to the oven for an additional 5 minutes, or until the cheese is melted and bubbly.
10. Garnish with fresh parsley before serving.

GRILLED LEMON HERB CHICKEN THIGHS WITH ROASTED BRUSSELS SPROUTS

Nutrition: Cal 360;Fat 17 g;Carb 23 g;Protein 33 g
Serving 2; Cook time 40 min

Ingredients
FOR THE CHICKEN:

- 4 bone-in, skin-on chicken thighs
- 1 lemon, juiced and zested
- 2 cloves garlic, minced
- 1 tablespoon fresh parsley, chopped
- 1 tablespoon fresh rosemary, chopped
- 1 tablespoon olive oil
- Salt and pepper to taste

FOR THE ROASTED BRUSSELS SPROUTS AND SWEET POTATOES:

- 1 cup Brussels sprouts, trimmed and halved
- 1 small sweet potato, peeled and diced
- 1 tablespoon olive oil
- Salt and pepper to taste

Instructions:

1. Preheat your grill to medium heat.
2. In a small bowl, combine the lemon juice, lemon zest, minced garlic, chopped parsley, chopped rosemary, olive oil, salt, and pepper to make the marinade for the chicken.
3. Place the chicken thighs in a resealable plastic bag or a shallow dish. Pour the marinade over the chicken, ensuring each piece is coated. Marinate in the refrigerator for at least 30 minutes.
4. In the meantime, preheat your oven to 400°F (200°C).
5. Toss the halved Brussels sprouts and diced sweet potatoes with olive oil, salt, and pepper. Spread them out on a baking sheet lined with parchment paper.
6. Roast the Brussels sprouts and sweet potatoes in the preheated oven for 20-25 minutes, or until they are tender and lightly browned.
7. While the vegetables are roasting, remove the chicken from the marinade and discard any excess marinade. Season the chicken thighs with salt and pepper.
8. Grill the chicken thighs over medium heat for about 8-10 minutes per side, or until they reach an internal temperature of 165°F (74°C) and the skin is crispy and golden.
9. Once the chicken is cooked through, remove it from the grill and let it rest for a few minutes before serving.

10. Serve the grilled lemon herb chicken thighs alongside the roasted Brussels sprouts and sweet potatoes.

TURKEY AND VEGETABLE STIR-FRY WITH SESAME

Nutrition: Cal 355;Fat 11 g;Carb 37 g;Protein 26 g
Serving 2; Cook time 20 min

Ingredients
FOR THE STIR-FRY:
• 8 ounces lean ground turkey
• 1 tablespoon sesame oil
• 1 bell pepper, thinly sliced
• 1 small zucchini, thinly sliced
• 1 cup broccoli florets
• 1 cup snap peas
• 2 green onions, sliced
• 1 tablespoon low-sodium soy sauce
• 1/2 teaspoon garlic powder
• 1/2 teaspoon ginger powder
• Salt and pepper to taste
FOR THE SESAME GINGER SAUCE:
• 2 tablespoons low-sodium soy sauce
• 1 tablespoon rice vinegar
• 1 tablespoon honey or a low-calorie sweetener
• 1 teaspoon sesame oil
• 1/2 teaspoon grated fresh ginger
• 1/2 teaspoon cornstarch (optional, for thickening)
FOR THE BROWN RICE:
• 1 cup cooked brown rice
Instructions:
1. Heat the sesame oil in a large skillet or wok over medium heat. Add the ground turkey and cook until browned, breaking it up into small pieces with a spoon.
2. Add the bell pepper, zucchini, broccoli, snap peas, and green onions to the skillet. Stir-fry for about 5-7 minutes, or until the vegetables are tender-crisp.
3. In a small bowl, whisk together the soy sauce, garlic powder, ginger powder, salt, and pepper. Pour the sauce over the stir-fry and toss to coat the ingredients evenly.
4. In another small bowl, whisk together the soy sauce, rice vinegar, honey (or low-calorie sweetener), sesame oil, grated ginger, and cornstarch (if using) to make the sesame ginger sauce.
5. Pour the sesame ginger sauce over the stir-fry and cook for an additional 2-3 minutes, or until the sauce thickens slightly.
6. Serve the turkey and vegetable stir-fry over cooked brown rice.

STUFFED BELL PEPPERS WITH QUINOA, BLACK BEANS, AND CORN

Nutrition: Cal 260;Fat 4 g;Carb 46 g;Protein 211g
Serving 2; Cook time 45 min

Ingredients
• 2 large bell peppers (any color)
• 1/2 cup cooked quinoa
• 1/2 cup canned black beans, rinsed and drained
• 1/2 cup frozen corn, thawed
• 1/4 cup diced red onion
• 1/4 cup diced tomatoes
• 1/4 cup shredded low-fat cheese (optional)
• 1 tablespoon chopped fresh cilantro
• 1/2 teaspoon cumin
• 1/2 teaspoon chili powder
• Salt and pepper to taste
Instructions:
1. Preheat your oven to 375°F (190°C).
2. Slice off the tops of the bell peppers and remove the seeds and membranes. Rinse the peppers and set them aside.
3. In a mixing bowl, combine the cooked quinoa, black beans, corn, red onion, tomatoes, cilantro, cumin, chili powder, salt, and pepper. Mix well to combine all the ingredients.
4. Stuff the bell peppers with the quinoa mixture, dividing it equally between the two peppers. Press the filling down gently to fill the peppers.
5. If desired, sprinkle the shredded cheese over the top of the stuffed peppers.
6. Place the stuffed peppers in a baking dish and cover with foil.
7. Bake in the preheated oven for about 25-30 minutes or until the peppers are tender and the filling is heated through.
8. Remove the foil and continue baking for an additional 5 minutes to allow the cheese to melt and slightly brown (if using).

9. Remove the stuffed peppers from the oven and let them cool slightly before serving.

SHRIMP AND BROCCOLI CAULIFLOWER FRIED RICE

Nutrition: Cal 280;Fat 11 g;Carb 18 g;Protein 23g
Serving 2; Cook time 20 min

Ingredients
- 1 head cauliflower
- 1 tablespoon vegetable oil
- 8 ounces shrimp, peeled and deveined
- 1 cup chopped broccoli florets
- 1/2 cup diced carrots
- 1/2 cup diced bell peppers (any color)
- 2 cloves garlic, minced
- 2 tablespoons low-sodium soy sauce
- 1 tablespoon sesame oil
- 1/2 teaspoon ground ginger
- Salt and pepper to taste
- Optional garnish: sliced green onions

Instructions:
1. Cut the cauliflower into florets and pulse in a food processor until it reaches a rice-like consistency. Set aside.
2. In a large skillet or wok, heat the vegetable oil over medium-high heat.
3. Add the shrimp to the skillet and cook until pink and cooked through, about 2-3 minutes per side. Remove the shrimp from the skillet and set aside.
4. In the same skillet, add the broccoli, carrots, bell peppers, and minced garlic. Stir-fry for 3-4 minutes until the vegetables are crisp-tender.
5. Push the vegetables to one side of the skillet and add the cauliflower rice to the other side. Cook for 2-3 minutes, stirring occasionally, until the cauliflower rice is heated through.
6. In a small bowl, whisk together the soy sauce, sesame oil, and ground ginger. Pour the sauce over the cauliflower rice and vegetables. Stir to combine everything well.
7. Return the cooked shrimp to the skillet and toss with the cauliflower rice and vegetables. Cook for an additional 1-2 minutes to warm the shrimp.
8. Season with salt and pepper to taste. Garnish with sliced green onions if desired.

LEMON GARLIC ROASTED PORK CHOPS WITH STEAMED GREEN BEANS

Nutrition: Cal 260;Fat 11 g;Carb 12 g;Protein 30 g
Serving 2; Cook time 30 min

Ingredients
- 2 boneless pork chops (4-6 ounces each)
- 2 tablespoons lemon juice
- 2 cloves garlic, minced
- 1 tablespoon olive oil
- 1/2 teaspoon dried thyme
- Salt and pepper to taste
- 1 cup fresh green beans, trimmed
- Optional garnish: lemon wedges and chopped parsley

Instructions:
1. Preheat your oven to 400°F (200°C).
2. In a small bowl, whisk together the lemon juice, minced garlic, olive oil, dried thyme, salt, and pepper.
3. Place the pork chops in a shallow dish and pour the lemon garlic marinade over them. Make sure the pork chops are well coated. Let them marinate for at least 15 minutes.
4. While the pork chops are marinating, prepare the green beans by washing them and trimming the ends.
5. Arrange the marinated pork chops on a baking sheet lined with parchment paper. Pour any remaining marinade over the pork chops.
6. Place the pork chops in the preheated oven and roast for about 20-25 minutes, or until they reach an internal temperature of 145°F (63°C).
7. While the pork chops are roasting, steam the green beans. Fill a pot with about 1 inch of water and bring it to a boil. Place the green beans in a steamer basket and place it over the boiling water. Cover the pot and steam the green beans for 5-7 minutes, or until they are tender-crisp.
8. Once the pork chops are cooked, remove them from the oven and let them rest for a few minutes before serving.
9. Serve the roasted pork chops with steamed green beans on the side. Garnish with lemon wedges and chopped parsley, if desired.

GREEK-STYLE STUFFED ZUCCHINI WITH GROUND TURKEY AND TOMATOES

Nutrition: Cal 250;Fat 13 g;Carb 10 g;Protein 30 g
Serving 2; Cook time 30 min

Ingredients
- 2 boneless pork chops (4-6 ounces each)
- 2 tablespoons lemon juice
- 2 cloves garlic, minced
- 1 tablespoon olive oil
- 1/2 teaspoon dried thyme
- Salt and pepper to taste
- 1 cup fresh green beans, trimmed
- Optional garnish: lemon wedges and chopped parsley

Instructions:
1. Preheat your oven to 400°F (200°C).
2. In a small bowl, whisk together the lemon juice, minced garlic, olive oil, dried thyme, salt, and pepper.
3. Place the pork chops in a shallow dish and pour the lemon garlic marinade over them. Make sure the pork chops are well coated. Let them marinate for at least 15 minutes.
4. While the pork chops are marinating, prepare the green beans by washing them and trimming the ends.
5. Arrange the marinated pork chops on a baking sheet lined with parchment paper. Pour any remaining marinade over the pork chops.
6. Place the pork chops in the preheated oven and roast for about 20-25 minutes, or until they reach an internal temperature of 145°F (63°C).
7. While the pork chops are roasting, steam the green beans. Fill a pot with about 1 inch of water and bring it to a boil. Place the green beans in a steamer basket and place it over the boiling water. Cover the pot and steam the green beans for 5-7 minutes, or until they are tender-crisp.
8. Once the pork chops are cooked, remove them from the oven and let them rest for a few minutes before serving.
9. Serve the roasted pork chops with steamed green beans on the side. Garnish with lemon wedges and chopped parsley, if desired.

CAULIFLOWER CRUST PIZZA WITH CHICKEN, SPINACH, AND FETA

Nutrition: Cal 280;Fat 12 g;Carb 18 g;Protein 24 g
Serving 2; Cook time 24 min

Ingredients
FOR THE CRUST:
- 1 medium cauliflower head, riced
- 1/2 cup grated Parmesan cheese
- 1/4 cup almond flour
- 1 egg, beaten
- 1/2 teaspoon dried oregano
- 1/2 teaspoon garlic powder
- Salt and pepper to taste

FOR THE TOPPINGS:
- 1/2 cup marinara sauce (look for a low-sugar option)
- 1 cup cooked chicken breast, shredded
- 1 cup fresh spinach leaves
- 1/4 cup crumbled feta cheese
- Fresh basil leaves for garnish

Instructions:
1. Preheat your oven to 425°F (220°C). Line a baking sheet with parchment paper.
2. Prepare the cauliflower crust by placing the riced cauliflower in a microwave-safe bowl. Microwave on high for 5-6 minutes, or until the cauliflower is cooked and softened. Allow it to cool slightly.
3. Transfer the cooked cauliflower to a clean kitchen towel or cheesecloth. Squeeze out as much liquid as possible from the cauliflower.
4. In a mixing bowl, combine the squeezed cauliflower, grated Parmesan cheese, almond flour, beaten egg, dried oregano, garlic powder, salt, and pepper. Mix well until a dough-like consistency forms.
5. Place the cauliflower dough on the prepared baking sheet. Use your hands to shape it into a round or rectangular pizza crust, about 1/4 inch thick.
6. Bake the cauliflower crust in the preheated oven for 15-20 minutes, or until it becomes golden and slightly crispy.
7. Remove the crust from the oven and let it cool for a few minutes.
8. Spread the marinara sauce evenly over the crust, leaving a small border around the edges.

9. Top the sauce with shredded chicken breast, fresh spinach leaves, and crumbled feta cheese.

10. Return the pizza to the oven and bake for an additional 10-15 minutes, or until the toppings are heated through and the cheese has melted.

11. Once the pizza is ready, remove it from the oven and garnish with fresh basil leaves.

12. Slice the cauliflower crust pizza and serve hot.

TERIYAKI GLAZED SALMON WITH CAULIFLOWER RICE AND STIR-FRIED VEGETABLES

Nutrition: Cal 380;Fat 18 g;Carb 16 g;Protein 30 g
Serving 2; Cook time 30 min

Ingredients
FOR THE TERIYAKI GLAZE:
- 2 tablespoons low-sodium soy sauce
- 2 tablespoons honey or a low-calorie sweetener
- 1 tablespoon rice vinegar
- 1 tablespoon sesame oil
- 1 teaspoon grated fresh ginger
- 1 clove garlic, minced

FOR THE SALMON:
- 2 salmon fillets (4-6 ounces each)
- Salt and pepper to taste

FOR THE CAULIFLOWER RICE:
- 1 medium cauliflower head, riced
- 1 tablespoon olive oil
- Salt and pepper to taste

FOR THE STIR-FRIED VEGETABLES:
- 1 tablespoon olive oil
- 1 cup mixed vegetables (such as bell peppers, broccoli, and carrots), thinly sliced
- 1 clove garlic, minced
- 1 teaspoon low-sodium soy sauce

Instructions:
1. Preheat your oven to 400°F (200°C). Line a baking sheet with parchment paper.

2. In a small bowl, whisk together the ingredients for the teriyaki glaze: soy sauce, honey, rice vinegar, sesame oil, grated ginger, and minced garlic.

3. Place the salmon fillets on the prepared baking sheet. Brush the teriyaki glaze over the salmon, coating it evenly. Set aside to marinate for a few minutes.

4. In the meantime, prepare the cauliflower rice. Place the riced cauliflower in a microwave-safe bowl and microwave on high for 3-4 minutes, or until it is cooked but still slightly firm. Drain any excess moisture.

5. Heat 1 tablespoon of olive oil in a skillet over medium heat. Add the cauliflower rice and sauté for 3-4 minutes, or until it is heated through. Season with salt and pepper to taste. Set aside.

6. In a separate skillet, heat 1 tablespoon of olive oil over medium-high heat. Add the mixed vegetables and minced garlic. Stir-fry for 4-5 minutes, or until the vegetables are crisp-tender. Drizzle with 1 teaspoon of low-sodium soy sauce and toss to coat. Remove from heat.

7. Place the marinated salmon in the preheated oven and bake for 12-15 minutes, or until it is cooked to your desired level of doneness.

8. Once the salmon is cooked, remove it from the oven and let it rest for a few minutes.

9. Divide the cauliflower rice between two plates and top each portion with a salmon fillet.

10. Serve the teriyaki glazed salmon with stir-fried vegetables on the side.

MEXICAN-STYLE STUFFED PORTOBELLO MUSHROOMS

Nutrition: Cal 270;Fat 11 g;Carb 18 g;Protein 22 g
Serving 2; Cook time 30 min

Ingredients
- 4 large portobello mushrooms
- 1/2 pound lean ground beef
- 1/2 cup canned black beans, rinsed and drained
- 1/4 cup diced onion
- 1/4 cup diced bell pepper
- 1 clove garlic, minced
- 1/2 teaspoon ground cumin
- 1/2 teaspoon chili powder
- Salt and pepper to taste
- 1/4 cup shredded reduced-fat cheese (such as cheddar or Mexican blend)
- Fresh cilantro, for garnish

Instructions:
1. Preheat the oven to 375°F (190°C).

2. Clean the portobello mushrooms and remove the stems.

3. In a skillet, cook the lean ground beef over medium heat until browned. Drain any excess fat.
4. Add the diced onion, bell pepper, and minced garlic to the skillet. Cook until the vegetables are softened.
5. Stir in the black beans, ground cumin, chili powder, salt, and pepper. Cook for an additional 2-3 minutes.
6. Spoon the beef and black bean mixture into the hollowed-out portobello mushrooms.
7. Place the stuffed mushrooms on a baking sheet and sprinkle with shredded cheese.
8. Bake in the preheated oven for 15-20 minutes, or until the mushrooms are tender and the cheese is melted and bubbly.
9. Garnish with fresh cilantro before serving.

GARLIC HERB GRILLED TURKEY TENDERLOIN WITH ROASTED ROOT VEGETABLES

Nutrition: Cal 330;Fat 10 g;Carb 30 g;Protein 25 g
Serving 2; Cook time 45 min

Ingredients
- 1 turkey tenderloin (approximately 1 pound)
- 2 cloves garlic, minced
- 1 teaspoon dried thyme
- 1 teaspoon dried rosemary
- Salt and pepper to taste
- 2 tablespoons olive oil
- 2 medium-sized carrots, peeled and cut into sticks
- 2 medium-sized parsnips, peeled and cut into sticks
- 1 medium-sized sweet potato, peeled and cut into cubes
- 1 medium-sized beet, peeled and cut into cubes
- Cooking spray

Instructions:
1. Preheat the grill to medium-high heat.
2. In a small bowl, mix together minced garlic, dried thyme, dried rosemary, salt, pepper, and olive oil to make a marinade.
3. Rub the turkey tenderloin with the marinade, coating it evenly. Let it marinate for about 15 minutes.
4. While the turkey is marinating, preheat the oven to 400°F (200°C).

5. Place the prepared carrots, parsnips, sweet potato, and beet in a roasting pan. Lightly spray them with cooking spray and season with salt and pepper to taste.
6. Roast the vegetables in the preheated oven for about 25-30 minutes or until they are tender and lightly browned.
7. Meanwhile, grill the marinated turkey tenderloin on the preheated grill for about 15-20 minutes, turning occasionally, until it reaches an internal temperature of 165°F (74°C).
8. Remove the turkey tenderloin from the grill and let it rest for a few minutes before slicing.
9. Serve the grilled turkey tenderloin with the roasted root vegetables.

SPAGHETTI SQUASH WITH TURKEY BOLOGNESE SAUCE AND A SIDE SALAD

Nutrition: Cal 400;Fat 12 g;Carb 35 g;Protein 32 g
Serving 2; Cook time 70 min

Ingredients
- 1 medium-sized spaghetti squash
- 1 pound lean ground turkey
- 1 small onion, diced
- 2 cloves garlic, minced
- 1 can (14 ounces) diced tomatoes
- 2 tablespoons tomato paste
- 1 teaspoon dried basil
- 1 teaspoon dried oregano
- Salt and pepper to taste
- Optional: 1/4 teaspoon red pepper flakes (for a spicy kick)
- Cooking spray

FOR THE SIDE SALAD:
- Mixed salad greens
- Cherry tomatoes, halved
- Cucumber, sliced
- Red onion, thinly sliced
- Dressing of your choice (low-fat or vinaigrette recommended)

Instructions:
1. Preheat the oven to 400°F (200°C).
2. Cut the spaghetti squash in half lengthwise and scoop out the seeds. Place the halves, cut side down, on a baking sheet lined with parchment paper. Bake for about 40-45 minutes, or until

the squash is tender and easily separates into strands with a fork.

3. While the spaghetti squash is baking, heat a large skillet over medium heat. Spray the skillet with cooking spray and add the ground turkey. Cook until browned, breaking it up into crumbles.

4. Add the diced onion and minced garlic to the skillet with the turkey. Cook for about 2-3 minutes, until the onion is softened.

5. Stir in the diced tomatoes (with their juice), tomato paste, dried basil, dried oregano, salt, pepper, and optional red pepper flakes. Reduce the heat to low and simmer for about 15-20 minutes, allowing the flavors to meld together.

6. Remove the spaghetti squash from the oven and use a fork to scrape the flesh, separating it into spaghetti-like strands. Transfer the squash strands to a serving dish.

7. Serve the spaghetti squash with the turkey Bolognese sauce on top. Garnish with fresh herbs if desired.

8. In a separate bowl, toss together the mixed salad greens, cherry tomatoes, cucumber, and red onion. Drizzle with your preferred dressing.

9. Serve the spaghetti squash and Bolognese sauce with the side salad.

LEMON GINGER GRILLED SHRIMP SKEWERS WITH QUINOA AND ROASTED ASPARAGUS

Nutrition: Cal 320;Fat 10 g;Carb 33 g;Protein 28 g
Serving 2; Cook time 30 min

Ingredients
FOR THE SHRIMP SKEWERS:
- 10-12 large shrimp, peeled and deveined
- 1 tablespoon fresh lemon juice
- 1 tablespoon low-sodium soy sauce
- 1 teaspoon grated ginger
- 1 clove garlic, minced
- Salt and pepper to taste
- Skewers (soaked in water if using wooden skewers)

FOR THE QUINOA:
- 1/2 cup quinoa

- 1 cup water or low-sodium chicken broth
- Salt to taste

FOR THE ROASTED ASPARAGUS:
- 1 bunch asparagus, ends trimmed
- 1 tablespoon olive oil
- Salt and pepper to taste

Instructions:
1. In a bowl, combine the lemon juice, soy sauce, grated ginger, minced garlic, salt, and pepper. Add the shrimp to the bowl and marinate for about 15 minutes.

2. While the shrimp is marinating, rinse the quinoa under cold water to remove any bitterness. In a small saucepan, bring the water or chicken broth to a boil. Add the quinoa and a pinch of salt, then reduce the heat to low. Cover and simmer for about 15 minutes, or until the liquid is absorbed and the quinoa is tender. Fluff with a fork.

3. Preheat the grill to medium-high heat. If using wooden skewers, make sure to soak them in water for about 15 minutes before grilling.

4. Thread the marinated shrimp onto the skewers.

5. In a separate bowl, toss the trimmed asparagus with olive oil, salt, and pepper.

6. Place the shrimp skewers and asparagus on the preheated grill. Grill the shrimp for about 2-3 minutes per side, or until they are pink and opaque. Grill the asparagus for about 5-7 minutes, turning occasionally, until they are tender and lightly charred.

7. Remove the shrimp skewers and asparagus from the grill.

8. Serve the grilled shrimp skewers on a bed of cooked quinoa, and arrange the roasted asparagus alongside.

9. Garnish with fresh herbs, if desired, and squeeze fresh lemon juice over the shrimp before serving.

STUFFED CABBAGE ROLLS WITH LEAN GROUND CHICKEN AND BROWN RICE

Nutrition: Cal 300;Fat 8 g;Carb 30 g;Protein 25 g
Serving 2; Cook time 60 min

Ingredients
FOR THE CABBAGE ROLLS:

- 8 large cabbage leaves
- 300 grams lean ground chicken
- 1/2 cup cooked brown rice
- 1 small onion, finely chopped
- 2 cloves garlic, minced
- 1/4 teaspoon dried thyme
- 1/4 teaspoon dried oregano
- 1/4 teaspoon paprika
- Salt and pepper to taste
- 1 cup low-sodium tomato sauce

FOR THE TOMATO SAUCE:
- 1 cup low-sodium tomato sauce
- 1/2 cup water
- 1/2 teaspoon dried basil
- 1/2 teaspoon dried oregano
- Salt and pepper to taste

Instructions:
1. Preheat the oven to 180°C (350°F).
2. Bring a large pot of water to a boil. Add the cabbage leaves and blanch for 2-3 minutes until they are slightly tender. Remove the leaves and set them aside to cool.
3. In a mixing bowl, combine the ground chicken, cooked brown rice, chopped onion, minced garlic, dried thyme, dried oregano, paprika, salt, and pepper. Mix well until all ingredients are combined.
4. Take one cabbage leaf and place a portion of the chicken and rice mixture in the center. Roll the leaf tightly, folding in the sides as you go. Repeat with the remaining cabbage leaves and filling.
5. In a baking dish, spread a thin layer of tomato sauce to prevent sticking. Arrange the cabbage rolls in the dish, seam side down.
6. In a small bowl, whisk together the tomato sauce, water, dried basil, dried oregano, salt, and pepper. Pour the sauce over the cabbage rolls, covering them evenly.
7. Cover the baking dish with foil and bake in the preheated oven for 40-45 minutes, or until the cabbage is tender and the filling is cooked through.
8. Remove from the oven and let the cabbage rolls cool slightly before serving.

CHICKEN FAJITA BOWLS WITH PEPPERS, ONIONS, BLACK BEANS, AND SALSA

Nutrition: Cal 350;Fat 12 g;Carb 45 g;Protein 30 g
Serving 2; Cook time 30 min

Ingredients
FOR THE CHICKEN FAJITAS:
- 2 boneless, skinless chicken breasts
- 1 red bell pepper, sliced
- 1 green bell pepper, sliced
- 1 small onion, sliced
- 1 tablespoon olive oil
- 1 teaspoon chili powder
- 1/2 teaspoon cumin
- 1/2 teaspoon paprika
- 1/2 teaspoon garlic powder
- Salt and pepper to taste

FOR THE BOWL:
- 1 cup cooked quinoa
- 1 cup canned black beans, rinsed and drained
- Salsa for serving
- Optional toppings: chopped cilantro, avocado slices, lime wedges

Instructions:
1. Preheat the oven to 200°C (400°F).
2. Season the chicken breasts with chili powder, cumin, paprika, garlic powder, salt, and pepper.
3. Heat a grill pan or skillet over medium-high heat. Add the olive oil and cook the chicken breasts for about 6-8 minutes on each side, or until cooked through. Remove the chicken from the pan and let it rest for a few minutes before slicing into strips.
4. In the same pan, add the sliced bell peppers and onions. Cook for 4-5 minutes, or until they are slightly softened and have some char marks.
5. In serving bowls, divide the cooked quinoa, black beans, sliced chicken, and sautéed peppers and onions.
6. Serve with salsa and optional toppings such as chopped cilantro, avocado slices, and lime wedges.

GREEK-STYLE STUFFED TOMATOES WITH QUINOA, SPINACH, AND FETA CHEESE

Nutrition: Cal 250;Fat 12 g;Carb 25 g;Protein 10 g
Serving 2; Cook time 45 min

Ingredients
- 4 large tomatoes
- 1/2 cup uncooked quinoa
- 1 cup water or vegetable broth
- 2 cups fresh spinach, chopped
- 1/2 cup crumbled feta cheese
- 1/4 cup chopped fresh parsley
- 2 tablespoons olive oil
- 2 cloves garlic, minced
- 1/2 teaspoon dried oregano
- Salt and pepper to taste

Instructions:
1. Preheat the oven to 200°C (400°F).
2. Cut off the top of each tomato and scoop out the pulp and seeds to create a hollow center. Set aside.
3. Rinse the quinoa under cold water. In a small saucepan, combine the quinoa and water (or vegetable broth). Bring to a boil, then reduce the heat, cover, and simmer for 15-20 minutes, or until the quinoa is cooked and the liquid is absorbed.
4. In a large mixing bowl, combine the cooked quinoa, chopped spinach, feta cheese, parsley, olive oil, minced garlic, dried oregano, salt, and pepper. Mix well to combine.
5. Stuff each tomato with the quinoa mixture, pressing it down gently.
6. Place the stuffed tomatoes in a baking dish and bake for 20-25 minutes, or until the tomatoes are tender and the filling is heated through.
7. Serve the Greek-style stuffed tomatoes as a main dish or as a side dish with a salad or steamed vegetables.

MOROCCAN-SPICED TURKEY MEATBALLS WITH CAULIFLOWER COUSCOUS

Nutrition: Cal 250;Fat 12 g;Carb 20 g;Protein 30 g
Serving 2; Cook time 40 min

Ingredients
FOR THE MEATBALLS:
- 250g lean ground turkey
- 1/4 cup almond flour
- 1 small onion, finely chopped
- 2 cloves garlic, minced
- 1 teaspoon ground cumin
- 1 teaspoon ground coriander
- 1/2 teaspoon ground cinnamon
- 1/2 teaspoon paprika
- 1/4 teaspoon ground ginger
- 1/4 teaspoon cayenne pepper (optional, for extra spice)
- 1 tablespoon chopped fresh parsley
- Salt and pepper to taste
- Cooking spray or olive oil for greasing

FOR THE CAULIFLOWER COUSCOUS:
- 1 small head cauliflower
- 1 tablespoon olive oil
- 2 tablespoons chopped fresh cilantro
- Juice of 1 lemon
- Salt and pepper to taste

Instructions:
1. Preheat the oven to 200°C (400°F).
2. In a large mixing bowl, combine the ground turkey, almond flour, chopped onion, minced garlic, cumin, coriander, cinnamon, paprika, ground ginger, cayenne pepper (if using), chopped parsley, salt, and pepper. Mix well until all the ingredients are evenly incorporated.
3. Shape the mixture into small meatballs, about 1 inch in diameter. Place them on a baking sheet lined with parchment paper or greased with cooking spray or olive oil.
4. Bake the meatballs in the preheated oven for 15-20 minutes, or until cooked through and lightly browned.
5. Meanwhile, prepare the cauliflower couscous. Cut the cauliflower into florets and place them in a food processor. Pulse several times until the cauliflower resembles couscous or rice-like texture.
6. Heat olive oil in a large skillet over medium heat. Add the cauliflower couscous and sauté for 5-7 minutes, or until tender but still slightly crisp.
7. Remove the skillet from heat and stir in the chopped cilantro, lemon juice, salt, and pepper.

8. Serve the Moroccan-spiced turkey meatballs over the cauliflower couscous and garnish with additional parsley or cilantro, if desired.

TERIYAKI TOFU AND VEGETABLE STIR-FRY WITH BROWN RICE

Nutrition: Cal 380;Fat 11 g;Carb 37 g;Protein 18 g
Serving 2; Cook time 25 min

Ingredients
FOR THE STIR-FRY:
• 200g firm tofu, drained and cubed
• 1 cup mixed vegetables (such as bell peppers, broccoli, carrots, snap peas)
• 1 small onion, thinly sliced
• 2 cloves garlic, minced
• 2 tablespoons low-sodium teriyaki sauce
• 1 tablespoon low-sodium soy sauce
• 1 tablespoon rice vinegar
• 1 tablespoon sesame oil
• 1 tablespoon cornstarch (optional, for thickening the sauce)
• Cooking spray or oil for frying
FOR THE BROWN RICE:
• 1 cup cooked brown rice
Instructions:
1. Heat a large skillet or wok over medium heat and lightly coat it with cooking spray or oil.
2. Add the tofu cubes to the skillet and cook for 5-7 minutes, or until they are lightly browned and crispy on the outside. Remove the tofu from the skillet and set aside.
3. In the same skillet, add the sliced onion and minced garlic. Sauté for 2-3 minutes until the onion becomes translucent.
4. Add the mixed vegetables to the skillet and stir-fry for another 3-5 minutes, or until they are tender-crisp.
5. In a small bowl, whisk together the teriyaki sauce, soy sauce, rice vinegar, sesame oil, and cornstarch (if using). Pour the sauce over the vegetables in the skillet.
6. Return the tofu to the skillet and toss everything together until the sauce coats the tofu and vegetables evenly. Cook for an additional 1-2 minutes, or until the sauce thickens slightly.

7. Remove the skillet from heat and let it sit for a few minutes to allow the flavors to meld together.
8. Serve the teriyaki tofu and vegetable stir-fry over a bed of cooked brown rice.

SPINACH AND FETA STUFFED CHICKEN ROLL-UPS WITH ROASTED CAULIFLOWER

Nutrition: Cal 250;Fat 10 g;Carb 10 g;Protein 30 g
Serving 2; Cook time 35 min

Ingredients
FOR THE CHICKEN ROLL-UPS:
• 2 boneless, skinless chicken breasts
• 2 cups fresh spinach leaves
• 1/4 cup crumbled feta cheese
• 1 teaspoon dried oregano
• Salt and pepper, to taste
FOR THE ROASTED CAULIFLOWER:
• 1 small head cauliflower, cut into florets
• 1 tablespoon olive oil
• 1 teaspoon garlic powder
• Salt and pepper, to taste
Instructions:
1. Preheat the oven to 400°F (200°C).
2. Butterfly the chicken breasts by slicing them horizontally but not all the way through. Open the chicken breasts like a book.
3. Place the chicken breasts between two sheets of plastic wrap and gently pound them with a meat mallet or rolling pin to flatten them to an even thickness.
4. In a bowl, combine the fresh spinach, crumbled feta cheese, dried oregano, salt, and pepper.
5. Spread the spinach and feta mixture evenly on one side of each flattened chicken breast.
6. Roll up the chicken breasts tightly, tucking in the filling as you go. Secure the roll-ups with toothpicks.
7. Place the chicken roll-ups in a baking dish and lightly season with salt and pepper.
8. In a separate bowl, toss the cauliflower florets with olive oil, garlic powder, salt, and pepper.
9. Spread the cauliflower evenly on a baking sheet lined with parchment paper.
10. Place both the baking dish with the chicken roll-ups and the baking sheet with the cauliflower in the preheated oven.

11. Bake for about 20-25 minutes, or until the chicken is cooked through and the cauliflower is tender and golden brown.
12. Remove the toothpicks from the chicken roll-ups before serving.
13. Serve the spinach and feta stuffed chicken roll-ups with the roasted cauliflower on the side.

GRILLED LEMON HERB SHRIMP WITH QUINOA AND ROASTED ASPARAGUS

Nutrition: Cal 330;Fat 10 g;Carb 25 g;Protein 30 g
Serving 2; Cook time 30 min

Ingredients
FOR THE GRILLED LEMON HERB SHRIMP:
- 1 pound shrimp, peeled and deveined
- 2 tablespoons olive oil
- 2 cloves garlic, minced
- 1 teaspoon lemon zest
- 2 tablespoons lemon juice
- 1 tablespoon chopped fresh herbs (such as parsley, basil, or dill)
- Salt and pepper, to taste
FOR THE QUINOA:
- 1 cup quinoa
- 2 cups water or low-sodium vegetable broth
- Salt, to taste
FOR THE ROASTED ASPARAGUS:
- 1 bunch asparagus, trimmed
- 1 tablespoon olive oil
- Salt and pepper, to taste

Instructions:
1. Preheat the grill to medium-high heat.
2. In a bowl, combine the olive oil, minced garlic, lemon zest, lemon juice, chopped herbs, salt, and pepper. Mix well.
3. Add the shrimp to the bowl and toss to coat them evenly with the marinade. Let them marinate for about 10-15 minutes.
4. While the shrimp is marinating, prepare the quinoa. Rinse the quinoa under cold water and drain. In a saucepan, bring the water or vegetable broth to a boil. Add the quinoa and salt, then reduce the heat to low and cover. Cook for about 15-20 minutes, or until the liquid is absorbed and the quinoa is tender. Fluff with a fork.
5. Toss the trimmed asparagus with olive oil, salt, and pepper. Place the asparagus on a baking sheet lined with parchment paper.
6. Place the shrimp on the preheated grill and cook for 2-3 minutes per side, or until they are opaque and cooked through. Be careful not to overcook.
7. At the same time, roast the asparagus in the oven at 400°F (200°C) for about 10-12 minutes, or until they are tender and slightly browned.
8. Serve the grilled lemon herb shrimp over a bed of cooked quinoa, alongside the roasted asparagus.

STUFFED CHICKEN BREASTS WITH SPINACH , FETA, AND SUN-DRIED TOMATOES

Nutrition: Cal 300;Fat 10 g;Carb 7 g;Protein 30 g
Serving 2; Cook time 45 min

Ingredients
- 2 boneless, skinless chicken breasts
- 2 cups fresh spinach, chopped
- 1/4 cup crumbled feta cheese
- 2 tablespoons sun-dried tomatoes, chopped
- 1 clove garlic, minced
- 1/2 teaspoon dried oregano
- Salt and pepper, to taste
- Cooking spray

Instructions:
1. Preheat the oven to 375°F (190°C).
2. In a bowl, combine the chopped spinach, crumbled feta cheese, sun-dried tomatoes, minced garlic, dried oregano, salt, and pepper. Mix well.
3. Using a sharp knife, cut a slit horizontally in each chicken breast to create a pocket.
4. Stuff each chicken breast with the spinach and feta mixture, pressing it gently to fill the pocket.
5. Secure the opening of the stuffed chicken breasts with toothpicks to keep the filling in place.
6. Lightly coat a baking dish with cooking spray and place the stuffed chicken breasts in the dish.

7. Season the chicken breasts with a sprinkle of salt, pepper, and dried oregano.
8. Bake in the preheated oven for 25-30 minutes, or until the chicken is cooked through and no longer pink in the center.
9. Remove the toothpicks before serving.
10. Serve the stuffed chicken breasts with a side of steamed vegetables or a mixed green salad.

BAKED COD WITH LEMON BUTTER SAUCE AND STEAMED BROCCOLI

Nutrition: Cal 220;Fat 11 g;Carb 5 g;Protein 26 g
Serving 2; Cook time 25 min

Ingredients
- 2 cod fillets (approximately 4-6 ounces each)
- 1 tablespoon olive oil
- Salt and pepper, to taste
- 1 lemon, sliced
- 2 tablespoons unsalted butter
- 1 garlic clove, minced
- 1 tablespoon fresh lemon juice
- 1 tablespoon chopped fresh parsley
- 2 cups broccoli florets

Instructions:
1. Preheat the oven to 400°F (200°C).
2. Place the cod fillets on a baking sheet lined with parchment paper or aluminum foil.
3. Drizzle the cod fillets with olive oil and season with salt and pepper.
4. Top each fillet with a few slices of lemon.
5. Bake the cod in the preheated oven for 12-15 minutes, or until it is opaque and easily flakes with a fork.
6. While the cod is baking, prepare the lemon butter sauce. In a small saucepan, melt the butter over medium heat.
7. Add the minced garlic to the melted butter and cook for 1-2 minutes, until fragrant.
8. Remove the saucepan from the heat and stir in the fresh lemon juice and chopped parsley.
9. Steam the broccoli florets in a steamer basket or microwave until tender, about 5-7 minutes.
10. Once the cod is cooked, remove it from the oven and drizzle the lemon butter sauce over the fillets.

11. Serve the baked cod with steamed broccoli on the side.

TURKEY AND VEGETABLE STIR-FRY WITH GINGER

Nutrition: Cal 250;Fat 10 g;Carb 15 g;Protein 20 g
Serving 2; Cook time 25 min

Ingredients
FOR THE STIR-FRY:
- 8 ounces lean ground turkey
- 1 tablespoon vegetable oil
- 2 cloves garlic, minced
- 1 tablespoon grated fresh ginger
- 1 cup broccoli florets
- 1 medium carrot, julienned
- 1 bell pepper, thinly sliced
- 1 cup snap peas
- Salt and pepper, to taste
FOR THE GINGER SOY SAUCE:
- 2 tablespoons low-sodium soy sauce
- 1 tablespoon rice vinegar
- 1 tablespoon honey or a low-calorie sweetener
- 1 teaspoon grated fresh ginger
- 1 teaspoon cornstarch
FOR THE CAULIFLOWER RICE:
- 1 medium head cauliflower
- 1 tablespoon vegetable oil
- Salt, to taste

Instructions:
1. Prepare the cauliflower rice by cutting the cauliflower into florets. Place the florets in a food processor and pulse until they resemble rice grains.
2. Heat 1 tablespoon of vegetable oil in a large skillet or wok over medium-high heat.
3. Add the ground turkey to the skillet and cook until browned, breaking it up into small pieces with a spoon. Remove the cooked turkey from the skillet and set aside.
4. In the same skillet, add the minced garlic and grated ginger. Cook for 1-2 minutes until fragrant.
5. Add the broccoli, carrot, bell pepper, and snap peas to the skillet. Stir-fry for 3-4 minutes until the vegetables are crisp-tender.
6. In a small bowl, whisk together the soy sauce, rice vinegar, honey, grated ginger, and cornstarch until well combined.

7. Pour the ginger soy sauce into the skillet with the vegetables. Return the cooked turkey to the skillet and stir-fry for another 2-3 minutes until the sauce thickens and coats the ingredients.
8. In a separate pan, heat 1 tablespoon of vegetable oil over medium heat. Add the cauliflower rice and cook for 5-7 minutes, stirring occasionally, until the cauliflower is tender. Season with salt to taste.
9. Divide the cauliflower rice onto two plates and top with the turkey and vegetable stir-fry.

SPINACH AND FETA STUFFED PORTOBELLO MUSHROOMS WITH A SIDE SALAD

Nutrition: Cal 200;Fat 10 g;Carb 10 g;Protein 10 g
Serving 2; Cook time 25 min

Ingredients
FOR THE STUFFED PORTOBELLO MUSHROOMS:
- 4 large portobello mushrooms
- 2 cups fresh spinach, chopped
- 1/2 cup crumbled feta cheese
- 2 cloves garlic, minced
- 1 tablespoon olive oil
- Salt and pepper, to taste
FOR THE SIDE SALAD:
- 4 cups mixed salad greens
- 1/2 cup cherry tomatoes, halved
- 1/4 cup sliced cucumber
- 1/4 cup sliced red onion
- 2 tablespoons balsamic vinegar
- 1 tablespoon extra virgin olive oil
Instructions:
1. Preheat the oven to 400°F (200°C).
2. Remove the stems from the portobello mushrooms and gently scrape out the gills using a spoon.
3. In a skillet, heat the olive oil over medium heat. Add the minced garlic and sauté for 1 minute until fragrant.
4. Add the chopped spinach to the skillet and cook until wilted, about 2-3 minutes. Season with salt and pepper to taste.
5. Remove the skillet from heat and let the spinach cool slightly. Stir in the crumbled feta cheese.

6. Divide the spinach and feta mixture evenly among the portobello mushrooms, filling the cavities.
7. Place the stuffed mushrooms on a baking sheet and bake in the preheated oven for 15-20 minutes, or until the mushrooms are tender and the cheese is melted.
8. While the mushrooms are baking, prepare the side salad by combining the mixed salad greens, cherry tomatoes, sliced cucumber, and sliced red onion in a large bowl.
9. In a small bowl, whisk together the balsamic vinegar and extra virgin olive oil to make the dressing.
10. Drizzle the dressing over the salad and toss to combine.
11. Once the mushrooms are done, remove them from the oven and let them cool for a few minutes.
12. Serve the stuffed portobello mushrooms alongside the side salad.

GARLIC HERB GRILLED PORK TENDERLOIN WITH ROASTED BRUSSELS SPROUTS

Nutrition: Cal 250;Fat 10 g;Carb 10 g;Protein 25 g
Serving 2; Cook time 40 min

Ingredients
FOR THE PORK TENDERLOIN:
- 1 lb (450g) pork tenderloin
- 2 cloves garlic, minced
- 1 tablespoon fresh herbs (such as rosemary, thyme, or parsley), chopped
- 1 tablespoon olive oil
- Salt and pepper, to taste
FOR THE ROASTED BRUSSELS SPROUTS:
- 1 lb (450g) Brussels sprouts, trimmed and halved
- 1 tablespoon olive oil
- Salt and pepper, to taste
Instructions:
1. Preheat the grill to medium-high heat.
2. In a small bowl, combine the minced garlic, fresh herbs, olive oil, salt, and pepper to make a marinade for the pork tenderloin.
3. Rub the marinade all over the pork tenderloin, ensuring it is evenly coated. Let it marinate for at least 15 minutes, or refrigerate for longer for more flavor.

4. While the pork is marinating, preheat the oven to 400°F (200°C) for the Brussels sprouts.

5. Toss the halved Brussels sprouts with olive oil, salt, and pepper in a large bowl until coated.

6. Spread the Brussels sprouts in a single layer on a baking sheet and roast in the preheated oven for 20-25 minutes, or until they are tender and lightly browned, tossing halfway through.

7. Meanwhile, grill the pork tenderloin on the preheated grill for about 12-15 minutes, turning occasionally, until it reaches an internal temperature of 145°F (63°C). Cooking time may vary depending on the thickness of the pork tenderloin.

8. Once the pork tenderloin is cooked, remove it from the grill and let it rest for a few minutes before slicing.

9. Serve the grilled pork tenderloin with the roasted Brussels sprouts as a side.

QUINOA AND BLACK BEAN BURGERS WITH WHOLE WHEAT BUNS AND AVOCADO

Nutrition: Cal 340;Fat 12 g;Carb 55 g;Protein 20 g
Serving 2; Cook time 30 min

Ingredients
FOR THE QUINOA AND BLACK BEAN BURGERS:
- 1 cup cooked quinoa
- 1 can (15 oz) black beans, rinsed and drained
- 1/2 cup bread crumbs (whole wheat or gluten-free)
- 1/4 cup diced onion
- 1 clove garlic, minced
- 1 teaspoon ground cumin
- 1/2 teaspoon chili powder
- Salt and pepper, to taste
- 1 tablespoon olive oil (for cooking)

FOR SERVING:
- 2 whole wheat burger buns
- 1 ripe avocado, sliced
- Optional toppings: lettuce, tomato, onion, mustard, etc.

Instructions:
1. In a large bowl, mash the black beans with a fork until they are mostly mashed but still have some texture.

2. Add the cooked quinoa, bread crumbs, diced onion, minced garlic, ground cumin, chili powder, salt, and pepper to the bowl. Mix well until all ingredients are combined.

3. Divide the mixture into two equal portions and shape them into burger patties.

4. Heat the olive oil in a skillet over medium heat. Cook the quinoa and black bean burgers for about 4-5 minutes per side, or until they are golden brown and heated through.

5. While the burgers are cooking, you can toast the whole wheat burger buns if desired.

6. Once the burgers are cooked, assemble the burgers by placing each patty on a whole wheat bun.

7. Top the burgers with sliced avocado and any other desired toppings, such as lettuce, tomato, onion, or mustard.

8. Serve the quinoa and black bean burgers with a side salad or a side of steamed vegetables.

CAULIFLOWER CRUST PIZZA WITH TURKEY PEPPERONI AND VEGETABLES

Nutrition: Cal 250;Fat 10 g;Carb 20 g;Protein 20 g
Serving 2; Cook time 45 min

Ingredients
FOR THE CAULIFLOWER CRUST:
- 1 medium-sized cauliflower head, riced (about 2 cups)
- 1 egg
- 1/4 cup grated Parmesan cheese
- 1/2 teaspoon dried oregano
- 1/2 teaspoon garlic powder
- Salt and pepper, to taste

FOR THE PIZZA TOPPINGS:
- 1/2 cup tomato sauce (low-sodium)
- 1 cup shredded mozzarella cheese (part-skim)
- 1/2 cup sliced turkey pepperoni
- 1/2 cup diced bell peppers
- 1/2 cup sliced mushrooms
- Optional toppings: sliced onions, black olives, spinach, etc.

Instructions:
1. Preheat the oven to 425°F (220°C).

2. Place the riced cauliflower in a microwave-safe bowl and microwave on high for 4-5 minutes, or until the cauliflower is tender.

3. Allow the cauliflower to cool for a few minutes, then transfer it to a clean kitchen towel or cheesecloth. Squeeze out as much liquid as possible from the cauliflower.

4. In a mixing bowl, combine the squeezed cauliflower, egg, grated Parmesan cheese, dried oregano, garlic powder, salt, and pepper. Mix well until all ingredients are evenly combined.

5. Line a baking sheet with parchment paper and lightly grease it with cooking spray. Transfer the cauliflower mixture to the baking sheet and press it into a thin, round crust shape.

6. Bake the cauliflower crust in the preheated oven for 15-20 minutes, or until it becomes golden brown and firm.

7. Remove the crust from the oven and let it cool slightly.

8. Spread the tomato sauce evenly over the crust, leaving a small border around the edges.

9. Sprinkle the shredded mozzarella cheese over the sauce, and then top with turkey pepperoni, diced bell peppers, sliced mushrooms, and any other desired toppings.

10. Return the pizza to the oven and bake for an additional 10-15 minutes, or until the cheese is melted and bubbly.

11. Once the pizza is cooked, remove it from the oven and let it cool for a few minutes before slicing and serving.

TERIYAKI GLAZED CHICKEN THIGHS WITH STIR-FRIED VEGETABLES

Nutrition: Cal 350;Fat 11 g;Carb 40 g;Protein 28 g
Serving 2; Cook time 45 min

Ingredients
FOR THE TERIYAKI GLAZE:
• 2 tablespoons low-sodium soy sauce
• 2 tablespoons honey
• 2 tablespoons rice vinegar
• 1 tablespoon sesame oil
• 1 clove garlic, minced
• 1 teaspoon grated ginger
• 1 teaspoon cornstarch (optional, for thickening)
FOR THE CHICKEN:
• 4 boneless, skinless chicken thighs

• Salt and pepper, to taste
• For the stir-fried vegetables:
• 1 tablespoon olive oil
• 2 cups mixed vegetables (such as bell peppers, broccoli, carrots, snap peas, etc.), sliced or chopped
• 1 clove garlic, minced
• Salt and pepper, to taste
FOR THE BROWN RICE:
• 1 cup brown rice
• 2 cups water
OPTIONAL GARNISH:
• Sesame seeds
• Chopped green onions
Instructions:
1. In a small bowl, whisk together the soy sauce, honey, rice vinegar, sesame oil, minced garlic, and grated ginger to make the teriyaki glaze. If desired, mix in the cornstarch to thicken the glaze.

2. Season the chicken thighs with salt and pepper on both sides.

3. Heat a non-stick skillet over medium heat. Place the chicken thighs in the skillet and cook for about 6-8 minutes per side, or until they reach an internal temperature of 165°F (74°C).

4. Pour the teriyaki glaze over the cooked chicken thighs and let them simmer in the glaze for a couple of minutes, turning the thighs to coat them evenly. Remove the chicken from the skillet and set aside.

5. In the same skillet, add olive oil and heat over medium-high heat. Add the mixed vegetables and minced garlic. Stir-fry the vegetables for 3-5 minutes, or until they are tender-crisp. Season with salt and pepper to taste.

6. Meanwhile, in a separate pot, cook the brown rice according to package instructions. This typically involves bringing the water and rice to a boil, then reducing the heat to low, covering the pot, and simmering for about 40-45 minutes until the rice is tender.

7. Serve the teriyaki glazed chicken thighs over a bed of brown rice, with the stir-fried vegetables on the side. Garnish with sesame seeds and chopped green onions, if desired.

GREEK-STYLE STUFFED ZUCCHINI BOATS WITH GROUND TURKEY AND QUINOA

Nutrition: Cal 350;Fat 10 g;Carb 40 g;Protein 25 g
Serving 2; Cook time 45 min

Ingredients
FOR THE TERIYAKI GLAZE:
- 2 tablespoons low-sodium soy sauce
- 2 tablespoons honey
- 2 tablespoons rice vinegar
- 1 tablespoon sesame oil
- 1 clove garlic, minced
- 1 teaspoon grated ginger
- 1 teaspoon cornstarch (optional, for thickening)

FOR THE CHICKEN:
- 4 boneless, skinless chicken thighs
- Salt and pepper, to taste

FOR THE STIR-FRIED VEGETABLES:
- 1 tablespoon olive oil
- 2 cups mixed vegetables (such as bell peppers, broccoli, carrots, snap peas, etc.), sliced or chopped
- 1 clove garlic, minced
- Salt and pepper, to taste

FOR THE BROWN RICE:
- 1 cup brown rice
- 2 cups water
- Optional garnish:
- Sesame seeds
- Chopped green onions

Instructions:
1. In a small bowl, whisk together the soy sauce, honey, rice vinegar, sesame oil, minced garlic, and grated ginger to make the teriyaki glaze. If desired, mix in the cornstarch to thicken the glaze.
2. Season the chicken thighs with salt and pepper on both sides.
3. Heat a non-stick skillet over medium heat. Place the chicken thighs in the skillet and cook for about 6-8 minutes per side, or until they reach an internal temperature of 165°F (74°C).
4. Pour the teriyaki glaze over the cooked chicken thighs and let them simmer in the glaze for a couple of minutes, turning the thighs to coat them evenly. Remove the chicken from the skillet and set aside.

5. In the same skillet, add olive oil and heat over medium-high heat. Add the mixed vegetables and minced garlic. Stir-fry the vegetables for 3-5 minutes, or until they are tender-crisp. Season with salt and pepper to taste.
6. Meanwhile, in a separate pot, cook the brown rice according to package instructions. This typically involves bringing the water and rice to a boil, then reducing the heat to low, covering the pot, and simmering for about 40-45 minutes until the rice is tender.
7. Serve the teriyaki glazed chicken thighs over a bed of brown rice, with the stir-fried vegetables on the side. Garnish with sesame seeds and chopped green onions, if desired.

TURKEY MEATLOAF WITH CAULIFLOWER MASH AND GREEN BEANS

Nutrition: Cal 360;Fat 18 g;Carb 18 g;Protein 37 g
Serving 2; Cook time 60 min

Ingredients
FOR THE TURKEY MEATLOAF:
- 1 pound lean ground turkey
- 1/2 cup almond flour
- 1/4 cup grated Parmesan cheese
- 1/4 cup finely chopped onion
- 1/4 cup finely chopped bell pepper
- 1 clove garlic, minced
- 1 large egg, beaten
- 1 tablespoon Worcestershire sauce
- 1 tablespoon low-sodium soy sauce
- 1/2 teaspoon dried thyme
- 1/2 teaspoon dried oregano
- Salt and pepper, to taste

FOR THE CAULIFLOWER MASH:
- 1 medium head cauliflower, cut into florets
- 2 tablespoons unsalted butter or olive oil
- 1/4 cup grated Parmesan cheese
- Salt and pepper, to taste

FOR THE GREEN BEANS:
- 1/2 pound fresh green beans, ends trimmed
- 1 tablespoon olive oil
- 1 clove garlic, minced
- Salt and pepper, to taste

Instructions:

1. Preheat the oven to 375°F (190°C). Line a baking sheet with parchment paper or lightly grease it.
2. In a large mixing bowl, combine the ground turkey, almond flour, grated Parmesan cheese, chopped onion, chopped bell pepper, minced garlic, beaten egg, Worcestershire sauce, soy sauce, dried thyme, dried oregano, salt, and pepper. Mix well until all the ingredients are evenly combined.
3. Shape the turkey mixture into a loaf shape and place it on the prepared baking sheet. Bake in the preheated oven for about 40-45 minutes, or until the internal temperature reaches 165°F (74°C).
4. While the meatloaf is baking, prepare the cauliflower mash. Steam the cauliflower florets until they are tender. Drain any excess water and transfer the cooked cauliflower to a food processor or blender. Add the butter or olive oil, grated Parmesan cheese, salt, and pepper. Process until smooth and creamy. Adjust the seasonings to taste.
5. In a separate skillet, heat olive oil over medium heat. Add the minced garlic and cook for about 1 minute, until fragrant. Add the green beans and sauté for 5-7 minutes, or until they are crisp-tender. Season with salt and pepper.
6. Once the turkey meatloaf is cooked through, remove it from the oven and let it rest for a few minutes before slicing.
7. Serve the turkey meatloaf slices with a side of cauliflower mash and sautéed green beans.

ZUCCHINI NOODLES WITH SHRIMP SCAMPI AND CHERRY TOMATOES

Nutrition: Cal 240;Fat 12 g;Carb 11 g;Protein 24 g
Serving 2; Cook time 20 min

Ingredients
- 2 medium zucchini
- 1/2 pound shrimp, peeled and deveined
- 2 tablespoons olive oil
- 3 cloves garlic, minced
- 1/4 teaspoon red pepper flakes (optional)
- 1 cup cherry tomatoes, halved
- 2 tablespoons fresh lemon juice
- 2 tablespoons chopped parsley
- Salt and pepper, to taste

Instructions:
1. Use a spiralizer or a vegetable peeler to create zucchini noodles from the zucchini. Set aside.
2. In a large skillet, heat the olive oil over medium heat. Add the minced garlic and red pepper flakes (if using) and sauté for about 1 minute, until fragrant.
3. Add the shrimp to the skillet and cook for 2-3 minutes on each side until they turn pink and are cooked through. Remove the shrimp from the skillet and set aside.
4. In the same skillet, add the cherry tomatoes and cook for 2-3 minutes until they start to soften and release their juices.
5. Return the cooked shrimp to the skillet with the cherry tomatoes. Add the zucchini noodles, lemon juice, and chopped parsley. Toss everything together and cook for another 2-3 minutes, until the zucchini noodles are tender.
6. Season with salt and pepper to taste.
7. Divide the zucchini noodles with shrimp scampi and cherry tomatoes between two plates.

CAPRESE CHICKEN WITH ROASTED VEGETABLES AND BALSAMIC GLAZE

Nutrition: Cal 330;Fat 12 g;Carb 12 g;Protein 33 g
Serving 2; Cook time 35 min

Ingredients
- 2 boneless, skinless chicken breasts
- 2 medium tomatoes, sliced
- 4 ounces fresh mozzarella cheese, sliced
- 2 tablespoons chopped fresh basil
- Salt and pepper, to taste
- 2 tablespoons balsamic glaze (store-bought or homemade)
- 2 cups mixed vegetables (e.g., bell peppers, zucchini, eggplant), chopped
- 1 tablespoon olive oil

Instructions:
1. Preheat the oven to 400°F (200°C).
2. Season the chicken breasts with salt and pepper on both sides.
3. In a large baking dish, place the chicken breasts and surround them with the mixed vegetables.

Drizzle the vegetables with olive oil and sprinkle with salt and pepper.

4. Roast in the preheated oven for about 20-25 minutes, or until the chicken is cooked through and the vegetables are tender.

5. While the chicken and vegetables are roasting, prepare the Caprese topping. In a small bowl, combine the sliced tomatoes, mozzarella cheese, and chopped basil. Season with salt and pepper to taste.

6. Once the chicken and vegetables are cooked, remove from the oven. Top each chicken breast with the Caprese mixture.

7. Drizzle the balsamic glaze over the chicken and vegetables.

8. Return the baking dish to the oven and broil for 2-3 minutes, or until the cheese has melted and started to bubble.

9. Remove from the oven and let it rest for a few minutes.

10. Serve the Caprese chicken with roasted vegetables on a plate, and drizzle any remaining balsamic glaze over the top.

CAULIFLOWER CRUST PIZZA WITH TURKEY SAUSAGE AND VEGETABLES

Nutrition: Cal 300;Fat 12 g;Carb 20 g;Protein 25 g
Serving 2; Cook time 45 min

Ingredients
FOR THE CAULIFLOWER CRUST:
- 1 medium head of cauliflower
- 1 egg
- 1/2 cup grated Parmesan cheese
- 1 teaspoon dried oregano
- 1/2 teaspoon garlic powder
- Salt and pepper, to taste

FOR THE TOPPINGS:
- 4 ounces turkey sausage, cooked and crumbled
- 1/2 cup pizza sauce (low-sugar or homemade)
- 1/2 cup shredded mozzarella cheese
- 1/2 cup chopped vegetables (e.g., bell peppers, mushrooms, onions)
- Fresh basil leaves, for garnish

Instructions:
1. Preheat the oven to 425°F (220°C).

2. Cut the cauliflower into florets and place them in a food processor. Pulse until the cauliflower resembles rice.

3. Transfer the cauliflower rice to a microwave-safe bowl and microwave on high for 5 minutes. Let it cool slightly.

4. Place the cooked cauliflower rice in a clean kitchen towel or cheesecloth. Squeeze out as much moisture as possible.

5. In a mixing bowl, combine the cauliflower rice, egg, grated Parmesan cheese, dried oregano, garlic powder, salt, and pepper. Mix well until a dough forms.

6. Line a baking sheet with parchment paper. Transfer the cauliflower dough to the baking sheet and shape it into a round pizza crust, about 1/4-inch thick.

7. Bake the cauliflower crust in the preheated oven for 15-20 minutes, or until golden brown and firm.

8. Remove the crust from the oven and let it cool slightly. Leave the oven on.

9. Spread the pizza sauce evenly over the crust, leaving a small border around the edges.

10. Sprinkle the cooked turkey sausage, shredded mozzarella cheese, and chopped vegetables over the sauce.

11. Place the pizza back in the oven and bake for an additional 10-15 minutes, or until the cheese is melted and bubbly.

12. Remove from the oven and let it cool for a few minutes.

13. Garnish with fresh basil leaves and slice the pizza into desired portions.

SPINACH AND FETA STUFFED PORK TENDERLOIN WITH ROASTED CARROTS

Nutrition: Cal 250;Fat 10 g;Carb 15 g;Protein 40 g
Serving 2; Cook time 40 min

Ingredients
FOR THE STUFFED PORK TENDERLOIN:
- 1 pork tenderloin (about 1 pound)
- 2 cups fresh spinach leaves
- 1/4 cup crumbled feta cheese
- 1 clove garlic, minced
- 1/2 teaspoon dried oregano

- Salt and pepper, to taste

FOR THE ROASTED CARROTS:
- 4 medium carrots, peeled and cut into sticks
- 1 tablespoon olive oil
- 1/2 teaspoon dried thyme
- Salt and pepper, to taste

Instructions:
1. Preheat the oven to 400°F (200°C).
2. Prepare the pork tenderloin by making a lengthwise cut down the center, but not all the way through. Open the tenderloin like a book.
3. Season the inside of the tenderloin with salt, pepper, minced garlic, and dried oregano.
4. Layer the spinach leaves and crumbled feta cheese evenly over the seasoned side of the tenderloin.
5. Fold the tenderloin back together, securing the stuffing inside. Use kitchen twine to tie the tenderloin at 1-inch intervals to hold its shape.
6. Place the stuffed tenderloin on a baking sheet lined with parchment paper.
7. In a bowl, toss the carrot sticks with olive oil, dried thyme, salt, and pepper until evenly coated.
8. Arrange the seasoned carrots around the stuffed tenderloin on the baking sheet.
9. Place the baking sheet in the preheated oven and roast for about 25-30 minutes, or until the pork reaches an internal temperature of 145°F (63°C) and the carrots are tender.
10. Remove the baking sheet from the oven and let the pork rest for a few minutes before slicing.
11. Slice the stuffed pork tenderloin into medallions and serve with roasted carrots.

SHRIMP AND BROCCOLI STIR-FRY WITH GINGER SOY SAUCE AND BROWN RICE

Nutrition: Cal 350;Fat 10 g;Carb 30 g;Protein 30 g
Serving 2; Cook time 25 min

Ingredients
FOR THE SHRIMP STIR-FRY:
- 8 ounces (225 grams) shrimp, peeled and deveined
- 2 cups broccoli florets
- 1 bell pepper, thinly sliced
- 1 small onion, thinly sliced
- 2 cloves garlic, minced

- 1 tablespoon vegetable oil

FOR THE GINGER SOY SAUCE:
- 2 tablespoons low-sodium soy sauce
- 1 tablespoon rice vinegar
- 1 tablespoon honey or low-calorie sweetener
- 1 teaspoon grated fresh ginger
- 1 teaspoon cornstarch (optional, to thicken the sauce)

FOR THE BROWN RICE:
- 1 cup cooked brown rice

Instructions:
1. In a small bowl, whisk together the soy sauce, rice vinegar, honey or sweetener, grated ginger, and cornstarch (if using). Set aside.
2. Heat the vegetable oil in a large skillet or wok over medium-high heat.
3. Add the minced garlic and stir-fry for about 30 seconds until fragrant.
4. Add the shrimp to the skillet and cook for 2-3 minutes until they turn pink and opaque. Remove the cooked shrimp from the skillet and set aside.
5. In the same skillet, add the broccoli florets, bell pepper, and onion. Stir-fry for about 5-6 minutes until the vegetables are tender-crisp.
6. Return the cooked shrimp to the skillet with the vegetables.
7. Pour the ginger soy sauce over the shrimp and vegetables. Stir well to coat everything evenly. Cook for an additional 1-2 minutes until the sauce thickens slightly.
8. Serve the shrimp and broccoli stir-fry over cooked brown rice.

LEMON GARLIC ROASTED CHICKEN WITH SAUTÉED SPINACH AND CAULIFLOWER RICE

Nutrition: Cal 350;Fat 10 g;Carb 10 g;Protein 40 g
Serving 2; Cook time 40 min

Ingredients
FOR THE LEMON GARLIC ROASTED CHICKEN:
- 2 boneless, skinless chicken breasts
- 2 tablespoons fresh lemon juice
- 2 cloves garlic, minced
- 1 teaspoon lemon zest
- 1 tablespoon olive oil

•Salt and pepper to taste

FOR THE SAUTÉED SPINACH:
•4 cups fresh spinach leaves
•1 tablespoon olive oil
•2 cloves garlic, minced
•Salt and pepper to taste

FOR THE CAULIFLOWER RICE:
•1 small head cauliflower, riced (or pre-riced cauliflower)
•1 tablespoon olive oil
•Salt and pepper to taste

Instructions:
1. Preheat the oven to 400°F (200°C).
2. In a small bowl, mix together the lemon juice, minced garlic, lemon zest, olive oil, salt, and pepper.
3. Place the chicken breasts in a baking dish and pour the lemon garlic marinade over them. Make sure the chicken is well coated. Let it marinate for at least 15 minutes.
4. Roast the chicken in the preheated oven for about 20-25 minutes or until the internal temperature reaches 165°F (74°C).
5. While the chicken is roasting, prepare the sautéed spinach. Heat olive oil in a skillet over medium heat. Add the minced garlic and sauté for about 1 minute until fragrant.
6. Add the spinach leaves to the skillet and sauté for 2-3 minutes until wilted. Season with salt and pepper to taste. Remove from heat and set aside.
7. In a separate skillet, heat olive oil over medium heat. Add the riced cauliflower and sauté for 5-6 minutes until tender. Season with salt and pepper to taste.
8. Serve the lemon garlic roasted chicken with a side of sautéed spinach and cauliflower rice.

EGGPLANT PARMESAN WITH A SIDE SALAD

Nutrition: Cal 350;Fat 14 g;Carb 35 g;Protein 15 g
Serving 2; Cook time 50 min

Ingredients
FOR THE EGGPLANT PARMESAN:
•1 medium-sized eggplant
•1 cup marinara sauce
•1/2 cup shredded mozzarella cheese
•1/4 cup grated Parmesan cheese

•1/4 cup breadcrumbs (optional)
•1 tablespoon olive oil
•Salt and pepper to taste

FOR THE SIDE SALAD:
•4 cups mixed salad greens
•1/2 cup cherry tomatoes, halved
•1/4 cup sliced cucumber
•2 tablespoons balsamic vinegar
•1 tablespoon olive oil
•Salt and pepper to taste

Instructions:
1. Preheat the oven to 375°F (190°C).
2. Slice the eggplant into 1/2-inch thick rounds. Sprinkle salt over each slice and let them sit for about 10 minutes to draw out excess moisture. Pat dry with paper towels.
3. Heat olive oil in a skillet over medium heat. Lightly coat each eggplant slice with olive oil and cook them in the skillet until browned on both sides, about 2-3 minutes per side. Remove from the skillet and set aside.
4. In a baking dish, spread a thin layer of marinara sauce. Arrange a layer of eggplant slices on top. Sprinkle with mozzarella and Parmesan cheese. Repeat the layers until all the eggplant slices are used.
5. Top the final layer with breadcrumbs (optional) for added crunch.
6. Bake in the preheated oven for 20-25 minutes or until the cheese is melted and bubbly.
7. While the Eggplant Parmesan is baking, prepare the side salad. In a large bowl, combine the mixed salad greens, cherry tomatoes, and sliced cucumber.
8. In a small bowl, whisk together balsamic vinegar, olive oil, salt, and pepper to make the dressing for the salad.
9. Drizzle the dressing over the salad and toss gently to combine.
10. Serve the Eggplant Parmesan hot with a side of fresh salad.

STUFFED ZUCCHINI BOATS WITH LEAN GROUND BEEF AND QUINOA

Nutrition: Cal 350;Fat 14 g;Carb 25 g;Protein 25 g
Serving 2; Cook time 50 min

Ingredients

- 2 medium-sized zucchini
- 1/2 pound lean ground beef
- 1/4 cup cooked quinoa
- 1/4 cup diced onion
- 1/4 cup diced bell pepper
- 1 clove garlic, minced
- 1/2 cup marinara sauce
- 1/4 cup shredded mozzarella cheese
- 1 tablespoon olive oil
- Salt and pepper to taste

Instructions:

1. Preheat the oven to 375°F (190°C).
2. Cut each zucchini in half lengthwise. Scoop out the flesh from each half, leaving about a 1/4-inch border to form a zucchini boat. Reserve the scooped-out flesh for later use.
3. In a skillet, heat olive oil over medium heat. Add the diced onion, bell pepper, and minced garlic. Sauté until the vegetables are softened, about 2-3 minutes.
4. Add the lean ground beef to the skillet and cook until browned, breaking it up into small pieces with a spatula.
5. Add the reserved zucchini flesh and cooked quinoa to the skillet. Stir to combine and cook for an additional 2 minutes. Season with salt and pepper to taste.
6. Place the zucchini boats in a baking dish and fill each boat with the ground beef and quinoa mixture.
7. Pour marinara sauce over the stuffed zucchini boats, covering them evenly.
8. Sprinkle shredded mozzarella cheese on top of each boat.
9. Cover the baking dish with foil and bake in the preheated oven for 20 minutes. Then, remove the foil and continue baking for another 10-15 minutes until the zucchini is tender and the cheese is melted and bubbly.
10. Once cooked, remove from the oven and let cool slightly before serving.

ROASTED DUCK BREAST WITH CARROT PUREE, CREAMY BATATA MASH

Nutrition: Cal 430;Fat 18 g;Carb 33 g;Protein 35 g

Serving 2; Cook time 50 min

Ingredients

- 2 duck breasts
- 2 large carrots, peeled and chopped
- 2 medium-sized batatas (sweet potatoes), peeled and cubed
- 1/4 cup heavy cream
- Salt and pepper to taste
- Olive oil for cooking

Instructions:

1. Preheat the oven to 400°F (200°C).
2. Score the skin of the duck breasts in a criss-cross pattern. Season both sides of the duck breasts with salt and pepper.
3. Heat a skillet over medium-high heat and add a drizzle of olive oil. Place the duck breasts in the skillet, skin-side down, and cook for 5-6 minutes until the skin is crispy and golden brown. Flip the duck breasts and sear for an additional 1-2 minutes.
4. Transfer the duck breasts to a baking dish, skin-side up, and roast in the preheated oven for about 10-12 minutes for medium-rare or until desired doneness. Allow the duck breasts to rest for a few minutes before slicing.
5. While the duck breasts are roasting, prepare the carrot puree and batata mash.
6. In a saucepan, add the chopped carrots and cover with water. Bring to a boil and cook until the carrots are tender, about 10-12 minutes. Drain the carrots and transfer them to a blender or food processor. Blend until smooth. Season with salt and pepper to taste.
7. In a separate saucepan, add the cubed batatas and cover with water. Bring to a boil and cook until the batatas are fork-tender, about 12-15 minutes. Drain the batatas and return them to the saucepan. Mash the batatas with a potato masher until smooth. Stir in the heavy cream and season with salt and pepper.
8. Serve the roasted duck breast slices alongside a generous dollop of carrot puree and a scoop of creamy batata mash.

BAKED COD WITH CREAMY SPINACH AND CARROT MASH

Nutrition: Cal 400;Fat 11 g;Carb 35 g;Protein 30 g
Serving 2; Cook time 45 min

Ingredients

- 2 cod fillets
- 2 cups fresh spinach leaves
- 1/4 cup heavy cream
- 2 medium carrots, peeled and diced
- 2 medium potatoes, peeled and diced
- 1 small onion, diced
- 1/4 cup shredded cheese (such as Parmesan or cheddar)
- Salt and pepper to taste
- Olive oil for cooking

Instructions:

1. Preheat the oven to 400°F (200°C).
2. Place the diced carrots and potatoes in a saucepan and cover with water. Bring to a boil and cook until the vegetables are fork-tender, about 10-12 minutes. Drain the vegetables and return them to the saucepan.
3. In a separate pan, heat some olive oil over medium heat. Add the diced onion and cook until softened and translucent, about 5 minutes. Add the fresh spinach leaves and cook until wilted. Remove from heat.
4. Mash the cooked carrots and potatoes using a potato masher or fork until smooth. Stir in the heavy cream and cooked spinach mixture. Season with salt and pepper to taste.
5. Place the cod fillets in a baking dish. Season with salt and pepper. Spoon the creamy spinach and carrot mash over the cod fillets, covering them evenly.
6. Sprinkle the shredded cheese over the top of the mash.
7. Bake in the preheated oven for about 15-20 minutes, or until the cod is cooked through and flakes easily with a fork.
8. Serve the baked cod with a generous portion of the creamy spinach and carrot mash.

CREAMY SHRIMP AND SALMON SKILLET WITH ROASTED BROCCOLI AND CAULIFLOWER

Nutrition: Cal 350;Fat 15 g;Carb 12 g;Protein 28 g
Serving 2; Cook time 30 min

Ingredients

- 8-10 large shrimp, peeled and deveined
- 6-8 ounces salmon fillet, cut into bite-sized pieces
- 1 cup broccoli florets
- 1 cup cauliflower florets
- 1/4 cup heavy cream
- 2 cloves garlic, minced
- 1 small onion, diced
- Salt and pepper to taste
- Olive oil for cooking

Instructions:

1. Preheat the oven to 400°F (200°C).
2. Place the broccoli and cauliflower florets on a baking sheet. Drizzle with olive oil and season with salt and pepper. Toss to coat. Roast in the preheated oven for about 15-20 minutes, or until the vegetables are tender and lightly browned.
3. In a skillet, heat some olive oil over medium heat. Add the minced garlic and diced onion. Sauté until the onion is softened and translucent, about 5 minutes.
4. Add the shrimp and salmon pieces to the skillet. Cook until the shrimp turns pink and the salmon is cooked through, about 3-4 minutes.
5. Reduce the heat to low and pour in the heavy cream. Stir gently to combine and coat the shrimp and salmon with the creamy sauce. Cook for an additional 2-3 minutes to warm the cream.
6. Season with salt and pepper to taste. Adjust the seasoning according to your preference.
7. Remove the roasted broccoli and cauliflower from the oven and add them to the skillet with the shrimp and salmon. Gently toss to combine and coat the vegetables with the creamy sauce.
8. Serve the creamy shrimp and salmon skillet with roasted broccoli and cauliflower.

DESSERTS

GREEK YOGURT WITH FRESH BERRIES

Nutrition: Cal 170;Fat 3 g;Carb 25 g;Protein 18 g
Serving 2; Cook time 5 min

Ingredients

- 1 cup Greek yogurt (low-fat or non-fat)
- 1 cup mixed fresh berries (such as strawberries, blueberries, raspberries)
- 1 tablespoon honey or sweetener of choice (optional)
- 1 tablespoon chopped nuts (optional, for added crunch and healthy fats)

Instructions:

1. In a bowl, spoon 1/2 cup of Greek yogurt for each serving.
2. Rinse the fresh berries and add them to the bowl, on top of the yogurt.
3. Drizzle honey or sweetener of choice over the yogurt and berries, if desired, for added sweetness.
4. Sprinkle chopped nuts on top for added texture and healthy fats.
5. Mix gently to combine all the ingredients.
6. Serve immediately and enjoy!

FROZEN YOGURT BITES MADE WITH GREEK YOGURT AND FRUIT PUREE

Nutrition: Cal 40;Fat 1 g;Carb 5 g;Protein 3 g
Serving 2; Cook time 3 hours

Ingredients

- 1 cup Greek yogurt (low-fat or non-fat)
- 1/2 cup fruit puree (such as blended berries, mango, or pineapple)
- 1 tablespoon honey or sweetener of choice (optional)

Instructions:

1. In a bowl, mix the Greek yogurt and fruit puree until well combined.
2. If desired, add honey or sweetener to taste and mix again.
3. Line a baking sheet with parchment paper.

4. Use a spoon or a piping bag to drop small dollops of the yogurt mixture onto the baking sheet, forming bite-sized portions.
5. Place the baking sheet in the freezer and let the yogurt bites freeze for at least 2-3 hours or until firm.
6. Once frozen, transfer the yogurt bites to an airtight container or zip-top bag for storage in the freezer.

GREEK YOGURT POPSICLES WITH MIXED BERRIES

Nutrition: Cal 40;Fat 1 g;Carb 5 g;Protein 3 g
Serving 2; Cook time 3-4 hours

Ingredients

- 1 cup Greek yogurt (low-fat or non-fat)
- 1/2 cup mixed berries (such as strawberries, blueberries, and raspberries)
- 1 tablespoon honey or sweetener of choice (optional)

Instructions:

1. In a blender or food processor, combine the Greek yogurt, mixed berries, and honey (if using). Blend until smooth and well combined.
2. Taste the mixture and adjust the sweetness by adding more honey if desired.
3. Pour the mixture into popsicle molds, leaving a small gap at the top for expansion.
4. Insert popsicle sticks into each mold.
5. Place the popsicle molds in the freezer and let them freeze for at least 4-6 hours or until completely frozen.
6. Once frozen, remove the popsicles from the molds by running them under warm water for a few seconds. Gently pull the popsicles out of the molds.
7. Serve immediately or store the popsicles in an airtight container or zip-top bag in the freezer.

GREEK YOGURT BERRY PARFAITS WITH LAYERS OF YOGURT, MIXED BERRIES, AND CRUSHED ALMONDS

Nutrition: Cal 170;Fat 5 g;Carb 17 g;Protein 13 g
Serving 2; Cook time 5 min

Ingredients
- 1 cup Greek yogurt (low-fat or non-fat)
- 1 cup mixed berries (such as strawberries, blueberries, and raspberries)
- 2 tablespoons crushed almonds
- 1 tablespoon honey or sweetener of choice (optional)

Instructions:
1. In a bowl, mix the Greek yogurt and honey (if using) until well combined. Set aside.
2. In serving glasses or bowls, create layers by starting with a spoonful of Greek yogurt at the bottom.
3. Add a layer of mixed berries on top of the yogurt.
4. Repeat the layers, alternating between Greek yogurt and mixed berries until the glasses or bowls are filled.
5. Top each parfait with a sprinkle of crushed almonds.
6. Serve immediately or refrigerate until ready to serve.

BAKED APPLE SLICES WITH CINNAMON AND A SPRINKLE OF GRANOLA

Nutrition: Cal 100;Fat 2 g;Carb 20 g;Protein 1 g
Serving 2; Cook time 20 min

Ingredients
- 2 medium-sized apples
- 1 teaspoon cinnamon
- 2 tablespoons granola (choose a low-sugar or sugar-free option)
- Cooking spray or a light coating of oil (optional)

Instructions:
1. Preheat the oven to 375°F (190°C).
2. Wash the apples, then core and slice them into thin rings or wedges.
3. Place the apple slices in a single layer on a baking sheet lined with parchment paper or lightly greased with cooking spray or oil.
4. Sprinkle the cinnamon evenly over the apple slices.
5. Bake in the preheated oven for about 15-20 minutes, or until the apples are tender.
6. Remove the baking sheet from the oven and let the apple slices cool for a few minutes.
7. Transfer the baked apple slices to serving plates or bowls.
8. Sprinkle the granola over the apple slices.
9. Serve warm or at room temperature.

CHOCOLATE PROTEIN PUDDING MADE WITH WHEY PROTEIN POWDER

Nutrition: Cal 150;Fat42 g;Carb 9 g;Protein 28 g
Serving 2; Cook time 5 min

Ingredients
- 1 cup unsweetened almond milk (or any other milk of your choice)
- 2 scoops chocolate whey protein powder
- 1 tablespoon unsweetened cocoa powder
- 1-2 tablespoons sweetener of your choice (e.g., stevia, erythritol, or sugar-free syrup)
- 1/2 teaspoon vanilla extract (optional)
- A pinch of salt

Instructions:
1. In a mixing bowl, whisk together the almond milk, chocolate whey protein powder, unsweetened cocoa powder, sweetener, vanilla extract, and salt until well combined.
2. Continue whisking until the mixture becomes smooth and creamy. Make sure there are no lumps.
3. Taste the mixture and adjust the sweetness if needed.
4. Pour the pudding mixture into two individual serving bowls or containers.
5. Place the bowls in the refrigerator for at least 30 minutes to allow the pudding to set.
6. Once set, you can optionally garnish the pudding with a sprinkle of cocoa powder or some sliced almonds.

BANANA ICE CREAM MADE WITH FROZEN BANANAS AND A SPLASH OF ALMOND MILK

Nutrition: Cal 120;Fat 2 g;Carb 25 g;Protein 2 g
Serving 2; Cook time 5 min

Ingredients
- 2 ripe bananas, peeled and sliced
- 1/4 cup unsweetened almond milk (or any other milk of your choice)
- Optional toppings: sliced almonds, shredded coconut, dark chocolate chips, or fresh berries

Instructions:
1. Slice the bananas into coins and place them in a single layer on a baking sheet lined with parchment paper.
2. Place the baking sheet in the freezer and freeze the banana slices for at least 2-3 hours until they are firm.
3. Once the banana slices are frozen, transfer them to a blender or food processor.
4. Add the almond milk to the blender.
5. Blend the mixture on high speed until the bananas break down and turn into a smooth and creamy consistency.
6. If needed, stop and scrape down the sides of the blender and continue blending until the mixture is well combined.
7. Taste the banana ice cream and adjust the sweetness if desired by adding a natural sweetener like honey or a few drops of liquid stevia.
8. Serve the banana ice cream immediately in bowls or cones.
9. Optionally, you can top the ice cream with sliced almonds, shredded coconut, dark chocolate chips, or fresh berries.

SUGAR-FREE JELLO WITH A DOLLOP OF WHIPPED CREAM

Nutrition: Cal 20;Fat 0 g;Carb 1 g;Protein 1 g
Serving 2; Cook time 2-4 hours

Ingredients
- 1 package (0.3 ounces) sugar-free gelatin mix (any flavor of your choice)
- 1 cup boiling water
- 1 cup cold water
- Sugar-free whipped cream or light whipped topping for garnish

Instructions:
1. In a heatproof bowl, combine the sugar-free gelatin mix with boiling water.
2. Stir the mixture until the gelatin is completely dissolved.
3. Add the cold water to the gelatin mixture and stir well to combine.
4. Pour the gelatin mixture into individual serving cups or a single serving dish.
5. Place the cups or dish in the refrigerator and let the gelatin set for about 2-4 hours, or until firm.
6. Once the gelatin is set, remove it from the refrigerator.
7. Add a dollop of sugar-free whipped cream or light whipped topping on top of each serving.
8. Serve the sugar-free Jello with whipped cream immediately.

PEANUT BUTTER AND BANANA SMOOTHIE MADE WITH ALMOND MILK

Nutrition: Cal 200;Fat 10 g;Carb 20 g;Protein 7 g
Serving 2; Cook time 5 min

Ingredients
- 2 medium ripe bananas, peeled and sliced
- 2 tablespoons natural peanut butter (no added sugar or oils)
- 1 cup unsweetened almond milk
- Ice cubes (optional)

Instructions:
1. Place the sliced bananas, peanut butter, and almond milk in a blender.
2. Blend on high speed until the ingredients are well combined and the smoothie is creamy.
3. If desired, add a few ice cubes to the blender and blend again until the smoothie is chilled and frothy.
4. Taste the smoothie and adjust the sweetness or thickness by adding more almond milk or peanut butter as desired.
5. Pour the smoothie into two glasses and serve immediately.

CHIA SEED PUDDING WITH COCONUT MILK AND BERRIES

Nutrition: Cal 180;Fat 10 g;Carb 15 g;Protein 5 g
Serving 2; Cook time 5 min

Ingredients
- 1/4 cup chia seeds
- 1 cup unsweetened coconut milk
- 1 tablespoon honey or sweetener of choice (optional)
- 1/2 teaspoon vanilla extract
- Assorted fresh berries (e.g., strawberries, blueberries, raspberries) for topping

Instructions:
1. In a mixing bowl, combine the chia seeds, coconut milk, honey (if using), and vanilla extract. Stir well to ensure the chia seeds are evenly distributed.
2. Let the mixture sit for 5 minutes, then stir again to prevent clumping.
3. Cover the bowl and refrigerate for at least 2 hours or overnight, allowing the chia seeds to absorb the liquid and form a pudding-like consistency.
4. Once the chia seed pudding has set, give it a good stir to break up any clumps that may have formed.
5. Divide the pudding into two serving bowls or glasses.
6. Top the pudding with a generous amount of fresh berries.

PROTEIN-PACKED CHOCOLATE TRUFFLES MADE WITH DATES AND PROTEIN POWDER

Nutrition: Cal 130;Fat 4 g;Carb 18 g;Protein 6 g
Serving 2; Cook time 20 min

Ingredients
- 1 cup pitted dates
- 1/4 cup chocolate protein powder
- 2 tablespoons unsweetened cocoa powder
- 2 tablespoons almond flour
- 1 tablespoon almond butter
- 1/4 teaspoon vanilla extract
- Unsweetened shredded coconut or cocoa powder for rolling (optional)

Instructions:
1. In a food processor, combine the pitted dates, chocolate protein powder, cocoa powder, almond flour, almond butter, and vanilla extract. Process until well combined and a sticky dough forms.
2. Scoop out small portions of the dough and roll them into bite-sized truffles using your hands.
3. If desired, roll the truffles in unsweetened shredded coconut or cocoa powder for additional flavor and texture.
4. Place the truffles on a baking sheet lined with parchment paper and refrigerate for at least 1 hour to allow them to firm up.
5. Once chilled, the truffles are ready to be enjoyed.

FROZEN GRAPES FOR A REFRESHING AND SWEET TREAT

Nutrition: Cal 100;Fat 0 g;Carb 18 g;Protein 1 g
Serving 2; Cook time 2 hours

Ingredients
- 2 cups grapes (any variety)
- Optional toppings: shredded coconut, chopped nuts, or a sprinkle of cinnamon (optional)

Instructions:
1. Rinse the grapes under cold water and pat them dry with a paper towel.
2. Spread the grapes in a single layer on a baking sheet lined with parchment paper.
3. Place the baking sheet with the grapes in the freezer.
4. Freeze the grapes for at least 2-3 hours or until completely frozen.
5. Once frozen, transfer the grapes to an airtight container or freezer bag for storage.

TO SERVE:
1. Remove the desired amount of frozen grapes from the freezer.
2. Enjoy them as a refreshing and sweet treat as is, or sprinkle them with shredded coconut, chopped nuts, or a sprinkle of cinnamon for added flavor and texture.

MINI CRUSTLESS PUMPKIN PIES MADE WITH CANNED PUMPKIN AND ALMOND FLOUR

Nutrition: Cal 100;Fat 7 g;Carb 8 g;Protein 4 g
Serving 2; Cook time 35 min

Ingredients

- 1 cup canned pumpkin puree
- 1/2 cup almond flour
- 1/4 cup granulated sweetener (such as stevia or erythritol)
- 1/4 cup unsweetened almond milk
- 1 large egg
- 1 teaspoon pumpkin pie spice
- 1/2 teaspoon vanilla extract
- Optional toppings: whipped cream, ground cinnamon (optional)

Instructions:

1. Preheat your oven to 350°F (175°C).
2. In a mixing bowl, combine the canned pumpkin puree, almond flour, granulated sweetener, unsweetened almond milk, egg, pumpkin pie spice, and vanilla extract. Mix well until all the ingredients are fully incorporated.
3. Lightly grease a muffin tin or line it with paper liners.
4. Pour the pumpkin mixture evenly into the muffin cups, filling each one about 3/4 full.
5. Bake in the preheated oven for 20-25 minutes or until the pies are set and a toothpick inserted in the center comes out clean.
6. Remove the mini crustless pumpkin pies from the oven and let them cool in the muffin tin for a few minutes. Then transfer them to a wire rack to cool completely.
7. Once cooled, you can optionally top the mini pies with a dollop of whipped cream and a sprinkle of ground cinnamon before serving.

PROTEIN PANCAKES MADE WITH WHEY PROTEIN POWDER AND TOPPED WITH SUGAR-FREE SYRUP

Nutrition: Cal 150;Fat 6 g;Carb 15 g;Protein 20 g
Serving 2; Cook time 20 min

Ingredients

- 1/2 cup whey protein powder (flavor of your choice)
- 1/2 cup oat flour or finely ground oats
- 1/2 teaspoon baking powder
- 1/2 cup unsweetened almond milk (or any milk of your choice)
- 2 large eggs
- 1 teaspoon vanilla extract
- Optional toppings: fresh berries, sliced banana, sugar-free syrup

Instructions:

1. In a mixing bowl, whisk together the whey protein powder, oat flour, and baking powder.
2. Add the almond milk, eggs, and vanilla extract to the dry ingredients. Stir well until a smooth batter forms.
3. Heat a non-stick skillet or griddle over medium heat and lightly coat it with cooking spray or a small amount of oil.
4. Pour 1/4 cup of the pancake batter onto the heated skillet for each pancake. Cook until bubbles form on the surface, then flip and cook the other side until golden brown.
5. Repeat the process with the remaining batter, adding more cooking spray or oil to the skillet as needed.
6. Once all the pancakes are cooked, serve them with your choice of toppings, such as fresh berries, sliced banana, or sugar-free syrup.

STRAWBERRY PROTEIN SMOOTHIE MADE WITH GREEK YOGURT AND ALMOND MILK

Nutrition: Cal 150;Fat 2 g;Carb 15 g;Protein 20 g
Serving 2; Cook time 5 min

Ingredients

- 1 cup frozen strawberries
- 1/2 cup Greek yogurt (plain or flavored)
- 1 cup unsweetened almond milk (or any milk of your choice)
- 1 scoop of strawberry-flavored protein powder
- Optional: sweetener (e.g., stevia) if desired

Instructions:

1. Place the frozen strawberries, Greek yogurt, almond milk, and protein powder in a blender.
2. Blend until smooth and creamy. If desired, add a sweetener of your choice and blend again.
3. Taste and adjust the sweetness or thickness by adding more almond milk or yogurt if needed.
4. Pour the smoothie into two glasses and serve immediately.

BAKED PEACHES WITH CINNAMON AND GREEK YOGUR

Nutrition: Cal 65;Fat 1 g;Carb 15 g;Protein 2 g

Serving 2; Cook time 25 min

Ingredients
- 2 peaches
- 1/2 teaspoon cinnamon
- 2 tablespoons Greek yogurt (plain or flavored)

Instructions:
1. Preheat your oven to 350°F (175°C).
2. Cut the peaches in half and remove the pits.
3. Place the peach halves, cut side up, on a baking sheet lined with parchment paper.
4. Sprinkle each peach half with cinnamon.
5. Bake the peaches in the preheated oven for about 15-20 minutes or until they are tender and juicy.
6. Remove the baked peaches from the oven and let them cool for a few minutes.
7. Serve each baked peach half with a dollop of Greek yogurt on top.

ALMOND BUTTER ENERGY BALLS

Nutrition: Cal 150;Fat 9 g;Carb 16 g;Protein 4 g
Serving 2; Cook time 30 min

Ingredients
- 1 cup rolled oats
- 1/2 cup almond butter (unsweetened)
- 1/4 cup honey (or alternative sweetener of your choice)
- 1/4 cup unsweetened shredded coconut (optional)
- 1/4 cup chopped almonds (optional)
- 1/4 cup mini dark chocolate chips (optional)
- 1/2 teaspoon vanilla extract
- Pinch of salt

Instructions:
1. In a mixing bowl, combine the rolled oats, almond butter, honey, vanilla extract, and salt.
2. Mix well until all the ingredients are evenly combined.
3. If desired, add in the shredded coconut, chopped almonds, and dark chocolate chips. Mix well to distribute them evenly.
4. Place the mixture in the refrigerator for about 15-30 minutes to allow it to firm up slightly.
5. Once chilled, remove the mixture from the refrigerator and roll it into small balls, about 1 inch in diameter.
6. Repeat the process until all the mixture is used.

7. Store the almond butter energy balls in an airtight container in the refrigerator.

SUGAR-FREE GELATIN CUPS WITH FRESH FRUIT SLICES

Nutrition: Cal 30;Fat 0 g;Carb 4 g;Protein 3 g
Serving 2; Cook time 4 hours

Ingredients
- 2 cups water
- 2 packets of sugar-free gelatin (your choice of flavor)
- Assorted fresh fruit slices (such as strawberries, blueberries, kiwi, or oranges)

Instructions:
1. In a small saucepan, bring the water to a boil.
2. Remove the saucepan from heat and add the sugar-free gelatin packets. Stir well until the gelatin is completely dissolved.
3. Allow the gelatin mixture to cool slightly.
4. Prepare two serving cups or glasses for the gelatin cups.
5. Divide the fresh fruit slices evenly between the cups, arranging them as desired.
6. Pour the gelatin mixture over the fruit slices in the cups, filling them up to the desired level.
7. Place the cups in the refrigerator and let them set for about 2-4 hours, or until the gelatin is firm.
8. Once the gelatin is set, you can serve the sugar-free gelatin cups chilled.

CHOCOLATE AVOCADO MOUSSE

Nutrition: Cal 160;Fat 12 g;Carb 12 g;Protein 4 g
Serving 2; Cook time 10 min

Ingredients

- 2 ripe avocados
- 1/4 cup unsweetened cocoa powder
- 1/4 cup low-calorie sweetener (such as stevia or erythritol)
- 1/4 cup almond milk (or any other preferred milk alternative)
- 1 teaspoon vanilla extract
- Optional toppings: sliced almonds, berries, or a sprinkle of cocoa powder

Instructions:

1. Cut the avocados in half, remove the pits, and scoop the flesh into a blender or food processor.
2. Add the cocoa powder, low-calorie sweetener, almond milk, and vanilla extract to the blender.
3. Blend the ingredients until smooth and creamy, scraping down the sides as needed.
4. Taste the mousse and adjust the sweetness or cocoa flavor to your preference.
5. Transfer the chocolate avocado mousse to serving dishes or ramekins, dividing it equally between two portions.
6. Refrigerate the mousse for at least 1-2 hours to chill and set.
7. Once chilled, you can garnish the mousse with sliced almonds, berries, or a sprinkle of cocoa powder if desired.
8. Serve and enjoy the chocolate avocado mousse!

MINI CHEESECAKES WITH GREEK YOGURT AND NUT CRUS

Nutrition: Cal 200;Fat 15 g;Carb 10 g;Protein 12 g
Serving 2; Cook time 20 min

Ingredients

FOR THE CRUST:

- 1/2 cup mixed nuts (such as almonds and walnuts)
- 2 tablespoons melted coconut oil
- 1 tablespoon low-calorie sweetener (such as stevia or erythritol)

FOR THE FILLING:

- 1 cup Greek yogurt (plain or flavored, low-fat or non-fat)
- 2 tablespoons low-calorie sweetener
- 1 teaspoon vanilla extract
- Optional toppings: Fresh berries or a drizzle of sugar-free syrup

Instructions:

1. Preheat the oven to 325°F (160°C).
2. In a food processor or blender, pulse the mixed nuts until finely chopped.
3. Add the melted coconut oil and low-calorie sweetener to the nuts and pulse a few more times until the mixture resembles wet sand.
4. Divide the nut mixture evenly among two mini cheesecake pans or individual ramekins, pressing it down firmly to form the crust.
5. Bake the crusts in the preheated oven for about 10 minutes, or until golden and fragrant. Remove from the oven and let them cool.
6. In a bowl, combine the Greek yogurt, low-calorie sweetener, and vanilla extract. Stir until well combined.
7. Once the crusts have cooled, spoon the Greek yogurt mixture over the crusts, dividing it equally between the two pans or ramekins.
8. Smooth the tops with a spatula or the back of a spoon.
9. Place the mini cheesecakes in the refrigerator and let them chill for at least 2-3 hours, or until set.
10. Once chilled and set, remove the mini cheesecakes from the pans or ramekins.
11. Top with fresh berries or a drizzle of sugar-free syrup, if desired.

PUMPKIN SPICE PROTEIN SHAKE

Nutrition: Cal 160;Fat 5 g;Carb 18 g;Protein 17 g
Serving 2; Cook time 10 min

Ingredients

- 1 cup unsweetened almond milk (or any other milk of your choice)
- 1/2 cup canned pumpkin puree
- 1 scoop vanilla protein powder
- 1/2 teaspoon pumpkin pie spice
- 1/2 teaspoon vanilla extract
- Ice cubes (optional)
- Optional toppings: a sprinkle of cinnamon or whipped cream (sugar-free)

Instructions:

1. In a blender, combine the almond milk, pumpkin puree, protein powder, pumpkin pie spice, and vanilla extract.
2. Blend until smooth and well combined. If desired, add a few ice cubes and blend again to chill the shake.
3. Taste and adjust the sweetness or spice level as desired by adding a sweetener or more pumpkin pie spice.
4. Pour the shake into two glasses.
5. If desired, top with a sprinkle of cinnamon or a dollop of sugar-free whipped cream.

PROTEIN-PACKED CHOCOLATE CHIP COOKIES

Nutrition: Cal 150;Fat 10 g;Carb 6 g;Protein 7 g
Serving 2; Cook time 25 min

Ingredients
- 1 cup almond flour
- 1/4 cup vanilla protein powder
- 1/4 cup sugar substitute (e.g., erythritol, stevia)
- 1/4 teaspoon baking powder
- 1/4 teaspoon salt
- 1/4 cup unsweetened almond butter
- 2 tablespoons melted coconut oil
- 1 teaspoon vanilla extract
- 1/4 cup sugar-free chocolate chips

Instructions:
1. Preheat the oven to 350°F (175°C). Line a baking sheet with parchment paper.
2. In a mixing bowl, whisk together the almond flour, protein powder, sugar substitute, baking powder, and salt.
3. Add the almond butter, melted coconut oil, and vanilla extract to the dry ingredients. Stir until well combined.
4. Fold in the sugar-free chocolate chips.
5. Using a tablespoon or cookie scoop, portion the dough into 12 equal-sized balls and place them onto the prepared baking sheet.
6. Flatten each ball slightly with the back of a fork.
7. Bake for 10-12 minutes or until the edges are golden brown.
8. Remove from the oven and let the cookies cool on the baking sheet for a few minutes before transferring them to a wire rack to cool completely.

RASPBERRY ALMOND CHIA PUDDING

Nutrition: Cal 180;Fat 12 g;Carb 15 g;Protein 7 g
Serving 2; Cook time 2 hours 10 min

Ingredients
- 1 cup unsweetened almond milk
- 1/4 cup chia seeds
- 1 tablespoon almond butter
- 1 tablespoon sugar-free raspberry syrup
- 1/4 teaspoon vanilla extract
- Fresh raspberries for topping

Instructions:
1. In a bowl, combine the almond milk, chia seeds, almond butter, sugar-free raspberry syrup, and vanilla extract. Stir well until all the ingredients are evenly mixed.
2. Let the mixture sit for 5 minutes, then give it another stir to prevent clumping.
3. Cover the bowl and refrigerate for at least 2 hours or overnight, allowing the chia seeds to absorb the liquid and thicken the pudding.
4. Once the chia pudding has set, give it a final stir to break up any clumps.
5. Divide the pudding into two serving bowls or glasses.
6. Top with fresh raspberries.

PEANUT BUTTER PROTEIN BALLS

Nutrition: Cal 90;Fat 6 g;Carb 7 g;Protein 4 g
Serving 2; Cook time 15 min

Ingredients
- 1/2 cup oats
- 1/4 cup natural peanut butter
- 2 tablespoons protein powder (flavor of your choice)
- 2 tablespoons honey or maple syrup
- 1/2 teaspoon vanilla extract
- Pinch of salt
- Optional toppings: shredded coconut, chopped nuts, or dark chocolate chips

Instructions:
1. In a mixing bowl, combine oats, peanut butter, protein powder, honey or maple syrup, vanilla extract, and salt. Stir until well combined.
2. If the mixture is too dry, you can add a splash of water or milk to moisten it.
3. Take small portions of the mixture and roll them into bite-sized balls using your hands.

4. If desired, roll the balls in shredded coconut, chopped nuts, or dark chocolate chips for added flavor and texture.
5. Place the protein balls on a plate or baking sheet lined with parchment paper.
6. Refrigerate the protein balls for at least 30 minutes to allow them to firm up.
7. Once chilled, the protein balls are ready to enjoy. Store any leftovers in an airtight container in the refrigerator.

BAKED PEAR SLICES WITH HONEY AND CINNAMON

Nutrition: Cal 80;Fat 0 g;Carb 20 g;Protein 0 g
Serving 2; Cook time 20 min

Ingredients
- 2 ripe pears
- 1 tablespoon honey
- 1/2 teaspoon ground cinnamon

Instructions:
1. Preheat the oven to 375°F (190°C) and line a baking sheet with parchment paper.
2. Wash the pears and slice them into thin slices, discarding the core and seeds.
3. Arrange the pear slices in a single layer on the prepared baking sheet.
4. Drizzle the honey evenly over the pear slices.
5. Sprinkle the ground cinnamon over the pears, ensuring it coats each slice.
6. Bake in the preheated oven for about 15-20 minutes or until the pears are tender and slightly caramelized.
7. Remove from the oven and let the baked pear slices cool for a few minutes before serving.

LEMON POPPY SEED MUFFINS

Nutrition: Cal 130;Fat 9 g;Carb 7 g;Protein 9 g
Serving 2; Cook time 30 min

Ingredients
- 1 cup almond flour
- 1/4 cup protein powder (vanilla or lemon-flavored)
- 2 tablespoons poppy seeds
- 1/4 cup granulated sweetener (such as stevia or erythritol)
- 1 teaspoon baking powder
- 1/4 teaspoon salt
- 1/4 cup unsweetened almond milk
- 2 tablespoons lemon juice
- Zest of 1 lemon
- 2 tablespoons melted coconut oil
- 2 large eggs

Instructions:
1. Preheat the oven to 350°F (175°C) and line a muffin tin with paper liners.
2. In a mixing bowl, combine the almond flour, protein powder, poppy seeds, granulated sweetener, baking powder, and salt. Stir well to combine.
3. In a separate bowl, whisk together the almond milk, lemon juice, lemon zest, melted coconut oil, and eggs.
4. Add the wet ingredients to the dry ingredients and stir until a thick batter forms.
5. Divide the batter evenly among the muffin cups, filling each about 3/4 full.
6. Bake in the preheated oven for 18-20 minutes or until the muffins are golden brown and a toothpick inserted into the center comes out clean.
7. Remove from the oven and let the muffins cool in the tin for a few minutes before transferring them to a wire rack to cool completely.

CHOCOLATE PROTEIN ICE CREAM

Nutrition: Cal 150;Fat 4 g;Carb 28 g;Protein 18 g
Serving 2; Cook time 10 min

Ingredients
- 2 ripe bananas, sliced and frozen
- 2 scoops chocolate protein powder
- 1/4 cup unsweetened almond milk (or any milk of your choice)
- Optional toppings: sliced almonds, dark chocolate chips, or fresh berries

Instructions:
1. Place the frozen banana slices, chocolate protein powder, and almond milk in a blender or food processor.
2. Blend on high speed until the mixture is smooth and creamy, scraping down the sides as needed. If the mixture is too thick, add a little more almond milk, a tablespoon at a time, until desired consistency is reached.

3. Once the mixture is creamy, transfer it to a freezer-safe container and freeze for at least 2 hours or until firm.
4. Before serving, let the ice cream sit at room temperature for a few minutes to soften slightly.
5. Scoop the ice cream into bowls or cones and garnish with your favorite toppings, such as sliced almonds, dark chocolate chips, or fresh berries.

GREEK YOGURT PARFAIT WITH LAYERS OF YOGURT, FRUIT, AND GRANOLA

Nutrition: Cal 220;Fat 4 g;Carb 33 g;Protein 17 g
Serving 2; Cook time 5 min

Ingredients
- 1 cup Greek yogurt
- 1 cup mixed fresh berries (strawberries, blueberries, raspberries)
- 1/4 cup granola (choose a low-sugar option)
- Optional: drizzle of honey or maple syrup for sweetness

Instructions:
1. In two serving glasses or bowls, start by layering half of the Greek yogurt at the bottom of each.
2. Add a layer of mixed fresh berries on top of the yogurt.
3. Sprinkle half of the granola over the berries.
4. Repeat the layers with the remaining yogurt, berries, and granola.
5. If desired, drizzle a small amount of honey or maple syrup over the top for added sweetness.
6. Serve immediately and enjoy!

MINI BLUEBERRY MUFFINS

Nutrition: Cal 160;Fat 11 g;Carb 11 g;Protein 9 g
Serving 2; Cook time 30 min

Ingredients
- 1 cup almond flour
- 1/4 cup protein powder (choose a low-sugar option)
- 1/2 teaspoon baking powder
- 1/4 teaspoon baking soda
- 1/4 teaspoon salt
- 2 tablespoons coconut oil, melted
- 2 tablespoons honey or maple syrup
- 2 large eggs
- 1/2 cup unsweetened almond milk
- 1 teaspoon vanilla extract
- 1/2 cup fresh blueberries

Instructions:
1. Preheat the oven to 350°F (175°C). Grease a mini muffin pan or line it with mini muffin liners.
2. In a mixing bowl, whisk together the almond flour, protein powder, baking powder, baking soda, and salt.
3. In a separate bowl, whisk together the melted coconut oil, honey or maple syrup, eggs, almond milk, and vanilla extract.
4. Pour the wet ingredients into the dry ingredients and stir until well combined.
5. Gently fold in the fresh blueberries.
6. Spoon the batter into the prepared mini muffin pan, filling each cavity about 3/4 full.
7. Bake in the preheated oven for 12-15 minutes, or until a toothpick inserted into the center of a muffin comes out clean.
8. Allow the muffins to cool in the pan for a few minutes, then transfer them to a wire rack to cool completely.

CHOCOLATE ALMOND PROTEIN BARS

Nutrition: Cal 180;Fat 10 g;Carb 12 g;Protein 11 g
Serving 2; Cook time 10 min

Ingredients
- 1 cup almonds
- 1/2 cup protein powder (choose a low-sugar option)
- 2 tablespoons cocoa powder
- 1/4 cup almond butter
- 1/4 cup honey or maple syrup
- 1 teaspoon vanilla extract
- 2-3 tablespoons unsweetened almond milk (if needed for binding)

Instructions:
1. Place the almonds in a food processor or blender and pulse until finely chopped. Be careful not to over-process and turn them into almond butter.
2. In a mixing bowl, combine the chopped almonds, protein powder, and cocoa powder.

3. In a small saucepan, melt the almond butter and honey or maple syrup over low heat, stirring until well combined.

4. Remove the saucepan from heat and stir in the vanilla extract.

5. Pour the almond butter mixture into the bowl with the dry ingredients. Mix well until all the ingredients are evenly combined. If the mixture appears too dry, add 1 tablespoon of almond milk at a time until the mixture holds together.

6. Line a baking dish or tray with parchment paper. Press the mixture firmly into the dish to form an even layer.

7. Place the dish in the refrigerator and let it chill for at least 1-2 hours, or until firm.

8. Once firm, remove the mixture from the dish and cut it into bars of your desired size.

9. Store the chocolate almond protein bars in an airtight container in the refrigerator for up to a week.

CHOCOLATE COVERED STRAWBERRIES

Nutrition: Cal 140;Fat 7 g;Carb 13 g;Protein 2 g
Serving 2; Cook time 20 min

Ingredients
- 12 fresh strawberries
- 50 grams of dark chocolate (70% cocoa or higher)
- Optional toppings: chopped nuts, shredded coconut, or sprinkles (choose low-sugar options)

Instructions:
1. Rinse the strawberries under cold water and pat them dry with a paper towel. Ensure they are completely dry before proceeding.

2. Line a baking sheet or tray with parchment paper.

3. In a microwave-safe bowl, break the dark chocolate into small pieces. Microwave the chocolate in 30-second intervals, stirring in between, until completely melted and smooth. Be careful not to overheat the chocolate.

4. Dip each strawberry into the melted chocolate, coating it halfway or entirely, depending on your preference. Allow any excess chocolate to drip off.

5. Place the chocolate-coated strawberries onto the prepared baking sheet or tray.

6. If desired, sprinkle the strawberries with your chosen toppings while the chocolate is still wet.

7. Repeat the process with the remaining strawberries.

8. Once all the strawberries are coated and decorated, place the baking sheet or tray in the refrigerator for at least 15-20 minutes, or until the chocolate has hardened.

9. Once the chocolate is firm, transfer the chocolate covered strawberries to a plate or serving dish.

10. Serve immediately or store in the refrigerator for up to 24 hours. Note that the strawberries are best enjoyed within a day of making.

ALMOND FLOUR CHOCOLATE CHIP COOKIES

Nutrition: Cal 170;Fat 13 g;Carb 10 g;Protein 6 g
Serving 2; Cook time 20 min

Ingredients
- 1 cup almond flour
- 1/4 cup dark chocolate chips (70% cocoa or higher)
- 2 tablespoons coconut oil, melted
- 2 tablespoons natural sweetener (such as stevia or erythritol)
- 1/2 teaspoon vanilla extract
- 1/4 teaspoon baking soda
- Pinch of salt

Instructions:
1. Preheat your oven to 350°F (175°C). Line a baking sheet with parchment paper.

2. In a mixing bowl, combine the almond flour, dark chocolate chips, natural sweetener, baking soda, and salt. Stir until well combined.

3. Add the melted coconut oil and vanilla extract to the dry ingredients. Mix until a thick dough forms.

4. Scoop tablespoon-sized portions of dough onto the prepared baking sheet, spacing them evenly apart. Use your hands to gently flatten each cookie, as they will not spread much during baking.

5. Bake the cookies in the preheated oven for 10-12 minutes, or until the edges are golden brown.

6. Remove from the oven and allow the cookies to cool on the baking sheet for a few minutes before transferring them to a wire rack to cool completely.

CHOCOLATE CHERRY PROTEIN SMOOTHIE

Nutrition: Cal 220;Fat 6 g;Carb 22 g;Protein 22 g
Serving 2; Cook time 5 min

Ingredients
- 1 cup unsweetened almond milk
- 1/2 cup Greek yogurt
- 1/2 cup frozen cherries
- 1 scoop chocolate protein powder
- 1 tablespoon unsweetened cocoa powder
- 1/2 teaspoon vanilla extract
- Ice cubes (optional, for desired thickness)
- Optional toppings: shaved dark chocolate or fresh cherries

Instructions:
1. In a blender, combine almond milk, Greek yogurt, frozen cherries, chocolate protein powder, cocoa powder, and vanilla extract.

2. Blend until smooth and creamy. If desired, add ice cubes for a thicker consistency and blend again.

3. Taste and adjust sweetness if needed by adding a natural sweetener like stevia or a small amount of honey.

4. Pour the smoothie into two glasses.

5. Optional: Top with shaved dark chocolate or fresh cherries for added texture and flavor.

6. Serve immediately and enjoy!

VANILLA PROTEIN SHAKE

Nutrition: Cal 170;Fat 5 g;Carb 8 g;Protein 26 g
Serving 2; Cook time 5 min

Ingredients
- 2 cups unsweetened almond milk
- 2 scoops vanilla protein powder
- 1 teaspoon vanilla extract
- Optional: Stevia or another natural sweetener to taste
- Ice cubes

Instructions:

1. In a blender, combine almond milk, vanilla protein powder, vanilla extract, and sweetener if desired.

2. Blend on high speed until the ingredients are well combined and the shake is smooth.

3. Add ice cubes to the blender and blend again until the shake is chilled and frothy.

4. Taste the shake and adjust sweetness if needed by adding more sweetener.

5. Pour the vanilla protein shake into two glasses and serve immediately.

LEMON COCONUT ENERGY BALLS

Nutrition: Cal 110;Fat 7 g;Carb 10 g;Protein 3 g
Serving 2; Cook time 10 min(plus chilling time)

Ingredients
- 1 cup rolled oats
- 1/2 cup shredded coconut
- Zest of 1 lemon
- 1/2 cup almond butter
- 1/4 cup honey or maple syrup
- 1 teaspoon vanilla extract
- Pinch of salt

Instructions:
1. In a food processor, pulse the rolled oats until they form a coarse texture.

2. In a mixing bowl, combine the pulsed oats, shredded coconut, and lemon zest.

3. Add almond butter, honey or maple syrup, vanilla extract, and salt to the bowl.

4. Mix well until all the ingredients are fully combined.

5. Shape the mixture into small balls, approximately 1 inch in diameter, and place them on a baking sheet lined with parchment paper.

6. Refrigerate the energy balls for at least 30 minutes to firm up.

7. Store the energy balls in an airtight container in the refrigerator until ready to serve.

BLUEBERRY PROTEIN MUFFINS

Nutrition: Cal 140;Fat 9 g;Carb 12 g;Protein 8 g
Serving 2; Cook time 30 min

Ingredients
- 1 cup almond flour

- 1/4 cup protein powder (flavor of your choice)
- 1 teaspoon baking powder
- 1/4 teaspoon salt
- 2 tablespoons melted coconut oil
- 1/4 cup honey or maple syrup
- 2 large eggs
- 1/2 cup unsweetened almond milk
- 1 teaspoon vanilla extract
- 1 cup fresh blueberries

Instructions:

1. Preheat the oven to 350°F (175°C). Line a muffin tin with paper liners.
2. In a mixing bowl, whisk together the almond flour, protein powder, baking powder, and salt.
3. In a separate bowl, whisk together the melted coconut oil, honey or maple syrup, eggs, almond milk, and vanilla extract until well combined.
4. Add the wet ingredients to the dry ingredients and stir until just combined.
5. Gently fold in the fresh blueberries.
6. Divide the batter evenly among the muffin cups, filling each about three-quarters full.
7. Bake for 18-20 minutes, or until a toothpick inserted into the center of a muffin comes out clean.
8. Remove from the oven and let the muffins cool in the pan for a few minutes, then transfer them to a wire rack to cool completely.

VANILLA ALMOND CHIA PUDDING

Nutrition: Cal 200;Fat 12 g;Carb 18 g;Protein 8 g
Serving 2; Cook time 2 hours 5 min

Ingredients
- 1/4 cup chia seeds
- 1 cup unsweetened almond milk
- 1 tablespoon almond butter
- 1 tablespoon honey or maple syrup (optional, for sweetness)
- 1/2 teaspoon vanilla extract
- Sliced almonds and berries for topping (optional)

Instructions:

1. In a bowl, combine the chia seeds, almond milk, almond butter, honey or maple syrup (if using), and vanilla extract. Stir well to ensure the chia seeds are evenly distributed.
2. Let the mixture sit for 5 minutes and then give it another stir to prevent clumping.
3. Cover the bowl and refrigerate for at least 2 hours or overnight, allowing the chia seeds to absorb the liquid and create a pudding-like consistency.
4. Once the chia pudding has set, give it a final stir to break up any clumps.
5. Divide the chia pudding into two serving bowls or jars.
6. Top with sliced almonds and berries, if desired.

CHOCOLATE CHERRY PROTEIN SHAKE

Nutrition: Cal 200;Fat 4 g;Carb 20 g;Protein 20 g
Serving 2; Cook time 5 min

Ingredients
- 1 cup unsweetened almond milk
- 1/2 cup frozen cherries
- 1 scoop chocolate protein powder
- 1 tablespoon unsweetened cocoa powder
- 1/2 teaspoon vanilla extract
- Ice cubes (optional, for a thicker shake)

Instructions:

1. In a blender, combine the almond milk, frozen cherries, chocolate protein powder, cocoa powder, and vanilla extract.
2. Blend on high speed until smooth and creamy. If desired, add a few ice cubes and blend again for a thicker consistency.
3. Taste the shake and adjust the sweetness or thickness by adding more protein powder, cocoa powder, or almond milk, as needed.
4. Pour the shake into two glasses and serve immediately.

PUMPKIN PROTEIN BARS

Nutrition: Cal 140;Fat 5 g;Carb 12 g;Protein 12 g
Serving 2; Cook time 35 min

Ingredients
- 1 cup canned pumpkin puree
- 1/2 cup protein powder (your choice of flavor)
- 1/2 cup almond flour
- 1/4 cup unsweetened almond milk
- 2 tablespoons honey or your preferred sweetener
- 1 teaspoon pumpkin pie spice
- 1/2 teaspoon vanilla extract

•Optional toppings: chopped nuts, pumpkin seeds, or dark chocolate chips

Instructions:

1. Preheat the oven to 350°F (175°C) and line a baking dish or pan with parchment paper.
2. In a mixing bowl, combine the canned pumpkin puree, protein powder, almond flour, almond milk, honey or sweetener, pumpkin pie spice, and vanilla extract. Stir well until all the ingredients are thoroughly combined.
3. Transfer the mixture to the prepared baking dish and spread it evenly, smoothing the top with a spatula.
4. If desired, sprinkle the optional toppings evenly over the top of the mixture, pressing them lightly into the batter.
5. Bake in the preheated oven for 20-25 minutes, or until the bars are set and lightly golden on the edges.
6. Remove from the oven and let the bars cool completely in the baking dish before cutting into individual bars.
7. Once cooled, slice the bars into desired sizes and serve.

PEANUT BUTTER CHOCOLATE CHIP PROTEIN BARS

Nutrition: Cal 170;Fat 11 g;Carb 8 g;Protein 11 g
Serving 2; Cook time 15 min

Ingredients

•1 cup creamy peanut butter
•1/2 cup protein powder (chocolate flavor)
•1/4 cup honey or your preferred sweetener
•1/4 cup dark chocolate chips
•1/4 cup unsweetened almond milk (or milk of choice)
•1/4 teaspoon vanilla extract
•Optional: pinch of salt

Instructions:

1. In a mixing bowl, combine the peanut butter, protein powder, honey, almond milk, vanilla extract, and salt (if using). Stir until well combined and the mixture forms a thick batter.
2. Fold in the dark chocolate chips, distributing them evenly throughout the batter.

3. Line a baking dish or pan with parchment paper. Transfer the batter into the prepared dish and press it down firmly to create an even layer.
4. Place the dish in the refrigerator and chill for at least 1-2 hours, or until the bars are firm and set.
5. Once chilled, remove the bars from the dish and cut them into desired sizes.
6. Serve immediately or store in an airtight container in the refrigerator for up to a week.

BLUEBERRY ALMOND FLOUR CRUMBLE

Nutrition: Cal 170;Fat 10 g;Carb 15 g;Protein 6 g
Serving 2; Cook time 35 min

Ingredients

•2 cups fresh or frozen blueberries
•1 cup almond flour
•2 tablespoons sweetener of your choice (such as stevia, erythritol, or honey)
•2 tablespoons unsalted butter, melted
•1/2 teaspoon vanilla extract
•Pinch of salt

Instructions:

1. Preheat the oven to 350°F (175°C). Lightly grease a baking dish.
2. In a mixing bowl, combine the blueberries, sweetener, and vanilla extract. Stir well to coat the blueberries evenly.
3. In a separate bowl, combine the almond flour, melted butter, and pinch of salt. Mix until it resembles a crumbly texture.
4. Spread the blueberry mixture evenly in the greased baking dish.
5. Sprinkle the almond flour mixture over the blueberries, covering them completely.
6. Bake in the preheated oven for 25-30 minutes, or until the top is golden brown and the blueberries are bubbling.
7. Remove from the oven and let it cool slightly before serving.
8. Serve warm as is or with a dollop of Greek yogurt or a scoop of sugar-free vanilla ice cream, if desired.

CHOCOLATE AVOCADO PROTEIN PUDDING

Nutrition: Cal 250;Fat 17 g;Carb 12 g;Protein 10 g
Serving 2; Cook time 10 min

Ingredients
- 2 ripe avocados
- 1/4 cup unsweetened cocoa powder
- 1/4 cup protein powder (chocolate flavor)
- 2-3 tablespoons sweetener of your choice (such as stevia, erythritol, or honey)
- 1/2 teaspoon vanilla extract
- Pinch of salt
- Optional toppings: sliced almonds, berries, or shredded coconut

Instructions:
1. Cut the avocados in half, remove the pits, and scoop out the flesh into a blender or food processor.
2. Add the cocoa powder, protein powder, sweetener, vanilla extract, and salt to the blender.
3. Blend all the ingredients until smooth and creamy. If needed, you can add a small amount of almond milk or water to adjust the consistency.
4. Taste the pudding and adjust the sweetness if desired.
5. Divide the pudding into two serving bowls or glasses.
6. Cover and refrigerate for at least 1 hour to allow the pudding to set and thicken.
7. Before serving, you can add optional toppings such as sliced almonds, berries, or shredded coconut for extra texture and flavor.

LEMON RASPBERRY PROTEIN MUFFINS

Nutrition: Cal 150;Fat 8 g;Carb 8 g;Protein 6 g
Serving 2; Cook time 30 min

Ingredients
- 1 cup almond flour
- 1/4 cup protein powder (vanilla or lemon flavor)
- 1/4 cup sweetener of your choice (such as stevia, erythritol, or honey)
- 1 teaspoon baking powder
- 1/4 teaspoon salt
- Zest of 1 lemon
- Juice of 1 lemon
- 2 large eggs
- 1/4 cup unsweetened almond milk
- 1/2 cup fresh or frozen raspberries

Instructions:
1. Preheat your oven to 350°F (175°C). Line a muffin tin with paper liners or grease with cooking spray.
2. In a mixing bowl, whisk together the almond flour, protein powder, sweetener, baking powder, salt, and lemon zest.
3. In a separate bowl, whisk together the eggs, lemon juice, and almond milk.
4. Pour the wet ingredients into the dry ingredients and stir until well combined. Gently fold in the raspberries.
5. Divide the batter evenly among the muffin cups, filling each about three-quarters full.
6. Bake in the preheated oven for 18-20 minutes, or until the muffins are golden brown and a toothpick inserted into the center comes out clean.
7. Remove from the oven and let the muffins cool in the pan for a few minutes, then transfer them to a wire rack to cool completely.

VANILLA COCONUT CHIA PUDDING

Nutrition: Cal 150;Fat 12 g;Carb 8 g;Protein 3 g
Serving 2; Cook time 2 hours

Ingredients
- 1 cup coconut milk (unsweetened)
- 2 tablespoons chia seeds
- 1 tablespoon sweetener of your choice (such as stevia, erythritol, or honey)
- 1/2 teaspoon vanilla extract
- Optional toppings: shredded coconut, berries, nuts

Instructions:
1. In a bowl or jar, combine the coconut milk, chia seeds, sweetener, and vanilla extract.
2. Stir well to make sure the chia seeds are evenly distributed and not clumping together.
3. Cover the bowl or jar and refrigerate for at least 2 hours or overnight. This allows the chia seeds to absorb the liquid and form a pudding-like consistency.

4. After the chia pudding has set, give it a good stir to break up any clumps and ensure a smooth texture.
5. Divide the pudding into two serving dishes or jars.
6. If desired, top the pudding with shredded coconut, fresh berries, or your favorite nuts for added flavor and texture.
7. Serve chilled and enjoy!

ALMOND FLOUR BLUEBERRY MUFFINS

Nutrition: Cal 120;Fat 12 g;Carb 8 g;Protein 8 g
Serving 2; Cook time 30 min

Ingredients
- 1 cup almond flour
- 1/4 cup sweetener of your choice (such as stevia, erythritol, or honey)
- 1/2 teaspoon baking powder
- 1/4 teaspoon salt
- 2 large eggs
- 1/4 cup unsweetened almond milk
- 1 teaspoon vanilla extract
- 1 cup fresh blueberries

Instructions:
1. Preheat your oven to 350°F (175°C) and line a muffin tin with paper liners.
2. In a mixing bowl, combine the almond flour, sweetener, baking powder, and salt. Stir until well combined.
3. In a separate bowl, whisk together the eggs, almond milk, and vanilla extract.
4. Pour the wet ingredients into the dry ingredients and mix until a smooth batter forms.
5. Gently fold in the fresh blueberries, being careful not to overmix.
6. Divide the batter evenly among the muffin cups, filling each about three-quarters full.
7. Bake in the preheated oven for 20-25 minutes, or until a toothpick inserted into the center of a muffin comes out clean.
8. Remove the muffins from the oven and allow them to cool in the muffin tin for a few minutes before transferring to a wire rack to cool completely.

MINT CHOCOLATE PROTEIN SMOOTHIE

Nutrition: Cal 220;Fat 8 g;Carb 17 g;Protein 22 g
Serving 2; Cook time 5 min

Ingredients
- 2 cups spinach leaves
- 1 scoop chocolate protein powder
- 1 cup unsweetened almond milk
- 1/2 cup plain Greek yogurt
- 1/4 teaspoon peppermint extract
- 1 tablespoon dark chocolate chips (70% cocoa or higher)
- Ice cubes, as desired

Instructions:
1. In a blender, add the spinach, protein powder, almond milk, Greek yogurt, peppermint extract, and dark chocolate chips.
2. Blend on high speed until all the ingredients are well combined and the smoothie reaches your desired consistency.
3. Add ice cubes and blend again until the smoothie becomes chilled and thick.
4. Taste and adjust the sweetness or mint flavor if desired by adding a sweetener like stevia or a bit more peppermint extract.
5. Pour the smoothie into two glasses and serve immediately.

CHOCOLATE COCONUT CHIA SEED PUDDING

Nutrition: Cal 150;Fat 10 g;Carb 16 g;Protein 6 g
Serving 2; Cook time 20 min

Ingredients
- 1/4 cup chia seeds
- 1 cup unsweetened coconut milk
- 2 tablespoons unsweetened cocoa powder
- 1-2 tablespoons sweetener of choice (e.g., stevia, honey, or maple syrup)
- Optional toppings: shredded coconut, dark chocolate shavings, or fresh berries

Instructions:
1. In a bowl, whisk together the chia seeds, coconut milk, cocoa powder, and sweetener until well combined.
2. Let the mixture sit for about 5 minutes to allow the chia seeds to start absorbing the liquid.
3. Whisk the mixture again to ensure there are no clumps of chia seeds.

4. Cover the bowl and refrigerate for at least 2 hours or overnight, allowing the chia seeds to fully absorb the liquid and form a pudding-like consistency.

5. Once the chia pudding has set, give it a good stir to ensure it is evenly mixed.

6. Divide the pudding into two serving bowls or jars.

7. Top with your choice of shredded coconut, dark chocolate shavings, or fresh berries.

8. Serve chilled and enjoy!

PEANUT BUTTER BANANA PROTEIN ICE CREAM

Nutrition: Cal 200;Fat 8 g;Carb 20 g;Protein 10 g
Serving 2; Cook time 2 hours 10 min

Ingredients
- 2 large ripe bananas, peeled and sliced
- 2 tablespoons natural peanut butter (no added sugar or oil)
- 1 scoop of your preferred vanilla protein powder
- Optional toppings: crushed peanuts, dark chocolate chips, sliced bananas

Instructions:
1. Place the sliced bananas in a zip-top bag and freeze them for at least 2 hours or until completely frozen.

2. In a blender or food processor, add the frozen banana slices, peanut butter, and protein powder.

3. Blend on high speed until the mixture becomes smooth and creamy. You may need to stop and scrape down the sides of the blender a few times.

4. Once the desired consistency is reached, transfer the mixture to a freezer-safe container.

5. Cover and freeze for an additional 1-2 hours to firm up the ice cream.

6. Remove from the freezer and let it sit at room temperature for a few minutes before serving.

7. Scoop the peanut butter banana protein ice cream into bowls or cones.

8. Optional: Sprinkle with crushed peanuts, dark chocolate chips, or sliced bananas as desired.

RASPBERRY ALMOND FLOUR MUFFINS

Nutrition: Cal 140;Fat 11 g;Carb 8 g;Protein 6 g
Serving 2; Cook time 30 min

Ingredients
- 1 cup almond flour
- 1/4 cup coconut flour
- 1/4 cup granulated sweetener of your choice (e.g., stevia, erythritol)
- 1 teaspoon baking powder
- 1/4 teaspoon salt
- 3 large eggs
- 1/4 cup unsweetened almond milk
- 2 tablespoons melted coconut oil
- 1 teaspoon vanilla extract
- 1 cup fresh raspberries

Instructions:
1. Preheat your oven to 350°F (175°C) and line a muffin tin with paper liners.

2. In a large bowl, whisk together the almond flour, coconut flour, sweetener, baking powder, and salt.

3. In a separate bowl, beat the eggs. Add the almond milk, melted coconut oil, and vanilla extract. Mix well.

4. Pour the wet ingredients into the dry ingredients and stir until just combined. Be careful not to overmix.

5. Gently fold in the fresh raspberries.

6. Divide the batter evenly among the prepared muffin cups, filling each about 3/4 full.

7. Bake for 18-20 minutes or until a toothpick inserted into the center of a muffin comes out clean.

8. Remove the muffins from the oven and let them cool in the pan for a few minutes. Then transfer them to a wire rack to cool completely.

CHOCOLATE MINT PROTEIN SHAKE

Nutrition: Cal 150;Fat 5 g;Carb 7 g;Protein 20 g
Serving 2; Cook time 5 min

Ingredients
- 2 cups unsweetened almond milk
- 1 handful of fresh mint leaves
- 2 tablespoons chocolate protein powder

• 1-2 tablespoons sweetener of your choice (e.g., stevia, honey) (optional)
• Ice cubes (optional)

Instructions:

1. In a blender, combine the almond milk, fresh mint leaves, chocolate protein powder, and sweetener (if desired).
2. Blend on high speed until all the ingredients are well combined and the mint leaves are finely chopped.
3. Taste the shake and adjust the sweetness if necessary by adding more sweetener.
4. If desired, add a few ice cubes to the blender and blend again until the shake becomes chilled and frothy.
5. Pour the shake into two glasses and garnish with a mint leaf, if desired.
6. Serve immediately and enjoy!

VANILLA COCONUT PROTEIN BALLS

Nutrition: Cal 120;Fat 9 g;Carb 7 g;Protein 7 g
Serving 2; Cook time 10 min

Ingredients

• 1 cup shredded coconut
• 1/2 cup vanilla protein powder
• 2 tablespoons almond flour
• 2 tablespoons coconut oil, melted
• 1 tablespoon honey or sweetener of your choice
• 1 teaspoon vanilla extract
• Pinch of salt

Instructions:

1. In a mixing bowl, combine the shredded coconut, vanilla protein powder, almond flour, and salt.
2. Add the melted coconut oil, honey, and vanilla extract to the dry ingredients.
3. Mix well until all the ingredients are thoroughly combined and form a sticky mixture.
4. Take small portions of the mixture and roll them into bite-sized balls using your hands.
5. Place the protein balls on a tray lined with parchment paper.
6. Repeat the process until all the mixture is used.
7. Place the tray of protein balls in the refrigerator for about 30 minutes to allow them to firm up.

8. Once firm, transfer the protein balls to an airtight container and store them in the refrigerator.
9. The protein balls can be enjoyed immediately or kept for up to a week.

LEMON POPPY SEED PROTEIN MUFFINS

Nutrition: Cal 140;Fat 8 g;Carb 7 g;Protein 10 g
Serving 2; Cook time 30 min

Ingredients

• 1 cup almond flour
• 1/2 cup vanilla protein powder
• 1/4 cup sweetener of your choice (e.g., erythritol, stevia)
• 1 tablespoon poppy seeds
• 1 teaspoon baking powder
• 1/4 teaspoon salt
• Zest of 1 lemon
• Juice of 1 lemon
• 1/4 cup unsweetened almond milk
• 2 tablespoons melted coconut oil
• 2 large eggs
• 1 teaspoon vanilla extract

Instructions:

1. Preheat the oven to 350°F (175°C). Line a muffin tin with paper liners.
2. In a large mixing bowl, combine the almond flour, vanilla protein powder, sweetener, poppy seeds, baking powder, salt, and lemon zest.
3. In a separate bowl, whisk together the lemon juice, almond milk, melted coconut oil, eggs, and vanilla extract.
4. Pour the wet ingredients into the dry ingredients and stir until well combined.
5. Divide the batter evenly among the muffin cups, filling each about 2/3 full.
6. Bake for 18-20 minutes or until a toothpick inserted into the center of a muffin comes out clean.
7. Remove the muffins from the oven and let them cool in the tin for a few minutes, then transfer them to a wire rack to cool completely.

PUMPKIN SPICE PROTEIN WAFFLES

Nutrition: Cal 350;Fat 25 g;Carb 15 g;Protein 18 g
Serving 2; Cook time 25 min

Ingredients
- 1/2 cup pumpkin puree
- 1/2 cup unsweetened almond milk
- 2 large eggs
- 2 tablespoons melted coconut oil
- 1 teaspoon vanilla extract
- 1 cup almond flour
- 1/4 cup vanilla protein powder
- 1 teaspoon baking powder
- 1 teaspoon pumpkin pie spice
- Pinch of salt

Instructions:
1. Preheat your waffle iron according to the manufacturer's instructions.
2. In a mixing bowl, whisk together the pumpkin puree, almond milk, eggs, melted coconut oil, and vanilla extract until well combined.
3. In a separate bowl, whisk together the almond flour, protein powder, baking powder, pumpkin pie spice, and salt.
4. Gradually add the dry ingredients to the wet ingredients, stirring until a smooth batter forms.
5. Spray the preheated waffle iron with non-stick cooking spray.
6. Pour enough batter onto the waffle iron to cover the surface, being careful not to overfill.
7. Close the waffle iron and cook until the waffles are golden brown and cooked through, according to the waffle iron instructions.
8. Carefully remove the cooked waffles from the iron and repeat with the remaining batter.
9. Serve the pumpkin spice protein waffles warm with your choice of toppings, such as Greek yogurt, chopped nuts, or a drizzle of sugar-free syrup.

CHOCOLATE COCONUT PROTEIN SMOOTHIE

Nutrition: Cal 150;Fat 7 g;Carb 10 g;Protein 15 g
Serving 2; Cook time 5 min

Ingredients
- 1 cup unsweetened almond milk
- 2 tablespoons cocoa powder
- 1 scoop chocolate protein powder
- 2 tablespoons unsweetened shredded coconut
- 1 tablespoon sweetener (optional)
- 1 cup ice cubes

Instructions:
1. In a blender, combine almond milk, cocoa powder, protein powder, shredded coconut, sweetener (if desired), and ice cubes.
2. Blend on high speed until all the ingredients are well combined and the smoothie reaches a creamy consistency.
3. Taste and adjust the sweetness or cocoa flavor if needed, by adding more sweetener or cocoa powder.
4. Pour the smoothie into two glasses and serve immediately.

VANILLA ALMOND FLOUR COOKIES

Nutrition: Cal 100;Fat 8 g;Carb 3 g;Protein 3 g
Serving 2; Cook time 25 min

Ingredients
- 1 cup almond flour
- 2 tablespoons sweetener of your choice (e.g., erythritol, stevia, or monk fruit)
- 1/2 teaspoon baking powder
- 1/4 teaspoon salt
- 2 tablespoons melted coconut oil or butter
- 1 large egg
- 1 teaspoon vanilla extract

Instructions:
1. Preheat your oven to 350°F (175°C) and line a baking sheet with parchment paper.
2. In a mixing bowl, combine almond flour, sweetener, baking powder, and salt.
3. In a separate bowl, whisk together melted coconut oil or butter, egg, and vanilla extract.
4. Add the wet ingredients to the dry ingredients and stir until well combined.
5. Use a tablespoon to scoop the dough and roll it into balls. Place the dough balls onto the prepared baking sheet, leaving space between each cookie.
6. Use the back of a fork to press down on each dough ball and create a crisscross pattern on top.

7. Bake in the preheated oven for about 10-12 minutes, or until the cookies are lightly golden around the edges.
8. Remove from the oven and allow the cookies to cool on the baking sheet for a few minutes before transferring them to a wire rack to cool completely.

BERRY PROTEIN SMOOTHIE BOWL

Nutrition: Cal 300;Fat 7 g;Carb 30 g;Protein 30 g
Serving 2; Cook time 5 min

Ingredients
- 1 cup dried apples, chopped
- 1 cup almonds
- 1/2 cup protein powder (flavor of your choice)
- 1/4 cup almond butter
- 2 tablespoons honey or maple syrup
- 1 teaspoon cinnamon
- 1/4 teaspoon vanilla extract
- Pinch of salt

Instructions:
1. In a blender, combine the frozen mixed berries, almond milk, and protein powder.
2. Blend until smooth and creamy, adding more almond milk if needed to achieve the desired consistency.
3. Pour the smoothie into a bowl.
4. Top the smoothie bowl with fresh berries, a handful of low-sugar granola, and a sprinkle of chia seeds or shredded coconut if desired.

CHOCOLATE PEANUT BUTTER PROTEIN BARS

Nutrition: Cal 150;Fat 8 g;Carb 15 g;Protein 8 g
Serving 2; Cook time 10 min

Ingredients
- 1 cup old-fashioned oats
- 1/2 cup natural peanut butter
- 1/4 cup honey or maple syrup
- 1/4 cup chocolate protein powder
- 1/4 cup unsweetened cocoa powder
- 1/4 cup unsweetened almond milk
- Optional: 2 tablespoons dark chocolate chips or chopped nuts for topping

Instructions:

1. In a mixing bowl, combine the oats, peanut butter, honey or maple syrup, chocolate protein powder, cocoa powder, and almond milk.
2. Stir until well combined and the mixture forms a thick dough-like consistency.
3. Line a baking dish or pan with parchment paper.
4. Transfer the mixture to the prepared pan and press it down evenly using a spatula or your hands.
5. If desired, sprinkle the top with dark chocolate chips or chopped nuts.
6. Place the pan in the refrigerator for at least 1 hour or until the mixture sets.
7. Once firm, remove from the pan and cut into bars or squares.
8. Store the bars in an airtight container in the refrigerator.

MINT CHOCOLATE CHIP PROTEIN ICE CREAM

Nutrition: Cal 170;Fat 7 g;Carb 12 g;Protein 17 g
Serving 2; Cook time 10 min

Ingredients
- 2 cups plain Greek yogurt
- 1 cup unsweetened almond milk
- 1/4 cup fresh mint leaves, finely chopped
- 2 tablespoons protein powder (chocolate or vanilla flavor)
- 2 tablespoons dark chocolate chips (sugar-free or at least 70% cocoa)

Instructions:
1. In a blender or food processor, combine the Greek yogurt, almond milk, fresh mint leaves, and protein powder. Blend until smooth and well combined.
2. Pour the mixture into an ice cream maker and churn according to the manufacturer's instructions until it reaches a soft-serve consistency.
3. Stir in the dark chocolate chips.
4. Transfer the ice cream to an airtight container and freeze for an additional 2-3 hours, or until it reaches your desired firmness.
5. Serve the mint chocolate chip protein ice cream in bowls or cones and enjoy!

VANILLA COCONUT FLOUR MUFFINS

Nutrition: Cal 120;Fat 7 g;Carb 8 g;Protein 5 g
Serving 2; Cook time 35 min

Ingredients
- 1/2 cup coconut flour
- 4 large eggs
- 1/4 cup coconut oil, melted
- 1/4 cup unsweetened almond milk
- 1/4 cup sweetener of your choice (e.g., stevia, erythritol, or monk fruit)
- 1 teaspoon vanilla extract
- 1/2 teaspoon baking powder
- 1/2 teaspoon cinnamon (plus extra for sprinkling on top)
- Pinch of salt

Instructions:
1. Preheat the oven to 350°F (175°C) and line a muffin tin with paper liners or grease the cups.
2. In a mixing bowl, whisk together the eggs, melted coconut oil, almond milk, sweetener, and vanilla extract until well combined.
3. In a separate bowl, whisk together the coconut flour, baking powder, cinnamon, and salt.
4. Gradually add the dry ingredients to the wet ingredients and mix until a smooth batter forms. Let the batter sit for a few minutes to allow the coconut flour to absorb the liquids.
5. Divide the batter evenly among the muffin cups, filling each about 2/3 full.
6. Sprinkle a pinch of cinnamon on top of each muffin.
7. Bake in the preheated oven for 20-25 minutes, or until a toothpick inserted into the center of a muffin comes out clean.
8. Allow the muffins to cool in the pan for a few minutes, then transfer them to a wire rack to cool completely.

STRAWBERRY BANANA PROTEIN POPSICLES

Nutrition: Cal 90;Fat 2 g;Carb 10 g;Protein 8 g
Serving 2; Cook time 4 hours

Ingredients
- 1 cup Greek yogurt
- 1 cup fresh strawberries, hulled and chopped
- 1 ripe banana
- 2 tablespoons protein powder (vanilla or strawberry flavor)
- 1 tablespoon honey or sweetener of your choice (optional)
- Popsicle molds

Instructions:
1. In a blender, combine the Greek yogurt, strawberries, banana, protein powder, and honey (if using). Blend until smooth and well combined.
2. Taste the mixture and adjust the sweetness if needed by adding more honey or sweetener.
3. Pour the mixture into popsicle molds, leaving a small space at the top for expansion when freezing.
4. Insert popsicle sticks into each mold.
5. Place the molds in the freezer and freeze for at least 4 hours or until completely firm.
6. Once frozen, remove the popsicles from the molds by running them under warm water for a few seconds.
7. Serve immediately or transfer the popsicles to an airtight container and store them in the freezer.

BLUEBERRY ALMOND FLOUR COFFEE CAKE

Nutrition: Cal 230;Fat 18 g;Carb 12 g;Protein 7 g
Serving 2; Cook time 45 min

Ingredients
FOR THE CAKE:
- 1 1/2 cups almond flour
- 1/4 cup coconut flour
- 1/4 cup granulated sweetener (e.g., stevia or monk fruit sweetener)
- 1/2 teaspoon baking powder
- 1/4 teaspoon baking soda
- 1/4 teaspoon salt
- 2 large eggs
- 1/4 cup unsweetened almond milk
- 1/4 cup melted coconut oil
- 1 teaspoon vanilla extract
- 1 cup fresh blueberries
FOR THE TOPPING:
- 1/4 cup almond flour
- 2 tablespoons coconut flour
- 2 tablespoons granulated sweetener
- 2 tablespoons melted coconut oil
- 1/2 teaspoon ground cinnamon

Instructions:

1. Preheat the oven to 350°F (175°C). Grease an 8x8-inch baking dish or line it with parchment paper.
2. In a large mixing bowl, whisk together the almond flour, coconut flour, sweetener, baking powder, baking soda, and salt.
3. In a separate bowl, whisk the eggs, almond milk, melted coconut oil, and vanilla extract.
4. Pour the wet ingredients into the dry ingredients and mix until well combined.
5. Gently fold in the fresh blueberries.
6. Transfer the batter into the prepared baking dish, spreading it out evenly.
7. In a small bowl, mix together the almond flour, coconut flour, sweetener, melted coconut oil, and cinnamon until crumbly.
8. Sprinkle the topping mixture over the batter in the baking dish.
9. Bake for 30-35 minutes, or until a toothpick inserted into the center comes out clean.
10. Allow the coffee cake to cool for a few minutes before slicing and serving.

PEANUT BUTTER SWIRL PROTEIN BROWNIES

Nutrition: Cal 130;Fat 7 g;Carb 12 g;Protein 9 g
Serving 2; Cook time 30 min

Ingredients
- 1/2 cup almond flour
- 1/4 cup cocoa powder
- 1/4 cup protein powder (chocolate or your preferred flavor)
- 1/4 teaspoon baking powder
- 1/4 teaspoon salt
- 1/4 cup unsweetened applesauce
- 2 tablespoons peanut butter (smooth or crunchy)
- 1/4 cup honey or sweetener of your choice
- 1/4 cup unsweetened almond milk
- 1 teaspoon vanilla extract
- 1 large egg

Instructions:

1. Preheat the oven to 350°F (175°C). Grease a small baking dish or line it with parchment paper for easier removal.
2. In a mixing bowl, combine the almond flour, cocoa powder, protein powder, baking powder, and salt.
3. In a separate bowl, whisk together the applesauce, peanut butter, honey, almond milk, vanilla extract, and egg until well combined.
4. Add the wet ingredients to the dry ingredients and stir until a thick batter forms.
5. Pour the batter into the prepared baking dish and spread it evenly.
6. Drop small dollops of peanut butter onto the batter and use a knife to swirl it into the batter to create a marbled effect.
7. Bake in the preheated oven for about 18-20 minutes, or until the edges are set and a toothpick inserted into the center comes out with a few moist crumbs.
8. Allow the brownies to cool in the baking dish for a few minutes, then transfer them to a wire rack to cool completely.
9. Once cooled, cut into squares and serve.

LEMON COCONUT PROTEIN BARS

Nutrition: Cal 8;Fat 7 g;Carb 9 g;Protein 9 g
Serving 2; Cook time 10 min

Ingredients
- 1 cup shredded coconut (unsweetened)
- 1/2 cup protein powder (vanilla or your preferred flavor)
- 2 tablespoons lemon zest (from about 2 lemons)
- 1/4 cup almond butter (or your preferred nut butter)
- 1/4 cup honey or sweetener of your choice
- 1/4 cup unsweetened almond milk
- 1 teaspoon vanilla extract

Instructions:

1. In a mixing bowl, combine the shredded coconut, protein powder, and lemon zest.
2. In a separate microwave-safe bowl, heat the almond butter and honey together for about 20 seconds until softened.
3. Add the almond milk and vanilla extract to the almond butter and honey mixture, and stir until well combined.
4. Pour the wet ingredients into the bowl with the dry ingredients. Mix well until all the ingredients are evenly incorporated.
5. Line a small baking dish with parchment paper. Transfer the mixture into the dish and press it down firmly to create an even layer.

6. Place the baking dish in the refrigerator for at least 1-2 hours to allow the mixture to set.
7. Once firm, remove the bars from the baking dish and cut them into desired sizes.
8. Store the bars in an airtight container in the refrigerator.

ALMOND FLOUR RASPBERRY THUMBPRINT COOKIES

Nutrition: Cal 70;Fat 6 g;Carb 4 g;Protein 2 g
Serving 2; Cook time 25 min

Ingredients
- 1 cup almond flour
- 2 tablespoons coconut flour
- 2 tablespoons sweetener of your choice (e.g., stevia, erythritol)
- 1/4 teaspoon baking powder
- 1/4 teaspoon salt
- 2 tablespoons coconut oil, melted
- 1 large egg
- 1/2 teaspoon vanilla extract
- Sugar-free raspberry jam (for filling)

Instructions:
1. Preheat your oven to 350°F (175°C) and line a baking sheet with parchment paper.
2. In a mixing bowl, whisk together the almond flour, coconut flour, sweetener, baking powder, and salt.
3. In a separate bowl, whisk together the melted coconut oil, egg, and vanilla extract.
4. Add the wet ingredients to the dry ingredients and stir until a dough forms. Let the dough rest for a few minutes to allow the coconut flour to absorb the moisture.
5. Shape the dough into small balls, about 1 inch in diameter, and place them onto the prepared baking sheet. Make an indentation in the center of each cookie using your thumb or the back of a spoon.
6. Fill each indentation with a small amount of sugar-free raspberry jam.
7. Bake the cookies in the preheated oven for 12-15 minutes, or until the edges are golden brown.
8. Allow the cookies to cool on the baking sheet for a few minutes, then transfer them to a wire rack to cool completely.

VANILLA ALMOND CHIA SEED PUDDING

Nutrition: Cal 170;Fat 10 g;Carb 10 g;Protein 6 g
Serving 2; Cook time 5 min

Ingredients
- 1/4 cup chia seeds
- 1 cup unsweetened almond milk
- 1/2 teaspoon vanilla extract
- 1/2 teaspoon sweetener of your choice (e.g., stevia, erythritol)
- Cinnamon (for sprinkling)
- 2 tablespoons almond butter (for topping)

Instructions:
1. In a bowl, combine the chia seeds, almond milk, vanilla extract, and sweetener. Stir well to mix everything together.
2. Let the mixture sit for about 5 minutes, then stir it again to prevent clumping.
3. Cover the bowl and refrigerate for at least 2 hours, or overnight, to allow the chia seeds to absorb the liquid and thicken into a pudding-like consistency.
4. When ready to serve, give the chia seed pudding a good stir. If it's too thick, you can add a little more almond milk to reach your desired consistency.
5. Divide the chia seed pudding into two serving bowls or glasses.
6. Sprinkle each portion with a pinch of cinnamon for added flavor.
7. Top each serving with a dollop of almond butter.
8. Enjoy the pudding immediately or refrigerate for later consumption.

CHOCOLATE ALMOND FLOUR MUFFINS

Nutrition: Cal 170;Fat 13 g;Carb 9 g;Protein 6 g
Serving 2; Cook time 30 min

Ingredients
- 1 cup almond flour
- 1/4 cup cocoa powder (unsweetened)
- 1/4 cup sweetener of your choice (e.g., stevia, erythritol)
- 1/2 teaspoon baking powder
- 1/4 teaspoon salt
- 2 large eggs
- 1/4 cup unsweetened almond milk
- 2 tablespoons melted coconut oil
- 1/2 teaspoon vanilla extract
- 1/4 cup dark chocolate chips

Instructions:
1. Preheat your oven to 350°F (175°C). Line a muffin tin with paper liners or lightly grease the tin.
2. In a large mixing bowl, whisk together the almond flour, cocoa powder, sweetener, baking powder, and salt.
3. In a separate bowl, whisk together the eggs, almond milk, melted coconut oil, and vanilla extract.
4. Pour the wet ingredients into the dry ingredients and stir until well combined.
5. Fold in the dark chocolate chips.
6. Divide the batter evenly among the muffin cups, filling each about 2/3 full.
7. Bake in the preheated oven for 18-20 minutes, or until a toothpick inserted into the center of a muffin comes out clean.
8. Remove from the oven and allow the muffins to cool in the tin for a few minutes before transferring them to a wire rack to cool completely.

MIXED BERRY PROTEIN SMOOTHIE

Nutrition: Cal 250;Fat 5 g;Carb 30 g;Protein 17 g
Serving 2; Cook time 5 min

Ingredients
- 1 cup frozen mixed berries (such as strawberries, blueberries, and raspberries)
- 1/2 ripe banana
- 1 cup unsweetened almond milk (or any milk of your choice)
- 1 scoop protein powder (vanilla or berry flavored)
- 1 tablespoon chia seeds (optional)
- 1/2 cup ice cubes (optional, for a colder smoothie)
- Additional sweetener (optional, if desired)

Instructions:
1. Place all the ingredients in a blender.
2. Blend on high speed until smooth and creamy. If the smoothie is too thick, you can add more

almond milk until desired consistency is reached.

3. Taste the smoothie and add sweetener if needed. Keep in mind that the sweetness of the mixed berries and protein powder may be sufficient for your taste.

4. Pour the smoothie into two glasses.

BAKED CINNAMON APPLES WITH A SPRINKLE OF GRANOLA

Nutrition: Cal 170;Fat 3 g;Carb 25 g;Protein 5 g
Serving 2; Cook time 25 min

Ingredients
- 2 medium-sized apples (such as Granny Smith or Honeycrisp)
- 1 teaspoon cinnamon
- 1 tablespoon granulated sweetener (such as stevia or erythritol)
- 1/4 cup low-sugar granola

Instructions:
1. Preheat the oven to 350°F (175°C).
2. Core the apples and cut them into thin slices.
3. In a bowl, combine the cinnamon and granulated sweetener.
4. Toss the apple slices in the cinnamon-sweetener mixture until they are evenly coated.
5. Arrange the coated apple slices in a baking dish.
6. Sprinkle the granola over the apple slices.
7. Bake in the preheated oven for about 15-20 minutes, or until the apples are tender and the granola is lightly golden.
8. Remove from the oven and let cool for a few minutes.

RASPBERRY ALMOND FLOUR CRUMBLE BARS

Nutrition: Cal 200;Fat 12 g;Carb 12 g;Protein 6 g
Serving 2; Cook time 44 min

Ingredients
FOR THE CRUST AND CRUMBLE:
- 1 1/2 cups almond flour
- 1/4 cup coconut flour
- 1/4 cup granulated sweetener (such as stevia or erythritol)
- 1/4 teaspoon salt
- 1/4 cup coconut oil, melted
- 1 teaspoon vanilla extract
FOR THE RASPBERRY FILLING:

- 2 cups fresh raspberries
- 2 tablespoons lemon juice
- 2 tablespoons granulated sweetener

Instructions:
1. Preheat the oven to 350°F (175°C) and line a baking dish with parchment paper.
2. In a mixing bowl, combine the almond flour, coconut flour, granulated sweetener, and salt for the crust and crumble. Mix well.
3. Add the melted coconut oil and vanilla extract to the dry ingredients. Stir until the mixture resembles coarse crumbs.
4. Set aside 1/2 cup of the crumble mixture for later use as the topping.
5. Press the remaining crumble mixture into the bottom of the prepared baking dish to form an even crust layer.
6. In a separate bowl, gently toss the raspberries, lemon juice, and granulated sweetener for the filling.
7. Spread the raspberry mixture evenly over the crust.
8. Sprinkle the reserved crumble mixture over the raspberries as the topping.
9. Bake in the preheated oven for about 25-30 minutes, or until the edges are golden brown.
10. Remove from the oven and let cool completely before cutting into bars.
11. Serve the raspberry almond flour crumble bars as a delicious bariatric-friendly dessert or snack.

CHOCOLATE PROTEIN MUG CAKE

Nutrition: Cal 200;Fat 7 g;Carb 10 g;Protein 20 g
Serving 2; Cook time 5 min

Ingredients
- 4 tablespoons protein powder (chocolate flavor)
- 2 tablespoons cocoa powder
- 2 tablespoons almond flour
- 1/2 teaspoon baking powder
- 1/4 teaspoon salt
- 2 tablespoons granulated sweetener (such as stevia or erythritol)
- 1/4 cup unsweetened almond milk
- 1/2 teaspoon vanilla extract
- 1 tablespoon sugar-free chocolate chips (optional)

Instructions:

1. In a microwave-safe mug, combine the protein powder, cocoa powder, almond flour, baking powder, salt, and granulated sweetener. Mix well.
2. Add the almond milk and vanilla extract to the dry ingredients. Stir until the batter is smooth and well combined. If desired, fold in the sugar-free chocolate chips.
3. Microwave the mug on high for approximately 1-2 minutes, or until the cake is set in the center. Cooking time may vary depending on the wattage of your microwave, so check the cake after 1 minute and adjust the cooking time accordingly.
4. Carefully remove the mug from the microwave (it will be hot) and let the cake cool for a few minutes before enjoying.
5. Optionally, you can top the mug cake with a dollop of Greek yogurt, a sprinkle of cocoa powder, or a drizzle of sugar-free syrup for added flavor.

VANILLA COCONUT CHIA SEED PUDDING PARFAIT

Nutrition: Cal 200;Fat 9 g;Carb 13 g;Protein 7 g
Serving 2; Cook time 10 min

Ingredients
- 1/4 cup chia seeds
- 1 cup unsweetened almond milk
- 1/2 teaspoon vanilla extract
- 2 tablespoons granulated sweetener (such as stevia or erythritol)
- 1 cup unsweetened coconut yogurt
- Fresh berries or nuts for topping (optional)

Instructions:

1. In a bowl, combine the chia seeds, almond milk, vanilla extract, and granulated sweetener. Stir well to ensure the chia seeds are evenly distributed. Let the mixture sit for about 10-15 minutes, stirring occasionally, until it thickens and forms a gel-like consistency.
2. Once the chia pudding has thickened, divide it into two serving glasses or jars.
3. Next, spoon a layer of unsweetened coconut yogurt on top of the chia pudding in each glass.
4. Repeat the layers, alternating between chia pudding and coconut yogurt until the glasses are filled.
5. Top the parfaits with fresh berries or nuts, if desired.
6. Place the parfaits in the refrigerator for at least 1 hour to allow the flavors to meld and the chia pudding to fully set.

PEANUT BUTTER CHOCOLATE CHIP PROTEIN COOKIES

Nutrition: Cal 120;Fat 8 g;Carb 5 g;Protein 7 g
Serving 2; Cook time 15 min

Ingredients
- 1/2 cup peanut butter (smooth or crunchy)
- 1/4 cup protein powder (vanilla or chocolate flavor)
- 1/4 cup almond flour
- 1/4 cup granulated sweetener (such as stevia or erythritol)
- 1/4 cup dark chocolate chips (sugar-free or high-quality dark chocolate, chopped)
- 1 egg
- 1/2 teaspoon vanilla extract

Instructions:

1. Preheat your oven to 350°F (175°C) and line a baking sheet with parchment paper.
2. In a mixing bowl, combine the peanut butter, protein powder, almond flour, granulated sweetener, dark chocolate chips, egg, and vanilla extract. Mix well until all the ingredients are evenly incorporated.
3. Scoop out tablespoon-sized portions of the dough and roll them into balls. Place the dough balls onto the prepared baking sheet, leaving some space between each cookie.
4. Use a fork to gently flatten each dough ball, creating a crisscross pattern on top.
5. Bake the cookies in the preheated oven for about 10-12 minutes or until the edges are slightly golden.
6. Remove the baking sheet from the oven and let the cookies cool on the sheet for a few minutes before transferring them to a wire rack to cool completely.

MIXED BERRY PROTEIN SMOOTHIE POPSICLES

Nutrition: Cal 100;Fat 2 g;Carb 10 g;Protein 12 g
Serving 2; Cook time 10 min

Ingredients
- 1 cup Greek yogurt (unsweetened)
- 1 cup mixed berries (such as strawberries, blueberries, and raspberries)
- 1 scoop protein powder (vanilla or berry flavor)
- 1 tablespoon honey or preferred sweetener (optional)

Instructions:
1. In a blender, combine the Greek yogurt, mixed berries, protein powder, and honey (if desired). Blend until smooth and well combined.
2. Taste the mixture and adjust the sweetness if needed by adding more honey or sweetener of your choice.
3. Pour the smoothie mixture into popsicle molds, leaving a little space at the top for expansion.
4. Insert popsicle sticks into each mold and place the molds in the freezer.
5. Freeze the popsicles for at least 4-6 hours or until completely frozen.
6. Once frozen, remove the popsicles from the molds and enjoy!

ALMOND FLOUR LEMON POPPY SEED MUFFINS

Nutrition: Cal 140 ;Fat 12 g;Carb 7 g;Protein 6 g
Serving 2; Cook time 25 min

Ingredients
- 1 cup almond flour
- 1/4 cup sweetener of your choice (e.g., stevia, erythritol)
- 1 tablespoon poppy seeds
- 1/2 teaspoon baking powder
- 1/4 teaspoon salt
- 2 large eggs
- 2 tablespoons melted coconut oil
- 1/4 cup unsweetened almond milk
- 1 tablespoon lemon zest
- 1 tablespoon lemon juice

Instructions:
1. Preheat the oven to 350°F (175°C) and line a muffin tin with paper liners.
2. In a mixing bowl, whisk together the almond flour, sweetener, poppy seeds, baking powder, and salt.
3. In a separate bowl, whisk the eggs, melted coconut oil, almond milk, lemon zest, and lemon juice.
4. Pour the wet ingredients into the dry ingredients and stir until well combined.
5. Divide the batter evenly among the muffin cups, filling each about 3/4 full.
6. Bake for 18-20 minutes or until a toothpick inserted into the center of a muffin comes out clean.
7. Remove the muffins from the oven and let them cool in the tin for a few minutes before transferring them to a wire rack to cool completely.

CHOCOLATE COCONUT PROTEIN FUDGE

Nutrition: Cal 120 ;Fat 11 g;Carb 4 g;Protein 5 g
Serving 2; Cook time 60 min

Ingredients
- 1/2 cup coconut oil
- 1/4 cup unsweetened cocoa powder
- 1/4 cup protein powder (chocolate flavor)
- 1/4 cup unsweetened shredded coconut
- 1-2 tablespoons sweetener of your choice (e.g., stevia, erythritol) (optional)

Instructions:
1. In a microwave-safe bowl, melt the coconut oil until it becomes liquid.
2. Add the cocoa powder, protein powder, shredded coconut, and sweetener (if using) to the melted coconut oil. Stir well until all the ingredients are thoroughly combined.
3. Line a small baking dish or container with parchment paper.
4. Pour the mixture into the lined dish and spread it out evenly.
5. Place the dish in the refrigerator and let it set for at least 1 hour or until firm.
6. Once the fudge is firm, remove it from the refrigerator and cut it into small squares or desired shapes.
7. Store the fudge in an airtight container in the refrigerator.

VANILLA COCONUT FLOUR WAFFLES

Nutrition: Cal 180 ;Fat 11 g;Carb 11 g;Protein 8 g
Serving 2; Cook time 20 min

Ingredients

- 1/2 cup coconut flour
- 4 large eggs
- 1/2 cup unsweetened almond milk (or any preferred milk)
- 2 tablespoons coconut oil, melted
- 1 tablespoon sweetener of your choice (e.g., stevia, erythritol)
- 1 teaspoon vanilla extract
- 1/2 teaspoon baking powder
- Pinch of salt

TOPPINGS:

- Sugar-free syrup
- Fresh fruit (e.g., berries, sliced banana)

Instructions:

1. Preheat a waffle iron according to its instructions.
2. In a mixing bowl, whisk together the eggs, almond milk, melted coconut oil, sweetener, and vanilla extract.
3. In a separate bowl, combine the coconut flour, baking powder, and salt.
4. Gradually add the dry ingredients to the wet ingredients, stirring until well combined. The batter will be thick.
5. Allow the batter to sit for a few minutes to allow the coconut flour to absorb the liquids.
6. Grease the preheated waffle iron with coconut oil or non-stick cooking spray.
7. Spoon the batter onto the waffle iron, spreading it out to cover the surface.
8. Close the waffle iron and cook until the waffles are golden brown and cooked through.
9. Carefully remove the waffles from the iron and repeat the process with the remaining batter.
10. Serve the waffles warm with a drizzle of sugar-free syrup and fresh fruit toppings.

STRAWBERRY PROTEIN CHEESECAKE CUPS

Nutrition: Cal 170 ;Fat 2 g;Carb 15 g;Protein 25 g
Serving 2; Cook time 10 min

Ingredients

- 1 cup Greek yogurt
- 1/2 cup strawberries, chopped
- 2 tablespoons protein powder (vanilla or strawberry flavor)
- 1 tablespoon sweetener of your choice (e.g., stevia, erythritol)
- 1/2 teaspoon vanilla extract

OPTIONAL TOPPINGS:

- Fresh strawberries, sliced

Instructions:

1. In a blender or food processor, combine the Greek yogurt, chopped strawberries, protein powder, sweetener, and vanilla extract.
2. Blend until smooth and well combined.
3. Taste and adjust the sweetness if needed by adding more sweetener.
4. Divide the mixture evenly into two serving cups or jars.
5. Refrigerate for at least 2 hours or until set.
6. Once set, remove from the refrigerator and top with fresh strawberry slices, if desired.

PEANUT BUTTER CHOCOLATE PROTEIN MUG BROWNIE

Nutrition: Cal 350 ;Fat 20 g;Carb 20 g;Protein 25 g
Serving 2; Cook time 5 min

Ingredients

- 4 tablespoons peanut butter (creamy or chunky)
- 2 tablespoons protein powder (chocolate flavor)
- 1 tablespoon cocoa powder
- 1 tablespoon sweetener of your choice (e.g., stevia, erythritol)
- 1/4 teaspoon baking powder
- 1/4 cup almond milk (unsweetened)
- 1/4 teaspoon vanilla extract

OPTIONAL TOPPINGS:

- Whipped cream (sugar-free)
- Dark chocolate chips (sugar-free)

Instructions:

1. In a microwave-safe mug, combine the peanut butter, protein powder, cocoa powder, sweetener, and baking powder. Mix well until all ingredients are thoroughly combined.
2. Add the almond milk and vanilla extract to the mug. Stir until the batter is smooth and well mixed.
3. Place the mug in the microwave and cook on high for approximately 60-90 seconds, or until the brownie is set and cooked through. Cooking times may vary depending on the

wattage of your microwave, so keep an eye on it to prevent overcooking.

4. Remove the mug from the microwave and allow the brownie to cool for a few minutes.

5. Top with a dollop of whipped cream and a sprinkle of dark chocolate chips, if desired.

6. Enjoy the peanut butter chocolate protein mug brownie while it's warm!

ALMOND FLOUR BLUEBERRY COFFEE CAKE

Nutrition: Cal 180 ;Fat 11 g;Carb 11 g;Protein 7 g
Serving 2; Соок time 40 min

Ingredients
- 1 cup almond flour
- 1/4 cup sweetener of your choice (e.g., stevia, erythritol)
- 1/2 teaspoon baking powder
- 1/4 teaspoon salt
- 2 large eggs
- 1/4 cup unsweetened almond milk
- 1 teaspoon vanilla extract
- 1 cup fresh blueberries

OPTIONAL TOPPING:
- 2 tablespoons sliced almonds

Instructions:
1. Preheat your oven to 350°F (175°C) and grease a small baking dish or cake pan.

2. In a mixing bowl, combine the almond flour, sweetener, baking powder, and salt. Stir until well mixed.

3. In a separate bowl, whisk the eggs, almond milk, and vanilla extract together.

4. Pour the wet ingredients into the dry ingredients and mix until just combined. Be careful not to overmix.

5. Gently fold in the fresh blueberries.

6. Pour the batter into the prepared baking dish, spreading it evenly.

7. If desired, sprinkle the sliced almonds on top of the batter.

8. Bake in the preheated oven for approximately 25-30 minutes, or until a toothpick inserted into the center comes out clean.

9. Remove from the oven and allow the coffee cake to cool before serving.

CHOCOLATE AVOCADO PROTEIN POPSICLES

Nutrition: Cal 120 ;Fat 10 g;Carb 10 g;Protein 8 g
Serving 2; Соок time 4-6 hours

Ingredients
- 2 ripe avocados
- 2 tablespoons cocoa powder
- 2 scoops of chocolate protein powder
- 1 cup unsweetened almond milk (or any other milk of your choice)
- 2 tablespoons sweetener of your choice (e.g., stevia, erythritol) (optional)

Instructions:
1. Cut the avocados in half, remove the pits, and scoop out the flesh into a blender or food processor.

2. Add the cocoa powder, protein powder, almond milk, and sweetener (if desired) to the blender.

3. Blend the ingredients until smooth and creamy. Taste the mixture and adjust the sweetness if needed.

4. Pour the mixture into popsicle molds, leaving a little space at the top for expansion.

5. Insert popsicle sticks into each mold.

6. Place the molds in the freezer and let them freeze for at least 4-6 hours or until fully set.

7. Once the popsicles are completely frozen, remove them from the molds by running the molds under warm water for a few seconds.

8. Serve and enjoy your delicious and nutritious chocolate avocado protein popsicles!

VANILLA ALMOND FLOUR BANANA BREAD MUFFINS

Nutrition: Cal 180 ;Fat 12 g;Carb 12 g;Protein 8 g
Serving 2; Соок time 35 min

Ingredients
- 2 ripe bananas, mashed
- 2 cups almond flour
- 3 eggs
- 1/4 cup honey or sweetener of your choice
- 1/4 cup unsweetened almond milk (or any other milk of your choice)
- 1 teaspoon vanilla extract
- 1 teaspoon baking powder
- 1/2 teaspoon cinnamon (optional)
- Pinch of salt

Instructions:

1. Preheat your oven to 350°F (175°C) and line a muffin tin with paper liners.
2. In a large bowl, combine the mashed bananas, eggs, honey, almond milk, and vanilla extract. Mix well until smooth.
3. In a separate bowl, whisk together the almond flour, baking powder, cinnamon (if using), and salt.
4. Gradually add the dry ingredients to the wet ingredients, stirring until well combined and there are no lumps.
5. Divide the batter evenly among the muffin cups, filling each about 3/4 full.
6. Bake for approximately 20-25 minutes or until a toothpick inserted into the center of a muffin comes out clean.
7. Remove the muffins from the oven and allow them to cool in the pan for a few minutes before transferring them to a wire rack to cool completely.
8. Once cooled, serve and enjoy these delicious and nutritious vanilla almond flour banana bread muffins!

RASPBERRY ALMOND PROTEIN SMOOTHIE

Nutrition: Cal 180 ;Fat 8 g;Carb 8 g;Protein 20 g
Serving 2; Cook time 5 min

Ingredients
- 1 cup unsweetened almond milk
- 1 cup fresh or frozen raspberries
- 1 scoop vanilla protein powder (approximately 20-25 grams)
- 1 tablespoon almond butter
- Ice cubes (optional, for a chilled smoothie)

Instructions:

1. In a blender, combine the almond milk, raspberries, protein powder, and almond butter.
2. Blend on high speed until all the ingredients are well combined and the smoothie is creamy and smooth.
3. If desired, add a few ice cubes and blend again to make the smoothie colder.
4. Pour the smoothie into two glasses and serve immediately.

PUMPKIN SPICE PROTEIN MUG CAKE

Nutrition: Cal 200 ;Fat 6 g;Carb 15 g;Protein 20 g
Serving 2; Cook time 5 min

Ingredients
- 1/4 cup pumpkin puree
- 1 scoop vanilla protein powder (approximately 20-25 grams)
- 1 tablespoon almond flour
- 1/2 teaspoon pumpkin pie spice
- 1/4 teaspoon baking powder
- 1/4 cup unsweetened almond milk
- Optional: Stevia or another low-calorie sweetener, to taste

Instructions:

1. In a microwave-safe mug, combine the pumpkin puree, vanilla protein powder, almond flour, pumpkin pie spice, and baking powder. Stir well to combine.
2. Add the unsweetened almond milk to the mug and mix until a smooth batter forms. If desired, add a small amount of sweetener to taste.
3. Place the mug in the microwave and cook on high for 1-2 minutes, or until the cake is set and springs back when lightly touched.
4. Carefully remove the mug from the microwave (it will be hot) and allow the cake to cool for a few minutes before serving.
5. Optionally, sprinkle with a pinch of pumpkin pie spice or add a dollop of whipped cream on top before enjoying.

CHOCOLATE COCONUT FLOUR PANCAKES

Nutrition: Cal 150 ;Fat 8 g;Carb 12 g;Protein 6 g
Serving 2; Cook time 20 min

Ingredients
- 1/4 cup coconut flour
- 2 tablespoons unsweetened cocoa powder
- 1/2 teaspoon baking powder
- Pinch of salt
- 2 large eggs
- 1/4 cup unsweetened almond milk (or any other non-dairy milk)
- 2 tablespoons unsweetened applesauce
- 1 tablespoon melted coconut oil
- 1 teaspoon vanilla extract

- Sugar-free syrup, for serving
- Shredded coconut, for topping

Instructions:

1. In a mixing bowl, whisk together the coconut flour, cocoa powder, baking powder, and salt.
2. In a separate bowl, whisk together the eggs, almond milk, applesauce, melted coconut oil, and vanilla extract.
3. Pour the wet ingredients into the dry ingredients and stir until well combined and no lumps remain.
4. Let the batter rest for a few minutes to allow the coconut flour to absorb the liquid. The batter will thicken slightly.
5. Heat a non-stick skillet or griddle over medium heat. Lightly grease with cooking spray or a small amount of coconut oil.
6. Spoon about 1/4 cup of the batter onto the skillet for each pancake. Use the back of the spoon to spread the batter into a circular shape.
7. Cook the pancakes for 2-3 minutes, or until the edges start to set and bubbles form on the surface. Flip the pancakes and cook for an additional 1-2 minutes, until cooked through.
8. Serve the pancakes with sugar-free syrup and a sprinkle of shredded coconut.

VANILLA COCONUT PROTEIN ICE CREAM

Nutrition: Cal 120 ;Fat 11 g;Carb 4 g;Protein 5 g
Serving 2; Cook time 60 min

Ingredients

- 1 can (13.5 oz) full-fat coconut milk
- 1/4 cup protein powder (vanilla flavored)
- 2 tablespoons powdered sweetener (such as erythritol or stevia)
- 1 teaspoon vanilla extract
- Optional toppings: shredded coconut, chopped nuts, fresh berries

Instructions:

1. Place the can of coconut milk in the refrigerator for a few hours or overnight to allow the cream to separate from the liquid.
2. Open the can of coconut milk and scoop out the solid coconut cream into a mixing bowl. Reserve the liquid for other uses (such as adding to smoothies).
3. Using an electric mixer or whisk, beat the coconut cream until smooth and creamy.
4. Add the protein powder, powdered sweetener, and vanilla extract to the bowl. Beat or whisk again until well combined and creamy.
5. Transfer the mixture to an ice cream maker and churn according to the manufacturer's instructions until the mixture reaches a soft-serve consistency.
6. If desired, add optional toppings like shredded coconut, chopped nuts, or fresh berries during the last few minutes of churning.
7. Transfer the ice cream to a lidded container and place it in the freezer for at least 2 hours to firm up.
8. When ready to serve, remove the ice cream from the freezer and let it soften for a few minutes before scooping into bowls or cones.

BLUEBERRY ALMOND FLOUR SCONES

Nutrition: Cal 170 ;Fat 14 g;Carb 7 g;Protein 5 g
Serving 2; Cook time 30 min

Ingredients

- 1 cup almond flour
- 1/4 cup coconut flour
- 1/4 cup powdered sweetener (such as erythritol or stevia)
- 1/2 teaspoon baking powder
- 1/4 teaspoon salt
- 2 tablespoons cold unsalted butter, cubed
- 1/4 cup unsweetened almond milk
- 1 teaspoon vanilla extract
- 1/2 cup fresh blueberries

Instructions:

1. Preheat the oven to 350°F (175°C) and line a baking sheet with parchment paper.
2. In a mixing bowl, whisk together the almond flour, coconut flour, powdered sweetener, baking powder, and salt.
3. Add the cold butter to the dry ingredients and use your fingers or a pastry cutter to cut it into the flour mixture until crumbly.
4. Stir in the almond milk and vanilla extract until the dough starts to come together.
5. Gently fold in the fresh blueberries, being careful not to crush them.

6. Transfer the dough onto a lightly floured surface and shape it into a round disc, about 1/2 to 3/4 inch thick.
7. Cut the disc into 6 equal wedges and place them onto the prepared baking sheet.
8. Bake in the preheated oven for 18-20 minutes, or until the scones are golden brown and firm to the touch.
9. Remove from the oven and let them cool on a wire rack before serving.

PEANUT BUTTER CHOCOLATE PROTEIN TRUFFLES

Nutrition: Cal 100 ;Fat 8 g;Carb 5 g;Protein 6 g
Serving 2; Cook time 60 min

Ingredients
- 1/2 cup natural peanut butter (smooth or crunchy)
- 1/4 cup protein powder (chocolate flavor)
- 2 tablespoons powdered sweetener (such as erythritol or stevia)
- 1/4 teaspoon vanilla extract
- 2-3 ounces dark chocolate, melted (70% cocoa or higher)

Instructions:
1. In a mixing bowl, combine the peanut butter, protein powder, powdered sweetener, and vanilla extract. Mix well until all the ingredients are evenly incorporated.
2. Place the mixture in the refrigerator for about 30 minutes to firm up.
3. Once the mixture is firm, remove it from the refrigerator and shape it into small truffle-sized balls using your hands.
4. Place the truffles on a baking sheet lined with parchment paper and return them to the refrigerator for another 15-20 minutes.
5. Meanwhile, melt the dark chocolate in a microwave-safe bowl or using a double boiler.
6. Take the chilled truffles out of the refrigerator and dip each one into the melted chocolate, coating them completely. Use a fork or spoon to remove any excess chocolate.
7. Place the chocolate-coated truffles back on the lined baking sheet and refrigerate for an additional 15-20 minutes to allow the chocolate to set.

8. Once the chocolate has hardened, the truffles are ready to serve. Enjoy them as a delicious and protein-packed treat.

MIXED BERRY PROTEIN MUFFINS

Nutrition: Cal 120 ;Fat 9 g;Carb 7 g;Protein65 g
Serving 2; Cook time 30 min

Ingredients
- 1 cup almond flour
- 1/4 cup protein powder (vanilla or berry flavor)
- 1 teaspoon baking powder
- 1/4 teaspoon salt
- 2 tablespoons sweetener of choice (such as erythritol or stevia)
- 2 eggs
- 1/4 cup almond milk (or any milk of choice)
- 1 teaspoon vanilla extract
- 1 cup mixed berries (such as blueberries, raspberries, and strawberries)

Instructions:
1. Preheat the oven to 350°F (175°C) and line a muffin tin with paper liners or grease with cooking spray.
2. In a mixing bowl, combine the almond flour, protein powder, baking powder, salt, and sweetener. Mix well to combine.
3. In a separate bowl, whisk the eggs, almond milk, and vanilla extract together until well combined.
4. Pour the wet ingredients into the dry ingredients and stir until just combined. Do not overmix.
5. Gently fold in the mixed berries into the batter.
6. Divide the batter evenly among the muffin cups, filling each about 3/4 full.
7. Bake in the preheated oven for 18-22 minutes, or until a toothpick inserted into the center of a muffin comes out clean.
8. Remove the muffins from the oven and let them cool in the pan for a few minutes, then transfer them to a wire rack to cool completely.
9. Once cooled, the muffins are ready to enjoy.

CHOCOLATE MINT PROTEIN POPSICLES

Nutrition: Cal 70 ;Fat 2 g;Carb 6 g;Protein 6 g
Serving 2; Cook time 6 hours

Ingredients

- 1 cup Greek yogurt
- 1/4 cup protein powder (chocolate flavor)
- 1 tablespoon unsweetened cocoa powder
- 1 tablespoon honey or sweetener of choice (optional)
- 1/4 cup fresh mint leaves, chopped
- 1/4 cup dark chocolate chips (optional, for extra chocolate flavor)
- Popsicle molds

Instructions:

1. In a mixing bowl, combine the Greek yogurt, protein powder, cocoa powder, and honey (if using). Stir well to ensure the ingredients are fully combined.
2. Add the chopped mint leaves to the yogurt mixture and stir until evenly distributed.
3. If desired, stir in the dark chocolate chips for extra chocolate flavor and texture.
4. Pour the mixture into popsicle molds, leaving a little space at the top for expansion.
5. Insert popsicle sticks into each mold.
6. Place the molds in the freezer and allow the popsicles to freeze for at least 4-6 hours, or until fully set.
7. Once the popsicles are frozen, remove them from the molds by briefly running the molds under warm water to loosen the popsicles. Gently pull the popsicles out.

COCONUT FLOUR CHOCOLATE CHIP COOKIES

Nutrition: Cal 80 ;Fat 6 g;Carb 5 g;Protein 2 g
Serving 2; Cook time 60 min

Ingredients

- 1/2 cup coconut flour
- 1/4 cup coconut oil, melted
- 1/4 cup sugar-free sweetener (e.g., stevia, erythritol)
- 2 large eggs
- 1 teaspoon vanilla extract
- 1/4 teaspoon baking soda
- 1/4 teaspoon salt
- 1/4 cup sugar-free chocolate chips

Instructions:

1. Preheat your oven to 350°F (175°C) and line a baking sheet with parchment paper.
2. In a mixing bowl, combine the coconut flour, sugar-free sweetener, baking soda, and salt.

3. In a separate bowl, whisk together the melted coconut oil, eggs, and vanilla extract until well combined.
4. Gradually add the wet ingredients to the dry ingredients and mix until a dough forms.
5. Fold in the sugar-free chocolate chips.
6. Shape the dough into small balls and place them on the prepared baking sheet. Flatten each cookie slightly with your palm.
7. Bake for 10-12 minutes or until the edges are golden brown.
8. Remove from the oven and let the cookies cool on the baking sheet for a few minutes before transferring them to a wire rack to cool completely.

VANILLA PROTEIN WAFFLES WITH FRESH BERRIES AND GREEK YOGURT

Nutrition: Cal 270 ;Fat 16 g;Carb 12 g;Protein 22 g
Serving 2; Cook time 20 min

Ingredients

- 1 cup almond flour
- 2 scoops vanilla protein powder
- 1 teaspoon baking powder
- 1/4 teaspoon salt
- 2 large eggs
- 1/4 cup unsweetened almond milk (or milk of choice)
- 1 teaspoon vanilla extract
- Cooking spray or coconut oil for greasing
- Fresh berries of choice (e.g., strawberries, blueberries, raspberries)
- Greek yogurt for topping

Instructions:

1. Preheat your waffle iron according to the manufacturer's instructions.
2. In a mixing bowl, whisk together the almond flour, vanilla protein powder, baking powder, and salt.
3. In a separate bowl, beat the eggs, almond milk, and vanilla extract until well combined.
4. Gradually add the wet ingredients to the dry ingredients, stirring until a thick batter forms. If needed, add a little more almond milk to achieve the desired consistency.
5. Lightly grease the waffle iron with cooking spray or coconut oil.

6. Pour the batter onto the preheated waffle iron, spreading it evenly. Cook according to your waffle iron's instructions until golden brown and crispy.

7. Once cooked, remove the waffles from the iron and let them cool slightly on a wire rack.

8. Serve the waffles topped with fresh berries and a dollop of Greek yogurt.

CHOCOLATE COCONUT PROTEIN BARS

Nutrition: Cal 150 ;Fat 11 g;Carb 11 g;Protein 8 g
Serving 2; Cook time 10 min

Ingredients
- 1 cup unsweetened shredded coconut
- 1/4 cup cocoa powder
- 1/2 cup vanilla protein powder
- 1/4 cup almond butter
- 1/4 cup sugar-free maple syrup or honey
- 1/4 cup unsweetened almond milk (or milk of choice)
- 1 teaspoon vanilla extract
- Pinch of salt

Instructions:
1. In a mixing bowl, combine the shredded coconut, cocoa powder, and vanilla protein powder. Stir until well mixed.

2. In a separate microwave-safe bowl, combine the almond butter and sugar-free maple syrup (or honey). Microwave for 20-30 seconds to soften the mixture.

3. Add the almond milk, vanilla extract, and pinch of salt to the almond butter mixture. Stir until smooth.

4. Pour the almond butter mixture into the dry ingredients and mix well until everything is evenly combined.

5. Line a baking dish or pan with parchment paper. Transfer the mixture into the dish and press it down firmly to form an even layer.

6. Place the dish in the refrigerator for at least 1-2 hours, or until the mixture is firm and set.

7. Once firm, remove the mixture from the refrigerator and cut it into bars or squares of your desired size.

8. Store the bars in an airtight container in the refrigerator for up to one week.

VANILLA CHIA SEED PUDDING

Nutrition: Cal 190 ;Fat 12 g;Carb 16 g;Protein 7 g
Serving 2; Cook time 45 min

Ingredients
- 1/4 cup chia seeds
- 1 cup unsweetened almond milk (or milk of choice)
- 1 tablespoon sugar-free vanilla extract or vanilla protein powder
- 1/2 teaspoon ground cinnamon
- 2 tablespoons almond butter (or nut butter of choice)

Instructions:
1. In a bowl, combine the chia seeds, unsweetened almond milk, sugar-free vanilla extract or vanilla protein powder, and ground cinnamon. Stir well to ensure the chia seeds are evenly distributed.

2. Let the mixture sit for about 5 minutes, then stir again to prevent clumping.

3. Cover the bowl and refrigerate for at least 2 hours, or overnight, to allow the chia seeds to absorb the liquid and thicken.

4. Once the pudding has reached the desired consistency, give it a final stir. If it's too thick, you can add a splash of almond milk to adjust the consistency.

5. Divide the chia seed pudding into two serving bowls or jars.

6. Sprinkle a pinch of cinnamon on top of each serving and add a dollop of almond butter.

ALMOND FLOUR CARROT CAKE MUFFINS

Nutrition: Cal 120 ;Fat 11 g;Carb 8 g;Protein 6 g
Serving 2; Cook time 30 min

Ingredients
- 1 cup almond flour
- 1/4 cup coconut flour
- 1/4 cup granulated sweetener of choice (e.g., stevia, erythritol)
- 1/2 teaspoon baking powder
- 1/2 teaspoon ground cinnamon
- 1/4 teaspoon ground nutmeg
- 1/4 teaspoon ground ginger
- Pinch of salt
- 2 large eggs
- 1/4 cup unsweetened applesauce

- 2 tablespoons melted coconut oil
- 1 teaspoon vanilla extract
- 1 cup grated carrots
- 1/4 cup chopped walnuts (optional)

Instructions:

1. Preheat the oven to 350°F (175°C). Line a muffin tin with paper liners or grease the cups.
2. In a mixing bowl, whisk together the almond flour, coconut flour, sweetener, baking powder, cinnamon, nutmeg, ginger, and salt.
3. In a separate bowl, beat the eggs. Add the applesauce, melted coconut oil, and vanilla extract. Mix well.
4. Pour the wet ingredients into the dry ingredients and stir until combined.
5. Fold in the grated carrots and chopped walnuts (if using).
6. Divide the batter evenly among the muffin cups, filling each about 3/4 full.
7. Bake for 18-20 minutes, or until a toothpick inserted into the center of a muffin comes out clean.
8. Allow the muffins to cool in the pan for a few minutes, then transfer them to a wire rack to cool completely.

CHOCOLATE CHERRY PROTEIN MUFFINS

Nutrition: Cal 120 ;Fat 8 g;Carb 6 g;Protein 6 g
Serving 2; Cook time 30 min

Ingredients

- 1 cup almond flour
- 1/4 cup cocoa powder
- 1/4 cup granulated sweetener of choice (e.g., stevia, erythritol)
- 1/2 teaspoon baking powder
- Pinch of salt
- 2 scoops chocolate protein powder
- 1/4 cup melted coconut oil
- 1/4 cup unsweetened almond milk
- 2 large eggs
- 1 teaspoon vanilla extract
- 1/4 cup dried cherries, chopped

Instructions:

1. Preheat the oven to 350°F (175°C). Line a muffin tin with paper liners or grease the cups.
2. In a mixing bowl, whisk together the almond flour, cocoa powder, sweetener, baking powder, salt, and chocolate protein powder.
3. In a separate bowl, whisk together the melted coconut oil, almond milk, eggs, and vanilla extract.
4. Pour the wet ingredients into the dry ingredients and stir until well combined.
5. Fold in the chopped dried cherries.
6. Divide the batter evenly among the muffin cups, filling each about 3/4 full.
7. Bake for 15-18 minutes, or until a toothpick inserted into the center of a muffin comes out clean.
8. Allow the muffins to cool in the pan for a few minutes, then transfer them to a wire rack to cool completely.

VANILLA COCONUT PROTEIN SHAKE

Nutrition: Cal 160 ;Fat 9 g;Carb 7 g;Protein 16 g
Serving 2; Cook time 5 min

Ingredients

- 1 cup unsweetened coconut milk
- 1 scoop vanilla protein powder
- 1/2 teaspoon vanilla extract
- 1-2 tablespoons sweetener of choice (optional)
- Ice cubes (as desired)

Instructions:

1. In a blender, combine the unsweetened coconut milk, vanilla protein powder, vanilla extract, and sweetener (if using).
2. Blend on high speed until all the ingredients are well combined and the shake is smooth.
3. If desired, add a few ice cubes to the blender and blend again until the shake is chilled and frothy.
4. Taste and adjust the sweetness if necessary by adding more sweetener.
5. Pour the shake into two glasses and serve immediately.

RASPBERRY ALMOND FLOUR COFFEE CAKE

Nutrition: Cal 205 ;Fat 16 g;Carb 12 g;Protein 7 g
Serving 2; Cook time 40 min

Ingredients

FOR THE CAKE:
- 1 cup almond flour
- 1/4 cup sweetener of choice (such as erythritol or stevia)
- 1/4 teaspoon baking powder
- 1/4 teaspoon salt
- 2 tablespoons melted coconut oil
- 2 eggs
- 1/4 cup unsweetened almond milk
- 1 teaspoon vanilla extract
- 1 cup fresh raspberries

FOR THE CRUMBLE TOPPING:
- 2 tablespoons almond flour
- 2 tablespoons sweetener of choice
- 2 tablespoons melted coconut oil
- 1/4 teaspoon cinnamon

Instructions:
1. In a mixing bowl, combine the almond flour, sweetener, baking powder, and salt.
2. In a separate bowl, whisk together the melted coconut oil, eggs, almond milk, and vanilla extract.
3. Add the wet ingredients to the dry ingredients and mix until well combined.
4. Gently fold in the fresh raspberries.
5. Pour the batter into the prepared baking dish, spreading it evenly.
6. In a small bowl, combine the almond flour, sweetener, melted coconut oil, and cinnamon to make the crumble topping. Mix until crumbly.
7. Sprinkle the crumble topping over the cake batter.
8. Bake in the preheated oven for 25-30 minutes, or until the cake is golden brown and a toothpick inserted into the center comes out clean.
9. Allow the cake to cool for a few minutes before serving.

VANILLA ALMOND FLOUR THUMBPRINT COOKIES

Nutrition: Cal 100 ;Fat 18g;Carb 5 g;Protein 3 g
Serving 2; Cook time 20 min

Ingredients
- 1 cup almond flour
- 2 tablespoons sweetener of choice (such as erythritol or stevia)
- 1/4 teaspoon baking powder
- 1/8 teaspoon salt
- 2 tablespoons melted coconut oil
- 1/2 teaspoon vanilla extract
- Sugar-free strawberry jam (or any other flavor of your choice)

Instructions:
1. Preheat the oven to 350°F (175°C) and line a baking sheet with parchment paper.
2. In a mixing bowl, combine the almond flour, sweetener, baking powder, and salt.
3. Add the melted coconut oil and vanilla extract to the dry ingredients. Mix until a dough forms.
4. Roll the dough into small balls, about 1 inch in diameter, and place them on the prepared baking sheet.
5. Use your thumb or the back of a spoon to make an indentation in the center of each cookie.
6. Fill each indentation with a small amount of sugar-free strawberry jam.
7. Bake in the preheated oven for 10-12 minutes, or until the edges are lightly golden.
8. Allow the cookies to cool on the baking sheet for a few minutes before transferring them to a wire rack to cool completely.

PUMPKIN PROTEIN MUG CAKE

Nutrition: Cal 180 ;Fat 7 g;Carb 12 g;Protein 18 g
Serving 2; Cook time 5 min

Ingredients
- 1/4 cup pumpkin puree
- 1/4 cup unsweetened almond milk
- 1 scoop vanilla protein powder
- 2 tablespoons almond flour
- 1 tablespoon sweetener of choice (such as erythritol or stevia)
- 1/2 teaspoon pumpkin pie spice
- 1/2 teaspoon baking powder
- Pinch of salt

Instructions:
1. In a microwave-safe mug, whisk together the pumpkin puree and almond milk until well combined.
2. Add the vanilla protein powder, almond flour, sweetener, pumpkin pie spice, baking powder, and salt to the mug. Stir until all the

ingredients are fully incorporated and no lumps remain.

3. Microwave the mug on high for 1-2 minutes, or until the cake has risen and is cooked through. Cooking time may vary depending on the wattage of your microwave, so keep an eye on it.

4. Carefully remove the mug from the microwave and let it cool for a few minutes.

5. Optionally, you can top the mug cake with a dollop of Greek yogurt, a sprinkle of cinnamon, or a drizzle of sugar-free syrup.

6. Enjoy the pumpkin protein mug cake warm directly from the mug.

CHOCOLATE ALMOND FLOUR COFFEE CAKE

Nutrition: Cal 180 ;Fat 15 g;Carb 8 g;Protein 6 g
Serving 2; Cook time 35 min

Ingredients
FOR THE CAKE:
- 1 cup almond flour
- 1/4 cup cocoa powder
- 1/4 cup sweetener of choice (such as erythritol or stevia)
- 1/2 teaspoon baking powder
- 1/4 teaspoon salt
- 2 large eggs
- 1/4 cup unsweetened almond milk
- 2 tablespoons melted coconut oil
- 1 teaspoon vanilla extract
- 1/4 cup dark chocolate chips (sugar-free if desired)

FOR THE TOPPING:
- 1/4 cup almond flour
- 2 tablespoons sweetener of choice
- 1 tablespoon melted coconut oil
- 1/4 teaspoon cinnamon

Instructions:
1. Preheat your oven to 350°F (175°C) and line an 8x8-inch baking dish with parchment paper.

2. In a large bowl, whisk together the almond flour, cocoa powder, sweetener, baking powder, and salt.

3. In a separate bowl, whisk the eggs, almond milk, melted coconut oil, and vanilla extract.

4. Pour the wet ingredients into the dry ingredients and stir until well combined. Fold in the dark chocolate chips.

5. Pour the batter into the prepared baking dish and spread it evenly.

6. In a small bowl, combine the almond flour, sweetener, melted coconut oil, and cinnamon for the topping. Mix until crumbly.

7. Sprinkle the topping mixture over the cake batter.

8. Bake in the preheated oven for 20-25 minutes, or until a toothpick inserted into the center comes out clean.

9. Allow the coffee cake to cool in the pan for a few minutes before transferring it to a wire rack to cool completely.

PRODUCT INDEX

E

F

G

V

Z

CONCLUSION

As we near the end of our bariatric cookbook, let's take some time to review why it's so important to have a resource that's specifically geared toward bariatric patients, as well as consider the transformational potential of eating a diet that's rich in a variety of foods.

Review of the Reasons Why a Bariatric Cookbook Is Necessary

Individuals who have undergone bariatric surgery or who are currently on a journey to lose weight will find a bariatric cookbook to be an indispensable resource. It gives you access to a plethora of mouthwatering and wholesome recipes that have been thoughtfully crafted to help you achieve your health objectives and satisfy your specific dietary requirements. The following are some of the reasons why this cookbook is so important:

Finding Your Way Through the Post-Operative Phase The process of recovering from bariatric surgery involves considerable adjustments to your eating routine and digestion. This new era of your life can be easier navigated with the assistance of the cookbook, which provides you with direction and support. It gives recipes that are ideal for your smaller stomach size, ensuring that you acquire the necessary nourishment while still enjoying the meals you eat despite having less room in your stomach.

Making informed and health-conscious decisions It is possible for you to make informed and health-conscious decisions when you have a wide variety of bariatric-friendly recipes at your disposal. The cookbook has an emphasis on nutrient-dense ingredients, controlling portion sizes, and engaging in mindful eating practices, all of which contribute to your success over the long run and your general well-being.

Preventing Dietary Monotony: Since variety is the spice of life, the bariatric cookbook ensures that your meals will not be monotonous in any way. You can consume a wide variety of meals that are both scrumptious and gratifying if you make use of a variety of flavors, cuisines, and innovative alterations to recipes. This helps keep you from getting bored with your diet and maintains your motivation to adhere to your healthy eating plan.

In Conclusion: The Importance of Eating a Variety of Food Groups

Beginning a bariatric journey is a life-changing experience on multiple levels, including both the physical and the emotional. It is an opportunity to take care of your health and well-being, and maintaining a diet that is both healthy and balanced is an essential component of this process. Keep these important considerations in mind as you move forward on your journey:

The aim of losing weight is a worthy one, but one must look beyond the numbers on the scale to determine whether or not they have been successful. Embrace the beneficial alterations that are taking place in your body, such as an increase in energy, an improvement in mobility, and an improvement in your general health. Honor these accomplishments and take pride in the strides that you've made.

The bariatric cookbook is not simply a short-term resource but rather a friend that you may keep with you for the rest of your life. It provides you with the education and resources necessary to maintain a healthy eating lifestyle for many years to come. Embrace this as a long-term strategy to ensure that you continue to put your health first by nourishing your body with nutritious foods and putting an emphasis on how you feel.

Your Bariatric Journey: Celebrate Your Own Progress and Accomplishments Because everyone's experience with bariatric surgery is different, it is essential to take stock of and take pride in one's own development and achievements. Keep your attention fixed on your own objectives and achievements, and resist the temptation to evaluate your progress in relation to that of others. It is important to keep in mind that this is a personal path of self-improvement and self-care.

In conclusion, the bariatric cookbook is more than just a collection of dishes that are appropriate for those with weight loss goals. It is a handbook that gives you the ability to make great adjustments in your life that will promote your health, happiness, and success over the long run. You are making a huge move toward a future that will be more nourishing for you by adhering to the recipes, dietary guidelines, and lifestyle advice contained in this book.

Your journey through the world of cuisine can now officially begin. Open up the cookbook, go through the different recipes, and see your taste buds light up with excitement. I wish for you on your path that you are blessed with happiness, flavor, and the many blessings that come with maintaining a healthy diet. Cheers to your physical and mental well-being, as well as to the bright future that lies ahead!

2023

SANDRA GRANT

Made in the USA
Monee, IL
15 November 2024

70213592R00122